DOCUMENTS SET

VOLUME I

OUT OF MANY

A HISTORY

OF THE

AMERICAN PEOPLE

Third Edition

JOHN MACK FARAGHER
Yale University

MARI JO BUHLE
Brown University

DANIEL CZITROM
Mount Holyoke College

SUSAN H. ARMITAGE
Washington State University

Prentice Hall, Upper Saddle River, New Jersey 07458

©2000, 1997 by Prentice-Hall, Inc.
Upper Saddle River, New Jersey 07458

Printed in the United States of America

10 9 8 7 6 5 4 3

ISBN 0-13-999566-8

Prentice Hall International (UK) Limited, *London*
Prentice Hall of Australia Pty. Limited, *Sydney*
Prentice Hall Canada Inc., *Toronto*
Prentice Hall Hispoamericana, S.A., *Mexico*
Prentice Hall of India Private Limited, *New Delhi*
Prentice Hall of Japan, Inc., *Tokyo*
Editora Prentice-Hall do Brasil, *Rio de Janeiro*

Documents Set

OUT OF MANY: A History of the American People, Third Edition

Volume I

by Faragher / Buhle / Czitrom / Armitage

Chapter 17. Reconstruction, 1863–1877   **219**

Preface

This Documents Reader is designed as a learning companion to the textbook OUT OF MANY. As teachers, we have found that having students engage primary source documents from the past is an effective technique for making history come alive. We have devised the Documents Reader to be read along with assignments from OUT OF MANY. For each chapter in the textbook we have selected approximately ten primary source documents keyed to that chapter's subject matter. Each document has been edited down to a suitable length and given an introductory headnote and source. Ideally, the documents should be discussed in class along with the corresponding chapter assignments. Toward that end, we have also included discussion questions at the end of each document.

We have chosen five types of primary source documents for each chapter. These include:

Community Documents: Keyed to the American Communities introduction in each chapter.

Social History Documents: Reflecting everyday life from diaries, letters, and journals.

Government/Political Documents: Covering laws, court cases, election campaigns, and debates over public policy.

Cultural/Intellectual Documents: Illustrating contemporary fiction, journalism, and essays.

Foreign Relations Documents: Demonstrating America's historical connections with the larger world community of nations.

The documents may be photocopied and distributed to your students free of charge as long as OUT OF MANY is your required textbook. The complete set of documents from each volume is available for purchase by your students at a nominal fee, shrinkwrapped to copies of the corresponding text volume. Please contact your local Prentice Hall sales representative for more information.

Faragher / Buhle / Czitrom / Armitage
OUT OF MANY: A HISTORY OF THE AMERICAN PEOPLE, COMBINED EDITION, *3e*

Faragher / Buhle / Czitrom / Armitage
OUT OF MANY: A HISTORY OF THE AMERICAN PEOPLE, COMBINED EDITION, *3e*
DOCUMENTS SET VOLUME I, *3e*, and DOCUMENTS SET VOLUME II, *3e* PACKAGE

Faragher / Buhle / Czitrom / Armitage
OUT OF MANY: A HISTORY OF THE AMERICAN PEOPLE, VOLUME I, *3e*

Faragher / Buhle / Czitrom / Armitage
OUT OF MANY: A HISTORY OF THE AMERICAN PEOPLE, VOLUME I, *3e*
and DOCUMENTS SET VOLUME I, *3e* PACKAGE

Faragher / Buhle / Czitrom / Armitage
OUT OF MANY: A HISTORY OF THE AMERICAN PEOPLE, VOLUME II, *3e*

Faragher / Buhle / Czitrom / Armitage
OUT OF MANY: A HISTORY OF THE AMERICAN PEOPLE, VOLUME II, *3e*
and DOCUMENTS SET VOLUME II, *3e* PACKAGE

We believe the Documents Reader will help deepen students' understanding of the complexity of the American past, and that it will encourage many of them to pursue historical research and study beyond the college survey course.

JMF

DC

A Continent of Villages, to 1500

1–1 The Story of the Creation of the World, Told by a Zuni Priest in 1885

All cultures use myth and legend to help explain the beginning of things. Many Indian myths tell of a creator who first lights up the darkness, then creates a world of water from which the land gradually emerges. This legend, told by Zuni elders to the ethnologist Frank Hamilton Cushing in the 1880s, features Mother-earth and Sky-father, the original parents.

SOURCE: Frank Hamilton Cushing, *Thirteenth Annual Report of the Bureau of American Ethnology, 1894–95* (Washington. D.C.: Smithsonian Institution, 1896).

Before the beginning of the new-making, Awonawilona (the Maker and Container of All, the All-father Father), solely had being. There was nothing else whatsoever throughout the great space of the ages save everywhere black darkness in it, and everywhere void desolation.

In the beginning of the new-made, Awonawilona conceived within himself and thought outward in space, whereby mists of increase, steams potent of growth, were evolved and uplifted. Thus, by means of his innate knowledge, the All-container made himself in person and form of the Sun whom we hold to be our father and who thus came to exist and appear. With his appearance came the brightening of the spaces with light and with the brightening of the spaces the great mist-clouds were thickened together and fell, whereby was evolved water in water; yea, and the world-holding sea.

With his substance of flesh outdrawn from the surface of his person, the Sun-father formed the seed-stuff of twain worlds, impregnating therewith the great waters, and lo! in the heat of his light these waters of the sea grew green and scums rose upon them, waxing wide and weighty until, behold! they became Awitelin Tsita, the "Four-fold Containing Mother-earth," and Apoyan Tächu, the "All-covering Father-sky."

From the lying together of these twain upon the great world-waters, so vitalizing, terrestrial life was conceived; whence began all beings of earth, men and the creatures, in the Fourfold womb of the World.

Thereupon the Earth-mother repulsed the Sky-father, growing big and sinking deep into the embrace of the waters below, thus separating from the Sky-father in the embrace of the waters above. As a woman forebodes evil for her first-born ere born, even so did the Earth-mother forebode, long withholding from birth her myriad progeny and meantime seeking counsel with the Sky-father. "How," said they to one another, "shall our children when brought forth, know one place from another, even by the white light of the Sun-father?"

Now like all the surpassing beings the Earth-mother and the Sky-father were changeable, even as smoke in the wind; transmutable at thought, manifesting themselves in any form at will, like as dancers may be mask-making.

Thus, as a man and woman, spake they, one to the other. "Behold!" said the Earth-mother as a great terraced bowl appeared at hand and within it water, "this is as upon me the homes of my tiny children shall be. On the rim of each world-country they wander in, terraced mountains shall stand, making in one region many, whereby country shall be known from country, and within each, place from place. Behold, again!" said she as she spat on the water and rapidly smote and stirred it with her fingers. Foam formed, gathering about the terraced rim, mounting higher and higher. "Yea," said she, "and from my bosom they shall draw nourishment, for in such as this shall they find the substance of life whence we were ourselves sustained, for see!" Then with her warm breath she blew across the terraces; white flecks of the foam broke away, and, floating over above the water, were shattered by the cold breath of the Sky-father attending, and forthwith shed downward abundantly fine mist and spray! "Even so, shall white clouds float up from the great waters at the borders of the world, and clustering about the mountain terraces of the horizons be borne aloft and abroad by the breaths of the surpassing of soul-beings, and of the children, and shall hardened and broken be by thy cold, shedding downward, in rain-spray, the water of life, even into the hollow places of my lap! For therein chiefly shall nestle our children mankind and creature-kind, for warmth in thy coldness."

Lo! even the trees on high mountains near the clouds and the Sky-father crouch low toward the Earth-mother for warmth and protection! Warm is the Earth-mother, cold the Sky-father, even as woman is the warm, man the cold being!

"Even so!" said the Sky-father; "Yet not alone shalt *thou* helpful be unto our children, for behold!" and he spread his hand abroad with the palm downward and into all the wrinkles and crevices thereof he set the semblance of shining yellow corn-grains; in the dark of the early world-dawn they gleamed like sparks of fire, and moved as his hand was moved over the bowl, shining up from and also moving in the depths of the water therein. "See!" said he, pointing to the seven grains clasped by his thumb and four fingers, "by such shall our children be guided; for behold, when the Sun-father is not nigh, and thy terraces are as the dark itself (being all hidden therein), then shall our children be guided by lights—like to these lights of all the six regions turning round the midmost one—as in and around the midmost place, where these our children shall abide, lie all the other regions of space! Yea! and even as these grains gleam up from the water, so shall seed-grains like to them, yet numberless, spring up from thy bosom when touched by my waters, to nourish our children." Thus and in other ways many devised they for their offspring.

SOURCE: Frank G. Speck, "Penobscot Tales and Religious Beliefs," *Journal of American Folklore* 48 (1935): 1–107.

* * * * * *

1. *How does this creation story compare to others with which you may be more familiar?*

2. *For the Pueblos, the sexual union between men and women was a symbol of the forces that ordered the universe. What elements of this idea can you find in this legend?*

1-2   The Discovery of Corn and Tobacco, as Recounted by a Penobscot Elder in 1907

The Penobscot Indians, an Algonquian-speaking people also known as the Eastern Abnekis, were hunters and farmers who made their homes in the forests and along the coasts of Maine. This tale was collected by Frank G. Speck (1881–1950), an anthropologist of Mohican Indian descent, who was the leading authority on the Indian people of eastern North America. It tells of the origins of the Penobscot's two most important crops.

A famine came upon the people and the streams and lakes dried up. No one knew what to do to make it different. At length a maid of great beauty appeared and one of the young men married her. But she soon became sad and retiring and spent much time in a secret place. Her husband followed her one day and discovered that she went to the forest and met a snake, her lover. He was sad, but he did not accuse her; he loved her so much he did not wish to hurt her feelings. He followed her, however, and she wept when she was discovered. Clinging to her ankle was a long green blade of a plant resembling grass. She then declared that she had a mission to perform and that he must promise to follow her instructions; if so, he would obtain a blessing that would comfort his mind in sorrow and nourish his body in want, and bless the people in time to come. She told him to kill her with a stone axe, and to drag her body seven times among the stumps of a clearing in the forest until the flesh was stripped from the bones, and finally to bury the bones in the center of the clearing. He was told to return to his wigwam and wait seven days before going again to the spot. During this period she promised to visit him in a dream and instruct him what to do afterward. He obeyed her. In his dream she told him that she was the mother of corn and tobacco and gave him instructions how to prepare these plants to be eaten and smoked. After seven days he went to the clearing and found the corn plant rising above the ground and the leaves of the tobacco plant coming forth. When the corn had born fruit and the silk of the corn ear had turned yellow he recognized in it the resemblance to his dead wife. Thus originated the cultivation of corn and tobacco. These plants have nourished the bodies of the Indians ever since and comforted their minds in trouble.

* * * * *

1. *Man and woman both figure prominently in this tale. How might their parts here reflect the real lives of Penobscot women and men?*

2. *"Remember her and think of her whenever you eat and whenever you smoke," ends another version of this myth; "she has given her life so that you might live." Consider the connection of life and death in this myth.*

1–3 A Cherokee Explains the Origins of Disease and Medicine in the 1890s

The ethnologist James Mooney collected many myths and stories from Cherokee families who had remained hiding in the Appalachian mountains when the majority of the people were exiled to Indian Territory (Oklahoma) in the 1830s. This myth attempts to make sense out of the existence of disease in the world.

SOURCE: *Nineteenth Annual Report of the Bureau of American Ethnology, 1897–98* (Washington, D.C.: Smithsonian Institution, 1900).

In the old days the beasts, birds, fishes, insects, and plants could all talk, and they and the people lived together in peace and friendship. But as time went on the people increased so rapidly that their settlements spread over the whole earth, and the poor animals found themselves beginning to be cramped for room. This was bad enough, but to make it worse Man invented bows, knives, blow-guns, spears, and hooks, and began to slaughter the larger animals, birds, and fishes for their flesh or their skins, while the smaller creatures, such as the frogs and worms, were crushed and trodden upon without thought, out of pure carelessness or contempt. So the animals resolved to consult upon measures for their common safety.

The Bears were the first to meet in council in their townhouse under Kuwǎ'hi mountain, the "Mulberry Place," and the old White Bear chief presided. After each in turn had complained of the way in which Man killed their friends, ate their flesh, and used their skins for his own purposes, it was decided to begin war at once against him. Someone asked what weapons Man used to destroy them. "Bows and arrows, of course," cried all the Bears in chorus. "And what are they made of?" was the next question. "The bow of wood, and the string of our entrails," replied one of the Bears. It was then proposed that they make a bow and some arrows and see if they could not use the same weapons against Man himself. So one Bear got a nice piece of locust wood and another sacrificed himself for the good of the rest in order to furnish a piece of his entrails for the string. But when everything was ready and the first Bear stepped up to make the trial, it was found that in letting the arrow fly after drawing back the bow, his long claws caught the string and spoiled the shot. This was annoying, but someone suggested that they might trim his claws, which was accordingly done, and on a second trial it was found that the arrow went straight to the mark. But here the chief, the old White Bear, objected, saying it was

necessary that they should have long claws in order to be able to climb trees. "One of us has already died to furnish the bowstring, and if we now cut off our claws we must all starve together. It is better to trust to the teeth and claws that nature gave us, for it is plain that Man's weapons were not intended for us."

No one could think of any better plan, so the old chief dismissed the council and the Bears dispersed to the woods and thickets without having concerted any way to prevent the increase of the human race. Had the result of the council been otherwise, we should now be at war with the Bears, but as it is, the hunter does not even ask the Bear's pardon when he kills one.

The Deer next held a council under their chief, the Little Deer, and after some talk decided to send rheumatism to every hunter who should kill one of them unless he took care to ask their pardon for the offense. They sent notice of their decision to the nearest settlement of Indians and told them at the same time what to do when necessity forced them to kill one of the Deer tribe. Now, whenever the hunter shoots a Deer, the Little Deer, who is swift as the wind and cannot be wounded, runs quickly up to the spot and, bending over the bloodstains, asks the spirit of the Deer if it has heard the prayer of the hunter for pardon. If the reply be "Yes," all is well, and the Little Deer goes on his way; but if the reply be "No," he follows on the trail of the hunter, guided by the drops of blood on the ground, until he arrives at his cabin in the settlement, when the Little Deer enters invisibly and strikes the hunter with rheumatism, so that he becomes at once a helpless cripple. No hunter who has regard for his health ever fails to ask pardon of the Deer for killing it, although some hunters who have not learned the prayer may try to turn aside the Little Deer from his pursuit by building a fire behind them in the trail.

Next came the Fishes and Reptiles, who had their own complaints against Man. They held their council together and determined to make their victims dream of snakes twining about them in slimy folds and blowing foul breath in their faces, or to make them dream of eating raw or decaying fish, so that they would lose appetite, sicken, and die. This is why people dream about snakes and fish.

Finally the Birds, Insects, and smaller animals came together for the same purpose, and the Grubworm was chief of the council. It was decided that each in turn should give an opinion, and then they would vote on the question as to whether or not Man was guilty. Seven votes should be enough to condemn him. One after another denounced Man's cruelty and injustice toward the other animals and voted in favor of his death. The Frog spoke first, saying: "We must do something to check the increase of the race, or people will become so numerous that we shall be crowded from off the earth. See how they have kicked me about because I'm ugly, as they say, until my back is covered with sores"; and here he showed the spots on his skin. Next came the Bird—no one remembers now which one it was—who condemned Man "because he burns my feet off," meaning the way in which the hunter barbecues birds by impaling them on a stick set over the fire, so that their feathers and tender feet are singed off. Others followed in the same strain. The Ground-squirrel alone ventured to say a good word for Man, who seldom hurt him because he was so small, but this made the others so angry that they fell upon the Ground-squirrel and tore him with their claws, and the stripes are on his back to this day.

They began then to devise and name so many new diseases, one after another, that had not their invention at last failed them, no one of the human race would have been able to survive. The Grubworm grew constantly more pleased as the name of each disease was called off, until at last they reached the end of the list, when someone proposed to make menstruation sometimes fatal to women. On this he rose up in his place and cried: "Wadân'! [Thanks!] I'm glad some more of them will die, for they are getting so thick that they tread on me." The thought fairly made him shake with joy, so that he fell over backward and could not get on his feet again, but had to wriggle off on his back, as the Grubworm has done ever since.

When the Plants, who were friendly to Man, heard what had been done by the animals, they determined to defeat the latters' evil designs. Each Tree, Shrub, and Herb, down even to the Grasses and Mosses, agreed to furnish a cure for some one of the diseases named, and each said: "I shall appear to help Man when he calls upon me in his need." Thus came medicine; and the plants, every one of which has its use if we only knew it, furnish the remedy to counteract the evil wrought by the revengeful animals. Even weeds were made for some good purpose, which we must find out for ourselves. When the doctor does not know what medicine to use for a sick man the spirit of the plant tells him.

* * * * *

1. According to the Bible, God gave man and woman "dominion over the fish of the sea and over the birds of the air and over every living thing that moves upon the earth." By contrast, what does this myth suggest about Cherokee beliefs concerning the relationship between people and the animals?

2. It is often said that Indian peoples viewed themselves as part of the natural world. Discuss the various elements in this tale that might support such an interpretation.

SOURCE: Charles G. Leland, Algonquin Legends (Boston: Houghton, Mifflin and Company, 1884), pp. 208–32.

1–4 A Story of the Trickster Rabbit, Told by a Micmac Indian in the 1870s

One of the recurring characters in Indian tales is the figure of the trickster. Portrayed by some cultures as Coyote and by others as Raven, for the Algonquians of the Northeast he was Rabbit, Matigwess, the magician. The Sioux medicine man John Lame Deer says that such tricksters "are a necessary part of us. A people who have so much to cry about as Indians do also need their laughter to survive." This tale was collected by Silas T. Rand, Baptist Missionary among the Micmac Indians of Nova Scotia in the 1870s.

Of old times, Mahtigwess, the Rabbit, who is called in the Micmac tongue Ableegumooch, lived with his grandmother. The Rabbit was waiting for better times; and truly he found it a hard matter in midwinter, when ice was on the river and snow was on the plain, to provide even for his small household. And running through the forest one day he found a lonely wigwam, and he that dwelt therein was Keeoony, the Otter. The lodge was on the bank of a river, and a smooth road of ice slanted from the door down to the water. And the Otter made him welcome, and directed his housekeeper to get ready to cook; saying which, he took the hooks on which he was wont to string fish when he had them, and went to fetch a mess for dinner. Placing himself on the top of the slide, he coasted in and under the water, and then came out with a great bunch of eels, which were soon cooked, and on which they dined.

"By my life," thought Master Rabbit, "but that is an easy way of getting a living! Truly these fishing-folk have fine fare, and cheap! Cannot I, who am so clever, do as well as this mere Otter? Of course I can. Why not?" Thereupon he grew so confident of himself as to invite the Otter to dine with him on the third day after that, and so went home.

"Come on!" he said to his grandmother the next morning; "let us remove our wigwam down to the lake." So they removed; and he selected a site such as the Otter had chosen for his home, and the weather being cold he made a road of ice, or a coast, down from his door to the water, and all was well. Then the guest came at the time set, and Rabbit, calling his grandmother, bade her get ready to cook a dinner. "But what am I to cook, grandson?" inquired the old dame.

"Truly I will see to that," said he, and made him a *nabogun*, or stick to string eels. Then going to the ice path, he tried to slide like one skilled in the art, but indeed with little luck, for he went first to the right side, then to the left, and so hitched and jumped till he came to the water, where he went in with a bob backwards. And this bad beginning had no better ending, since of all swimmers and divers the Rabbit is the very worst, and this one was no better than his brothers. The water was cold, he lost his breath, he struggled, and was well-nigh drowned.

"But what on earth ails the fellow?" said the Otter to the grandmother, who was looking on in amazement.

"Well, he has seen somebody do something, and is trying to do likewise," replied the old lady.

"Ho! come out of that now," cried the Otter, "and hand me your *nabogun!*" And the poor Rabbit, shivering with cold, and almost frozen, came from the water and limped into the lodge. And there he required much nursing from his grandmother, while the Otter, plunging into the stream, soon returned with a load of fish. But, disgusted at the Rabbit for attempting what he could not perform, he threw them down as a gift, and went home without tasting the meal.

Now Master Rabbit, though disappointed, was not discouraged, for this one virtue he had, that he never gave up. And wandering one day in the wilderness, he found a wigwam well filled with young women, all wearing red head-dresses; and no wonder, for they were Woodpeckers. Now, Master Rabbit was a well-bred Indian, who made himself as a melody to all voices, and so he was cheerfully bidden to bide to dinner, which he did. Then one of the red-polled pretty girls, taking a *wottes*, or wooden dish, lightly climbed a tree, so that she seemed to run; and while ascending, stopping here and there and tapping now and then, took from this place and that many of those insects called by the Indians *apchel-moal-timpkawal*, or rice, because they so much resemble it. And note that this rice is a dainty dish for those who like it. And when it was boiled, and they had dined, Master Rabbit again reflected, "La! how easily some folks live! What is to hinder me from doing the same? Ho, you girls! come over and dine with me the day after to-morrow!"

And having accepted this invitation, all the guests came on the day set, when Master Rabbit undertook to play woodpecker. So having taken the head of an eel-spear and fastened it to his nose to make a bill, he climbed as well as he could—and bad was the best—up a tree, and tried to get his harvest of rice. Truly he got none; only in this did he succeed in resembling a Woodpecker, that he had a red poll; for his pate was all torn and bleeding, bruised by the fishing-point. And the pretty birds all looked and laughed, and wondered what the Rabbit was about.

"Ah!" said his grandmother, "I suppose he is trying again to do something which he has seen someone do. 'Tis just like him."

"Oh, come down there!" cried Miss Woodpecker, as well as she could for laughing. "Give me your dish!" And having got it she scampered up the trunk, and soon brought down a dinner. But it was long ere Master Rabbit heard the last of it from these gay tree-tappers.

Now, truly, one would think that after all that had befallen Master *Mahtigwess*, the Rabbit, that he would have had enough of trying other people's trades; but his nature was such that, having once set his mighty mind to a thing, little short of sudden death would cure him. And being one day with the Bear in his cave, he beheld with great wonder how *Mooin* fed his folk. For, having put a great pot on the fire, he did but cut a little slice from his own foot and drop it into the boiling water, when it spread and grew into a mess of meat which served for all.* Nay, there was a great piece given to Rabbit to take home to feed his family.

"Now, truly," he said, "this is a thing which I can indeed do. Is it not recorded in the family wampum that whatever a Bear can do well a Rabbit can do better?" So, in fine, he invited his friend to come and dine with him the day after to-morrow.

And the Bear being there, Rabbit did but say, "*Noogume' kuesawal' wohu!*" "Grandmother, set your pot to boiling!" And, whetting his knife on a stone, he tried to do as the Bear had done; but little did he get from his small, thin soles, though he cut himself madly and sadly.

"What can he be trying to do?" growled the guest.

"Ah!" sighed the grandmother, "something which he has seen someone else do."

"Ho! I say there! Give me the knife," quoth Bruin. And, getting it, he took a slice from his sole, which did him no harm, and then, what with magic and fire, gave them a good dinner. But Master Rabbit was in sad case, and it was many a day ere he got well.

There are men who are bad at copying, yet are good originals, and of this kind was Master Rabbit, who, when he gave up trying to do as others did, succeeded very well. And, having found out his foible, he applied himself to become able in good earnest, and studied *m'téoulin*, or magic, so severely that in time he grew to be an awful conjurer, so that he could raise ghosts, crops, storms, or devils whenever he wanted them. For he had perseverance, and out of this may come anything, if it be only brought into the right road.

*Editor's note: This is evidently an illusion to the bear's ability to survive on stored fat during hibernation.

1. Stories such as this one were frequently told to Indian children. What message do you think this tale communicates?

* * * * *

2. Trickster Rabbit may be a fool, but he also has his admirable traits. Discuss.

1–5 A Spanish Priest Speculates on the Origin of the Indians in 1590

The Jesuit priest Jose de Acosta (1540–1600) spent seventeen years, from 1570 to 1587, in Spanish America, working in areas as widely separated as Peru and Mexico. His book Historia natural y moral de las Indias (1590) is invaluable for Acosta's astute observations of the native cultures of the Americas and the dramatic effects of colonization. It also contains his logical speculations on the origins of the Indians, a portion of which is reprinted below. In these pages, Acosta was first to propose that the Americas had been populated by migration from the Old World.

SOURCE: Jose de Acosta, *The Naturall and Morall Historie of the East and West Indies*, translated by Edward Grimston (London: V. Sims, 1604).

The reason that inforceth us to yeeld that the first men of the Indies are come from Europe or Asia, is the testimonie of the holy scripture, which teacheth us plainely that all men came from Adam. We can therefore give no other beginning to those at the Indies, seeing the holy scripture saieth, that all beasts and creatures of the earth perished but such as were reserved in the Arke of Noah, for the multiplication and maintenance of their kinde; so as we must necessarily referre the multiplication of all beastes to those which came out of the Arke of Noah, on the mountaines of Ararat, where it staied. And by this meanes we must seeke out both for men and beastes the way whereby they might passe from the old world to this new....

I conjecture...that the new world, which we call Indies, is not altogether severed and disjoyned from the other world; and to speake my opinion, I have long beleeved that the one and the other world are joyned and continued one with another in some part, or at the least are very neere. And yet to this day there is no certaine knowledge of the contrary. For towards the Articke or Northerne Pole all the longitude of the earth is not discovered, and many hold that above Florida the Land runnes out very large towards the North, and as they say joynes with the Scithike or German Sea. Others affirme that a Ship sayling in that Sea reported to have seene the coast of Bacalaos [Newfoundland] which stretcheth

almost to the confines of Europe. Moreover, no man knowes how farre the land runnes beyond the Cape of Mendocino [in California] in the South sea, but that they affirme it is a great Continent which runnes an infinite length; and returning to the Southerne Pole no man knowes the lands on the other part of the Straight of Magellan. A ship belonging to the Bishoppe of Plasencia, which passed the Straight, reports to have sayled alwayes within sight of land; the like Hernando Lamero a Pilot doth affirme, who, forced by foule weather, passed two or three degrees above the sayd Straight. So as there is no reason or experience that doth contradict my conceit and opinion, which is, that the whole earth is united and joyned in some part, or at the least the one approcheth neere unto the other. If this be true, as in effect there is some likelyhood, the answere is easie to the doubt we have propounded, how the first Inhabitants could passe to the Indies. For that wee must beleeve they could not so conveniently come thither by Sea as travelling by Land, which might be done without consideration in changing by little and little their lands and habitations. Some people, in time they came to inhabite and people the Indies, with so many nations, people, and tongues as we see....

Some (following Plato's opinion) affirme that these men parted from Europe or Afficke to go to that famous and renowned island of Atlantis, and so passed from one island unto another, until they came to the maine land of the Indies....But, to say the truth, I do not so much respect the authoritie of Plato (whom they call Divine), as I will beleeve he could write these things of the Atlantis island for a true Historie, the which are but meere fables, seeing hee confesseth that hee learned them of Critias, being a little childe, who, among other songs, sung that of the Atlantis island. But whether that Plato did write it for a true Historie or a fable, for my part I beleeve that all which he hath written of this island...cannot be held for true but among children and old folkes.

Others say that the Indians are descended from the Jews; for, commonly you shall see them fearfull, submisse, ceremonious, and subtill in lying. And, moreover, they say their habites are like unto those the Jewes used; for they weare a short coat or waste-coat, and a cloake imbroidered all about; they goe bare-footed, or with soles tied with latchets over the foot. And they say, that it appears by their Histories, as also by their ancient pictures, which represent them in this fashion, that this attire was the ancient habite of the Hebrewes, and that these two kinds of garments, which the Indians onely use, were used by Samson, which the Scripture calleth *Tunicam et Syndonem*; beeing the same which the Indians terme waste-coate and cloake. But all these conjectures are light, and rather against them then with them; for wee know well, that the Hebrewes used letters, whereof there is no shew among the Indians; they were great lovers of silver, these make no care of it; the Jews, if they were not circumcised, held not themselves for Jewes, and contrariwise the Indians are not at all, neyther did they ever use any ceremonie neere it as many in the East have done. But what reason of conjecture is there in this, seeing the Jewes are so carefull to preserve their language and Antiquities, so as in all parts of the world they differ and are known from others, and yet at the Indies alone, they have forgotten their Lineage, their Law, their Ceremonies, their Messiahs; and, finally, their whole Indaisme. And whereas they say, the Indians are fearefull cowards, superstitious, and subtill in lying; for the first, it is not common to all, there are some nations among the Barbarians free from these vices, there are some valiant and hardy, there are some blunt and dull of understanding....

It is easier to refute and contradict the false opinions conceyved of the Originall of the Indians, then to set downe a true and certaine resolution; for that there is no writing among the Indians, nor any certaine remembrances of their founders; neyther is there any mention made of this new world in their bookes that have knowledge of letters; our Ancients held, that in those parts, there were neyther men, land, nor haven. So as hee should seeme rash and presumptuous, that should thinke to discover the first beginning of the Indians. But we may judge a farre off, by the former discourse, that these Indians came by little and little to this newe world, and that by the helpe and meanes of the neerenesse of lands, or by some navigation; the which seemes to mee the meanes whereby they came, and not that they prepared any armie to goe thither of purpose; neyther that they have been caried thither by any ship-wracke or tempest, although some of these things may chance in

some part of the Indies; for these Regions being so great, as they containe Nations without number, we may beleeve, that some came to inhabite after one sort, and some after an other. But in the ende I resolve upon this point, that the true and principall cause to people the Indies, was, that the lands and limits thereof are joyned and continued in some extremities of the world, or at the least were very neere. And I beleeve it is not many thousand yeeres past since men first inhabited this new world and West Indies, and that the first men that entred, were rather savage men and hunters, then bredde up in civill and well governed Common-weales; and that they came to this new world, having lost their owne land, or being in too great numbers, they were forced of necessitie to seeke some other habitations; the which found, they begame by little and little to plant, having no other law, but some instinct of nature, and that very darke, and some customes remayning of their first Countries. And although they came from Countries well governed, yet is it not incredible to thinke that they had forgotten all through the tract of time and want of use, seeing that in Spaine and Italie we find companies of men, which have nothing but the shape and countenance onely, whereby we may conjecture in what sort this new world grew so barbarous and uncivill.

* * * * * *

1. *What are the elements of Acosta's argument about the origins of the Indians? How well does it stand up to the modern Beringian migration hypothesis?*

2. *Acosta briefly discusses what Europeans knew of the coastal geography of the Americas by the late sixteenth century. Use an atlas to review the state of this knowledge.*

3. *One of the most common theories about Indian origins was that they were descended from one or more of the lost tribes of the Israelites. What did Acosta think of this claim?*

1–6 Two Nineteenth-Century Archaeologists Provide the First Scientific Description of the Indian Mounds of the Mississippi Valley in 1848

In the 1840s the archaeologists Ephraim George Squier (1821–1888) and Edwin H. Davis (1811–1888) researched and wrote Ancient Monuments of the Mississippi Valley (1848), the first work issued by the newly-organized Smithsonian Institution. Squier and Davis provided detailed surveys of hundreds of Indian mounds, many of which have since been destroyed by agriculture and town building. In the following passages they offer their concluding observations on the mystery of the mounds.

THE ancient monuments of the Western United States consist, for the most part, of elevations and embankments of earth and stone, erected with great labor and manifest design. In connection with these, more or less intimate, are found various minor relics of art, consisting of ornaments and implements of many kinds, some of them composed of metal, but most of stone.

These remains are spread over a vast extent of country. They are found on the sources of the Alleghany, in the western part of the State of New York, on the east; and extend thence westwardly along the southern shore of Lake Erie, and through Michigan and Wisconsin, to Iowa and the Nebraska territory, on the west. We have no record of their occurrence above the great lakes. Carver mentions some on the shores of Lake Pepin, and some are said to occur near Lake Travers, under the 46th parallel of latitude. Lewis and Clarke saw them on the Missouri river, one thousand miles above its junction with the Mississippi; and they have been observed on the Kansas and Platte, and on other remote western rivers. They are found all over the intermediate country, and spread over the valley of the Mississippi to the Gulf of Mexico. They line the shores of the Gulf from Texas to Florida, and extend, in diminished numbers, into South Carolina. They occur in great numbers in Ohio, Indiana, Illinois, Wisconsin, Missouri, Arkansas, Kentucky, Tennessee, Louisiana, Mississippi, Alabama, Georgia, Florida, and Texas. They are found, in less numbers, in the western

portions of New York, Pennsylvania, Virginia, and North and South Carolina; as also in Michigan, Iowa, and in the Mexican territory beyond the Rio Grande del Norte. In short, they occupy the entire basin of the Mississippi and its tributaries, as also the fertile plains along the Gulf....

...We find numberless mounds, most of them conical but many pyramidal in form, and often of great dimensions. The pyramidal structures are always truncated, sometimes terraced, and generally have graded ascents to their summits. They bear a close resemblance to the Teocallis of Mexico; and the known uses of the latter are suggestive of the probable purposes to which they were applied. Accompanying these, and in some instances sustaining an intimate relation to them, are numerous enclosures of earth and stone, frequently of vast size, and often of regular outline. These are by far the most imposing class of our aboriginal remains, and impress us most sensibly with the numbers and power of the people who built them. The purposes of many of these are quite obvious; and investigation has served to settle, pretty clearly, the character of most of the other works occurring in connection with them....

Without undertaking to point out the affinities, or to indicate the probable origin of the builders of the western monuments, and the cause of their final disappearance,—inquiries of deep interest and vast importance in an archaeological and ethnological point of view we may venture to suggest that the facts thus far collected point to a connection more or less intimate between the race of the mounds and the semi-civilized nations which formerly had their seats among the sierras of Mexico, upon the plains of Central America and Peru, and who erected the imposing structures which from their number, vastness, and mysterious significance, invest the central portions of the continent with an interest not less absorbing than that which attaches to the valley of the Nile. These nations alone, of all those found in possession of the continent by the European discoverers, were essentially stationary and agricultural in their habits,—conditions indispensable to large population, to fixedness of institutions, and to any considerable advance in the economical or ennobling arts. That the mound-builders, although perhaps in a less degree, were also stationary and agricultural, clearly appears from a variety of facts and circumstances, most of which will no doubt recur to the mind of the reader, but which will bear recapitulation here.

It may safely be claimed, and will be admitted without dispute, that a large local population can only exist under an agricultural system. Dense commercial and manufacturing communities, the apparent exceptions to the remark, are themselves the offspring of a large agricultural population, with which nearly or remotely they

SOURCE: E. G. Squier and E. H. Davis, *Ancient Monuments of the Mississippi Valley* (Washington, D.C.: Smithsonian Institution, 1848), pp. 1–3, 301–306.

are connected, and upon which they are dependent. Now it is evident that works of art, so numerous and vast as we have seen those of the Mississippi valley to be,—could only have been erected by a numerous people,—and especially must we regard as numerous the population capable of constructing them, when we reflect how imperfect at the best must have been the artificial aids at their command, as compared with those of the present age. Implements of wood, stone, and copper, could hardly have proved very efficient auxiliaries to the builders, who must have depended mainly upon their own bare hands and weak powers of transportation, for excavating and collecting together the twenty millions of cubic feet of material which make up the solid contents of the great mound at Cahokia alone.

But the conclusion that the ancient population was exceedingly dense, follows not less from the capability which they possessed to erect, than from the circumstance that they required, works of the magnitude we have seen, to protect them in danger, or to indicate in a sufficiently imposing form their superstitious zeal, and their respect for the dead. As observed by an eminent archaeologist, whose opinions upon this and collateral subjects are entitled to a weight second to those of no other author, "it is impossible that the population, for whose protection such extensive works were necessary, and which was able to defend them, should not have been eminently agricultural." The same author elsewhere observes, of the great mound at Grave creek, that "it indicates not only a dense agricultural population, but also a state of society essentially different from that of the modern race of Indians north of the tropic. There is not, and there was not in the sixteenth century, a single tribe of Indians (north of the semi-civilized nations) between the Atlantic and the Pacific, which had means of subsistence sufficient to enable them to apply, for such purposes, the unproductive labor necessary for the work; nor was there any in such a social state as to compel the labor of the people to be thus applied.'" ...

* [Albert] GALLATIN'S "Notes on the semi-civilized nations of Mexico," *Transactions of American Ethnological Society*, Vol. I, p. 207.

In respect to the extent of territory occupied at one time, or at successive periods, by the race of the mounds, so far as indicated by the occurrence of their monuments, little need be said in addition to the observations presented in the first chapter. It cannot, however, have escaped notice, that the relics found in the mounds,—composed of materials peculiar to places separated as widely as the ranges of the Alleghanies on the east, and the Sierras of Mexico on the west, the waters of the great lakes on the north, and those of the Gulf of Mexico on the south,—denote the contemporaneous existence of communication between these extremes. For we find, side by side in the same mounds, native copper from Lake Superior, mica from the Alleghanies, shells from the Gulf, and obsidian (perhaps porphyry) from Mexico. This fact seems seriously to conflict with the hypothesis of a migration, either northward or southward. Further and more extended investigations and observations may, nevertheless, serve satisfactorily to settle not only this, but other equally interesting questions connected with the extinct race, whose name is lost to tradition itself, and whose very existence is left to the sole and silent attestation of the rude but often imposing monuments which throng the valleys of the West.

* * * * * *

1. What explanations do Squier and Davis offer for the building of mounds in the Mississippi Valley?

2. The authors argue that only an agricultural people could construct the mounds. On the basis of your reading in the text, is this strictly true?

3. According to the authors, the builders of the mounds must have "disappeared," for when the Europeans arrived there was not a single tribe of Indians between the Atlantic and the Pacific with "the means of subsistence sufficient" to build them. What is wrong with this interpretation?

1–7 A Jesuit Missionary Reports on the Society of the Natchez of the Lower Mississippi in 1730

Jesuit missionary Mathurin Le Petit (1693–1739) was born in France and came to Louisiana in 1726. After several years working among the Choctaws he was appointed superior of the Louisiana missions and moved to New Orleans. The Natchez Indians opposed the expansion of French influence into their country, and they attacked and killed many colonists, including two missionaries under Le Petit's charge. In the following report, written to his superiors in France, Father Le Petit provides one of the best descriptions of the Natchez. But it is important to keep in mind that Father Le Petit was attempting to justify the planned French attack on these Indians, which would destroy them in 1731.

SOURCE: Reuben Gold Thwaites. ed., *The Jesuit Relations and Allied Documents* (Cleveland: The Burrows Brothers Company, 1896–1901). 68: 123–39.

This Nation of Savages inhabits one of the most beauti-ful and fertile countries in the World, and is the only one on this continent which appears to have any regular wor-ship. Their Religion in certain points is very similar to that of the ancient Romans. They have a Temple filled with Idols, which are different figures of men and of animals, and for which they have the most profound veneration. Their Temple in shape resembles an earthen oven, a hun-dred feet in circumference. They enter it by a little door about four feet high, and not more than three in breadth. No window is to be seen there. The arched roof of the edi-fice is covered with three rows of mats, placed one upon the other, to prevent the rain from injuring the masonry. Above on the outside are three figures of eagles made of wood, and painted red, yellow, and white. Before the door is a kind of shed with folding-doors, where the Guardian of the Temple is lodged; all around it runs a circle of pal-isades, on which are seen exposed the skulls of all the heads which their Warriors had brought back from the bat-tles in which they had been engaged with the enemies of their Nation.

In the interior of the Temple are some shelves arranged at a certain distance from each other, on which are placed cane baskets of an oval shape, and in these are enclosed the bones of their ancient Chiefs, while by their side are those of their victims who had caused themselves to be strangled, to follow their masters into the other world. Another separate shelf supports many flat baskets very gorgeously painted, in which they preserve their Idols. These are figures of men and women made of stone or baked clay, the heads and the tails of extraordinary serpents, some stuffed owls, some pieces of crystal, and some jaw-bones of large fish. In the year 1699, they had there a bottle and the foot of a glass, which they guarded as very precious.

In this Temple they take care to keep up a perpetu-al fire, and they are very particular to prevent its ever blazing; they do not use anything for it but dry wood of the walnut or oak. The old men are obliged to carry, each one in his turn, a large log of wood into the enclosure of the palisade. The number of the Guardians of the Temple is fixed, and they serve by the quarter. He who is on duty is placed like a sentinel under the shed, from whence he examines whether the fire is not in danger of going out. He feeds it with two or three large logs, which do not burn except at the extremity, and which they never place one on the other, for fear of their getting into a blaze.

Of the women, the sisters of the great Chief alone have liberty to enter within the Temple. The entrance is forbidden to all the others, as well as to the common peo-ple, even when they carry something there to feast to the memory of their relatives, whose bones repose in the Temple. They give the dishes to the Guardian, who carries them to the side of the basket in which are the bones of the dead; this ceremony lasts only during one moon. The dish-es are afterward placed on the palisades which surround the Temple, and are abandoned to the fallow-deer.

The Sun is the principal object of veneration to these people; as they cannot conceive of anything which can be above this heavenly body, nothing else appears to them more worthy of their homage. It is for the same reason that the great Chief of this Nation, who knows nothing on the earth more dignified than himself, takes the title of broth-er of the Sun, and the credulity of the people maintains him in the despotic authority which he claims. To enable them better to converse together, they raise a mound of artificial soil, on which they build his cabin, which is of the same construction as the Temple. The door fronts the East, and every morning the great Chief honors by his presence the rising of his elder brother, and salutes him with many howlings as soon as he appears above the hori-zon. Then he gives orders that they shall light his calumet; he makes him an offering of the first three puffs which he draws; afterward raising his hand above his head, and turning from the East to the West, he shows him the direc-tion which he must take in his course....

This Government is hereditary; it is not, however, the son of the reigning Chief who succeeds his father, but the son of his sister, or the first Princess of the blood. This policy is founded on the knowledge they have of the licen-tiousness of their women. They are not sure, they say, that the children of the chief's wife may be of the blood Royal, whereas the son of the sister of the great Chief must be, at least on the side of the mother.

The Princesses of the blood never espouse any but men of obscure family, and they have but one husband, but they have the right of dismissing him whenever it pleases them, and of choosing another among those of the Nation, provided he has not made any other alliance among them. If the husband has been guilty of infidelity, the Princess may have his head cut off in an instant; but she is not her-self subject to the same law, for she may have as many Lovers as she pleases, without the husband having any power to complain. In the presence of his wife he acts with the most profound respect, never eats with her, and salutes her with howls, as is done by her servants. The only satis-faction he has is, that he is freed from the necessity of laboring, and has entire authority over those who serve the Princess....

Each year the people assemble to plant one vast field with Indian corn, beans, pumpkins, and melons, and then again they collect in the same way to gather the harvest. A large cabin situated on a beautiful prairie is set apart to hold the fruits of this harvest. Once in the summer, toward the end of July, the people gather by order of the great Chief, to be present at a grand feast which he gives them. This Festival lasts for three days and three nights, and each one contributes what he can to furnish it; some bring game, others fish, etc. They have almost constant dances, while the great Chief and his sister are in an elevated lodge covered with boughs, from whence they can see the joy of their subjects. The Princes, the Princesses, and those who by their office are of distinguished rank, are arranged very near the Chief, to whom they show their respect and submission by an infinite variety of ceremonies.

The great Chief and his sister make their entrance in the place of the assembly on a litter borne by eight of their greatest men: the Chief holds in his hand a great scepter ornamented with painted plumes, and all the people dance and sing about him in testimony of the public joy. The last day of this Feast he causes all his subjects to approach, and makes them a long harangue, in which he exhorts them to fulfill all their duties to Religion; he recommends them above all things to have a great veneration for the spirits who reside in the Temple, and carefully to instruct their children. If any one has distinguished himself by some act of zeal, he is then publicly praised. Such a case happened in the year 1702. The Temple having been struck by lightning and reduced to ashes, seven or eight women cast their infants into the midst of the flames to appease the wrath of Heaven. The great Chief called these heroines, and gave

them great praises for the courage with which they had made the sacrifice of that which they held most dear; he finished his panegyric by exhorting the other women to imitate so beautiful an example in similar circumstances.

* * * * *

1. Many historians believe that the Natchez continued to practice many of the traits of the great Mississippian societies that had dominated the South in the centuries before European conquest. What supporting evidence for that view can you find in the account of Father Le Petit?

2. How does Father Le Petit explain the building of mounds by the Natchez? How do this views compare with the interpretation of Squier and Davis in the previous document?

3. Father Le Petit suggests that the hereditary patterns of Natchez royalty were the result of "the licentiousness of their women." Can you provide an alternative explanation?

1–8   The Constitution of the Five Nation Confederacy Records the Innovations of an Iroquois Founding Father of the Fifteenth Century

The Five Nation Iroquois Confederacy was founded in the mid-fifteenth century by the legendary Onondaga chief Deganawida. Renowned for his wisdom, Deganawida proposed this union of the nations as a way to end the persistent violence and warfare among themselves. Communicated orally for generations, the constitution was finally written down in the mid-nineteenth century. The version from which the following excerpts are taken was published in 1880 by Seth Newhouse, a Seneca.

SOURCE: Thomas R. Henry, *Wilderness Messiah: The Story of Hiawatha and the Iroquois* (New York, 1955).

This is wisdom and justice of the part of the Great Spirit to create and raise chiefs, give and establish unchangeable laws, rules and customs between the Five Nation Indians, viz the Mohawks, Oneidas, Onondagas, Cayugas and Senecas and the other nations of Indians here in North America. The object of these laws is to establish peace between the numerous nations of Indians, hostility will be done away with, for the preservation and protection of life, property and liberty.

Laws, rules and customs as follows:

I. And the number of chiefs in this confederation of the five Nation Indians are fifty in number, no more and no less. They are the ones to arrange, to legislate and to look after the affairs of their people....

7. And when the Five Nation Indians confederation chiefs assemble to hold a council, the council shall be duly opened and closed by the Onondaga chiefs, the Fire keepers. They will offer thanks to the Great Spirit that dwells in heaven above: the source and ruler of our lives, and it is him that sends daily blessings upon us, our daily wants and daily health, and they will then declare the council open for the transaction of business, and give decisions of all that is done in the council....

10. And the business of the council of the Five Nation Indians is transacted by two combination of chiefs; viz first the Mohawks and Senecas, and second the Oneidas and Cayugas.

11. And when a case or proposition is introduced in the council of the five nations, the Mohawk chiefs with the Senecas shall first consider the matter, and whatever the decision may be; then the speaker will refer the matter to the other side of the council fire; to the second combination chiefs, the Oneidas and Cayugas, for their consideration, and if they all agree unanimously then the speaker of the council shall refer the matter to the Fire keepers; and it is

then their duty to sanction it; and their speaker will then pronounce the case as passed in council.

12. And if a dissention arises between the two combination chiefs in council, and they agree to refer the matter to the Fire keepers to decide, then the Fire keepers shall decide which of the two or more propositions is most advantageous to their people, and their decision is final.

13. And when any case or proposition has passed unanimously between the two combination chiefs, and the case or proposition is then referred to the Fire keepers for their sanction: and if the Fire keepers see that the case or proposition is such that it will be injurious and not to the advantage of their people, then they will refer the case or proposition back to the Mohawk chiefs, and point out where it would be injurious to the people and then they will reconsider the case. When it is right the case is then referred again to the Fire keepers and then they will pass it....

24. And the duty of the Head Principal Chief of the Onondagas, Ododarho, is to keep the Five Nation Indians confederation council fire clean all around, that no dust or dirt is to be seen. There is a long wing of a bird, and a stick is placed by his side, and he will take the long wing and sweep or dust the dirt away from the council fire, and if he sees any creeping creature crawling towards the Five Nation Indians council fire he will take the stick and pitch the crawling creature away from the fire, and his cousin chiefs of the Onondagas will act with him at all times, and the crawling creature signifies any case or proposition or the crawling creature signifies any case or proposition or subject brought before the Five Nation Indians council which would be ruinous and injurious to their people, and they are to reject anything which on the nature would be ruinous and injurious and not to the advantage of their people, and they are to consider first by themselves during the council, and then call the attention of the council to the fact, case or proposition, and the council are not to receive it after it had been rejected by the council....

26. The duty of the two head Seneca chiefs, viz Ke non keri dawi and De yo nin ho hakarawen, who are stationed at the door of the Five Nations Indians confederation session, is to watch and if they see any crawling creature entering in the session they will disallow to enter in the session; Crawling creature signifies any case of proposition which brought before the session would be ruinous, or injurious to the people; and also if they see stranger near the door they will bring the stranger in their session and ask what is their message have they with them....

28. And if the principal chief or chiefs of the Five Nation Indians confederation, disregards the constitution of the Five Nation Indians, then his female relatives will come to him and warn him or they to come back, and

walk according to this constitution; if he or they disregards the warning after the first and second warnings, then she will refer the matter to the war chief, and the war chief will now say to him, so you did not listen to her warnings, now it is just where the bright noonday sun stands, an its before that sun's brightness I now discharge you as a chief an I now disposses you of the office of chieftainship. I now give her the chieftainship for she is the proprietor, and as I have now discharged you as a chief, so you are no longer a chief you will now go where you want it to go, an you will now go alone, an the rest of the people will not go with you for we know not of what kind of a spirit has got in you, and as the Great Spirit could not handle sin therefore he could not come to take you out of the prespice in the place of destruction, and you will never be restored again to the place you did occupy once. Then the war chief will notify the Five Nation Indians confederation of his dismissal and they will sanction it.

29. Kariwhiyho, the good message is the love of the Great Spirit, the Supreme Being, now this Kariwhiyho is the surrounding guard of the Five Nation Indians confederation principal chiefs, an this Kariwhiyho it loves all alike the members of the Five Nation Indians confederation, and other nations of Indians that are attached to it by and through customary way of treaties....

30. And there is Five arrows bound together. This is the symbol of Union, Power, Honour, and Dominion of the Five Nation Indians confederation, an if one of the Five arrows was to be taken out then the remainder is easily broken asunder. This signifies if one of the Five Nations were to emagrate to a distant country of course they now withdrawn from the confederation therefore the Power of the Five Nation Indians confederation decreased.

* * * * * *

1. *The model for the Iroquois confederacy was based on the idea of the longhouse. What evidence do you find in this document for the use of the metaphor of longhouse?*

2. *Some scholars believe that the Iroquois constitution influenced the men who drafted the constitution of the United States, while others believe that by the time Iroquois law was written down, the oral tradition had shaped it to conform with American law. In either case, what similarities do you find between these two constitutions?*

3. *What does the constitution suggest about the political roles of Iroquois women?*

When Worlds Collide, 1492–1588

2–1 Christopher Columbus Writes of His First View of the New World in 1492

An Italian sailor working for the King and Queen of Spain, Columbus made the first recorded European crossing of the Atlantic. Despite evidence of earlier Scandinavian contact with the northern coast of North America, Columbus's voyage opened up contact between the continents for future European migration. Columbus's mission was twofold: To establish himself as governor-general and viceroy of new lands for Spain, and to open broader diplomatic, commercial, and religious contact for Spain. His journal provides a record of his scientific, spiritual, and imperial explorations.

SOURCE: Christopher Columbus, "Journal of the First Voyage to America," in Julius E. Olson and Edward Gaylord Bourne, ed., *The Northmen, Columbus, and Cabot, 985–1503. Original Narratives of Early American History* (New York: Charles Scribner's Sons. 1906).

Sunday, Oct. 21st [1492]. At 10 o'clock, we arrived at a cape of the island, and anchored, the other vessels in company. After having dispatched a meal, I went ashore, and found no habitation save a single house, and that without an occupant; we had no doubt that the people had fled in terror at our approach, as the house was completely furnished. I suffered nothing to be touched, and went with my captains and some of the crew to view the country. This island even exceeds the others in beauty and fertility. Groves of lofty and flourishing trees are abundant, as also large lakes, surrounded and overhung by the foliage, in a most enchanting manner. Everything looked as green as in April in Andalusia. The melody of the birds was so exquisite that one was never willing to part from the spot, and the flocks of parrots obscured the heavens. The diversity in the appearance of the feathered tribe from those of our country is extremely curious. A thousand different sorts of trees, with their fruit were to be met with, and of a wonderfully delicious odour. It was a great affliction to me to be ignorant of their natures, for I am very certain they are all valuable; specimens of them and of the plants I have preserved: Going round one of these lakes, I saw a snake, which we killed, and I have kept the skin for your

Highnesses; upon being discovered he took to the water, whither we followed him, as it was not deep, and dispatched him with our lances; he was seven spans in length; I think there are many more such about here. I discovered also the aloe tree, and am determined to take on board the ship to-morrow, ten quintals of it, as I am told it is valuable. While we were in search of some good water, we came upon a village of the natives about half a league from the place where the ships lay; the inhabitants on discovering us abandoned their houses, and took to flight, carrying off their goods to the mountain. I ordered that nothing which they had left should be taken, not even the value of a pin. Presently we saw several of the natives advancing towards our party, and one of them came up to us, to whom we gave some hawk's bells and glass beads, with which he was delighted. We asked him in return, for water, and after I had gone on board the ship, the natives came down to the shore with their calabashes full, and showed great pleasure in presenting us with it. I ordered more glass beads to be given them, and they promised to return the next day. It is my wish to fill all the water casks of the ships at this place, which being executed, I shall depart immediately, if the weather serve, and sail round the island, till I succeed in meeting with the king, in order to see if I can acquire any of the gold, which I hear he possesses. Afterwards I shall set sail for another very large island which I believe to be *Cipango*, according to the indications I receive from the Indians on board. They call the Island *Colba*, Cuba, and say there are many large ships, and sailors there. This other island they name *Bosio*, and inform me that it is very large; the others which lie in our course, I shall examine on the passage, and according as I find gold or spices in abundance, I shall determine what to do; at all events I am determined to proceed on to the continent, and visit the city of *Guisay* where I shall deliver the letters of your Highnesses to the *Great Can*, and demand an answer, with which I shall return.

Monday, Oct. 22d. Through the night, and today we remained waiting here to see if the king, or any others would bring us gold or anything valuable. Many of the natives visited us, resembling those of the other islands, naked like them, and painted white, red, black and other colours; they brought javelins and clews of cotton to barter, which they exchanged with the sailors for bits of glass, broken cups, and fragments of earthenware. Some of them wore pieces of gold at their noses; they readily gave them away for hawk's bells and glass beads; the amount collected in this manner, however, was very inconsiderable. Any small matter they received from us, they held in high estimation, believing us to have come from heaven. We took in water for the ships from a lake in the neighbourhood of this cape, which I have named *Cabo del Isleo*: in this lake Martin Alonzo Pinzon, captain of the Pinta, killed a snake similar to that of yesterday, seven spans long. I ordered as much of the aloe to be collected as could be found.

Tuesday, Oct. 23d. It is now my determination to depart for the island of *Cuba*, which I believe to be *Cipango*, from the accounts I have received here, of the multitude and riches of the people. I have abandoned the intention of staying here and sailing round the island in search of the king, as it would be a waste of time, and I perceive there are no gold mines to be found. Moreover it would be necessary to steer many courses in making the circuit, and we cannot expect the wind to be always favourable. And as we are going to places where there is great commerce, I judge it expedient not to linger on the way, but to proceed and survey the lands we met with, till we arrive at that most favourable for our enterprise. It is my opinion that we shall find much profit there in spices; but my want of knowledge in these articles occasions me the most excessive regrets, inasmuch as I see a thousand sorts of trees, each with its own species of fruit, and as flourishing at the present time, as the fields in Spain, during the months of May and June; likewise a thousand kinds of herbs and flowers, of all which I remain in ignorance as to their properties, with the exception of the aloe, which I have directed to-day to be taken on board in large quantities for the use of your Highnesses. I did not set sail to-day for want of wind, a dead calm and heavy rain prevailing. Yesterday it rained much without cold; the days here are hot, and the nights mild like May in Andalusia.

Wednesday, Oct. 24th. At midnight weighed anchor and set sail from *Cabo del Isleo* of the island of *Isabela*, being in the North part, where I had remained preparing to depart for the island of *Cuba*, in which place the Indians tell me I shall find a great trade, with abundance of gold and spices, and large ships, and merchants; they directed me to steer toward the W.S.W., which is the course I am pursuing. If the accounts which the natives of the islands and those on board the ships have communicated to me by signs (for their language I do not understand) may be relied on, this must be the island of *Cipango*, of which we have heard so many wonderful things; according to my geographical knowledge it must be somewhere in this neighbourhood....

1. *How do Columbus's journal entries reflect the purposes of his mission? Why would Columbus keep a journal? What would he include, or leave out, to affect its later usage?*

* * * * * *

2. *What can we tell about the indigenous people Columbus encountered from his journal?*

2–2   An Aztec Remembers the Conquest of Mexico a Quarter Century Afterwards, in 1550

The following is a native account of Cortés's conquest of the Aztecs. The first part, describing the looting of gold from Montezuma, is taken from the Codex Florentino, a compilation of oral histories by those who survived the conquest. The story of the massacre at the Fiesta of Toxcatl, an Aztec celebration to honor the god Huitzilopochtli, comes from the Codex Ramirez and the Codex Aubin. The Codexes are important documents of the Indian people of Mexico at the time of the conquest, mostly assembled by Spanish priests.

SOURCE: From *The Broken Spears* by Miguel Leon-Portilla. © 1962, 1990 by Beacon Press. Reprinted by Permission of Beacon Press.

The Aztecs believed that Cortés was Quetzalcoatl, god and culture hero who had departed to the east, promising that someday he would return from across the seas. It is thus ironic that when Cortés and his men entered Mexico, they were often welcomed not only as guests but also as gods coming home. The Aztec desire to honor the "gods" coincided with the Spanish desire for gold. Thus Montezuma sent out messengers with gifts. But as Cortés's forces moved toward Tenochtitlan (Mexico City), the initial "golden age" disintegrated into suspicion, manipulation, and distrust. Such distrust was often translated into brutality...

When Montezuma had given necklaces to each one, Cortés asked him: "Are you Montezuma? Are you the king? Is it true that you are the king Montezuma?"

And the king said: "Yes, I am Montezuma." Then he stood up to welcome Cortés; he came forward, bowed his head low and addressed him in these words: "Our lord, you are weary. The journey has tired you, but now you have arrived on the earth. You have come to your city, Mexico. You have come here to sit on your throne, to sit under its canopy.

"The kings who have gone before, your representatives, guarded it and preserved it for your coming. The kings Itzcoatl, Motecuhzoma the Elder, Axayacatl, Tizoc and Ahuitzol ruled for you in the City of Mexico. The people were protected by their swords and sheltered by their shields.

"Do the kings know the destiny of those they left behind, their posterity? If only they are watching! If only they can see what I see!

"No, it is not a dream. I am not walking in my sleep. I am not seeing you in my dreams....I have seen you at last! I have met you face to face! I was in agony for five days, for ten days, with my eyes fixed on the Region of the Mystery. And now you have come out of the clouds and mists to sit on your throne again.

"This was foretold by the kings who governed your city, and now it has taken place. You have come back to us; you have come down from the sky. Rest now, and take possession of your royal houses. Welcome to your land, my lords !"

When Montezuma had finished, La Malinche translated his address into Spanish so that the Captain could understand it. Cortés replied in his strange and savage tongue, speaking first to La Malinche: "Tell Montezuma that we are his friends. There is nothing to fear. We have wanted to see him for a long time, and now we have seen his face and heard his words. Tell him that we love him well and that our hearts are contented."

Then he said to Montezuma: "We have come to your house in Mexico as friends. There is nothing to fear."

La Malinche translated this speech and the Spaniards grasped Montezuma's hands and patted his back to show their affection for him....

When the Spaniards were installed in the palace, they asked Montezuma about the city's resources and reserves and about the warriors' ensigns and shields. They questioned him closely and then demanded gold.

Montezuma guided them to it. They surrounded him and crowded close with their weapons. He walked in the center, while they formed a circle around him.

When they arrived at the treasure house called Teucalco, the riches of gold and feathers were brought out to them: ornaments made of quetzal feathers, richly worked shields, disks of gold, the necklaces of the idols, gold nose plugs, gold greaves and bracelets and crowns.

The Spaniards immediately stripped the feathers from the gold shields and ensigns. They gathered all the gold into a great mound and set fire to everything else, regardless of its value. Then they melted down the gold into ingots. As for the precious green stones, they took only the best of them; the rest were snatched up by the Tlaxcaltecas. The Spaniards searched through the whole treasure house, questioning and quarreling, and seized every object they thought was beautiful.

Next they went to Montezuma's storehouse, in the place called Totocalco [Place of the Palace of the Birds], where his personal treasures were kept. The Spaniards grinned like little beasts and patted each other with delight.

When they entered the hall of treasures, it was as if they had arrived in Paradise. They searched everywhere and coveted everything; they were slaves to their own greed. All of Montezuma's possessions were brought out: fine bracelets, necklaces with large stones, ankle rings with little gold bells, the royal crowns and all the royal finery—everything that belonged to the king and was reserved to him only. They seized these treasures as if they were their own, as if this plunder were merely a stroke of good luck. And when they had taken all the gold, they heaped up everything else in the middle of the patio.

La Malinche called the nobles together. She climbed up to the palace roof and cried: "Mexicanos, come forward! The Spaniards need your help! Bring them food and pure water. They are tired and hungry; they are almost fainting from exhaustion! Why do you not come forward? Are you angry with them?"

The Mexicans were too frightened to approach. They were crushed by terror and would not risk coming forward. They shied away as if the Spaniards were wild beasts, as if the hour were midnight on the blackest night of the year. Yet they did not abandon the Spaniards to hunger and thirst. They brought them whatever they needed, but shook with fear as they did so. They delivered the supplies to the Spaniards with trembling hands, then turned and hurried away.....

Cortés had been absent from the city for twenty days when the massacre at the fiesta of Tuxcatl took place; he had gone out to fight Panfilo de Narvaez, who was coming to arrest him by order of Diego Velazquez, governor of Cuba. Cortés' deputy, Pedro de Alvarado, treacherously murdered the celebrants when the festival was at its height.....

At the fiesta, when the dance was loveliest and when song was linked to song, the Spaniards were seized with an urge to kill the celebrants. They all ran forward, armed as if for battle. They closed the entrances and passageways, all the gates of the patio: the Eagle Gate in the lesser palace, the Gate of the Canestalk and the Gate of the Serpent of Mirrors. They posted guards so that no one could escape, and then rushed into the Sacred Patio to slaughter the celebrants. They came on foot, carrying their swords and their wooden or metal shields.

They ran in among the dancers, forcing their way to the place where the drums were played. They attacked the man who was drumming and cut off his arms. Then they cut off his head, and it rolled across the floor.

They attacked all the celebrants, stabbing them, spearing them, striking them with their swords. They attacked some of them from behind, and these fell instantly to the ground with their entrails hanging out. Others they beheaded: they cut off their heads, or split their heads to pieces.

They struck others in the shoulders, and their arms were torn from their bodies. They wounded some in the thigh and some in the calf. They slashed others in the abdomen, and their entrails all spilled to the ground. Some attempted to run away, but their intestines dragged as they ran; they seemed to tangle their feet in their own entrails. No matter how they tried to save themselves, they could find no escape.

Some attempted to force their way out, but the Spaniards murdered them at the gates. Others climbed the walls, but they could not save themselves. Those who ran into the communal houses were safe there for a while; so were those who lay down among the victims and pretended to be dead. But if they stood up again, the Spaniards saw them and killed them.

The blood of the warriors flowed like water and gathered into pools. The pools widened, and the stench of blood and entrails filled the air. The Spaniards ran into the communal houses to kill those who were hiding. They ran everywhere and searched everywhere; they invaded every room, hunting and killing.

When the news of this massacre was heard outside the Sacred Patio, a great cry went up: "Mexicanos, come running! Bring your spears and shields! The strangers have murdered our warriors!"

This cry was answered with a roar of grief and anger: the people shouted and wailed and beat their palms against their mouths. The captains assembled at once, as if the hour had been determined in advance. They all carried their spears and shields.

Then the battle began. The Aztecs attacked with javelins and arrows, even with the light spears that are used for hunting birds. They hurled their javelins with all their strength, and the cloud of missiles spread out over the Spaniards like a yellow cloak.

The Spaniards immediately took refuge in the palace. They began to shoot at the Mexicans with their iron arrows and to fire their cannons and arquebuses. And they shackled Montezuma in chains.

The Mexicans who had died in the massacre were taken out of the patio one by one and inquiries were made to discover their names. The fathers and mothers of the dead wept and lamented.

* * * * * *

1. As portrayed in this account, what is the Spanish conquistador's purpose in the new world? How does it compare to Christopher Columbus's story in his journal?

2. La Malinche becomes an important symbol in Mexican literature and history. How is she portrayed in this account?

3. What do you think of oral history as a means of documenting historical events? What possible problems might arise when oral histories are collected several years after the events, as these accounts were? What possible effect could the priests who collected the oral histories have on their recording? How might they have been different?

2–3 An Early Proponent for Native Rights Condemns the Torture of the Indians in 1565

Bartolomé de las Casas was one of the first proponents of Indian rights in the New World. A priest and historian of his day, responsible for preserving Christopher Columbus's journals, de las Casas also wrote works such as The Devastation of the Indies and Apologetic History of the Indics. Labeled a heretic and traitor, de las Casas documented the war on the Indians by the Spaniards and argued the Indians' cause, at great personal risk, before the Spanish court. The following account gives a sympathetic description of the natives, outlines the Spanish lust for gold, and details a nearly unbelievable torture of several Indians.

SOURCE: From The Devastation of the Indies by Bartolomé de las Casas. English Translation Copyright © 1974 by The Crossroad Publishing Company. Reprinted by permission of The Crossroad Publishing Company.

And of all the infinite universe of humanity, these people are the most guileless, the most devoid of wickedness and duplicity, the most obedient and faithful to their native masters and to the Spanish Christians whom they serve. They are by nature the most humble, patient, and peaceable, holding no grudges, free from embroilments, neither excitable nor quarrelsome. These people are the most devoid of rancors, hatreds, or desire for vengeance of any people in the world. And because they are so weak and complaisant, they are less able to endure heavy labor and soon die of no matter what malady. The sons of nobles among us, brought up in the enjoyments of life's refinements, are no more delicate than are these Indians, even those among them who are of the lowest rank of laborers. They are also poor people, for they not only possess little but have no desire to possess worldly goods. For this reason they are not arrogant, embittered, or greedy. Their repasts are such that the food of the holy fathers in the desert can scarcely be more parsimonious, scanty, and poor. As to their dress, they are generally naked, with only their pudenda covered somewhat. And when they cover their shoulders it is with a square cloth no more than two varas in size. They have no beds, but sleep on a kind of matting or else in a kind of suspended net called *hamacas.* They are very clean in their persons, with alert, intelligent minds, docile and open to doctrine, very apt to receive our holy Catholic faith, to be endowed with virtuous customs, and to behave in a godly fashion. And once they begin to hear the tidings of the Faith, they are so insistent on knowing more and on taking the sacraments of the Church and on observing the divine cult that, truly, the missionaries who are here need to be endowed by God with great patience in order to cope with such eagerness. Some of the secular Spaniards who have been here for many years say that the goodness of the Indians is undeniable and that if this gifted people could be brought to know the one true God they would be the most fortunate people in the world....

The common ways mainly employed by the Spaniards who call themselves Christian and who have gone there to extirpate those pitiful nations and wipe them off the earth is by unjustly waging cruel and bloody wars. Then, when they have slain all those who fought for their lives or to escape the tortures they would have to endure, that is to say, when they have slain all the native rulers and young men (since the Spaniards usually spare only the women and children, who are subjected to the hardest and bitterest servitude ever suffered by man or beast), they enslave any survivors. With these infernal methods of tyranny they debase and weaken countless numbers of those pitiful Indian nations.

Their reason for killing and destroying such an infinite number of souls is that the Christians have an ultimate aim, which is to acquire gold, and to swell themselves with riches in a very brief time and thus rise to a high estate disproportionate to their merits. It should be kept in mind that their insatiable greed and ambition, the greatest ever seen in the world, is the cause of their villainies. And also, those lands are so rich and felicitous, the native peoples so meek and patient, so easy to subject, that our Spaniards have no more consideration for them than beasts. And I say this from my own knowledge of the acts I witnessed. But I should not say "than beasts" for, thanks be to God, they have treated beasts with some respect; I should say instead like excrement on the public squares....

I once saw this, when there were four or five Indian nobles lashed on grids and burning; I seem even to recall that there were two or three pairs of grids where others were burning, and because they uttered such loud screams that they disturbed the Spanish captain's sleep, he ordered them to be strangled. And the constable, who was worse than an executioner, did not want to obey that order (and I know the name of that constable and know his relatives in Seville), but instead put a stick over the victims' tongues, so they could not make a sound, and he stirred up the fire, but not too much, so that they roasted slowly, as he liked. I saw all these things I have described, and countless others.

And because all the people who could do so fled to the mountains to escape these inhuman, ruthless, and fero-

cious acts, the Spanish captains, enemies of the human race, pursued them with the fierce dogs they kept which attacked the Indians, tearing them to pieces and devouring them. And because on few and far between occasions, the Indians justifiably killed some Christians, the Spaniards made a rule among themselves that for every Christian slain by the Indians, they would slay a hundred Indians....

Among the noteworthy outrages they committed was the one they perpetrated against a cacique, a very important noble, by name Hatuey, who had come to Cuba from Hispaniola with many of his people, to flee the calamities and inhuman acts of the Christians. When he was told by certain Indians that the Christians were now coming to Cuba, he assembled as many of his followers as he could and said this to them: "Now you must know that they are saying the Christians are coming here, and you know by experience how they put So and So and So and So, and other nobles to an end. And now they are coming from Haiti (which is Hispaniola) to do the same here. Do you know why they do this?" The Indians replied: "We do not know. But it may be that they are by nature wicked and cruel." And he told them: "No, they do not act only because of that, but because they have a God they greatly worship and they want us to worship that God, and that is why they struggle with us and subject us and kill us." ...

He had a basket full of gold and jewels and he said: "You see their God here, the God of the Christians. If you agree to it, let us dance for this God, who knows, it may please the God of the Christians and then they will do us no harm." And his followers said, all together, "Yes, that is good, that is good!" And they danced round the basket of gold until they fell down exhausted. Then their chief, the cacique Hatuey, said to them: "See here, if we keep this basket of gold they will take it from us and will end up by killing us. So let us cast away the basket into the river." They all agreed to do this, and they flung the basket of gold into the river that was nearby.

This cacique, Hatuey, was constantly fleeing before the Christians from the time they arrived on the island of Cuba, since he knew them and of what they were capable. Now and then they encountered him and he defended himself, but they finally killed him. And they did this for the sole reason that he had fled from those cruel and wicked Christians and had defended himself against them. And when they had captured him and as many of his followers as they could, they burned them all at the stake.

When tied to the stake, the cacique Hatuey was told by a Franciscan friar who was present, an artless rascal, something about the God of the Christians and of the articles of the Faith. And he was told what he could do in the brief time that remained to him, in order to be saved and go to Heaven. The cacique, who had never heard any of this before, and was told he would go to Inferno where if he did not adopt the Christian Faith, he would suffer eternal torment, asked the Franciscan friar if Christians all went to Heaven. When told that they did he said he would prefer to go to Hell. Such is the fame and honor that God and our Faith have earned through the Christians who have gone out to the Indies.

* * * * * *

1. In the writings of Bartolomé de las Casas we have a very different interpretation of events than those presented by Cortés, or most of the histories of the

Spanish conquest of Mexico. What does this tell us about the interpretive nature of history?

2. Does de las Casas imply that cruelty is typical of the Spanish as a whole or only of individuals? What does de las Casas indicate the motivation of the Conquistadors to be?

3. De las Casas personalizes the narrative of his story. Do you find this convincing? Does it lend validity to the account or call it into question?

2–4 A Shipwrecked Spaniard Writes of His Incredible Journey through North America from 1528–1536

Alvar Nuñez Cabeza de Vaca came to America as the second in command for Pánfilo de Narváez's expedition to conquer Florida in 1527. Abandoned and shipwrecked with three companions, Cabeza de Vaca made an incredible journey across the American Southwest from 1528 to 1536. Cabeza de Vaca and his companions were captives of several Indian tribes in Texas, but eventually they walked from Texas through New Mexico and Arizona to Mexico. Cabeza de Vaca's detailed descriptions provide important insights into early 16th century native American life and material culture. His stories, told in Mexico City, fueled the Spanish drive for gold and led to Coronado's conquest of New Mexico in 1540.

SOURCE: Cabeza de Vaca, Adventures in the Unknown Interior of America, translated and edited by Cyclone Covey (Albuquerque: University of New Mexico Press, 1961).

The Indians are so accustomed to running that, without resting or getting tired, they run from morning till night in pursuit of a deer, and kill a great many, because they follow until the game is worn out, sometimes catching it alive. Their huts are of matting placed over four arches. They carry them on their back and move every two or three days in quest of food; they plant nothing that would be of any use.

They are very merry people, and even when famished do not cease to dance and celebrate their feasts and ceremonials. Their best times are when "tunas" (prickly pears) are ripe, because then they have plenty to eat and spend the time in dancing and eating day and night. As long as these tunas last they squeeze and open them and set them to dry. When

dried they are put in baskets like figs and kept to be eaten on the way. The peelings they grind and pulverize.

All over this country there are a great many deer, fowl and other animals which I have before enumerated. Here also they come up with cows; I have seen them thrice and have eaten their meat. They appear to me of the size of those in Spain. Their horns are small, like those of the Moorish cattle; the hair is very long, like fine wool and like a peajacket; some are brownish and others black, and to my taste they have better and more meat than those from here. Of the small hides the Indians make blankets to cover themselves with, and of the taller ones they make shoes and targets. These cows come from the north, across the country further on, to the coast of Florida, and are found all over the land for over four hundred leagues. On this whole stretch, through the valleys by which they come, people who live there descend to subsist upon their flesh. And a great quantity of hides are met with inland.

We remained with the Avavares Indians for eight months, according to our reckoning of the moons. During that time they came for us from many places and said that verily we were children of the sun. Until then Donates and the negro had not made any cures, but we found ourselves so pressed by the Indians coming from all sides, that all of us had to become medicine men. I was the most daring and reckless of all in undertaking cures. We never treated anyone that did not afterwards say he was well, and they had such confidence in our skills as to believe that none of them would die as long as we were among them....

The women brought many mats, with which they built us houses, one for each of us and those attached to him. After this we would order them to boil all the game, and they did it quickly in ovens built by them for the purpose. We partook of everything a little, giving the rest to the principal man among those who had come with us for distribution among all. Every one then came with the share he had received for us to breathe on it and bless it, without which they left it untouched. Often we had with us three to four thousand persons. And it was very tiresome to have to breathe on and make the sign of the cross over every morsel they ate or drank. For many other things they wanted to do they would come to ask our permission, so that it is easy to realize how greatly we were bothered. The women brought us tunas, spiders, worms, and whatever else they could find, for they would rather starve than partake of anything that had not first passed through our hands.

While travelling with those, we crossed a big river coming from the north and, traversing about thirty leagues of plains, met a number of people that came from afar to meet us on the trail, who treated us like the foregoing ones.

Thence on there was a change in the manner of reception, insofar as those who would meet us on the trail with gifts were no longer robbed by the Indians of our company, but after we had entered their homes they tendered us all they possessed, and the dwellings also. We turned over everything to the principals for distribution. Invariably those who had been deprived of their belongings would follow us, in order to repair their losses, so that our retinue became very large. They would tell them to be careful and not conceal anything of what they owned, as it could not be done without our knowledge, and then we would cause their death. So much did they frighten them that on the first few days after joining us they would be trembling all the time, and would not dare to speak or lift their eyes to Heaven.

Those guided us for more than fifty leagues through a desert of very rugged mountains, and so arid that there was no game. Consequently we suffered much from lack of food, and finally forded a very big river, with its water reaching to our chest. Thence on many of our people began to show the effects of the hunger and hardships they had undergone in those mountains, which were extremely barren and tiresome to travel.

The next morning all those who were strong enough came along, and at the end of three journeys we halted. Alonso del Castillo and Estevanico, the negro, left with the women as guides, and the woman who was a captive took them to a river that flows between mountains where there was a village in which her father lived, and these were the first adobes we saw that were like unto real houses. Castillo and Estevanico went to these and, after holding parley with the Indians, at the end of three days Castillo returned to where he had left us, bringing with him five or six of the Indians. He told how he had found permanent houses, inhabited, the people of which ate beans and squashes, and that he had also seen maize.

Of all things upon earth that caused us the greatest pleasure, and we gave endless thanks to our Lord for this news. Castillo also said that the negro was coming to meet us on the way, near by, with all the people of the houses. For that reason we started, and after going a league and a half met the negro and the people that came to receive us, who gave us beans and many squashes to eat, gourds to carry water in, robes of cowhide, and other things. As those people and the Indians of our company were enemies, and did not understand each other, we took leave of the latter, leaving them all that had been given to us, while we went on with the former and, six leagues beyond, when night was already approaching, reached their houses, where they received us with great ceremonies. Here we remained one day, and left on the next, taking them with us to other permanent houses, where they subsisted on the same food also, and thence on we found a new custom....

Having seen positive traces of Christians and become satisfied they were very near, we gave many thanks to our Lord for redeeming us from our sad and gloomy condition. Any one can imagine our delight when he reflects how long we had been in that land, and how many dangers and hardships we had suffered. That night I entreated one of my companions to go after the Christians, who were moving through the part of the country pacified and quieted by us, and who were three days ahead of where we were. They did not like my suggestion, and excused themselves from going, on the ground of being tired and worn out, although any of them might have done far better than I, being younger and stronger.

Seeing their reluctance, in the morning I took with me the negro and eleven Indians and, following the trail, went in search of the Christians. On that day we made ten leagues, passing three places where they slept. The next morning I came upon four Christians on horseback, who seeing me in such a strange attire, and in company with Indians, were greatly startled. They stared at me for quite awhile, speechless; so great was their surprise that they could not find words to ask me anything. I spoke first, and told them to lead me to their captain, and we went together to Diego de Alcaraz, their commander.

* * * * *

1. *How does the Indian's view of Cabeza de Vaca compare to the Aztec's view of Cortés?*

2. *How does Cabeza de Vaca's view of Indians differ from that of Bartolomé de las Casas or Father Paul Le Jeune? Is he sympathetic to them?*

3. *What do you think was Cabeza de Vaca's purpose in writing the account of his journey? How did his journal change the geographical knowledge of North America at the time?*

2–5   A French Captain Describes His First Contact with the Indians in 1534

Jacques Cartier was responsible for France's early possession of Canada, landing at Cape Gaspé while on a mission for King Frances I in 1534. Cartier's search for a route to the Western Sea led him to discover and later explore in depth the Saint Lawrence River. Despite several voyages to Canada, Cartier's dreams for riches were never fulfilled, and for a multitude of reasons, including wars at home, the French lost interest in Canada and didn't return until the seventeenth century. Cartier's detailed description of the natives was probably expanded from his ship's log.

SOURCE: "The First Relation of Jacques Cartier of S. Malo," in Henry S. Burrage, ed., Early English and French Voyages, Chiefly from Hakluyt. Original Narratives of Early American History (New York: Charles Scribner's Sons, 1906).

Upon Thursday being the eight of the month, because the winde was not good to go out with our ships, we set our boates in a readiness to goe to discover the said Bay, and that day wee went 25. leagues within it. The next day the wind and weather being faire, we sailed until noone, in which time we had notice of a great part of the said Bay, and how that over the low lands, there were other lands with high mountaines: but seeing that there was no passage at all, wee began to turne back againe, taking our way along the coast: and sayling, we saw certaine wilde men that stood upon the shoare of a lake, that is among the low grounds, who were making fires and smokes: wee went thither, and found that there was a channel of the sea that did enter into the lake, and setting our boats at one of the banks of the chanell, the wilde men with one of their boates came unto us, and brought up pieces of Seales ready sodden, putting them upon pieces of wood: then retiring themselves, they would make signes unto us, that they did give them us. We sent two men unto them with hatchets, knives, beads, and other such like ware, where

at they were very glad, and by and by in clusters they came to the shore where wee were, with their boates, bringing with them skinnes and other such things as they had, to have of our wares. They were more than 300. men, women, and children: Some of the women which came not over, wee might see stand up to the knees in water, singing and dancing: the other that had passed the river where we were, came very friendly to us, rubbing our armes with their owne handes, then would they lift them up toward heaven, shewing many signes of gladnesse: and in such wise were we assured one of another, that we very familiarly began to trafique for whatsoever they had, til they had nothing but their naked bodies; for they gave us all whatsoever they had, and that was but of small value. We perceived that this people might very easily be converted to our Religion. They goe from place to place. They live onely with fishing. They have an ordinarie time to fish for their provision. The countrey is hotter than the country of Spaine, and the fairest that can possibly be found, altogether smooth, and level. There is no place be it never so little, but it hath some trees (yea albeit it be sandie) or else is full of wilde corne, that hath an eare like unto Rie: the corne is like oates, and smal peason as thicke as if they had bene sowen and plowed, white and red gooseberies, strawberies, black-beries, white and red Roses, with many other floures of very sweet and pleasant smell. There be also many goodly medowes full of grasse, and lakes wherein great plentie of salmons be. They call a hatchet in their tongue Cochi, and a knife Bacon: we named it The bay of heat.

* * * * * *

1.   What is France's primary purpose in coming to the New World? How does this difference of intent affect French interactions with the Indians? How does it compare to the Spanish?

2.   How is the possibility of Cartier's account being reconstructed from his ship's log reflected in his writing ? How does his narrative differ from that of Father Paul le Jeune (Document 2–6)?

2–6   A French Jesuit Describes the Cosmology of Montagnais Indians in 1534

When the French reentered Canada in the early seventeenth century, a French Jesuit priest by the name of Paul Le Jeune came with them. Le Jeune spent a winter with the Montagnais Indians and became familiar with their language and their mythology. Le Jeune records here the winter he spent with the Indians as well as their story of the great flood.

SOURCE: Reuben Gold Thwaites, ed., The Jesuit Relations and Allied Documents (Cleveland: Burrows Brothers, 1897).

I have already reported that the Savages believe that a

certain one named Atachocam had created the world, and that one named Messou had restored it. I have questioned upon this subject the famous Sorcerer and the old man with whom I passed the Winter; they answered that they did not know who was the first Author of the world,—that it was perhaps Atahocam, but that was not certain; that they only spoke of Atahocam as one speaks of a thing so far distant that nothing sure can be known about it;...

As to the Messou, they hold that he restored the world, which was destroyed in the flood; whence it appears that they have some tradition of that great universal deluge which happened in the time of Noah....

They also say that all animals, of every species, have an elder brother, who is, as it were, the source and origin of all individuals, and this elder brother is wonderfully great and powerful...Now these elders of all the animals are the juniors of the Messou. Behold him well related, this worthy restorer of the Universe, he is elder brother to all beasts. If any one, when asleep, sees the elder or progenitor of some animals, he will have a fortunate chase; if he sees the elder of the Beavers, he will take Beavers; if he sees the elder of the Elks, he will take Elks, possessing the juniors through the favor of their senior whom he has seen in the dream....

Their Religion, or rather their superstition, consists besides in praying; but O, my God, what prayers they make! In the morning, when the little children come out from their Cabins, they shout, *Cacouakhi, Pakhais Amiscouakhi, Pakhais Mousouakhi, Pakhais,* "Come Porcupines; come, Beavers; come, Elk;" and this is all of their prayers.

When the Savages sneeze, and sometimes even at other times, during the Winter, they cry out in a loud voice, *Etouctaian miraouinam an Mirouscamikhi,* "I shall be very glad to see the Spring."

At other times, I have heard them pray for the Spring, or for deliverance from evils and other similar things; and they express all these things in the form of desires, crying out as loudly as they can, "I would be very glad if this day would continue, if the wind would change," etc. I could not say to whom these wishes are addressed, for they themselves do not know, at least those whom I have asked have not been able to enlighten me....

These are some of their superstitions. How much dust there is in their eyes, and how much trouble there will be to remove it that they may see the beautiful light of truth! I believe, nevertheless, that any one who knew their language perfectly, in order to give them good reasons promptly, would soon make them laugh at their own stupidity; for sometimes I have made them ashamed and confused, although I speak almost entirely by my hands, I mean by signs....

In order to have some conception of the beauty of this edifice, its construction must be described. I shall speak from knowledge, for I have often helped to build it. Now, when we arrived at the place where we were to camp, the women, armed with axes, went here and there in the great forests, cutting the framework of the hostelry where we were to lodge; meantime the men, having drawn the plan thereof, cleared away the snow with their snowshoes, or with shovels which they make and carry expressly for this purpose. Imagine now a great ring or square in the snow, two, three or four feet deep, according to the weather or the place where they encamp. This depth of snow makes a white wall for us, which surrounds us on all sides, except the end where it is broken through to form the door. The framework having been brought, which consists of twenty or thirty poles, more or less, according to the size of the cabin, it is planted, not upon the ground but upon the snow; then they throw upon these poles, which converge a little at the top, two or three rolls of bark sewed together, beginning at the bottom, and behold, the house is made. The ground inside, as well as the wall of snow which extends all around the cabin, is covered with little branches of fir; and, as a finishing touch, a wretched skin is fastened to two poles to serve as a door, the doorposts being the snow itself....

You cannot stand upright in this house, as much on account of its low roof as the suffocating smoke; and consequently you must always lie down, or sit flat upon the ground, the usual posture of the Savages. When you go out, the cold, the snow, and the danger of getting lost in these great woods drive you in again more quickly than the wind, and keep you a prisoner in a dungeon which has neither lock nor key.

This prison, in addition to the uncomfortable position that one must occupy upon a bed of earth, has four other great discomforts,—cold, heat, smoke, and dogs. As to the cold, you have the snow at your head with only a pine branch between, often nothing but your hat, and the winds are free to enter in a thousand places.... When I lay down at night I could study through this opening both the Stars and the Moon as easily as if I had been in the open fields.

Nevertheless, the cold did not annoy me as much as the heat from the fire. A little place like their cabins is easily heated by a good fire, which sometimes roasted and broiled me on all sides, for the cabin was so narrow that I could not protect myself against the heat. You cannot move to right or left, for the Savages, your neighbors, are at your elbows; you cannot withdraw to the rear, for you encounter the wall of snow, or the bark of the cabin which shuts you in. I did not know what position to take. Had I stretched myself out, the place was so narrow that my legs would have been halfway in the fire; to roll myself up in a ball, and crouch down in their way, was a position I could not retain as long as they could; my clothes were all scorched and burned. You will ask me perhaps if the snow at our backs did not melt under so much heat. I answer, "no," that if sometimes the heat softened it in the least, the cold immediately turned it into ice. I will say, however, that both the cold and the heat are endurable, and that some remedy may be found for these two evils.

But, as to the smoke, I confess to you that it is martyrdom. It almost killed me, and made me weep continually, although I had neither grief nor sadness in my heart. It sometimes grounded all of us who were in the cabin; that is, it caused us to place our mouths against the earth in order to breathe. For, although the Savages were accustomed to this torment, yet occasionally it became so dense that they, as well as I, were compelled to prostrate themselves, and as it were to eat the earth, so as not to drink the smoke. I have sometimes remained several hours in this position, especially during the most severe cold and when it snowed; for it was then the smoke assailed us with the greatest fury, seizing us by the throat, nose, and eyes....

As to the dogs, which I have mentioned as one of the discomforts of the Savages' houses, I do not know that I ought to blame them, for they have sometimes rendered me good service....These poor beasts, not being able to live outdoors, came and lay down sometimes upon my shoulders, sometimes upon my feet, and as I only had one blanket to serve both as covering and mattress, I was not sorry for this protection, willingly restoring to them a part of the heat which I drew from them. It is true that, as they were large and numerous, they occassionally crowded and annoyed me so much, that in giving me a little heat they robbed me of my sleep, so that I very often drove them away....

* * * * * *

1. Father Le Jeune refers to the Indian's cosmological beliefs as "superstitions." What does this tell us about his view of them? What are the similarities between the Montagnais's animal elder brothers and Catholic saints? Their flood and the story of Noah? How do the Montagnais myths compare to the pueblo myths you have read about in other chapters?

2. What does Le Jeune's detailed description regarding the material culture of the Montagnais tell us about their day to day life? How can we use material culture to inform our historical narrative?

2–7   *An English Scientist Writes of the Algonquian Peoples of the Atlantic Coast in 1588*

Thomas Harriot's Brief and True Report of the New Found Land of Virginia *is one of the few surviving accounts of Sir Walter Raleigh's first American colony. Harriot made extensive contributions as a scientist and astronomer in his native England, but is more widely known in America for his detailed accounting of the Indians, as well as his description of the commercial potential of the surrounding countryside. Harriot's recounting of the Indian's religion provides an important historical insight to indigenous people in America in the sixteenth century.*

SOURCE: Thomas Harriot, *A Brief And True Report Of The New Found Land Of Virginia* (New York: Dover Publications, Inc., 1972), pp. 24–27.

It refseth I fpeake a word or two of the naturall inhabitants, their natures and maners, leauing large difcourfe thereofvntill time more conuenient hereafter: nowe onely fo farre foorth, as that you may know, how that they in refpect of troubling our inhabiting and planting, are not to be feared; but that they shall haue caufe both to feare and loue vs, that shall inhabite with them.

They are a people clothed with loofe mantles made of Deere skins; & aprons of the fame rounde about their middles; all els naked; of fuch a difference of features only as wee in England; hauing no edge tooles or weapons of yron or fteele to offend vs withall, neither know they how to make any: thofe weapos that they haue, are onlie bowes made of Witchhazle, & arrowes of reeds; flat edged truncheons alfo of wood about a yard long, neither haue they any thing to defend themfelues but targets made of barcks; and fome armours made of ftickes wickered together with thread.

Their townes are but fmall, & neere the fea coaft but few, fome cotaining but 10. or 12. houfes: fome 20. the greateft that we haue feene haue bene but of 30. houfes: if they be walled it is only done with barks of trees made faft to flakes, or els with poles onely fixed vpright and clofe one by another.

Their houfes are made of fmall poles made faft at the tops in roude forme after the maner as is vfed in many arbories in our gardens of England, in moft townes couered with barkes, and in fome towne with artificiall mattes made of long rushes; from the tops of the houfes downe to the ground. The length of them is commonly double to the breadth, in fome places they are but 12. and 16. yardes long, and in other fome wee haue feene of foure and twentie....

Some religion they haue alreadie, which although it he farre from the truth, yet beyng at it is, there is hope it may bee the eafier and fooner reformed.

They beleeue that there are many Gods which they call *Mantóac*, but of different fortes and degrees; one onely chiefe and great God, which hath bene from all eternitie. Who as they affirme when hee purpofed to make the worlde, made firft other goddes of a principall order to bee as meanes and inftruments to bee vfed in the creation and gouernment to follow; and after the Sunne, Moone, and Starres, as pettie goddes and the inftruments of the other order more principall. Fifrt they fay were made waters, out of which by the gods was made all diuerfitie of creatures that are vifible or inuifible.

For mankind they fay a woman was made firft, which by the woorking of one of the goddes, coenciued and brought foorth children: And in fuch fort they fay they had their beginning.

But how manie yeeres or ages haue paffed fince, they fay they can make no relation, hauing no letters nor other fuch meanes as we to keepe recordes of the particularities of times paft, but onelie tradition from father to fonne....

Manie times and in euery towne where I came, according as I was able, I made declaration of the contentes of the Bible; that therein was fet foorth the true and onelie GOD, and his mightie woorkes, that therein was contayned the true doctrine of faluation through Chrift, with manie particularities of Miracles and chiefe poyntes of religion, as I was able then to vtter, and thought fitte for the time. And although I told them the booke materially & of itfelf was not of anie fuch vertue, as I thought they did conceiue, but onely the doctrine therein côtained; yet would many be glad to touch it, to embrace it, to kiffe it, to hold it to their brefts and heades, and ftroke ouer all their bodie with it; to shewe their hungrie defire of that knowledge which was fpoken of.

* * * * *

1. *According to Harriot's report, what seems to be his purpose in being among the Indians? How would this have been used by the English?*

2. *How does the Indian cosmology, as related in this report, compare to Christianity? To other Native American mythology?*

3. *What does Thomas Harriot's report tell you about changes within the English language since 1590? What effect does this have on history and historical documents?*

2-8   The Governor of Roanoke Describes His Return to the "Lost Colony" in 1590

Part of Sir Walter Raleigh's original exploration of Virginia in 1585, John White later returned as governor in 1587 to set up the new colony at Roanoke. After going to England to resupply the colony; White and the others found Roanoke abandoned in 1590. The fate of the planters at Roanoke remains one of early America's great historical mysteries.

SOURCE: "The Fifth Voyage of M. John White," in Henry S. Burrage, ed., *Early English and French Voyages, Chiefly from Hakluyt, Original Narratives of American History* (New York: Charles Scribner's Sons, 1906).

Our boats and all things fitted again, we pit off from Hatorask, being the number of nineteen persons in both boats: but before we could get to the place, where our planters were left, it was so exceedingly dark, that we over-shot the place a quarter of a mile. There we spied towards the North end of the island the light of a great fire thought the woods, to the which we presently rowed. When we came right over against it, we let fall our grapnel near the shore, and sounded with a trumpet a call, and afterwards many familiar English tunes of songs, and called to them friendly; but we had no answer. We therefore landed at day-break, and coming to the fire, we found the grass and sundry rotten trees burning about the place. From hence we went though the woods to that part of the island directly over against Dasamongwepeuk, and from thence we returned by the water side, round tabour the North point of the island, until we came to the place where I left our Colony in the year 1587.

In all this way we saw in the sand the print of the savages' feet of two of three sort trodden the night, and as we entered up the sandy bank upon a tree, in the very brow thereof were curiously carved these fair Roman letter C R O: which letters presently we knew to signify the place, where I should find the planters seated, according to a secret token agreed upon between them and me at my last departure from them, which was, that in any ways they should not fail to write or carve on the trees or posts of the doors the name of the place where they should be seated; for at my coming away they were prepared to remove from Roanoke 50 miles into the main. Therefore at may departure from them in A.D. 1587 I willed them, that if they should happen to be distressed in any of those places, that then they should carve over the letters or name, a Cross ✠

in this form, but we found no such sign of distress.

And having well considered of this, we passed toward the place where they were left in sundry houses, but we found the houses taken down, and the place very strongly enclosed with a high palisade of great trees, with continues and flankers very Fort-like, and one of the chief trees or posts at the right side of the entrance had the bark taken off, and 5 foot from the ground in fair Capital letters was graven CROATOAN without any cross or sign of distress. This done, we entered into the palisade, where we found many bars of iron, two pigs of lead, four iron fowlers, iron sacker-shot, and such like heavy things, thrown here and there, almost overgrown with grass and weeds. From thence we went along by the water side, towards the point of the Creek to see if we could find any of their boats or pinnace, but we could perceive no sign of them, nor any of the last falkons and small ordinance which were left with them, at my departure from them.

At our return from the Creek, some of our sailors meeting us, told us that they had found where divers chests had been hidden, and long since dug up again and broken up, and much of the goods in them spoiled and scattered about, but nothing lett, of such things as the Savages knew any use of, undefaced. Presently Captain Cooke and I went to the place, which was in the end of an old trench, made two years past by Captain Amadas: where we found five chests, that had been carefully hidden of the Planters, and of the same chests three were my own, and about the place many of my things spoiled and broken, and my books torn from the covers, the frames of some of my pictures and maps rotten and spoiled with rain, and my armor almost eaten through with rust. This could be no other but the deed of the Savages our enemies at Dasamongwepeuk, who had watched the departure of our men to Croatoan; and as soon as they were departed, dug up every place where they suspected any thing to be buried. But although it much grieved me to see such spoil of my goods, yet on the other side I greatly joyed that I had safely found a certain token of their safe being at Croatan, which is the place where Manteo was born, and the savages of the island our friends....

* * * * * *

1. *What were Raleigh's purposes in establishing a colony in Virginia? How does this compare to colonization by the French and the Spanish? What were their purposes?*

2. *This passage is in a more modern English than the piece by Thomas Harriot from A Brief and True Report....How does this affect its readability? Its veracity?*

3. *What do you think happened to the colonists at Roanoke?*

Planting Colonies in North America, 1588–1700

3–1   The Spanish Governor Reports on the Pueblo Revolt of 1680

The following is a letter sent September 8, 1680, by the Spanish Governor of New Mexico, Don Antonio de Otermín, to Fray Francisco de Ayeta, recounting the events of the Pueblo Revolt. In this segment from a longer account, Otermín describes several terrifying days of life under siege and an unsuccessful attempt at negotiation with an Indian leader.

SOURCE: Charles W. Hackett. ed., *Historical Documents Relating to New Mexico* (1937). pp. 433 ff.

My very reverend father, Sir, and friend, most beloved Fray Francisco de Ayeta: The time has come when, with tears in my eyes and deep sorrow in my heart, I commence to give an account of the lamentable tragedy, such as has never before happened in the world, which has occurred in this miserable kingdom and holy *custodia.*

After I sent my last letter to your reverence by the *maese de campo,* Pedro de Leyba, I received information that a plot for a general uprising of the Christian Indians was being formed and was spreading rapidly. This was wholly contrary to the existing peace and tranquility in this miserable kingdom, not only among the Spaniards and natives, but even on the part of the heathen enemy, for it had been a long time since they had done us any considerable damage. It was my misfortune that I learned of it on the eve of the day set for the beginning of the said uprising, and though I immediately, at that instant, notified the lieutenant-general on the lower river and all the other *alcaldes mayores*—so that they could take every care and precaution against whatever might occur, and so that they could make every effort to guard and protect the religious ministers and the temples—the cunning and cleverness of the rebels were such, and so great, that my efforts were of little avail. To this was added a certain degree of negligence by reason of the [report of the] uprising not having been given entire credence, as is apparent from the ease with which they captured and killed both those who were escorting some of the religious, as well as some citizens in their houses, and, particularly, in the efforts that they made to prevent my orders to the lieutenant-general passing through.

Seeing myself with notices of so many and such untimely deaths, and that not having received any word from the lieutenant-general was probably due to the fact that he was in the same exigency and confusion, or that the Indians had killed most of those on the lower river, I endeavored to send a relief of soldiers. Marching out for that purpose, they learned that in La Cañada, as in Los Taos and Pecuries, the Indians had risen in rebellion, joining the Apaches of the Achos nation. Thereupon I sent an order to the *alcalde mayor,* Luis de Quintana, to come at once to the villa with all the people whom he had assembled in his house, so that, joined with those of us who were in the *casa reales,* we might endeavor to defend ourselves against the enemy's invasions. It was necessarily supposed that they would join all their forces to take our lives, as was seen later by experience.

On Tuesday, the thirteenth of the said month, at about nine o'clock in the morning, there came in sight of us in the suburb of Analco, in the cultivated field of the hermitage of San Miguel, and on the other side of the river of the villa, all the Indians of the Tanos and Pecos nations and the Querez of San Marcos, armed and giving war-whoops. As I learned that one of the Indians who was leading them was from the villa and had gone to join them shortly before, I sent some soldiers to summon him and tell him on my behalf that he could come to see me in entire safety, so that I might ascertain from him the purpose for which they were coming. Upon receiving this message he came to where I was, and, since he was known, as I say, I asked him how it was that he had gone crazy too—being an Indian who spoke our language, was so intelligent, and had lived all his life in the villa among the Spaniards, where I had placed such confidence in him—and was now coming as a leader of the Indian rebels. He replied to me that they had elected him as their captain, and that they were carrying two banners, one white and the other red, and that the white one signified peace and the red one war. Thus if we wished to choose the white it must be [upon our agreeing] to leave the country, and if we chose the red, we must perish, because the rebels were numerous and we were very few; there was no alternative, inasmuch as they had killed so many religious and Spaniards.

On hearing his reply, I spoke to him very persuasively, to the effect that he and the rest of his followers were Catholic Christians, [asking] how they expected to live without the religious; and said that even though they had committed so many atrocities, still there was a remedy, for if they would return to the obedience of his Majesty they would be pardoned; and that thus he should go back to his people and tell them in my name all that had been said to him, and persuade them to [agree to] it and to withdraw from where they were; and that he was to advise me of what they might reply. He came back from there after a short time, saying that his people asked that all classes of Indians who were in our power be given up to them, both those in the service of the Spaniards and those of the Mexican nation of that suburb of Analco. He demanded also that his wife and children be given up to him, and likewise that all the Apache men and women whom the Spaniards had captured in war [be turned over to them], inasmuch as some Apaches who were among them were asking for them. If these things were not done they would declare war immediately, and they were unwilling to leave the place where they were because they were awaiting the Taos, Pecuries, and Theguas nations, with whose aid they would destroy us.

On the next Friday, the nations of the Taos, Pecuries, Hemes, and Querez having assembled during the past night, when dawn came more than 2,500 Indians fell upon us in the villa, fortifying and entrenching themselves in all its houses and at the entrances of all the streets, and cutting off our water, which comes through the arroyo and the irrigation canal in front of the casas reales. They burned the holy temple and many houses in the villa. We had several skirmishes over possession of the water, but seeing that it was impossible to hold even this against them, and almost all the soldiers of the post being already wounded, I endeavored to fortify myself in the casas reales and to make a defense without leaving their walls. [The Indians were] so dexterous and so bold that they came to set fire to the doors of the fortified tower of Nuestra Señora de las Casas Reales, and, seeing such audacity and the manifest risk that we ran of having the casas reales set on fire, I resolved to make a sally into the plaza of the said casas reales with all my available force of soldiers, without any protection, to attempt to prevent the fire which the enemy was trying to set. With this endeavor we fought the whole afternoon, Night overtook us thus and God was pleased that they should desist somewhat from shooting us with arquebuses and arrows. We passed this night, like the rest, with much care and watchfulness, and suffered greatly from thirst because of the scarcity of water.

On the next day, Saturday, they began at dawn to press us harder and more closely with gunshots, arrows, and stones, saying to us that now we should not escape them, and that besides their own numbers, they were expecting help from the Apaches whom they had already summoned. They fatigued us greatly on this day, because all was fighting, and above all we suffered from thirst, as we were already oppressed by it. At nightfall, because of the evident peril in which we found ourselves, by their gaining the two stations where cannon were mounted, which we had at the doors of the casas reales, aimed at the entrances of the streets, in order to bring them inside it was necessary to assemble all the forces that I had with me, because we realized that this was their [the Indians'] intention. Instantly all the said Indian rebels began a chant of victory and raised war-whoops, burning all the houses of the villa, and they kept us in this position the entire night, which I assure your reverence was the most horrible that could be thought of or imagined, because the whole villa was a torch and everywhere were war chants and shouts. What grieved us most were the dreadful flames from the church and the scoffing and ridicule which the wretched and miserable Indian rebels made of the sacred things, intoning the alabado and the other prayers of the church with jeers.

* * * * * *

1. What importance does religion have in the events Otermin describes? How important is Otermin's own religion in his perception of the events?

2. What reasons does Otermin give for the success of the uprising? Why, according to him, did the Indians rebel? What reasons for the rebellion does he seem to ignore?

3-2 A Pueblo Rebel in 1681 Explains the Reasons behind the Pueblo Revolt

During the several years following the Pueblo Revolt, Governor Otermin struggled in vain to recapture New Mexico for the Spanish crown. Spanish forces captured Pedro Naranjo, a member of the Queres nation and a native of the San Felipe pueblo, during an attack on the La Isleta pueblo in 1681. The following is a record of the testimony given by Naranjo, who spoke Castilian, to the Spanish authorities in December of that year:

SOURCE: Charles Wilson Hackett. *Revolt of the Pueblo Indians of New Mexico and Otermin's Attempted Reconquest 1680–1682* (Albuquerque, N.M.: 1942) pp. 245–49.

Asked whether he knows the reason or motives which the Indians of this kingdom had for rebelling, forsaking the law of God and obedience to his Majesty, and committing such grave and atrocious crimes, and who were the leaders and principal movers, and by whom and how it was ordered; and why they burned the images, temples, crosses, rosaries, and things of divine worship, committing such atrocities as killing priests, Spaniards, women, and children, and the rest that he might know touching the question, he said that since the government of Señor General Hernando Ugarte y la Concha they have planned to rebel on various occasions through conspiracies of the Indian sorcerers, and that although in some pueblos the messages were accepted, in other parts they would not agree to it; and that it is true that during the government of the said señor general seven or eight Indians were hanged for this same cause, whereupon the unrest subsided. Some time thereafter they [the conspirators] sent from the pueblo of Los Taos through the pueblos of the custodia two deerskins with some pictures on them signifying conspiracy after their manner, in order to convoke the people to a new rebellion, and the said deerskins passed to the province of Moqui, where they refused to accept them. The pact which they had been forming ceased for the time being, but they always kept in their hearts the desire to carry it out, so as to live as they are living to-day. Finally, in the past years, at the summons of an Indian named Popé who is said to have communication with the devil, it happened that in an estufa of the pueblo of Los Taos there appeared to the said Popé three figures of Indians who never came out of the estufa. They gave the said Popé to understand that they were going underground to the lake of Copala. He saw these figures emit fire from all the extremities of their bodies, and that one of them was called Caudi, another Tilini, and the other Tleume; and these three beings spoke to the said Popé, who was in hiding from the secretary, Francisco Xavier, who wished to punish him as a sorcerer. They told him to make a cord of maguey fiber and tie some knots in it which would signify the number of days that they must wait before the rebellion. He said that the cord was passed through all the pueblos of the kingdom so that the ones which agreed to it [the rebellion] might untie one knot in sign of obedience, and by the other knots they would know the days which were lacking; and this was to be done on pain of death to those who refused to agree to it. As a sign of agreement and notice of having concurred in the treason and perfidy they were to send up smoke signals to that effect in each one of the pueblos singly. The said cord was taken from pueblo to pueblo by the swiftest youths under the penalty of death if they revealed the secret. Everything being thus arranged, two days before the time set for its execution, because his lordship had learned of it and had imprisoned two Indian accomplices from the pueblo of Tesuque, it was carried out prematurely that night, because it seemed to them that they were now discovered; and they killed religious, Spaniards, women, and children. This being done, it was proclaimed in all the pueblos that everyone in common should obey the commands of their father whom they did not know, which would be given through El Caydi or El Popé. This

was heard by Alonso Catití, who came to the pueblo of this declarant to say that everyone must unite to go to the villa to kill the governor and the Spaniards who had remained with him, and that he who did not obey would, on their return, be beheaded; and in fear of this they agreed to it. Finally the señor governor and those who were with him escaped from the siege, and later this declarant saw that as soon as the Spaniards had left the kingdom an order came from the said Indian, Popé, in which he commanded all the Indians to break the lands and enlarge their cultivated fields, saying that now they were as they had been in ancient times, free from the labor they had performed for the religious and the Spaniards, who could not now be alive. He said that this is the legitimate cause and the reason they had for rebelling, because they had always desired to live as they had when they came out of the lake of Copala. Thus he replies to the question.

Asked for what reason they so blindly burned the images, temples, crosses, and other things of divine worship, he stated that the said Indian, Popé, came down in person, and with him El Saca and El Chato from the pueblo of Los Taos, and other captains and leaders and many people who were in his train, and he ordered in all the pueblos through which he passed that they instantly break up and burn the images of the holy Christ, the Virgin Mary and the other saints, the crosses, and everything pertaining to Christianity, and that they burn the temples, break up the bells, and separate from the wives whom God had given them in marriage and take those whom they desired. In order to take away their baptismal names, the water, and the holy oils, they were to plunge into the rivers and wash themselves with amole, which is a root native to the country, washing even their clothing, with the understanding that there would thus be taken from them the character of the holy sacraments. They did this, and also many other things which he does not recall, given to understand that this mandate had come from the Caydi and the other two who emitted fire from their extremities in the said estufa of Taos, and that they thereby returned to the state of their antiquity, as when they came from the lake of Copala; that this was the better life and the one they desired, because the God of the Spaniards was worth nothing and theirs was very strong, the Spaniard's God being rotten wood. These things were observed and obeyed by all except some who, moved by the zeal of Christians, opposed it, and such persons the said Popé caused to be killed immediately. He saw to it that they at once erected and rebuilt their houses of idolatry which they call estufas, and made very ugly masks in imitation of the devil in order to dance the dance of the cacina; and he said likewise that the devil had given them to understand that living thus in accordance with the law of their ancestors, they would harvest a great deal of maize, many beans, a great abundance of cotton, calabashes, and very large watermelons and cantaloupes; and that they could erect their houses and enjoy abundant health and leisure. As he has said, the people were very much pleased, living at their ease in this life of their antiquity, which was the chief cause of their falling into such laxity. Following what has already been stated, in order to terrorize them further and cause them to observe the diabolical commands, there came to them a pronouncement from the three demons already described, and from El Popé, to the effect that he who might still keep in his heart a regard for the priests, the governor, and the Spaniards would be known from his unclean face and clothes, and would be punished. And he stated that the said four persons stopped at nothing to have their commands obeyed. Thus he replies to the question.

Asked what arrangements and plans they had made for the contingency of the Spaniards' return, he said that what he knows concerning the question is that they were always saying they would have to fight to the death, for they do not wish to live in any other way than they are living at present; and the demons in the estufa of Taos had given them to understand that as soon as the Spaniards began to move toward this kingdom they would warn them so that they might unite, and none of them would be caught. He having been questioned further and repeatedly touching the case, he said that he has nothing more to say except that they should be always on the alert, because the said Indians were continually planning to follow the Spaniards and fight with them by night, in order to drive off the horses and catch them afoot, although they might have to follow them for many leagues. What he has said is the truth, and what happened, on the word of a Christian who confesses his guilt. He said that he has come to the pueblos through fear to lead in idolatrous dances, in which he greatly fears in his heart that he may have offended God, and that now having been absolved and returned to the fold of the church, he has spoken the truth in everything he has been asked.

* * * * *

1. Who is the author of this document? How much do the beliefs and prejudices of the author color this retelling of Naranjo's testimony? How much is Naranjo's testimony colored also by his desire to please his captors?

2. Why did Indians, many of whom were converts to the Catholic Church, make symbolic attacks on Christianity in their revolt against Spanish domination? Think about the role that religion and Spanish religious leaders played in the Spanish conquest of the region.

3. According to Naranjo, did all of the Indians who followed El Popé do so freely?

4. Based on the information provided in this passage, what were the principal causes of the Pueblo Revolt?

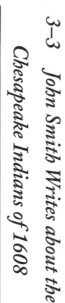

3–3 John Smith Writes about the Chesapeake Indians of 1608

A member of the expedition that established the English settlement at Jamestown, Virginia, in 1607, Captain John Smith was the elected leader of the colony in 1608–1609. His firm leadership brought the colony through much hardship. Returning to England in 1609, Smith devoted himself to promoting the colonies and publicizing his own exploits. In the following passage Smith offers his impressions of the Chesapeake Indians as part of his general description and promotion of Virginia.

SOURCE: Captain John Smith. Works: 1608–1631. Edited by Edward Arber, The English Scholars' Library, No. 16, (Birmingham, 1884), pp. 63–67.

The land is not populous, for the men be fewe; their far greater number is of women and children. Within 60 miles of James Towne there are about some 5000 people, but of able men fit for their warres scarse 1500. To nourish so many together they have yet no means, because they make so small a benefit of their land, be it never so fertill.

6 or 700 have been the most [that] hath seen together, when they gathered themselves to have surprised Captaine Smyth at Pamaunke, having but 15 to withstand the worst of their furie. As small as the proportion of ground that hath yet beene discovered, is in comparison of that yet unknowne. The people differ very much in stature, especially in language, as before is expressed.

Since being very great as the Sesquesahamocks, others very little as the Wighcocomocoes: but generally tall and straight, of a comely proportion, and of a colour browne, when they are of any age, but they are borne white. Their haire is generally black; but few have any beards. The men weare halfe their heads shaven, the other halfe long. For Barbers they use their women, who with 2 shels will grate away the haire, of any fashion they please. The women are cut in many fashions agreeable to their yeares, but ever some part remaineth long.

They are very strong, of an able body and full of

agilitie, able to endure to lie in the woods under a tree by the fire, in the worst of winter, or in the weedes and grasse, in *Ambuscado* in the Sommer.

They are inconstant in everie thing, but what feare constraineth them to keepe. Craftie, timerous, quicke of apprehension and very ingenuous. Some are of disposition feareful, some bold, most cautelous, all *Savage.* Generally covetous of copper, beads, and such like trash. They are soone moved to anger, and so malitious, that they seldome forget an injury: they seldome steale one from another, least their conjurors should reveale it, and so they be pursued and punished. That they are thus feared is certaine, but that any can reveale their offences by conjuration I am doubtful. Their women are carefull not to bee suspected of dishonesty without the leave of their husbands.

Each household knoweth their owne lands and gardens, and most live of their owne labours.

For their apparell, they are some time covered with the skinnes of wilde beasts, which in winter are dressed with the haire, but in sommer without. The better sort use large mantels of deare skins not much differing in fashion from the Irish mantels. Some imbrodered with white beads, some with copper, other painted after their manner. But the common sort have scarce to cover their nakednesse but with grasse, the leaves of trees, or such like. We have seene some use mantels made of Turkey feathers, so prettily wrought and woven with threeds that nothing could bee discerned but the feathers, that was exceeding warme and very handsome. But the women are alwaies covered about their midles with a skin and very shamefast to be seene bare.

They adorne themselves most with copper beads and paintings. Their women some have their legs, hands, breasts and face cunningly imbrodered with diverse workes, as beasts, serpentes, artificially wrought into their flesh with blacke spots. In each eare commonly they have 3 great holes, whereat they hange chaines, bracelets, or copper. Some of their men weare in those holes, a small greene and yellow coloured snake, neare halfe a yard in length, which crawling and lapping her selfe about his necke often times familiarly would kiss his lips. Others wear a dead Rat tied by the tail. Some on their heads weare the wing of a bird or some large feather, with a Rattell. Those Rattels are somewhat like the chape of a Rapier but lesse, which they take from the taile of a snake. Many have the whole skinne of a hawke or some strange fowle, stuffed with the wings abroad. Others a broad peece of copper, and some the hand of their enemy dryed. Their heads and shoulders are painted red with the roote *Pocone* braied to powder mixed with oyle; this they hold in somer to preserve them from the heate, and in winter from the cold. Many other formes of paintings they use, but he is the most gallant that is the most monstrous to

behould.

Their buildings and habitations are for the most part by the rivers or not farre distant from some fresh spring. Their houses are built like our Arbors of small young springs bowed and tyed, and so close covered with mats or the barkes of trees very handsomely, that notwithstanding either winde raine or weather, they are as warme as stooves, but very smoaky, yet at the toppe of the house there is a hole made for the smoake to goe into right over the fire.

Against the fire they lie on little hurdles of Reedes covered with a mat, borne from the ground a foote and more by a hurdle of wood. On these round about the house, they lie heads and points one by thother against the fire: some covered with mats, some with skins, and some starke naked lie on the ground, from 6 to 20 in a house.

Their houses are in the midst of their fields or gardens; which are smal plots of ground, some 20, some 40, some 100, some 200, some more, some lesse. Some times from 2 to 100 of these houses [are] togither, or but a little separated by groves of trees. Neare their habitations is little small wood, or old trees on the ground, by reason of their burning of them for fire. So that a man may gallop a horse amongst these woods any waie, but where the creekes or Rivers shall hinder.

Men women and children have their severall names according to the severall humor of their Parents. Their women (they say) are easilie delivered of childe, yet doe they love children verie dearly. To make them hardy, in the coldest mornings they wash them in the rivers, and by painting and ointments so tanne their skins, that after year or two, no weather will hurt them.

The men bestowe their times in fishing, hunting, wars, and such manlike exercise, scorning to be seene in any woman like exercise, which is the cause that the women be verie painefull and the men often idle. The women and children do the rest of the worke. They make mats, baskets, pots, morters, pound their corne, make their bread, prepare their victuals, plant their corne, gather their corne, beare all kind of burdens, and such like....

* * * * * *

1. *What does Smith's account reveal about gender relations among the native peoples of Virginia? How did the Indian people Smith describes divide work among men and women?*

2. *What does Smith mean when he calls the Indians "all savage?" Which of the characteristics that he describes in this passage might Smith and his European contemporaries have considered savage?*

3. Why does Smith choose to emphasize the differences between Indian and European cultures rather than the similarities? What influence might a vision of Indians as exotic and strange have on the policies employed by colonists for dealing with them?

4. Given Smith's assessment that Indians are "inconstant in everything but what feare constraith them to keepe," what sort of attitude would you expect him to take in diplomatic negotiations with them?

3–4 An Indentured Servant Writes from Virginia in 1623

Richard Frethorn was a young Englishman who settled in the Jamestown colony as an indentured servant in 1623. The following is one of three letters Frethorn sent his parents that same year reporting dissatisfaction with his lot and begging them to free him of his indenture. The letter describes a bleak life in Jamestown marked by disease, near starvation, and the constant threat of annihilation by Indians.

SOURCE: Paul Lauter et. al. eds., *The Heath Anthology of American Literature* (1990).

Loving and kind father and mother:

My most humble duty remembered to you, hoping in God of your good health, as I myself am at the making hereof. This is to let you understand that I your child am in a most heavy case by reason of the nature of the country, [which] is such that it causeth much sickness, as the scurvy and the bloody flux and diverse other diseases, which maketh the body very poor and weak. And when we are sick there is nothing to comfort us; for since I came out of the ship I never ate anything but peas, and loblollie (that is, water gruel). As for deer or venison I never saw any since I came into this land. There is indeed some fowl, but we are not allowed to go and get it, but must work hard both early and late for a mess of water gruel and a mouthful of bread and beef. A mouthful of bread for a penny loaf must serve for four men which is most pitiful....People cry out day and night—Oh! that they were in England without their limbs—and would not care to lose any limb to be England again, yea, though they beg from door to door. For we live in fear of the enemy every hour, yet we have had a combat with them on the Sunday before Shrovetide[1], and we took two alive and made slaves of them. But it was by policy, for we are in great danger; for our plantation is very weak by reason of the death and sickness of our company. For we came but twenty for the merchants, and they are half dead just; and we look every hour when two more should go. Yet there came some four other men yet to live with us, of which there is but one alive; and our Lieutenant is dead,

and his father and his brother. And there was some five or six of the last year's twenty, of which there is but three left, so that we are fain to get other men to plant with us; and yet we are but 32 to fight against 3000 if they should come. And the highest help that we have is ten miles of us, and when the rogues overcame this place last they slew 80 persons. How then shall we do, for we lie even in their teeth? They may easily take us, but that God is merciful and can save with few as well as with many, as he showed to Gilead[2]....

And I have nothing to comfort me, nor there is nothing to be gotten here but sickness and death, except that one had money to lay out in some things for profit. But I have nothing at all—no, not a shirt to my back but two rags (2), nor no clothes but one poor suit, nor but one pair of shoes, but one pair of stockings, but one cap, but two bands. My cloak is stolen by one of my own fellows, and to his dying hour [he] would not tell me what he did with it; but some of my fellows saw him have butter and beef out of a ship, which my cloak, I doubt [not], paid for. So that I have not a penny, nor a penny worth, to help me to either spice or sugar or strong waters, without the which one cannot live here. For as strong beer in England doth fatten and strengthen them, so water here doth wash and weaken these here [and] only keeps life and soul together. But I am not half a quarter so strong as I was in England, and all is for want of victuals; for I do protest unto you that I have eaten more in [one] day at home than I have allowed me here for a week. You have given more than my day's allowance to a beggar at the door; and if Mr. Jackson had not relieved me, I should be in a poor case. But he like a father and she like a loving mother doth still help me....

Goodman Jackson pitied me and made me a cabin to lie in always when I come up...which comforted me more than peas or water gruel. Oh, they be very godly folks, and love me very well, and will do anything for me. And he much marvelled that you would send me a servant to the Company; he saith I had been better knocked on the head. And indeed so I find it now, to my great grief and misery; and saith that if you love me you will redeem me suddenly, for which I do entreat and beg. And if you cannot get the merchants to redeem me for some little money, then for God's sake get a gathering or entreat some good folks to lay out some little sum of money in meal and cheese and butter and beef. Any eating meat will yield great profit. Oil and vinegar is very

[1] The three days before Ash Wednesday, formerly set aside as a period of confession and a time of festivity preceding Lent in Christian practice.

[2] A region east of the Jordan River settled in Biblical times by, among others, Israelites who were successfully defended in battle against vastly superior numbers of invaders by Judas Maccabeus and his warriors.

good; but, father, there is great loss in leaking. But for God's sake send beef and cheese and butter, or the more of one sort and none of another. But if you send cheese, it must be very old cheese; and at the cheese-monger's you may buy very good cheese for twopence farthing or halfpenny, that will be liked very well. But if you send cheese, you must have a care how you pack it in barrels; and you must put cooper's chips between every cheese, or else the heat of the hold will rot them. And look whatsoever you send me—be it never so much—look, what[ever] I make of it, I will deal truly with you. I will send it over and beg the profit to redeem me; and if I die before it come, I have entreated Goodman Jackson to send you the worth of it, who hath promised he will....Good father, do not forget me, but have mercy and pity my miserable case. I know if you did but see me, you would weep to see me; for I have but one suit....Wherefore, for God's sake, pity me. I pray you to remember my love to all my friends and kindred. I hope all my brothers and sisters are in good health, and as for my part I have set down my resolution that certainly will be; that is, that the answer of this letter will be life or death to me. Therefore, good father, send as soon as you can; and if you send me any thing let this be the mark.

ROT

Richard Frethorne,
Martin's Hundred

Moreover, on the third day of April we heard that after these rogues had gotten the pinnace and had taken all furnitures [such] as pieces, swords, armor, coats of mail, powder, shot and all the things that they had to trade withal, they killed the Captain and cut off his head. And rowing with the tail of the boat foremost, they set up a pole and put the Captain's head upon it, and so rowed home. Then the Devil set them on again, so that they furnished about 200 canoes with above 1000 Indians, and came, and thought to have taken the ship; but she was too quick for them—which thing was very much talked of, for they always feared a ship. But now the rogues grow very bold and can use pieces, some of them, as well or better than an Englishman; for an Indian did shoot with Mr. Charles, my master's kinsman, at a mark of white paper, and he hit it at the first, but Mr. Charles could not hit it. But see the envy of these slaves, for when they could not take the ship, then our men saw them threaten Accomack, that is the next plantation. And now there is no way but starving;...For they had no crop last year by reason of these rogues, so that we have no corn but as ships do relieve us, nor we shall hardly have any crop this year; and we are as like to perish first as any plantation. For we have but two hogsheads of meal left to serve us this two months....that is but a halfpennyloaf a day for a man. Is it not strange to me, think you? But what will it be when we shall go a month or two and never see a bit of bread, as my master doth say we must do? And he said he is not able to keep us all. Then we shall be turned up to the land and eat barks of trees or molds of the ground; therefore with weeping tears I beg of you to help me. Oh, that you did see my daily and hourly sighs, groans, and tears, and thumps that I afford mine own breast, and rue and curse the time of my birth, with holy Job. I thought no head had been able to hold so much water as hath and doth daily flow from mine eyes.

But this is certain: I never felt the want of father and mother till now; but now, dear friends, full well I know and rue it, although it were too late before I knew it....

Your loving son,
Richard Frethorne

Virginia, 3rd April, 1623

* * * * *

* * *

1. What is Frethorn's view of Indians? How does his view compare with the view expressed by John Smith or Antonio de Otermin?

2. To what extent is Frethorn's misery the result of his being an indentured servant? Which of his complaints were probably common to all settlers of Virginia?

3. In the midst of his tale of woe, Frethorn describes in great detail the manner in which one might "lay out in some things for profit." What was the importance of profit to the early settlers of Virginia? What information does Frethorn's letter give about the difficulties involved in getting English goods to market in Jamestown?

3-5 John Winthrop Defines the Puritan Ideal of Community 1630

John Winthrop (1588–1649), born in Suffolk, England, and educated at Cambridge, settled in the Massachusetts Bay colony in 1630. That same year he was elected the first governor of the colony, and though he was replaced as governor for several intermittent terms, he was a political and religious leader of the colony until the death in 1649. Winthrop's discourse, "A Modell of Christian Charity," written in 1630, outlines a project for the Puritan settlers of Massachusetts. He argues that the colony has a covenant with God to build a holy community:

SOURCE: John Winthrop, "A Modell of Christian Charity," in Winthrop Papers (Boston Massachusetts Historical Society, 1929), 2:282–84.

It rests now to make some application of this discourse by the present designe which gave the occasion of writing of it. Herein are 4 things to be propounded: first the persons, 2ly, the worke, 3ly, the end, 4ly the meanes.

1. For the persons, wee are a Company professing our selves fellow members of Christ, In which respect onely though wee were absent from each other many miles, and had our implymentes as farre distant, yet wee ought to account our selves knitt together by this bond of love, and live in the exercise of it, if wee would have comforte of our being in Christ....

2ly, for the worke wee have in hand, it is by a mutuall consent through a special overruleing providence, and a more than an ordinary approbation of the Churches of Christ to seeke out a place of Cohabitation and Consorteshipp under a due forme of Government both civill and ecclesiasticall. In such cases as this the care of the publique must oversway all private respects, by which not onely conscience, but meare Civill policy doth binde us; for it is a true rule that perticuler estates cannott subsist in the ruine of the publique.

3ly. The end is to improve our lives to doe more service to the Lord the comforte and encrease of the body of christe whereof wee are members that our selves and posterity may be the better preserved from the Common corrupcions of this evill world to serve the Lord and worke out our Salvacion under the power and purity of his holy Ordinances.

4ly. for the meanes whereby this must bee effected, they are 2fold, a Conformity with the worke and end wee aime at, these, wee see are extraordinary, therefore wee must not content our selves with usuall ordinary meanes whatsoever wee did or ought to have done when wee lived in England, the same must wee doe and more allsoe where

wee goe: That which the most in theire Churches maintetine as a truthe in profession onely, wee must bring into familiar and constant practise, as in this duty of love wee must love brotherly without dissimulation, wee must love one another with a pure hearte fervently wee must beare one anothers burthens, wee must not looke onely on our owne things, but allsoe on the things of our brethren, neither must wee think that the lord will beare with such faileings at our hands as hee dothe from those among whome wee have lived.... Thus stands the cause betweene God and us, wee are entered into Covenant with him for this worke, wee have taken out a Commission, the Lord hath given us leave to drawe our owne Articles wee have professed to enterprise these Accions upon these and these ends, wee have hereupon besought him of favour and blessing: Now if the Lord shall please to heare us, and bring us in peace to the place wee desire, then hath hee ratified this Covenant and sealed our Commission, [and] will expect a strickt performance of the Articles contained in it, but if wee shall neglect the observacion of these Articles which are the ends wee have propounded, and dissembling with our God, shall fall to embrace this present world and prosecute our carnall intencions, seeking greate things for our selves and our posterity, the Lord will surely breake out in wrathe against us be revenged of such a periured people and make us knowe the price of the breache of such a Covenant.

Now the onely way to avoyde this shipwracke and to provide for our posterity is to followe the Counsell of Micah, to doe Justly, to love mercy, to walke humbly with our God, for this end, wee must be knitt together in this worke as one man, wee must entertaine each other in brotherly Afeccion, wee must be willing to abridge our selves of our superfluities, for the supply of others necessities, wee must uphold a familiar Commerce together in all meekenes, gentlenes, patience and liberallity, wee must delight in eache other, make others Condicions our owne rejoyce together, mourne together, labour, and suffer together, allwayes haveing before our eyes our Commission and Community in the worke, our Community as members of the same body, soe shall wee keepe the unitie of the spirit in the bond of peace, the Lord will be our God and delight to dwell among us, as his owne people and will command a blessing upon us in all our wayes, soe that wee shall see much more of his wisdome power goodnes and truthe then formerly wee have beene acquainted with, wee shall finde that the God of Iseraell is among us, when tenn of us shall be able to resist a thousand of our enemies, when hee shall make us a prayse and glory, that men shall say of succeeding plantacions; the lord make it like that of New England: for wee must Consider that wee shall be as a Citty upon a Hill, the eies of all people are uppon us; soe that if wee shall deale falsely with our god in this worke wee have undertaken and soe cause him to withdrawe his present help from us, wee shall be made a story and a byword through the world, wee shall open the mouthes of enemies to speake evill of the wayes of god and all professours for Gods sake; wee shall shame the faces of many of gods worthy servants, and cause theire prayers to be turned in Cursses upon us till wee be consumed out of the good land whether wee are goeing: And to shutt upp this discourse with that exhortacion of Moses that faithfull servant of the Lord in his last farewell to Israell Deut. 30. Beloved there is now sett before us life, and good, deathe and evill in that wee are Commaunded this day to love the Lord our God, and to love one another to walke in his wayes and to keepe his Commaundements and his Ordinance, and his lawes, and the Articles of our Covenant with him that wee may live in the land whether wee goe to possesse it: But if our heartes shall turne away soe that wee will not obey, but shall be seduced and worshipp [serve cancelled] other Gods our pleasures, and proffitts, and serve them; it is propounded unto us this day; wee shall surely perishe out of the good Land whether wee passe over this vast Sea to possesse it;

Therefore lett us choose life,
that wee, and our Seede,
may live, by obeyeing his
voyce, and cleaveing to him,
for hee is our life, and
our prosperity.

* * * * *

1. *What balance does Winthrop propose for the relationship between the individual and the community? Is one more important to him than the other? Why?*

2. *What is the meaning of Winthrop's metaphor, "city on a hill?" How does his notion of a colony as an exceptional moral community differ from the self-conception of Jamestown's settlers?*

3. *Is there a conflict, for Winthrop, between service to God and the attempt to build a prosperous or economically successful community? Is there a place for profit in the city on a hill?*

3–6 Roger Williams Argues for Freedom of Conscience in 1644

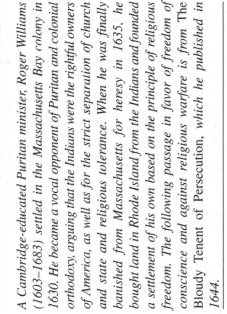

A Cambridge-educated Puritan minister, Roger Williams (1603–1683) settled in the Massachusetts Bay colony in 1630. He became a vocal opponent of Puritan and colonial orthodoxy, arguing that the Indians were the rightful owners of America, as well as for the strict separation of church and state and religious tolerance. When he was finally banished from Massachusetts for heresy in 1635, he bought land in Rhode Island from the Indians and founded a settlement of his own based on the principle of religious freedom. The following passage in favor of freedom of conscience and against religious warfare is from The Bloudy Tenent of Persecution, which he published in 1644.

SOURCE: Perry Miller, ed., *The Complete Writings of Roger Williams* (1963), p. 148.

First, That the blood of so many hundred thousand soules of Protestants and Papists, spilt in the Wars of present and former Ages, for their respective Consciences, is not required nor accepted by Jesus Christ the Prince of Peace.

Secondly, Pregnant Scriptures and Arguments are throughout the Worke proposed against the Doctrine of persecution for cause of Conscience.

Thirdly, Satisfactorie Answers are given to Scriptures, and objections produced by Mr. Calvin, Beza, Mr. Cotton, and the Ministers of the New English Churches and others former and later, tending to prove the Doctrine of persecution for cause of Conscience.

Fourthly, The Doctrine of persecution for cause of Conscience, is proved guilty of all the blood of the Soules crying for vengeance under the Altar.

Fifthly, All Civill States with their Officers of justice in their respective constitutions and administrations are proved essentially Civill, and therefore not Judges, Governours or Defendours of the Spirituall or Christian state and Worship.

Sixthly, It is the will and command of God, that (since the comming of his Sonne the Lord Jesus) a permission of the most Paganish, Jewish, Turkish, or Antichristian consciences and worships, bee granted to all men in all Nations and Countries: and they are onely to bee fought against with that Sword which is only (in Soule matters) able to conquer, to wit, the Sword of Gods Spirit, the Word of God.

Seventhly, The State of the Land of Israel, the Kings and people thereof in Peace & War, is proved figurative and ceremoniall, and no patterne nor president for any Kingdome or civill state in the world to follow.

Eightly, God requireth not an uniformity of Religion to be inacted and inforced in any civill state; which inforced uniformity (sooner or later) is the greatest occasion of Civill Warre, ravishing of conscience, persecution of Christ Jesus in his servants, and of the hypocrisie and destruction of millions of souls.

Ninthly, In holding an inforced uniformity of Religion in a civill state, wee must necessarily disclaime our desires and hopes of the Jewes conversion to Christ.

Tenthly, An inforced uniformity of Religion through-out a Nation or civill state, confounds the Civill and Religious, denies the principles of Christianity and civility, and that Jesus Christ is come in the Flesh.

Eleventhly, The permission of other consciences and worships then a state professeth, only can (according to God) procure a firme and lasting peace, (good assurance being taken according to the wisdome of the civill state for uniformity of civill obedience from all sorts.)

Twelfthly, lastly, true civility and Christianity may both flourish in a state or Kingdome, notwithstanding the permission of divers and contrary consciences, either of Jew or Gentile.

* * * * * *

1. According to Williams, what is the proper relationship between church and state? Why might his view have been considered heretical by the Puritan leadership of the Massachusetts Bay colony?

2. What arguments does Williams bring against "wars of conscience"? To what events in England and Europe might he be alluding?

3. Compare Roger Williams's state of "true Christianity and civility" with John Winthrop's "city on a hill." Which of these visions of the ideal community has had a greater or more permanent influence on American society?

3-7 Two Poems on Family by Anne Bradstreet Published in 1650

Born in Northhampton, England, Anne Bradstreet (1612-1672) traveled to America in 1630 with the first Massachusetts Bay colonists. There she settled with her husband to raise eight children and to write poetry. When a collection of her work was printed (without her knowledge) in London in 1650, she became the first American poet to be published. The following are two poems in Bradstreet's distinctively pious verse, one written for her husband, the other for one of her children.

To My Dear and Loving Husband

If ever two were one, then surely we.
If ever man were loved by wife, then thee;
If ever wife was happy in a man,
Compare with me, ye women, if you can.
I prize thy love more than whole mines of gold
Or all the riches that the East doth hold.
My love is such that rivers cannot quench,
Nor ought but love from thee, give recompense.
Thy love is such I can no way repay,
The heavens reward thee manifold, I pray.
Then while we live, in love let's so persevere
That when we live no more, we may live ever.

Before the Birth of One of Her Children

All things within this fading world hath end,
Adversity doth still our joys attend;
No ties so strong, no friends so dear and sweet,
But with death's parting blow is sure to meet.
The sentence past is most irrevocable,
A common thing, yet oh inevitable;
How soon, my dear, death may my steps attend,
How soon't may be thy lot to lose thy friend,
We both are ignorant, yet love bids me
These farewell lines to recommend to thee,
That when that knot's untied that made us one,
I may seem thine, who in effect am none.
And if I see not half my days that's due,
What nature would, God grant to yours and you;
The many faults that well you know I have,
Let be inter'd in my oblivion's grave;
If any worth or virtue were in me,
Let that live freshly in thy memory,
And when thou feel'st no grief, as I no harms,
Yet love thy dead, who long lay in thine arms:
And when thy loss shall be repaid with gains,
Look to my little babes, my dear remains.
And if thou love thy self, or loved'st me,
These O protect from step-dame's injury.
And if chance to thine eyes shall bring this verse,
With some sad sighs honor my absent hearse;
And kiss the paper for thy love's dear sake,
Who with salt tears this last farewell did take.

* * * * *

1. Why are the birth of her child and Bradstreet's own death so closely linked in "Before the Birth of One of Her Children?" How does the high probability that she will die giving birth influence Bradstreet's thinking?

2. How does Bradstreet's poem "To My Dear and Loving Husband" compare to the image of the Puritans as cold and heartless people?

3–8 Selections from the New England Primer of 1683

In 1647 Massachusetts passed a law requiring all towns with populations greater than 50 to open public schools for the basic education of the towns' children in reading, writing, and mathematics. Many of the towns in the other New England colonies opened schools as well. The following is an excerpt form the 1683 edition of the New England Primer, the standard reader in colonial schoolhouses used to teach both literacy and religious tenets.

SOURCE: Paul Lauter et at.. eds., *The Heath Anthology of American Literature* (1990), pp. 308–310.

A In *Adam's* Fall
We Sinned all.

B Thy Life to Mend
This *Book* Attend.

C The *Cat* doth play
And after slay.

D A *Dog* will bite
A *Thief* at night.

E An *Eagle's* flight
is out of sight.

F The idle *Fool*
Is whipt at School.

G As runs the *Glass*
Man's life doth pass.

H My *Book* and *Heart*
Shall never part.

J *Job* feels the Rod
Yet blesses GOD.

K Our *KING* the good
No man of blood.

L The *Lion* bold
The *Lamb* doth hold.

M The *Moon* gives light
In time of night.

N *Nightengales* sing
In time of Spring.

O The *Royal Oak*
it was the Tree
That sav'd His
Royal Majestie.

P *Peter* denies
His Lord and cries

Q *Queen Esther* comes
in Royal State
To Save the JEWS
from dismal Fate

R *Rachel* doth mourn
For her first born.

S *Samuel* anoints
Whom God appoints.

T *Time* cuts down all
Both great and small.

U *Uriah's* beauteous
Wife
Made David seek his
Life.

W *Whales* in the Sea
God's Voice obey.

X *Xerxes* the great did
die,
And so must you & I.

Y *Youth* forward slips
Death soonest nips.

Z *Zacheus* he
Did climb the Tree
His Lord to see.

Now the Child being entred in his Letters and Spelling, let him learn these and such like Sentences by Heart, whereby he will be both instructed in his Duty, and encouraged in his Learning.

The Dutiful Child's Promises

I will fear GOD, and honour the KING.
I will honour my Father & Mother.
I will Obey my Superiours.
I will Submit to my Elders,
I will Love my Friends.
I will hate no Man.
I will forgive my Enemies, and pray to God for them.
I will as much as in me lies keep all God's Holy
Commandments.
I will learn my Catechism.
I will keep the Lord's Day Holy.
I will Reverence God's Sanctuary,
For our GOD is a consuming Fire.

Verses

I in the Burying Place may see
Graves shorter there than I;
From Death's Arrest no Age is free,
Young Children too may die;
My God, may such an awful Sight,
Awakening be to me!
Oh! that by early Grace I might
For Death prepared be.

* * * * * *

1. On the basis of this document, what seems to have been the preferred method of teaching in colonial New England's schoolhouses? What sorts of assignments might teachers have given students using the Primer?

2. What, besides literacy, were the main purposes of primary education in 17th-century New England?

3. What aspects of Puritan ideas about death are evident in the poem "Verses?" What does it say about Puritan society that instilling a fervent preoccupation with death was considered an important element of the basic education of young children?

3-9   William Penn's 1681 Plans for the Province of Pennsylvania

In 1681, in payment for a debt of 16,000 pounds, Charles II gave William Penn (1644–1718) a charter to create a new colony in the Delaware Valley. To regulate the sale and settlement of land in the new colony, Penn wrote up a set of Conditions and Concessions, sections of which follow. Not a frame of government, the Concessions deal mostly with property arrangements and relations with Indians, but Penn also provides some insight into his plans for the colony.

SOURCE: F. N. Thorpe, ed., Federal and State Constitutions, Vol V, p. 3044 ff.

Certain conditions, or concessions, agreed upon by William Penn, Proprietary and Governor of the province of Pennsylvania, and those who are the adventurers and purchasers in the same province....

I. That so soon as it pleaseth God that the above-said persons arrive there, a certain quantity of land, or ground plat, shall be laid out, for a large town or city, in the most convenient place, upon the river, for health and navigation; and every purchaser and adventurer shall, by lot, have so much land therein as will answer to the proportion, which he hath bought, or taken up, upon rent: but it is to be noted, that the surveyors shall consider what roads or highways will be necessary to the cities, towns or through the lands. Great roads from city to city not to contain less than forty foot, in breadth, shall be first laid out and declared to be for high-ways, before the dividend of acres be laid out for the purchaser, and the like observation to be had for the streets in the towns and cities, that there may be convenient roads and streets preserved, not to be encroached upon by any planter or builder, that none may build irregularly to the damage of another. In this, custom governs....

III. That, when the country lots are laid out, every purchaser, from one thousand, to ten thousand acres, or more, not to have above one thousand acres together, unless in three years they plant a family upon every thousand acres; but that all such as purchase together, lie together; and, if as many as comply with this condition,

that the whole be laid out together,

VII. That, for every fifty acres, that shall be allotted to a servant, at the end of his service, his quit-rent shall be two shillings per annum, and the master, or owner of the servant, when he shall take up the other fifty acres, his quit-rent, shall be four shillings by the year, or, if the master of the servant (by reason in the indentures he is so obliged to do) allot out to the servant fifty acres in his own division, the said master shall have, on demand, allotted him, from the governor, the one hundred acres, at the chief rent of six shillings per annum.

VIII. And, for the encouragement of such as are ingenious and willing to search out gold and silver mines in this province, it is hereby agreed, that they have liberty to bore and dig in any man's property, fully paying the damages done; and in case a discovery should be made, that the discoverer have one-fifth, the owner of the soil (if not the discoverer) a tenth part, the Governor, two-fifths, and the rest to the public treasury, saving to the king the share reserved by patent.

IX. In every hundred thousand acres, the Governor and Proprietary, by lot, reserveth ten to himself, what shall lie but in one place.

X. That every man shall be bound to plant, or man, so much of his share of land as shall be set out and surveyed, within three years after it is so set out and surveyed, or else it shall be lawful for newcomers to be settled thereupon, paying to them their survey money, and they go up higher for their shares.

XI. There shall be no buying and selling, be it with an Indian, or one among another, of any goods to be exported, but what shall be performed in public market, when such places shall be set apart, or erected, when they shall pass the public stamp, or mark. If bad ware, and prized as good, or deceitful in proportion or weight, to forfeit the value, as if good and full weight and proportion, to the public treasury of this province, whether it be the merchandize of the Indian, or that of the planters.

XII. And forasmuch, as it is usual with the planters to over-reach the poor natives of the country, in trade, by goods not being good of the kind, or debased with mixtures, with which they are sensibly aggrieved, it is agreed, whatever is sold to the Indians, in consideration of their furs, shall be sold in the market place, and there suffer the test, whether good or bad; if good, to pass; if not good, not to be sold for good, that the natives may not be abused, nor provoked.

XIII. That no man shall, by any ways or means, in word, or deed, affront, or wrong any *Indian*, but he shall incur the same penalty of the law, as if he had committed it against his fellow planter, and if any *Indian* shall abuse, in word, or deed, any planter of this province, that he shall not be his own judge upon the *Indian*, but he shall make his complaint to the governor of the province, or his lieutenant, or deputy, or some inferior magistrate near him, who shall, to the utmost of his power, take care with the king of the said *Indian*, that all reasonable satisfaction be made to the said injured planter....

XV. That the *Indians* shall have liberty to do all things relating to improvement of their ground, and providing sustenance for their families, that any of the planters shall enjoy.

XVI. That the laws, as to slanders, drunkenness, swearing, cursing, pride in apparel, trespasses, distresses, replevins, weights, and measures, shall be the same as in *England*, till altered by law in this province....

XVIII. That, in clearing the ground, care be taken to leave *one* acre of trees for every *five* acres cleared, especially to preserve oak and mulberries, for silk and shipping....

WILLIAM PENN.

* * * * * *

1. *How does the plan for settlement of Pennsylvania differ from the plans laid out for earlier colonies in New England and Virginia? Is Penn, like Winthrop, planning a city on a hill?*

2. *What is Penn's attitude towards Indians? Why were regulations about relations with Indians (notice that most of these are regulations intended to protect Indians) important for the new colony? What do the regulations suggest about the white settlers Penn intended to attract?*

3. *How was land to be distributed in Pennsylvania? In what ways does Penn's organization of land ownership resemble that of feudal Europe? In what ways does it resemble later American settlement patterns such as homesteading?*

3–10 Iroquois Chiefs Address the Governors of New York and Virginia in 1684

The Five Nations of the Iroquois was the most powerful Indian confederacy in North America. Transferring their alliance to the English after New Holland became New York, the Iroquois came under increasing pressure from the French and their Indian allies to the north. In these addresses by spokesmen for three of the Iroquois nations—the Onondagas, Cayugas, and Senecas—the Iroquois appeal for the assistance of the New Yorkers and lay down their conditions for a continuing alliance.

SOURCE: Cadwallader Colden, *The History of the Five Nations of Canada*, 3d ed., (London: 1755), Vol. I., pp. 46–51.

[Spokesman for the Onondagas and Cayugas:]

Brother Corlear,

Your Sachem is a great Sachem, and we are but a small People; but when the English came first to Manhatan [New York], to Aragiske [Virginia] and to Yako-kranagary [Maryland], they were then but a small People, and we were great. Then, because we found you a good People, we treated you kindly, and gave you Land; we hope therefore, now that you are great, and we small, you will protect us from the French. If you do not, we shall lose all our Hunting and Bevers: The French will get all the Bevers. The Reason they are now angry with us is, because we carry our Bever to our Brethren.

We have put our Lands and ourselves under the Protection of the great Duke of York, the Brother of your great Sachem, who is likewise a great Sachem.

We have annexed the Susquehana River, which we won with the Sword, to this Government; and we desire it may be a Branch of the great Tree that grows in this Place, the Top of which reaches the Sun, and its Branches shelter us from the French, and all other Nations. Our Fire burns in your Houses, and your Fire burns with us; we desire it may be so always. But we will not that any of the great Penn's People settle upon the Susquehana River, for we have no other Land to leave to our Children.

Our young Men are Soldiers, and when they are provoked, they are like Wolves in the Woods, as you, Sachem of Virginia, very well know.

We have put ourselves under the great Sachem Charles, that lives on the other Side the great Lake. We give you these two white dressed Deer-skins, to send to the great Sachem, that he may write on them, and put a great red Seal to them, to confirm what we now do; and put the Susquehana River above the Falls, and all the rest of our Land under the great Duke of York, and give that Land to none else. Our Brethren, his People, have been like Fathers to our Wives and Children, and have given us

Bread when we were in Need of it; we will not therefore join ourselves, or our Land, to any other Government but this. We desire Corlear, our Governor, may send this our Proposition to the great Sachem Charles, who dwells on the other Side the great Lake, with this Belt of Wampum, and this other smaller Belt to the Duke of York his Brother: And we give you, Corlear, this Bever, that you may send over this Proposition.

You great Man of Virginia, we let you know, that great Penn did speak to us here in Corlear's House by his Agents, and desired to buy the Susquehana River of us, but we would not hearken to him, for we had fastened it to this Government.

We desire you therefore to bear witness of what we now do, and that we now confirm what we have done before. Let your Friend, that lives on the other Side the great Lake, know this, that we being a free People, though united to the English, may give our Lands, and be joined to the Sachem we like best. We give this Bever to remember what we say.

[Spokesman for the Senecas:]

We have heard and understood what Mischief hath been done in Virginia; we have it as perfect as if it were upon our Fingers Ends. O Corlear! we thank you for having been our Intercessor, so that the Axe has not fallen upon us.

And you Assarigoa, great Sachem of Virginia, we thank you for burying all Evil in the Pit. We are informed, that the Mohawks, Oneydoes, Onnondagas, and Cayugas, have buried the Axe already; now we that live remotest off, are come to do the same, and to include in this Chain the Cahnawaas, your Friends. We desire therefore, that an Axe, on our Part, may be buried with one of Assarigoa's. O Corlear! Corlear! we thank you for laying hold of one End of the Axe; and we thank you, great Governor of Virginia, not only for throwing aside the Axe, but more especially for your putting all Evil from your Heart. Now we have a new Chain, a strong and a straight Chain, that cannot be broken. The Tree of Peace is planted so firmly, that it cannot be moved, let us on both Sides hold the Chain fast.

We understand what you said of the great Sachem, that lives on the other Side the great Water.

You tell us, that the Cahnawaas will come hither, to strengthen the Chain. Let them not make any Excuse, that they are old and feeble, or that their Feet are sore. If the old Sachems cannot, let the young Men come. We shall not fail to come hither, tho' we live farthest off, and then the new Chain will be stronger and brighter.

We understand, that because of the Mischief that has been done to the People and Castles of Virginia and Maryland, we must not come near the Heads of your Rivers, nor near your Plantations; but keep at the Foot of the Mountains; for tho' we lay down our Arms, as Friends, we shall not be trusted for the future, but looked on as Robbers. We agree however to this Proposition, and shall wholly stay away from Virginia: And this we do in Gratitude to Codear, who has been at so great Pains to persuade you, great Governor of Virginia, to forget what is past. You are wise in giving Ear to Corlear's good Advice, for we shall now go a Path which was never trod before.

We have now done speaking to Corlear, and the Governor of Virginia; let the Chain be for ever kept clean and bright by him, and we shall do the same.

The other Nations from the Mohawks Country to the Cayugas, have delivered up the Susquehana River, and all that Country, to Corlear's Government. We confirm what they have done by giving this Belt.

* * * * * *

1. What terms did the Iroquois propose to the New Yorkers? Might it be described as a quid pro quo arrangement?

2. Note the distinction the Iroquois make between the colonies of New York, Pennsylvania, and Virginia. What did the Onondaga and Cayuga spokesman mean when he declared "that we being a free People, though united to the English, may give our Lands, and be joined to the Sachem we like best"?

3. Note the formality and rituals of Indian diplomacy. What was the meaning of giving the beaver pelts and wampum belts as part of this occasion?

chapter 4

Slavery and Empire, 1441–1770

4–1 England Asserts Her Dominion through Legislation in 1660

In conjunction with the restoration of the Stuart dynasty in 1660, England sought to strengthen the American colony's dependence on her for trade goods. British Parliament's passage of the Navigation Act of 1660 made it necessary for all trade goods bound for the colonies to enter England first and, likewise, for all goods sent to market from the colonies to travel through England. Although the Navigation Act was not strictly enforced, it set the basis for the increasingly constrictive British trade practices that led to the American Revolution. The following section outlines the main points of the legislation.

SOURCE: Owen Ruffhead, *The Statutes at Large* (London: M. Baskett, 1763–65).

An act for the encouraging and increasing of shipping and navigation

For the increase of shipping and encouragement of the navigation of this nation, wherein, under the good providence and protection of God, the wealth, safety and strength of this kingdom is so much concerned; be it enacted by the King's most excellent majesty, and by the lords and commons in this present parliament assembled, and by the authority thereof. That from and after the first day of *December* one thousand six hundred and sixty, and from thenceforward, no goods or commodities whatsoever shall be imported into or exported out of any lands, islands, plantations or territories to his Majesty belonging or in his possession, or which may hereafter belong unto or be in the possession of his Majesty, his heirs and successors, in *Asia, Africa* or *America,* in any other ship or ships, vessel or vessels whatsoever, but in such ships or vessels as do truly and without fraud belong only to the people of *England* or *Ireland,* dominion of *Wales* or town of *Berwick* upon *Tweed,* or are of the built of and belonging to any the said lands, islands, plantations or territories, as the proprietors and right owners thereof, and whereof the master and three fourths

of the mariners at least are *English;* under the penalty of the forfeiture and loss of all the goods and commodities which shall be imported into or exported out of any the aforesaid places in any other ship or vessel, as also of the ship or vessel....

II. And be it enacted, That no alien or person not born within the allegiance of our sovereign lord the King, his heirs and successors, or naturalized, or made a free denizen, shall from and after the first day of *February,* 1661, exercise the trade or occupation of a merchant or factor in any the said places; upon pain of the forfeiture and loss of all his goods and chattels,...and all governors of the said lands, islands, plantations or territories, and every of them, are hereby strictly required and command-ed, and all who hereafter shall be made governors of any such islands, plantations or territories, by his Majesty, his heirs or successors, shall before their entrance into their government take a solemn oath, to do their utmost, that every the afore-mentioned clauses, and all the matters and things therein contained, shall be punctually and *bona fide* observed according to the true intent and meaning thereof; and upon complaint and proof made before his Majesty, his heirs or successors, or such as shall be by him or them thereunto authorized and appointed, that any the said governors have been willingly and wittingly neg-ligent in doing their duty accordingly, that the said gover-nor so offending shall be removed from his government.

III. And it is further enacted...,That no goods or commodities whatsoever, of the growth, production or manufacture of *Africa, Asia* or *America,* or of any part thereof, of which are described or laid down in the usual maps or cards of those places, be imported into *England, Ireland* or *Wales,* islands of *Guernsey* and *Jersey,* or town of *Berwick* upon *Tweed,* in any other ship or ships, vessel or vessels whatsoever, but in such as do truly and without fraud belong only to the people of *England* or *Ireland,* dominion of *Wales,* or town of *Berwick* upon *Tweed* or of the lands, islands, plantations or territories in *Asia, Africa* or *America,* to his Majesty belonging, as the proprietors and right owners thereof, and whereof the master, and three fourths at least of the mariners are *English;* (2) under the penalty of the forfeiture of all such goods and commodities, and of the ship or vessel in which they were imported....

IV. And it is further enacted...,That no goods or commodities that are of foreign growth, production or manufacture, and which are to be brought into *England, Ireland, Wales,* the islands of *Guernsey* and *Jersey,* or town of *Berwick* upon *Tweed,* in *English*-built shipping, or other shipping belonging to some of the aforesaid places, and navigated by *English* mariners, as aforesaid, shall be shipped or brought from any other place or places, country or countries, but only from those of the said growth, production or manufacture, or from those

39

ports where the said goods and commodities can only, or are, or usually have been, first shipped for transportation, and from none other places or countries; under the penalty of the forfeiture of all such of the aforesaid goods as shall be imported from any other place or country contrary to the true intent and meaning hereof, as also of the ship in which they were imported....

V. And it is further enacted.... That any sort of ling, stock-fish, pilchard, or any other kind of dried or salted fish, usually fished for and caught by the people of England, Ireland, Wales, or town of Berwick upon Tweed; or any sort of cod-fish or herring, or any oil or blubber made or that shall be made of any kind of fish whatsoever, or any whale-fins or whale-bones, which shall be imported into England, Ireland, Wales, or town of Berwick upon Tweed, not having been caught in vessels truly and properly belonging thereunto as proprietors and right owners thereof, and the said fish cured saved and dried, and the oil and blubber aforesaid (which shall be accounted and pay as oil) not made by the people thereof, and shall be imported into England, Ireland or Wales, or town of Berwick upon Tweed, shall pay double aliens custom.

VI. And be it further enacted.... That from henceforth it shall not be lawful to any person or persons whatsoever, to load or cause to be loaden and carried in any bottom or bottoms, ship or ships, vessel or vessels whatsoever, whereof any stranger or strangers-born (unless such as shall be denizens or naturalized) be owners, partowners or master, and whereof three fourths of the mariners at least shall not be English, any fish, victual, wares, goods, commodities or things, of what kind or nature soever the same shall be, from one port or creek of England, Ireland, Wales, islands of Guernsey or Jersey, or town of Berwick upon Tweed, to another port or creek of the fame, or of any of them; under penalty for every one that shall offend contrary to the true meaning of this branch of this present act, to forfeit all such goods shall be loaden and carried in any such ship or vessel, together with the ship or vessel....

VIII. And it is further enacted....That no goods or commodities of the growth, production or manufacture of Muscovy or to any the countries, dominions or territories to the...emperor of Muscovy, or Russia belonging, as also that no sort of masts, timber or boards, no foreign salt, pitch, tar, rosin, hemp or flax, raisins, figs, prunes, olive-oils, no sorts of corn or grain, sugar, potashes, wines, vinegar, or spirits called aqua-vitae, or brandywine, shall from after the first day of April, 1662, be imported into England, Ireland, Wales, or town of Berwick upon Tweed, in any ship or ships...but in such as do truly and without fraud belong to the people thereof...and whereof the master and three fourths of the mariners at least are English; and that no currans nor commodities of the growth, production or manufacture of any of the countries, islands, dominions or territories to the Othoman or Turkish empire belonging, shall from after the first day of September, 1661, be imported into any of the afore-mentioned places in any ship or vessel, but which is of English-built, and navigated....

XIII. Provided also, That this act or any thing therein contained, extend not, or be meant, to restrain the importing of any East-India commodities loaden in English-built shipping, and whereof the master and three-fourths of the mariners at least are English, from the usual place or places for lading of them in any part of those seas, to the southward and eastward of Cabo bona Esperanza, although the said ports be not the very places of their growth....

XVIII. And it is further enacted....That from and after the first day of April, 1661, no sugars, tobacco, cotton-wool, indicoes, ginger, fustick, or other dying wood, of the growth, production or manufacture of any English plantations in America, Asia or Africa shall be shipped, carried, conveyed or transported from any of the said English plantations to any land...other than to such other English plantations as do belong to his Majesty....

* * * * * *

1. What effect did the Navigation Act of 1660 have on trade at the time? How would the act have established England as a superpower in its day?

2. Where were manufactured goods made in the mid-seventeenth century?

3. How does the Navigation Act of 1660 establish a legal precedent for our current trade laws?

4-2   Maryland Addresses the Status of Slaves in 1664

Although slavery dates back before 2000 B.C.E. to the Sumerians, the status of black slaves in the early years of colonization in Maryland was unclear. Were they to serve a limited number of years? Were they the property of their owners to do with as they saw fit? The Maryland Statute on Negroes and Other Slaves, a portion of which follows, established that all blacks, as well as their children and their families, would be slaves durante vita, that is, for their entire lives.

SOURCE: William H. Browne, ed., *Archives of Maryland* (Baltimore: Maryland Historical Society, 1883), pp. 533–34.

Bee itt Enacted by the Right Honourable the Lord Proprietary, by the advice and Consent of the upper and lower house of this present Generall Assembly, That all Negroes or other slaves already within the Province And all Negroes and other slaves to bee hereafter imported into the Province shall serve Durante Vita. And all Chilldren born of any Negro or other slave shall be Slaves as their ffathers were for the terme of their lives. And forasmuch as divers freeborne English women forgettfull of their free Condition and to the disgrace of our Nation doe intermarry with Negro Slaves, by which alsoe divers suites may arise touching the Issue of such woemen and a great damage doth befall the Masters of such Negros—for prevention whereof and for deterring such freeborne women from such shamefull Matches, Bee itt further Enacted by the Authority advice and Consent aforesaid, That whatsoever free borne woman shall inter marry with any slave from and after the Last day of this present Assembly shall Serve the master of such slave dureing the life of her husband, And that all the Issue of such freeborne woemen soe marryed shall be Slaves as their fathers were. And Bee itt further Enacted that all the Issues of English or other freeborne woemen that have already marryed Negroes shall serve the Masters of their Parents till they be Thirty years of age and noe longer.

* * * * * *

1. *What do you think was the legislator's intent in enacting the Maryland Statute on the Negroes and Other Slaves? What were they trying to protect?*

2. *Why would the statute address the intermarriage of "freeborne English women" with black men, but neglect to mention anything regarding the marriage of white men to black women?*

4-3   A Slave Tells of His Capture in Africa in 1798

The son of an African prince, Venture Smith was captured at the age of eight and shipped to America to be sold as a slave. One of the few surviving slave narratives of the colonial period of American history, Smith's story gives us valuable insight as to how Africans were captured by black slave traders and transported. Smith recounted his oral history when he was an old man living in Connecticut. The following excerpt from his narrative tells of his capture.

SOURCE: Venture Smith, *A Narrative of the Life and Adventures of Venture* (New London: n.p., 1798).

I was born at Dukandarra, in Guinea, about the year 1729. My father's name was Saungm Furro, Prince of the tribe of Dukandarra. My father had three wives. Polygamy was not uncommon in that country, especially among the rich, as every man was allowed to keep as many wives as he could maintain. By his first wife he had three children. The eldest of them was myself, named by my father, Broteer. The other two were named Cundazo and Soozaduka. My father had two children by his second wife, and one by his third. I descended from a very large, tall and stout race of beings, much larger than the generality of people in other parts of the globe, being commonly considerably above six feet in height, and every way well proportioned....

I was then about six years old...[One day] a message was brought...to my father, that the place had been invaded by a numerous army, from a nation not far distant, furnished with all kinds of arms then in use; that they were instigated by some white nation who equipped and sent them to subdue and possess the country....A detachment from the enemy came to my father and informed him that the whole army was encamped not far out of his dominions, and would invade the territory and deprive his people of their liberties and rights if he did not comply with the following terms. These were to pay them a large sum of money, three hundred fat cattle, and a great number of goats, sheep, asses, &c.

My father told the messenger he would comply rather than that his subjects should be deprived of their rights and privileges, which he was not then in circumstances to defend from so sudden an invasion. Upon turning out those articles, the enemy pledged their faith and honor that they would not attack him. On these he relied and therefore thought it unnecessary to be on his guard against the enemy. But their pledges of faith and honor proved no better than those of other unprincipled hostile nations; for a few days after a certain relation of the king came and informed him, that the enemy who sent terms of accommodation to him and received tribute to their satisfaction, yet meditated an attack upon his subjects by surprise, and that probably they would commence their attack in less than one day, and concluded with advising him, as he was not prepared for war, to order a speedy retreat of his family and subjects. He complied with this advice.

The same night which was fixed upon to retreat, my father and his family set off about the break of day. The king and his two younger wives went in one company, and my mother and her children in another. We left our dwellings in succession, and my father's company went on first. We directed our course for a large shrub plain, some distance off, where we intended to conceal ourselves from the approaching enemy, until we could refresh ourselves a little. But we presently found that our retreat was not secure. For having struck up a little fire for the purpose of cooking victuals, the enemy who happened to be encamped a little distance off, had sent out a scouting party who discovered us by the smoke of the fire, just as we were extinguishing it, and about to eat. As soon as we had finished eating, my father discovered the party, and immediately began to discharge arrows at them. This was what I first saw, and it alarmed both me and the women, who being unable to make any resistance, immediately betook ourselves to the tall thick reeds not far off, and left the old king to fight alone. For some time I beheld him from the reeds defending himself with great courage and firmness, till at last he was obliged to surrender himself into their hands.

They then came to us in the reeds, and the very first salute I had from them was a violent blow on the back part of the head with the fore part of a gun, and at the same time a grasp round the neck. I then had a rope put about my neck, as had all the women in the thicket with me, and was immediately led to my father, who was likewise pinioned and haltered for leading. In this condition we were all led to the camp. The women and myself being pretty submissive, had tolerable treatment from the enemy, while my father was closely interrogated respecting his money which they knew he must have. But as he gave them no account of it, he was instantly cut and pounded on his body with great inhumanity, that he might be induced by the torture he suffered to make the discovery. All this availed not in the least to make him give up his money, but he despised all the tortures which they inflicted, until the continued exercise and increase of torment, obliged him to sink and expire. He thus died without informing his enemies where his money lay. I saw him while he was thus tortured to death. The shocking scene is to this day fresh in my mind, and I have often been overcome while thinking on it. He was a man of remarkable stature. I should judge as much as six feet and six or seven inches high, two feet across his shoulders, and every way well proportioned. He was a man of remarkable strength and resolution, affable, kind and gentle, ruling with equity and moderation.

The army of the enemy was large, I should suppose consisting of about six thousand men. Their leader was called Baukurre. After destroying the old prince, they decamped and immediately marched towards the sea, lying to the west, taking with them myself and the women prisoners. In the march a scouting party was detached from the main army. To the leader of this party I was made waiter, having to carry his gun, &c. As we were a-scouting we came across a herd of fat cattle, consisting of about thirty in number. These we set upon, and immediately wrested from their keepers, and afterwards converted them into food for the army. The enemy had remarkable success in destroying the country wherever they went. For as far as they had penetrated, they laid the habitations waste and captured the people. The distance they had now brought me was about four hundred miles. All the march I had very hard tasks imposed on me, which I must perform on pain of punishment. I was obliged to carry on my head a large flat stone used for grinding our corn, weighing as I should suppose, as much as twenty-five pounds; besides victuals, mat and cooking utensils. Though I was pretty large and stout of my age, yet these burdens were very grievous to me, being only six years and a half old.

We were then come to a place called Malagasco. When we entered the place we could not see the least appearance of either houses or inhabitants, but upon stricter search found, that instead of houses above ground they had dens in the sides of hillocks, contiguous to ponds and streams of water. In these we perceived they had all hid themselves, as I suppose they usually did on such occasions. In order to compel them to surrender, the enemy contrived to smoke them out with faggots. These they put to the entrance of the caves and set them on fire. While they were engaged in this business, to their great surprise some of them were desperately wounded with arrows which fell from above on them. This mystery they soon found out. They perceived that the enemy discharged these arrows through holes on the top of the dens directly into the air. Their weight brought them back, point downwards on their enemies heads, whilst they were smoking the inhabitants out. The points of their arrows were poisoned, but their enemy had an antidote for it, which they instantly applied to the wounded part. The smoke at last obliged the people to give themselves up.

They came out of their caves, first spatting the palms of their hands together, and immediately after extended their arms, crossed at their wrists, ready to be bound and pinioned. I should judge that the dens above mentioned were extended about eight feet horizontally into the earth, six feet in height and as many wide. They were arched over head and lined with earth, which was of the clay kind, and made the surface of their walls firm and smooth.

The invaders then pinioned the prisoners of all ages and sexes indiscriminately, took their flocks and all their effects, and moved on their way towards the sea. On the march the prisoners were treated with clemency, on account of their being submissive and humble. Having come to the next tribe, the enemy laid siege and immediately took men, women, children, flocks, and all their valuable effects. They then went on to the next district which was contiguous to the sea, called in Africa, Anamaboo. The enemies' provisions were then almost spent, as well as their strength. The inhabitants knowing what conduct they had pursued, and what were their present intentions, improved the favorable opportunity, attacked them, and took enemy, prisoners, flocks and all their effects. I was then taken a second time. All of us were then put into the castle, and kept for market. On a

certain time I and other prisoners were put on board a canoe, under our master, and rowed away to a vessel belonging to Rhode Island, commanded by Captain Collingwood, and the mate Thomas Mumford. While we were going to the vessel, our master told us all to appear to the best possible advantage for sale. I was bought on board by one Robertson Mumford, steward of said vessel, for four gallons of rum, and a piece of calico, and called VENTURE, on account of his having purchased me with his own private venture. Thus I came by my name. All the slaves that were bought for that vessel's cargo, were two hundred and sixty.

* * * * *

1. How does Venture Smith's oral history inform our historical narrative regarding slavery? How does the personalization of one person's enslavement affect our understanding of what slavery meant?

2. Why would Africans be involved in selling their fellow countrymen into slavery? What would be their motivations?

4-4   A Slave Ship Surgeon Writes about the Slave Trade in 1788

Alexander Falconbridge was forced through poverty to work as a surgeon on slave ships. Witnessing the horrors of the trade, Falconbridge became an advocate for the slaves. He went on to become involved in Sierra Leone, a British antislavery resettlement colony in West Africa. The following passage outlines how slaves were obtained in Africa by kidnapping and examined by traders before being sold.

SOURCE: Alexander Falconbridge, An Account of the Slave Trade on the Coast of Africa (London, 1788).

The Manner in which the Slaves are Procured

After permission has been obtained for *breaking trade*, as it is termed, the captains go ashore from time to time, to examine the Negroes that are exposed to sale, and to make their purchases. The unhappy wretches thus disposed of, are bought by the black traders at fairs, which are held for that purpose, at the distance of upwards of two hundred miles from the sea coast, and these fairs are said to be supplied from an interior part of the country. Many Negroes, upon being questioned relative to the

places of their nativity, have asserted, that they have travelled during the revolution of several moons (their usual method of calculating time), before they have reached the places they were purchased by the black traders. At these fairs, which are held at uncertain periods, but generally every six weeks, several thousands are frequently exposed to sale, who had been collected from all parts of the country for a very considerable distance round. While I was upon the coast, during one of the voyages I made, the black traders brought down, in different canoes, from twelve to fifteen hundred Negroes, which had been purchased at one fair. They consisted chiefly of men and boys, the women seldom exceeding a third of the whole number. From forty to two hundred Negroes are generally purchased at a time by the black traders, according to the opulence of the buyer; and consist of those of all ages, from a month to sixty years and upwards. Scarce any age or situation is deemed an exception, the price being proportional. Women sometimes form a part of them, who happen to be so far advanced in their pregnancy, as to be delivered during their journey from the fairs to the coast; and I have frequently seen instances of deliveries on board ship. The slaves purchased at these fairs are only for the supply of the markets at Bonny, and Old and New Calabar.

There is great reason to believe, that most of the Negroes shipped off from the coast of Africa, are kidnapped. But the extreme care taken by the black traders to prevent the Europeans from gaining any intelligence of their modes of proceeding; the great distance inland from whence the Negroes are brought; and our ignorance of their language (with which, very frequently, the black traders themselves are equally unacquainted), prevent our obtaining such information on this head as we could wish. I have, however, by means of occasional inquiries, made through interpreters, procured some intelligence relative to the point, and such, as I think, puts the matter beyond a doubt.

From these I select the following striking instances; While I was in employ in board one of the slave ships, a Negro informed me that being in evening invited to drink with some of the black traders, upon his going away, attempted to seize him. As he was very active, he evaded their design and got out of their hands. He was, however, prevented from effecting his escape by a large dog, which laid hold of him, and compelled him to submit. These creatures are kept by many of the traders for that purpose; and being trained to the inhuman sport, they appear to be much pleased with it.

I was likewise told by a Negro woman that as she was on her return home, one evening, from some neighbors, to whom she had been making a visit by invitation, she was kidnapped; and notwithstanding she was big with child, sold for a slave. This transaction happened a considerable way up the country, and she had passed through the hands of several purchasers before she reached the ship. A man and his son, according to their own information, were seized by professional kidnappers, while they were planting yams, and sold for slaves. This likewise happened in the interior pans of the country, and after passing through several hands, they were purchased for the ship to which I belonged. It frequently happens that those who kidnap others are themselves, in their turns, seized and sold. A Negro in the West Indies informed me that after having been employed in kidnapping others, he had experienced this reverse. And he assured me that it was a common incident among his countrymen.

...During my stay on the coast of Africa, I was an eye-witness of the following transaction: a black trader invited a Negro, who resided a little way up the country, to come and see him. After the entertainment was over, the trader proposed to his guest, to treat him with a sight of one of the ships lying in the river. The unsuspicious countryman readily consented, and accompanied the trader in a canoe to the side of the ship, which he viewed with pleasure and astonishment. While he was thus employed, some black traders on board, who appeared to be in the secret, leaped into the canoe, seized the unfortunate man, and dragging him into the ship, immediately sold him...

When the Negroes, whom the black traders have to dispose of, are shown to the European purchasers, they first examine them relative to their age. They then minutely inspect their persons, and inquire into the state of their health; if they are afflicted with any infirmity, or are deformed; or have bad eyes or teeth; if they are lame, or weak in their joints, or distorted in the back, or of a slender make, or are narrow in the chest; in short, if they have been, or are afflicted in any manner, so as to render them incapable of much labour; if any of the foregoing defects are discovered in them, they are rejected. But if approved of, they are generally taken on board the ship the same evening. The purchaser has liberty to return on the following morning, but not afterwards, such as upon re-examination are found exceptionable.

The traders frequently beat those Negroes which are objected to by the captains and use them with great severity. It matters not whether they are refused on account of age, illness, deformity, or for any other reason. At New Calabar, in particular, the traders have frequently been known to put them to death. Instances have happened at that place that the traders, when any of their Negroes have been objected to, have dropped their canoes under the stern of the vessel, and instantly beheaded them, in sight of the captain.

* * * * * *

1. *Why would Falconbridge's account of the brutalities of the slave trade have been imperative to the antislavery movement?*

2. *What does Falconbridge tell us about how the slaves were obtained? Who obtained them? What sort of commercial network was necessary to sustain the slave trade?*

4–5 An African Captive Tells the Story of Crossing the Atlantic in a Slave Ship in 1789

Captured in Nigeria, Olaudah Equiano shared the fear of many captured Africans that the white men were going to eat him. More widely traveled than most slaves, Equiano was sold to the British and worked on ships for much of his life. Later able to purchase his freedom from his Quaker master, Equiano went on to become a staunch advocate in the British antislavery movement. This passage describes Equiano's trip from Africa to America.

SOURCE: Olaudah Equiano, *The Interesting Narrative of the Life of Olaudah Equiano or Gustavus Vasa, The African* (New York: n.p., 1791).

The first object which saluted my eyes when I arrived on the coast was the sea, and a slave ship, which was then riding at anchor, and waiting for its cargo. These filled me with astonishment, which was soon converted into terror, when I was carried on board. I was immediately handled, and tossed up, to see if I were sound, by some of the crew; and I was now persuaded that I had got into a world of bad spirits, and that they were going to kill me. Their complexions too differing so much from ours, their long hair, and the language they spoke (which was very different from any I had ever heard) united to confirm me in this belief. Indeed such were the horrors of my views and fears at the moment, that, if ten thousand worlds had been my own, I would have freely parted with them all to have exchanged my condition with that of the meanest slave in my own country. When I looked round the ship too and saw a large furnace or copper boiling, and a multitude of black people of every description chained together, every one of their countenances expressing dejection and sorrow, I no longer doubted of my fate; and, quite overpowered with horror and anguish, I fell motionless on the deck and fainted. When I recovered a little I found some black people about me, who I believed were some of those who had brought me on board, and had been receiving their pay; they talked to me in order to cheer me, but all in vain. I asked them if we were not to be eaten by those white men with horrible looks, red faces, and long hair. They told me I was not; and one of the crew brought me a small portion of spirituous liquor in a wine-glass; but being afraid of him, I would not take it out of his hand. One of the blacks therefore took it from him and gave it to me, and I took a little down my palate, which, instead of reviving me, as they thought it would, threw me into the greatest consternation at the strange feeling it

produced, having never tasted any such liquor before. Soon after this the blacks who brought me on board went off, and left me abandoned to despair. I now saw myself deprived of all chance of returning to my native country, or even the least glimpse of hope of gaining the shore, which I now considered as friendly; and I even wished for my former slavery in preference to my present situation, which was filled with horrors of every kind, still heightened by my ignorance of what I was to undergo. I was not long suffered to indulge my grief; I was soon put down under the decks, and there I received such a salutation in my nostrils as I had never experienced in my life: so that with the loathsomeness of the stench, and crying together, I became so sick and low that I was not able to eat, nor had I the least desire to taste any thing. I now wished for the last friend, death, to relieve me; but soon, to my grief, two of the white men offered me eatables; and, on my refusing to eat, one of them held me fast by the hands, and laid me across, I think the windlass, and tied my feet, while the other flogged me severely. I had never experienced any thing of this kind before: and, although not being used to the water, I naturally feared that element the first time I saw it, yet, nevertheless, could I have got over the nettings, I would have jumped over the side, but I could not; and, besides, the crew used to watch us very closely who were not chained down to the decks, lest we should leap into the water: and I have seen some of these poor African prisoners most severely cut for attempting to do so, and hourly whipped for not eating. This indeed was often the case with myself. In a little time after, amongst the poor chained men, I found some of my own nation, which in a small degree gave ease to my mind. I inquired of these what was to be done with us? They gave me to understand we were to be carried to these white people's country to work for them. I then was a little revived, and thought, if it were no worse than working, my situation was not so desperate: but still I feared I should be put to death, the white people looked and acted, as I thought, in so savage a manner; for I had never seen among any people such instances of brutal cruelty; and this not only shown towards us blacks, but also to some of the whites themselves. One white man in particular I saw, when we were permitted to be on deck, flogged so unmercifully with a large rope near the foremast, that he died in consequence of it; and they tossed him over the side as they would have done a brute. This made me fear these people the more; and I expected nothing less than to be treated in the same manner....

At last, when the ship we were in, had got in all her cargo, they made ready with many fearful noises, and we were all put under deck, so that we could not see how they managed the vessel. But this disappointment was the least of my sorrow. The stench of the hold while we were on the coast was so intolerably loathsome, that it was dangerous to remain there for any time, and some of us had been permitted to stay on the deck for the fresh air; but now that the whole ship's cargo were confined together, it became absolutely pestilential. The closeness of the place, and the heat of the climate, added to the number in the ship, which was so crowded that each had scarcely room to turn himself, almost suffocated us. This produced copious perspirations, so that the air soon became unfit for respiration, from a variety of loathsome smells, and brought on a sickness amongst the slaves, of which many died, thus falling victims to the improvident avarice, as I may call it, of their purchasers. This wretched situation was again aggravated by the galling of the chains, now become insupportable; and the filth of the necessary tubs, into which the children often fell, and were almost suffocated. The shrieks of the women, and the groans of the dying, rendered the whole a scene of horror almost inconceivable. Happily perhaps for myself I was soon reduced so low here that it was thought necessary to keep me almost always on deck; and from my extreme youth I was not put in fetters. In this situation I expected every hour to share the fate of my companions, some of whom were almost daily brought upon deck at the point of death, which I began to hope would soon put an end to my miseries. Often did I think many of the inhabitants of the deep much more happy than myself, I envied them the freedom they enjoyed, and as often wished I could change my condition for theirs. Every circumstance I met with served only to render my state more painful, and heightened my apprehensions and my opinion of the cruelty of the whites. One day they had taken a number of fishes; and when they had killed and satisfied themselves with as many as they thought fit, to our astonishment who were on the deck, rather than give any of them to us to eat, as we expected, they tossed the remaining fish into the sea again, although we begged and prayed for some as well as we could, but in vain; and some of my countrymen, being pressed by hunger, took an opportunity, when they thought no one saw them, of trying to get a little privately; but they were discovered, and the attempt procured them some very severe floggings. One day, when we had a smooth sea and moderate wind, two of my wearied countrymen who were chained together (I was near them at the time), preferring death to such a life of misery, somehow made through the nettings and jumped into the sea: immediately another quite dejected fellow, who on account of his illness, was suffered to be out of irons, also followed their example; and I believe many more would very soon have done the same if they had not been prevented by the ship's crew who were instantly alarmed. Those of us that were the most active were in a moment put down under the deck, and there was such a noise and confusion amongst the people of the ship as I never heard before, to stop her, and get the boat out to go after the slaves. However two of the wretches were drowned, but they got the other, and afterwards flogged him unmercifully for thus attempting to prefer death to slavery.

* * * * * *

1. How does Olaudah Equiano's view of the white men as spirits, "possessed of magic," compare to the Aztec or Pueblo views of the Spaniards?

2. Why do you think the sailors on the slave ships were cruel to the slaves to a point that could not possibly have been in their best commercial interests?

3. How does Equiano's story help us to understand the cruelty and brutality that characterized the slave trade?

4-6   A Virginian Describes the Difference between Servants and Slaves in 1722

Robert Beverly, who wrote The History and Present State of Virginia *in 1705, worked at various government positions in the early Virginia colony before being dismissed for criticizing several public events. Beverly published a revised version in 1722, from which the following passage is taken. Here he tries to distinguish between the role of servants and slaves and outlines some of the legal rights accorded servants, which, by omission, also illustrates the legal rights that were denied slaves.*
SOURCE: Robert Beverly, *The History of Virginia in Four Parts,* (London, 1722).

Their servants they distinguish by the names of slaves for life, and servants for a time.

Slaves are the negroes and their posterity, following the condition of the mother, according to the maxim, *partus frequitur ventrem.* They are called slaves, in respect of the time of their servitude, because it is for life.

Servants, are those which serve only for a few years, according to the time of their indenture, or the custom of the country. The custom of the country takes place upon such as have no indentures. The law in this case is, that if such servants be under nineteen years of age, they must be brought into court to have their age adjudged; and from the age they are judged to be of, they must serve until they reach four and twenty; but if they be adjudged upwards of nineteen, they are then only to be servants for the term of five years.

The male servants, and slaves of both sexes, are employed together in tilling and manuring the ground, in sowing and planting tobacco, corn, &c. Some distinction indeed is made between them in their clothes, and food; but the work of both is no other than what the overseers, the freemen, and the planters themselves do.

Sufficient distinction is also made between the female servants, and slaves; for a white woman is rarely or never put to work in the ground, if she be good for anything else; and to discourage all planters from using any women so, their law makes female servants working in the ground tithables, while it suffers all other white women to be absolutely exempted; whereas, on the other hand, it is a common thing to work a woman slave out of doors, nor does the law make any distinction in her taxes, whether her work be abroad or at home.

Because I have heard how strangely cruel and severe the service of this country is represented in some parts of England, I can't forbear affirming, that the work of their servants and slaves is no other than what every common freeman does; neither is any servant required to do more in a day than his overseer; and I can assure you, with great truth, that generally their slaves are not worked near so hard, nor so many hours in a day, as the husbandmen, and day laborers in England. An overseer is a man, that having served his time, has acquired the skill and character of an experienced planter, and is therefore entrusted with the direction of the servants and slaves.

But to complete this account of servants, I shall give you a short relation of the care their laws take, that they be used as tenderly as possible:

By the Laws of their Country

1. All servants whatsoever have their complaints heard without fee or reward; but if the master be found faulty, the charge of the complaint is cast upon him, otherwise the business is done *ex officio*.

2. Any justice of the peace may receive the complaint of a servant, and order everything relating thereto, till the next county court; where it will be finally determined.

3. All masters are under the correction and censure of the country courts, to provide for their servants good and wholesome diet, clothing and lodging.

4. They are always to appear upon the first notice given of the complaint of their servants, otherwise to forfeit the service of them until they do appear.

5. All servants' complaints are to be received at any time in court, without process, and shall not be delayed for

want of form; but the merits of the complaint must be immediately enquired into by the justices; and if the master cause any delay therein, the court may remove such servants, if they see cause, until the master will come to trial.

6. If a master shall at any time disobey an order of court, made upon any complaint of a servant, the court is empowered to remove such servant forthwith to another master who will be kinder, giving to the former master the produce only, (after fees deducted,) of what such servants shall be sold for by public outcry.

7. If a master should be so cruel, as to use his servant ill, that is fallen sick or lame in his service, and thereby rendered unfit for labor, he must be removed by the church wardens out of the way of such cruelty, and boarded in some good planter's house, till the time of his freedom, the charge of which must be laid before the next county court, which has power to levy the same, from time to time, upon the goods and chattels of the master, after which, the charge of such boarding is to come upon the parish in general.

8. All hired servants are entitled to these privileges.

9. No master of a servant can make a new bargain for service, or other matter with his servant, without the privity and consent of the county court, to prevent the masters overreaching, or scaring such servant into an unreasonable compliance.

10. The property of all money and goods sent over thither to servants, or carried in with them, is reserved to themselves, and remains entirely at their disposal.

11. Each servant at his freedom receives of his master ten bushels of corn, (which is sufficient for almost a year,) two new suits of clothes, both linen and woolen, and a gun, twenty shillings value, and then becomes as free in all respects, and as much entitled to the liberties and privileges of the country, as any of the inhabitants or natives are, if such servants were not aliens.

12. Each servant has then also a right to take up fifty acres of land, where he can find any unpatented.

This is what the laws prescribe in favor of servants, by which you may find, that the cruelties and severities imputed to that country, are an unjust reflection. For no people more abhor the thoughts of such usage, than the Virginians, nor take more precaution to prevent it now, whatever it was in former days.

* * * * * *

1.   Why would Robert Beverly write such a report? Why would he make the lives of servants in America seem so positive?

2.   Beverly's summary of the laws regarding servants carefully omits the word slave. What does this tell us about slave's rights under the then-current laws?

4-7 The Slaves Revolt in South Carolina in 1739

One may wonder why the slaves, vastly outnumbering their masters in many quarters, didn't raise up and revolt. The fact is, they did on occasion. In the early 1700s, the King of Spain promised political asylum to all runaway slaves who could make it to Florida. The following account of the Stono rebellion in South Carolina documents what happened and why slaves might have been reluctant to run away. The narrative comes from a letter dated October 9, 1739, which was circulated for publication in the newspaper by General Oglethorpe, the founder of the Georgia colony.

SOURCE: Allen D. Candler, ed., *The Colonial Records of the State of Georgia*, 26 vols. (Atlanta: Chas. P Byrd, 1913), 22:232-36.

Sometime since there was a Proclamation published at Augustine, in which the King of Spain (then at Peace with Great Britain) promised Protection and Freedom to all Negroes Slaves that would resort thither. Certain Negroes belonging to Captain Davis escaped to Augustine, and were received there. They were demanded by General Oglethorpe who sent Lieutenant Demere to Augustine, and the Governour assured the General of his sincere Friendship, but at the same time showed his Orders from the Court of Spain, by which he was to receive all Run away Negroes. Of this other Negroes having notice, as it is believed, from the Spanish Emissaries, four or five who were Cattel-Hunters, and knew the Woods, some of whom belonged to Captain Macpherson, ran away with His Horses, wounded his Son and killed another Man. These marched f [sic] for Georgia, and were pursued, but the Rangers being then newly reduced [sic] the Country people could not overtake them, though they were discovered by the Saltzburghers, as they passed by Ebenezer [a religious community near Savannah, founded by German dissenters]. They reached Augustine, one only being killed and another wounded by the Indians in their flight. They were received there with great honours, one of them had a Commission given to him, and a Coat faced with Velvet. Amongst the Negroe Slaves there are a people brought from the Kingdom of Angola in Africa, many of these speak Portugueze [which Language is as near Spanish as Scotch is to English,] by reason that the Portugueze have considerable Settlement, and the Jesuits have a Mission and School in that Kingdom and many Thousands of the Negroes there profess the Roman Catholic Religion. Several Spaniards upon diverse Pretences have for some time past been strolling about

Carolina, two of them, who will give no account of themselves have been taken up and committed to Jayl in Georgia. The good reception of the Negroes at Augustine was spread about, Several attempted to escape to the Spaniards, & were taken, one of them was hanged at Charles Town. In the latter end of July last Don Pedro, Colonel of the Spanish Horse, went in a Launch to Charles Town under pretence of a message to General Oglethorpe and the Lieutenant Governour.

On the 9th day of September last being Sunday which is the day the Planters allow them to work for themselves, Some Angola Negroes assembled, to the number of Twenty; and one who was called Jemmy was their Captain, they suprized a Warehouse belonging to Mr. Hutchenson at a place called Stonehow [sic—]; they there killed Mr. Robert Bathurst, and Mr. Gibbs, plundered the House and took a pretty many small Arms and Powder, which were there for Sale. Next they plundered and burnt Mr. Godfrey's house, and killed him, his Daughter and Son. They then turned back and marched Southward along Pons Pons, which is the Road through Georgia to Augustine, they passed Mr. Wallace's Tavern towards day break, and said they would not hurt him, for he was a good Man and kind to his Slaves, but they broke open and plundered Mr. Lemy's House, and killed him, his wife and Child. They marched on towards Mr. Rose's resolving to kill him; but he was saved by a Negroe, who having hid him went out and pacified the others. Several Negroes joyned them, they calling out Liberty, marched on with Colours displayed, and two Drums beating, pursuing all the white people they met with, and killing Man Woman and Child when they could come up to them. Colonel Bull Lieutenant Governour of South Carolina, who was then riding along the Road, discovered them, was pursued, and with much difficulty escaped & raised the Countrey. They then burnt Colonel Hext's house and killed his Overseer and his Wife. They then burnt Mr. Sprye's house, then Mr. Sacheverell's, and then Mr. Nash's house, all lying upon the Pons Pons Road, and killed all the white People they found in them. Mr. Bullock got off, but they burnt his House, by this time many of them were drunk with the Rum they had taken in the Houses. They increased every minute by new Negroes coming to them, so that they were above Sixty, some say a hundred, on which they halted in a field, and set to dancing, Singing and beating Drums, to draw more Negroes to them, thinking they were now victorious over the whole Province, having marched ten miles & burnt all before them without Opposition, but the Militia being raised, the Planters with great briskness pursued them and when they came up, dismounting; charged them on foot. The Negroes were soon routed, though they behaved boldly several being killed on the Spot, many ran back to their

Plantations thinking they had not been missed, but they were there taken and [sic] Shot, Such as were taken in the field also, were after being examined, shot on the Spot, And this is to be said to the honour of the Carolina Planters, that notwithstanding the Provocation they had received from so many Murders, they did not torture one Negroe, but only put them to an easy death. All that proved to be forced & were not concerned in the Murders & Burnings were pardoned, And this sudden Courage in the field, & the Humanity afterwards hath had so good an Effect that there hath been no farther Attempt, and the very Spirit of Revolt seems over. About 30 escaped from the fight, of which ten marched about 30 miles Southward, and being overtaken by the Planters on horseback, fought stoutly for some time and were all killed on the Spot. The rest are yet untaken. In the whole action about 40 Negroes and 20 whites were killed. The Lieutenant Governour sent an account of this to General Oglethorpe, who met the advices on his return from the Indian Nation. He immediately ordered a Troop of Rangers to be ranged, to patrole through Georgia, placed some Men in the Garrison at Palichocolas, which was before abandoned, and near which the Negroes formerly passed, being the only place where Horses can come to swim over the River Savannah for near 100 miles, ordered out the Indians in pursuit, and a Detachment of the Garrison at Port Royal to assist the Planters on any Occasion, and published a Proclamation ordering all the Constables &c. of Georgia to pursue and seize all Negroes, with a Reward for any that should be taken. It is hoped these measures will prevent any Negroes from getting down to the Spaniards.—

* * * * * *

1. Why would the King of Spain have offered slaves asylum in Spain's territory? What could the motivation have been?

2. Why would General Oglethorpe have wanted this story published in the newspaper? What did he stand to gain? Or lose?

3. Why do you think more slaves didn't revolt?

4-8 An Early Abolitionist Speaks Out Against Slavery in 1757

John Woolman was a Quaker who dedicated much of his life to eradicating slavery and the mistreatment of the poor and oppressed. Woolman's methodology was one of compassion and kindness, in keeping with Quaker tradition. He felt the slave owner was injured as much as the slave through slavery, at least in his soul and inner conscience. Woolman's thinking would become the foundation of abolitionism. The following selection, taken from Woolman's journal, exemplifies the sort of argument Woolman used in making his antislavery message.

SOURCE: John Woolman, A Journal of the Life, Gospel Labors, and Christian Experiences of that Faithful Minister of Jesus Christ, John Woolman (Dublin: R. M. Jackson, 1776)

Journey to Maryland and Virginia, 1757

9TH OF 5TH MONTH—Breakfasted at a Friend's house who afterwards putting us a little on our way, I had conversation with him, in the fear of the Lord, concerning his slaves, in which my heart was tender, and I used much plainness of speech with him, which he appeared to take it kindly. We pursued our journey without appointing meetings, being pressed in my mind to be at the Yearly Meeting in Virginia. In my travelling on the road I often felt a cry rise from the center of my mind thus—"Oh Lord, I am a stranger in the earth, hide not Thy face from me." On the 11th we crossed the rivers at Patowmack and Rapahannock, and lodged at Port Royal. On the way, happening in company with a Colonel of the Militia, who appeared to be a thoughtful man, I took occasion to remark on the difference in general betwixt a people used to labour moderately for their living, training up their children in frugality and business, and those who live on the labour of slaves; the former, in my view, being the most happy life. He concurred in the remark, and mentioned the trouble arising from the untoward, slothful disposition of the Negroes, adding that one of our labourers would do as much in a day as two of their slaves. I replied that free men whose minds were properly on their business, found a satisfaction in the improving, cultivating, and providing for their families; but Negroes, labouring to support those who claim them as their property, and expecting nothing but slavery during life, had not the like inducement to be industrious.

After some further conversation I said that men having power too often misapplied it; that though we made slaves of the Negroes, and the Turks made slaves of the Christians, I believed that liberty was the natural right of all men equally. This he did not deny, but said the lives of the Negroes were so wretched in their own country that many of them lived better here than there. I only said, "There's great odds in regard to us on what principle we act"; and so the conversation on that head ended. I may here add that another person some time afterwards mentioned the wretchedness of the Negroes occasioned by their intestine wars as an argument in favor of our fetching them away for slaves. To which I replied, if compassion for the Africans, on account of their domestic troubles, was the real motive of our purchasing them, that spirit of tenderness being attended to would incite us to use them kindly, that as strangers brought out of affliction their lives might be happy among us. And as they are human creatures, whose souls are as precious as ours, and who may receive the same help and comfort from the Holy Scriptures as we do, we could not omit suitable endeavours to instruct them therein; but while we manifest by our conduct that our views in purchasing them are to advance ourselves, and while our buying captives taken in war animates those parties to push on that war and increase desolation amongst them, to say they live unhappy in Africa is far from being an argument in our favour. I further said, the present circumstances of these provinces to me appear difficult; the slaves look like a burdensome stone to such as burden themselves with them; and that if the white people retain a resolution to prefer their own outward prospect of gain to all other considerations, and do not act conscientiously toward them as fellow creatures, I believe that burden will grow heavier and heavier until times change in a way disagreeable to us. At which the person appeared very serious and acknowledged that in considering their condition and the manner of their treatment in these provinces he had sometimes thought it might be just in the Almighty to so order it....

The prospect of a road lying open to the same degeneracy in some parts of this newly settled land of America in respect to our conduct towards the Negroes hath deeply bowed my mind in this journey, and though to briefly relate how these people are treated is no agreeable work, yet, after reading over the notes I made as I travelled, I find my mind engaged to preserve them. Many of the white people in those provinces take little or no care of Negro marriages; and when Negroes marry after their own way, some make so little account of those marriages that with views of outward interest they often part men from their wives by selling them far asunder, which is common when estates are sold by executors at vendue. Many whose labour is heavy being followed in the field by a man with a whip, hired for that purpose, have in common little else to eat but one peck of Indian corn and some salt, for one week, with a few potatoes; and the latter they commonly raise by their labour on the first day of the week. The correction ensuing on their disobedience to overseers, or slothfulness in business, is often very severe, and sometimes desperate.

Men and women have many times scarce clothes sufficient to hide their nakedness, and boys and girls ten and twelve years old are often stark naked amongst their master's children. Some of our Society, and some of the society called Newlights, use some endeavours to instruct those they have in reading; but in common this is not only neglected, but disapproved. These are a people by whose labour the other inhabitants are in a great measure supported, and many of them in the luxuries of life. These are a people who have made no agreement to serve us, and who have not forfeited their liberty that we know of. These are the souls for whom Christ died, and for our conduct towards them we must answer before that Almighty Being who is no respecter of persons. They who know the only true God, and Jesus Christ whom He hath sent, and are thus acquainted with the merciful, benevolent, Gospel Spirit, will therein perceive that the indignation of God is kindled against oppression and cruelty, and in beholding the great distress of so numerous a people will find cause for mourning.

* * * * * *

1. How do John Woolman's sentiments reflect the views of what would later become the abolitionist movement? What is Woolman's economic argument for the abolition of slavery? Do you think his humanitarian ideals are ahead of his time?

2. Does Woolman really believe slaves to be equal to white men? What evidence to you find in this passage to support this?

4–9 Slave Stories Told to a Folklorist in South Carolina in the 1910s

Folktales play an important part in any culture's identity and survival. The characters within the story often become spokespersons for a people, much as Brer Rabbit represents the slave in the following tales where he constantly outwits his oppressors. Having their origins in Africa, animal tales were modified in America by the slaves and still survive. The tales here were collected in the South Carolina Sea Islands by Elsie Clews Parsons, an American folklorist, in the 1910s.

SOURCE: Elsie Clews Parsons, Folk-Lore of the Sea Islands of South Carolina (Cambridge, MA: American Folk-Lore Society, 1923).

Ber Wolf had a pease-patch. An' every night somebody go in de pease-patch an' eat de pease. So Ber Wolf made a tar baby an' set him up in de yard. So Ber Rabbit went in de patch, an' he meet de tar baby standin' up. So Ber Rabbit said, "Good-mornin', gal!" Tar Baby ain't got no manners, say nothin'. Say, "Man, I slap you." His hand fasten. Ber Rabbit say, "I got anoder han'." So he hit him wid dat han'. Dat one fasten. Ber Rabbit said, "I got a head." Said he butt him wid de head. De head fasten. "Gal, you don't see I got a foot?" So he kick him wid de foot. De foot fasten. "I kick him wid de oder foot." Dat one fasten. Ber Rabbit said, "I got a mout'." De mout' fasten. Den Rabbit say, "Tu'n me loose!"

Next t'ing come along Wolf. Wolf say, "I ketch yer, t'ief! you eat all my pease. I putshyer head down on de choppin'-block an' chop em off."—"Oh, don't duh dat! Dat will kill me." Say, "I want ter kill you." Say, "I'll t'row you in de creek, drown you."—"Ah, don't duh dat!" he say. "I'll t'row you in de briar-patch," he say. "Yes, Ber Wolf, t'row me in de briar-patch! Den you'll kill me." When Ber Wolf t'row him in de briar-patch, Rabbit say, "Ping! Ping! Dat's de place my mammy done born me!" So dat ol' rabbit git away.

☆

Oncet Rabbit an' Wolf go out; an' Rabbit tol' Wolf dat ef he would le' him tie um to a tree, he would get um two fat hen. So he tie um to a tree wid wine [vine], tie um fas'. An' Wolf say, "Don' tie me too tight, Ber Rabbit!" Ber Rabbit say "Couldn' get de hen ef he don' tie um tight." So Wolf say, "Tie me tight, Ber Rabbit! Tie me tight!" So Ber Rabbit wen' to de barnyard an' call two houn'. An' dey chase um. An' he run back to de tree whey he tie Ber Wolf. Ber Wolf see de houn' comin', an' cry out, "Go 'roun', Ber Rabbit, go 'roun'!" But Rabbit keep straight on. An' de houn' get Ber Wolf; an' he call out, "I tol' you to go 'roun'! I tol' you to go 'roun'! Dat wasn' right."

☆

De fox had a way goin' to de man hawg-pen an' eatin' up all his hawg. So de people didn' know how to ketch de fox. An' so de rabbit was goin' along one Sunday mornin'. Say was goin' to church. Ber Fox singin', "Good-mornin', Ber Rabbit!" Ber Rabbit singin', "Good-mornin', Ber Fox!" Say, "Whey you goin'?" Say, "I'm goin' to church." Ber Fox say, "Dis is my time. I'm hungry dis mornin'. I'm goin' to ketch you."—"O Ber Fox! leave me off dis mornin'! I will sen' you to a man house where he got a penful of pretty little pig, an' you will get yet brakefus' fill. Ef you don' believe me, you can tie me here, an' you can go down to de house, an' I'll stay here until you come back." So Ber Fox tie him. When he wen' down to de house, de man had about fifty head of houn'-dawg. An' de man tu'n de houn'-dawg loose on him. An' de fox made de long run right by Ber Rabbit. Ber Fox say, "O Ber Rabbit! dose is no brakefus', dose is a pile of houn'-dawg."—"Yes, you was goin' to eat me, but dey will eat you for your brakefus' and supper to-night." An' so dey did. Dey cut [caught] de fox. An' Ber Rabbit give to de dawgs, "Gawd bless yer soul! dat what enemy get for meddlin' Gawd's people when dey goin' to church." Said, "I was goin' to school all my life an' learn every letter in de book but d an' D was death, an' death was de en' of Ber Fox."

☆

One day the wolf said, "Brother Rabbit, I am going to eat you up."—"No," said Brother Rabbit, "don't eat me! I know where some fine geese is. If you let me tie you here, I will go and get them for you." — "All right," said the wolf. So the rabbit tied the wolf. Then the rabbit went on his way until he came to a farmyard. Then he said, "Farmer, give me trouble." So the farmer went into the yard and get a hound-dog and two hound-puppies and put them in a bag, and said, "When you get out in the field, you must open the bag, and you will have all the trouble you want." — "All right," said the rabbit. So the rabbit went back to the wolf. He waited until he came near the wolf, then he loose the bag and ran the dogs behind him. He ran right straight for the wolf. Wolf said, "Bear off, Rabbit, bear off?" So he saw the rabbit was close upon him, he called out harder, "Bear off, Rabbit, bear off!" The Rabbit said, "Not a bit. I am running in straight deal this morning." So the dogs killed the wolf and eat him up. The story is end.

* * * * *

1. The clever trickster is a figure common to many mythologies. How does Brer Rabbit compare to the rabbit in the Micmac tale (Document 1–4)?

2. What purpose do you think the character of a trickster rabbit who could outwit its oppressors would serve for an enslaved people?

5–1 The Rev. John Williams Tells
of His Experiences as an Indian
Captive, 1707

John Williams recounted his experiences of captivity with the publication of The Redeemed Captive Returning to Zion in 1707. Written immediately after Williams's return to Massachusetts, The Redeemed Captive captured the attention of English colonists with its detailed descriptions of Indian customs and a glimpse into the lives of the French colonists in Canada. The book proved immensely popular; it went through six editions before the end of the eighteenth century.

SOURCE: John Williams, The Redeemed Captive Returning to Zion, Edward W. Clark, ed. (Amherst: University of Massachusetts Press, 1971) 54–55, 60–65.

My youngest daughter, aged seven years, was carried all the journey and looked after with a great deal of tenderness. My youngest son, aged four years, was wonderfully preserved from death; for, though they that carried him or drew him on sleighs were tired with their journeys, yet their savage cruel tempers were so overruled by God that they did not kill him, but in their pity he was spared and others would take care of him, so that four times on the journey he was spared and others would take care of him, till at last he arrived at Montreal where a French gentlewoman, pitying the child, redeemed it out of the hands of the heathen. My son Samuel and my eldest daughter were pitied so as to be drawn on sleighs when unable to travel. And though they suffered very much through scarcity of food and tedious journeys, they were carried through to Montreal. And my son Stephen, about eleven years of age, [was] wonderfully preserved from death in the famine whereof three English persons died and after eight months brought into Chambly.

My master returned on the evening of the Sabbath and told me he had killed five moose. The next day we removed to the place where he killed them. We tarried there three days till we had roasted and dried the meat. My master made me a pair of snowshoes, "For," said he, "you cannot possibly travel without, the snow being knee-deep." We parted from there heavy laden; I traveled with a burden on my back, with snowshoes, twenty-five

miles the first day of wearing them and again the next day till afternoon, and then we came to the French River. My master at this place took away my pack and drew the whole load on the ice, but my bones seemed to be misplaced and I unable to travel with any speed. My feet were very sore, and each night I wrung blood out of my stockings when I pulled them off. My shins also were very sore, being cut with crusty snow in the time of my traveling without snowshoes. But finding some dry oak leaves by the river banks, I put them to my shins and in once applying of them they were healed. And here my master was very kind to me, would always give me the best he had to eat, and by the goodness of God, I never wanted a meal's meat during my captivity though some of my children and neighbors were greatly wounded (as I may say) with the arrows of famine and pinching want, having for many days nothing but roots to live upon and not much of them either. My master gave me a piece of a Bible, never disturbed me in reading the Scriptures, or in praying to God. Many of my neighbors also found that mercy in their journey to have Bibles, Psalm books, Catechisms, and good books put into their hands with liberty to use them; and yet after their arrival at Canada all possible endeavors were used to deprive them of them. Some of them say their Bibles were demanded by the French priests and never re-delivered to them, to their great grief and sorrow.

One day a certain savagess taken prisoner in King Philip's War, who had lived at Mr. Buckley's at Wethersfield, called Ruth, who could speak English very well, who had been often at my house but was now proselyted to the Romish faith, came into the wigwam. And with her [came] an English maid who was taken the last war, who was dressed up in Indian apparel, could not speak one word of English, who said she could neither tell her own name or the name of the place from where she was taken. These two talked in the Indian dialect with my master a long time after which my master bade me to cross myself. I told him I would not; he commanded me several times, and I as often refused.

Ruth said, "Mr. Williams, you know the Scripture and therefore act against your own light, for you know the Scripture says, 'Servants, obey your masters.' He is your master and you his servant."

I told her she was ignorant and knew not the meaning of the Scripture, telling her [that] I was not to disobey the great God to obey any master, and that I was ready to suffer for God if called thereto. On which she talked to my master; I suppose she interpreted what I said.

My master took hold of my hand to force me to cross myself, but I struggled with him and would not suffer him to guide my hand; upon this he pulled off a crucifix from his own neck and bade me kiss it, but I refused once again. He told me he would dash out my brains with his hatchet if I refused. I told him I should sooner choose death than to sin against God; then he ran and caught up his hatchet and acted as though he would have dashed out my brains. Seeing I was not moved, he threw down his hatchet, saying he would first bite off all my nails if I still refused; I gave him my hand and told him I was ready to suffer. He set his teeth in my thumbnails and gave a grip with his teeth, and then said, "No good minister, no love God, as bad as the devil," and so left off.

I have reason to bless God who strengthened me to withstand; by this he was so discouraged as nevermore to meddle with me about my religion. I asked leave of the Jesuits to pray with those English of our town that were with me, but they absolutely refused to give us permission to pray one with another and did what they could to prevent our having any discourse together.

* * * * * *

1. *What is Williams's purpose in writing an account of his captivity? What do you think he hoped to accomplish with The Redeemed Captive? How would his encounters with Indians and French colonists be interpreted by settlers in Massachusetts?*

2. *What does Williams's retelling of his and his family's treatment suggest about his view toward his Indian captors? In his opinion, were they "savages"?*

3. *What does this passage tell us about the relationship between Puritans in Massachusetts and the French colonists and the Jesuits in Canada?*

5–2 An Iroquois Chief Argues for his Tribe's Property Rights in 1742

The concept of land ownership was a point of serious conflict for early settlers and the Native Americans who had previously lived there. The Indians could allow others to use land—for hunting, fishing, or even farming, but they did not have a concept of permanent ownership, and hence some of the many problems they had with the settlers over this issue. In the argument between the Iroquois Chief Canassateego and Lieutenant Governor Thomas of Pennsylvania, this difference of ownership was central to their conflict.

SOURCE: Cadwallader Colden, *The History of the Five Indian Nations of Canada.* (London, 1747).

Canassateego:

Brethren, the Governor and Council, and all present,

According to our Promise we now propose to return you an Answer to the several Things mentioned to us Yesterday, and shall beg Leave to speak to publick Affairs first, tho' they were what you spoke to last. On this Head you Yesterday put us in Mind, first, of William Penn's early and constant Care to cultivate Friendship with all the Indians; of the Treaty we held with one of his Sons, about ten Years ago; and of the Necessity there is at this Time of keeping the Roads between us clear and free from all Obstructions. We are all very sensible of the kind Regard that good Man William Penn had for all the Indians, and cannot but be pleased to find that his Children have the same. We well remember the Treaty you mention, held with his Son on his Arrival here, by which we confirmed our League of Friendship, that is to last as long as the Sun and Moon endure. In Consequence of this, we, on our Part, shall preserve the Road free from all Incumbrances; in Confirmation whereof we lay down this String of Wampum....

Brethren, we received from the Proprietor Yesterday, some Goods in Consideration of our Release of the Lands on the West-side of the Susquehannah. It is true, we have the full Quantity according to Agreement; but if the Proprietor had been here himself, we think, in Regard of our Numbers and Poverty, he would have made an Addition to them. If the Goods were only to be divided amongst the Indians present, a single Person would have but a small Portion, but if you consider what Numbers are left behind, equally entitled with us to a Share, there will be extremely little. We therefore desire, if you have the Keys of the Proprietor's Chest, you will open it, and take out a little more for us.

We know our Lands are now become more valuable. The white People think we do not know their Value; but we are sensible that the Land is everlasting, and the few Goods we receive for it are soon worn out and gone. For the future, we will sell no Lands but when the Proprietor is in the Country; and we will know beforehand, the Quantity of the Goods we are to receive. Besides, we are not well used with respect to the Lands still unsold by us. Your People daily settle on these Lands, and spoil our Hunting. We must insist on your removing them, as you know they have no Right to settle to the Northward of Kittochtinny-Hills. In particular, we renew our Complaints against some People who are settled at the Juniata, a Branch of the Susquehannah, and all the

Banks of that River, as far as Mahaniay; and we desire they may be forthwith made to go off the Land, for they do great Damage to our Cousins the Delawares.

We have further to observe, with respect to the Lands lying on the Westside of the Susquehannah, that though the Proprietor has paid us for what his People possess, yet some Parts of that Country have been taken up by Persons, whose Place of Residence is to the South of this Province, from whom we have never received any Consideration. This Affair was recommended to you by our Chiefs at our last Treaty; and you then, at our earnest Desire, promised to write a Letter to that Person who has the Authority over those People, and to procure us his Answer. As we have never heard from you on this Head, we want to know what you have done in it. If you have not done any Thing, we now *renew* our Request, and desire you will inform the Person whose People are seated on our Lands, that that Country belongs to us, in Right of Conquest—we having bought it with our Blood, and taken it from our Enemies in fair War; and we expect, as Owners of that Land, to receive such a Consideration for it as the Land is worth. We desire you will press him to send a positive Answer. Let him say Yes or No. If he says Yes, we will treat with him; if No, we are able to do ourselves Justice; and we will do it, by going to take Payment ourselves.

It is customary with us to make a Present of Skins, whenever we renew our Treaties. We are ashamed to offer our Brethren so few, but your Horses and Cows have eat the Grass our Deer used to feed on. This has made them scarce, and will, we hope, plead in Excuse for our not bringing a larger Quantity. If we could have spared more, we would have given more, but we are really poor; and desire you'll not consider the Quantity, but few as they are, accept them in Testimony of our Regard.

Lieutenant Governor Thomas:

Brethren,

We thank you for the many Declarations of Respect you have given us, in this solemn Renewal of our Treaties. We receive, and shall keep your String and Belts of Wampum, as Pledges of your Sincerity, and desire those we gave you may be carefully preserved, as Testimonies of ours.

In answer to what you say about the Proprietaries; they are all absent, and have taken the Keys of their Chest with them; so that we cannot, on their Behalf, enlarge the Quantity of Goods. Were they here, they might perhaps be more generous; but we cannot be liberal for them. The Government will, however, take your Request into Consideration; and in Regard to your Poverty, may perhaps make you a Present....

The Number of Guns, as well as every Thing else, answers exactly with the Particulars specified in your Deed of Conveyance, which is more than was agreed to be given you. It was your own Sentiments, that the Lands on the West-side of the Susquehannah, were not so valuable as those on the East; and an Abatement was to be made, proportionable to the Difference in Value. But the Proprietor overlooked this, and ordered the full Quantity to be delivered, which you will look on as a Favour.

It is very true, that Lands are of late becoming more valuable; but what raises their Value? Is it not entirely owing to the Industry and Labour used by the white People, in their Cultivation and Improvement? Had not they come amongst you, these Lands would have been of no Use to you, any further than to maintain you. And is there not, now you have sold so much, enough left for all the Purposes of Living? What you say of the Goods, that they are soon worn out, is applicable to every Thing; but you know very well, that they cost a great deal of Money; and the Value of Land is no more, than it is worth in Money.

* * * * * *

1. The interchange between Canassateego and Governor Thomas seems to reveal starkly divergent views regarding the use and value of land. Outline these views and discuss them.

2. The Iroquois had a long history of self-government and treaty making, both within their own tribe and with outside bodies. How is this reflected in Canassateego's speech?

5-3   A Boston Woman Writes about her Trip to New York in 1704

Sarah Kemble Knight's Journal Kept on a Journey from Boston to New York in the Year 1704 provides a marvelous record of colonial life and conditions. But even more remarkable is Knight herself. Undertaking such a journey by herself was no mean feat in its day. Knight also developed a reputation as a lay lawyer, settling several estates, including the one of her cousin Caleb Trowbridge, which was the purpose of her journey to New York. In this excerpt, Knight describes a leg of the journey, the conditions along the way, some Indians, and the manner in which commerce was conducted at the time.

SOURCE: Sarah Kemble Knight, *The Journal of Madam Knight* (Boston: Small, Maynard & Co., 1920).

Monday, Octb'r. ye second, 1704.—About three o'clock afternoon, I begun my Journey from Boston to New-Haven; being about two Hundred Mile. My Kinsman, Capt. Robert Luist, waited on me as farr as Dedham, where I was to meet ye Western post.

I vissitted the Reverd. Mr. Belcher, ye Minister of ye town, and tarried there till evening, in hopes ye post would come along. But he not coming, I resolved to go to Billingses where he used to lodg, being 12 miles further. But being ignorant of the way, Madm Billings, seing no persuasions of her good spouses or hers could prevail with me to Lodg there that night, Very kindly went wyth me to ye Tavern, where I hoped to get my guide, And desired the Hostess to inquire of her guests whether any of them would go with mee. But they [were] tyed by the Lipps to a pewter engine....

When we had Ridd about an how'r, wee come into a thick swamp, wch. by Reason of a great fogg, very much startled mee, it being now very Dark. But nothing dismay'd John: Hee had encountered a thousand and a thousand such Swamps, having a Universall Knowledge in the woods; and readily Answered all my inquiries wch. were not a few.

In about an how'r, or something more, after we left the Swamp, we come to Billinges, where I was to Lodg. My Guide dismounted and very Complasantly help't me down and shewd the door, signing to me wth his hand to Go in; wch I Gladly did—But had not gone many steps into the Room, ere I was Interogated by a young Lady I understood afterwards was the Eldest daughter of the family, with these, or words to this purpose, (viz.) Law for mee—what in the world brings You here at this time a night?—I never see a woman on the Rode so Dreadfull late, in all the days of my versall life. Who are You? Where are You going? I'me scar'd out of my witts—with much now of the same Kind. I stood aghast, Preparing to reply, when in comes my Guide—to him Madam turn'd, Roreing out: Lawfull heart, John, is it You?—how de do! Where in the world are you going with this woman? Who is she? John made no Ansr. but sat down in the corner, fumbled out his black Junk, [a pipe] and saluted that instead of Debb; she then turned agen to mee and fell anew into her silly questions, without asking me to sitt down.

I told her shee treated me very Rudely, and I did not think it my duty to answer her unmannerly Questions. But to get rid of them, I told her I come there to have the post's company with me to-morrow on my Journey, &c. Miss star'd awhile, drew a chair, bid me sitt, And then run up stairs and putts on two or three Rings, (or else I had not seen them before,) and returning, sett herself just before me, showing the way to Reding, that I might see her Ornaments, perhaps to gain the more respect. But her Graham's new Rung sow, had it appeared, would affected me as much. I paid honest John wth money and dram according to contract, and Dismist him, and pray'd Miss to shew me where I must Lodg. Shee conducted me to a parlour in a little back Lento, wch was almost fill'd wth the bedsted, wch was so high that I was forced to climb on a chair to gitt up to ye wretched bed that lay on it; on wch having Stretcht my tired Limbs, and lay'd my head on a Sad-colourd pillow, I began to think on the transac-tions of ye past day.

Tuesday, October ye third, about 8 in the morning, I with the Post proceeded forward without observing any thing remarkable; And about two, afternoon, Arrived at the Post's second stage, where the western Post mett him and exchanged Letters. Here, having called for something to eat, ye woman bro't in a Twisted thing like a cable, but something whiter; and laying it on the bord, tugg'd for life to bring it into a capacity to spread; wch having wth great pains accomplished, shee serv'd in a dish of Pork and Cabage, I suppose the remains of Dinner. The sause was of a deep Purple, wch I tho't was boil'd in her dye Kettle; the bread was Indian, and every thing on the Table service Agreeable to these. I, being hungry, gott a little down; but my stomach was soon cloy'd, and what cabbage I swallowed serv'd me for a Cudd the whole day after,...

There are every where in the Towns as I passed, a Number of Indians the Natives of the Country, and are the most salvage of all the salvages of that kind that I had ever Seen: little or no care taken (as I heard upon enquiry) to make them otherwise. They have in some places Landes of their owne, and Govern'd by Law's of their own making;—they marry many wives and at pleasure put them away, and on the ye least dislike or fickle humour, on either side, saying *stand away* to one another is a sufficient Divorce. And indeed those uncomely *Stand aways* are too much in Vougue among the English in this (Indulgent Colony) as their Records plentifully prove, and that on very trivial matters, of which some have been told me, but are not proper to be Related by a Female pen, tho some of that foolish sex have had too large a share in the story.

If the natives commit any crime on their own precincts among themselves, ye English takes no Cognezens of. But if on the English ground, they are punishable by our Laws. They mourn for their Dead by blacking their faces, and cutting their hair, after an Awkerd and frightfull manner; But can't bear You should mention the names of their dead Relations to them: they trade most for Rum, for wch theyd hazzard their very lives; and the English fit them Generally as well, by seasoning it plentifully with water.

They give the title of merchant to every trader; who Rate their Goods according to the time and spetia they pay in: viz. Pay, mony, Pay as mony, and trusting. *Pay* is Grain, Pork, Beef, &c. at the prices sett by the General Court that Year; *mony* is pieces of Eight, Ryalls, or Boston or Bay shillings (as they call them,) or Good hard money, as sometimes silver coin is termed by them; also Wampom, vizt. Indian beads wch serves for change. *Pay as mony* is provisions, as aforesd one Third cheaper then as the Assembly or Genel Court sets it; and *Trust* as they and the mercht agree for time.

Now, when the buyer comes to ask for a comodity, sometimes before the merchant answers that he has it, he sais, *is Your pay redy?* Perhaps the Chap Reply's Yes: what do You pay in? say's the merchant. The buyer having answered, then the price is set; as suppose he wants a sixpenny knife, in pay it is 12d—in pay as money eight pence, and hard money its own price, viz. 6d. It seems a very Intricate way of trade and what Lex Mercatoria [the law of merchants] had not thought of.

Being at a merchants house, in comes a tall country fellow, wth his alfogeos [saddlebags] full of Tobacco; for they seldom Loose their Cudd, but keep Chewing and Spitting as long as they'r eyes are open,—he advanc't to the middle of the Room, makes an Awkward Nodd, and spitting a Large deal of Aromatick Tincture, he gave a scrape with his shovel like shoo, leaving a small shovel full of dirt on the floor, made a full stop, Hugging his own pretty Body with his hands under his arms, Stood staring rown'd him, like a Cart let out of a Baskett. At last, like the creature Balaam Rode on, he opened his mouth and said: have You any Ribinet for Hatbands to sell I pray? The Questions and Answers about the pay being past, the Ribin is bro't and opened. Bumpkin Simpers, cryes its confounded Gay I vow; and becking to the door, in comes Jone Tawdry, dropping about 50 curtsees, and stands by him: hee shows her the Ribin. *Law, You,* sais shee, *its right Gent, do You, take it, tis dreadfull pretty.* Then she enquires, *have You any hood silk I pray?* wch being brought and bought, Have You any *thred silk to sew it with* says shee, wch being accomodated with they Departed. They Generally stand after they come in a great while wth speachless, and sometimes dont say a word till they are askt what they want, which I Impute to the Awe they stand in of the merchants, who they are constantly almost Indebted too; and must take what they bring without Liberty to choose for themselves; but they serve them as well, making the merchants stay long enough for their pay.

1. What is so striking about Knight's journey, given the role of women within colonial New England society? What does her story tell us about travel in colonial New England? About colonial New England itself?

2. What do you think of Knight's writing style? How does it compare to the style of other documents from this period in this chapter?

* * * * * *

5-4 A Colonial Planter Tours the Backcountry in 1728

William Byrd in many ways embodied the epitome of the colonial planter. Educated in England, a lawyer, as well as member of the Council of State, Byrd owned one of the largest libraries in the colonies (over 4,000 volumes) and a large plantation of 180,000 acres. This excerpt describes his journey along the Virginia-Carolina border

and the people he encountered there.

...WHILE WE continued here [at the eastern end of the Virginia-Carolina border], we were told that on the South Shore, not far from the Inlet, dwelt a Marooner, that Modestly call'd himself a Hermit, tho' he forfeited that Name by Suffering a wanton Female to cohabit with Him.

His Habitation was a Bower, cover'd with Bark after the Indian Fashion, which in that mild Situation protected

SOURCE: William Byrd, *Histories of the Dividing Line Betwixt Virginia and North Carolina.* (Raleigh: North Carolina Historical Commission, 1929).

him pretty well from the Weather. Like the Ravens, he neither plow'd nor sow'd, but Subsisted chiefly upon Oysters, which his Handmaid made a Shift to gather from the Adjacent Rocks. Sometimes, too, for Change of Dyet, he sent her to drive up the Neighbour's Cows, to moisten their Mouths with a little Milk. But as for raiment, he depended mostly upon his Length of Beard, and She upon her Length of Hair, part of which she brought decently forward, and the rest dangled behind quite down to her Rump, like one of Herodotus's East Indian Pigmies.

Thus did these Wretches live in a dirty State of Nature, and were mere Adamites, Innocence only excepted....

...We observed [advancing westward along the boundary] very few corn-fields in our Walks, and those very small, which seem'd the Stranger to us, because we could see no other Tokens of Husbandry or Improvement. But, upon further Inquiry, we were given to understand People only made Corn for themselves and not for their Stocks, which know very well how to get their own Living.

Both Cattle and Hogs ramble in the Neighbouring Marshes and Swamps, where they maintain themselves the whole Winter long, and are not fetch'd home till the Spring. Thus these Indolent Wretches, during one half of the Year, lose the Advantage of the Milk of their cattle, as well as their Dung, and many of the poor Creatures perish in the Mire, into the Bargain, by this ill Management.

Some, who pique themselves more upon Industry than their Neighbours, will, now and then, in compliment to their Cattle, cut down a Tree whose Limbs are loaden with the Moss aforemention'd. The trouble wou'd be too great to Climb the Tree in order to gather this Provender, but the Shortest way (which in this Country is always counted the best) is to fell it, just like the Lazy Indians, who do the same by such Trees as bear fruit, and so make one Harvest for all. By this bad Husbandry Milk is so Scarce, in the Winter Season, that were a Big-belly'd Woman to long for it, She would lose her Longing. And, in truth, I believe this is often the Case, and at the same time a very good reason why so many People in this Province are markt with a Custard Complexion.

The only Business here is raising of Hogs, which is manag'd with the least Trouble, and affords the Diet they are most fond of. The Truth of it is, the Inhabitants of N Carolina devour so much Swine's flesh, that it fills them full of gross Humours. For want too of a constant Supply of Salt, they are commonly obliged to eat it Fresh, and that begets the highest taint of Scurvy. Thus, whenever a Severe Cold happens to Constitutions thus Vitiated, tis apt to improve into the Yaws, called there very justly the country-Distemper. This has all the Symptoms of the Pox, with this Aggravation, that no Preparation of Mercury will touch it. First it seizes the Throat, next the Palate, and lastly shews its spite to the poor Nose, of which tis apt in a small time treacherously to undermine the Foundation.

This Calamity is so common and familiar here, that it ceases to be a Scandal, and in the disputes that happen about Beauty, the Noses have in some Companies much ado to carry it. Nay, tis said that once, after three good Pork years, a Motion had like to have been made in the House of Burgesses, that a Man with a Nose shou'd be incapable of holding any Place of Profit in the Province; which Extraordinary Motion could never have been intended without Some Hope of a Majority.

Thus, considering the foul and pernicious Effects of Eatin Swine's Flesh in a hot Country, it was wisely forbidden and made an Abomination to the Jews, who liv'd much in the same Latitude with Carolina....

We had encampt so early, that we found time in the Evening to walk near half a Mile into the Woods. There we came upon a Family of Mulattoes, that call'd themselves free, tho' by the Shyness of the Master of the House, who took care to keep least in Sight, their Freedom seem'd a little Doubtful. It is certain many Slaves Shelter themselves in this Obscure Part of the World, nor will any of their righteous Neighbours discover them. On the Contrary, they find their Account in Settling such Fugitives on some out-of-the-way corner of their Land, to raise Stocks for a mean and inconsiderable Share, well knowing their Condition makes it necessary for them to Submit to any Terms.

Nor were these worthy Borderers content to Shelter Runaway Slaves, but Debtors and Criminals have often met with the like Indulgence. But if the Government of North Carolina has encourag'd this unneighbourly Policy in order to increase their People, it is no more than what Ancient Rome did before them, which was made a City of Refuge for all Debtors and Fugitives, and from that wretched Beginning grew up in time to be Mistress of a great Part of the World. And, considering how Fortune delights in bringing great things out of Small, who knows but Carolina may, one time or other, come to be the Seat of some other great Empire?....

For want of men in Holy Orders, but the Members of the Council and Justices of the Peace are empower'd by the Laws of that Country to marry all those who will not take One another's Word; but for the ceremony of Christening their children, they trust that to chance. If a Parson come in their way, they will crave a Cast of his office, as they call it, else they are content their Offspring should remain as Arrant Pagans as themselves. They account it among their greatest advantages that they are not Priest-ridden, not remembering that the Clergy is rarely guilty of Bestriding such as have the misfortune to be poor.

One thing may be said for the Inhabitants of that Province, that they are not troubled with any Religious Fumes, and have the least Superstition of any People living. They do not know Sunday from any other day, any more than Robinson Crusoe did, which would give them a great Advantage were they given to be industrious. But they keep so many Sabbaths every week, that their disregard of the Seventh Day has no manner of cruelty in it, either to Servants or Cattle....

Surely there is no place in the World where the Inhabitants live with less Labour than in N Carolina. It approaches nearer to the Description of Lubberland than any other, by the great felicity of the Climate, the easiness of raising Provisions, and the Slothfulness of the People.

Indian Corn is of so great increase, that a little Pains will Subsist a very large Family with Bread, and then they may have meat without any pains at all, by the Help of the Low Grounds, and the great Variety of Mast that grows on the High-land. The Men, for their Parts, just like the Indians, impose all the Work upon the poor Women. They make their Wives rise out of their Beds early in the Morning, at the same time that they lye and Snore, till the Sun has run one third of his course, and disperst all the unwholesome Damps. Then, after Stretching and Yawning for half an Hour, they light their Pipes, and, under the Protection of a cloud of Sinoak, venture out into the open Air: tho', if it happens to be never so little cold, they quick-ly return Shivering into the Chimney corner. When the weather is mild, they stand leaning with both their arms upon the corn-field fence, and gravely consider whether they had best go and take a Small Heat at the Hough: but generally find reasons to put it off till another time.

Thus they loiter away their Lives, like Solomon's Sluggard, with their Arms across, and at the Winding up of the Year Scarcely have Bread to Eat.

To speak the Truth, tis a thorough Aversion to Labor that makes People file off to N Carolina, where Plenty and a Warm Sun confirm them in their Disposition to Laziness for their whole Lives....

* * * * *

1. What can we learn about rural colonial American life from William Byrd's journal entry? What did they raise for crops? How did they live?

2. What is Byrd's attitude towards the people he encounters? How is this evidenced in his writing? Give specific examples.

5–5   A Swedish Visitor Tells about Philadelphia, 1748

A member of the Swedish Academy of Sciences, Peter Kalm was a botanist sent to North America to collect seeds that could be grown in Sweden. During his three years in America, Kalm kept a journal with descriptions of not only natural history, but American Society as well. Here, Kalm describes Philadelphia.

SOURCE: Peter Kalm, *Travels in North America* (London, 1771)

All the streets except two which are nearest to the river, run in a straight line, and make right angles at the intersections. Some are paved, others are not; and it seems less necessary, since the ground is sandy, and therefore soon absorbs the wet. But in most of the streets is a pavement of flags, a fathom or more broad, laid before the houses, and posts put on the outside three or four fathom asunder. Under the roofs are gutters which are carefully connected with pipes, and by this means, those who walk under them, when it rains, or when the snow melts, need not fear being wet by the dropping from the roofs.

The houses make a good appearance, are frequently several stories high, and built either of bricks or of stone; but the former are more commonly used, since bricks are made before the town, and are well burnt. The stone which has been employed in the building of other houses, is a mixture of black or grey *glimmer*, running in undulated veins, and of a loose, and quite small grained *limestone*, which runs scattered between the bendings of the other veins, and are of a grey colour, excepting here and there some single grains of sand, of a paler hue. The glimmer makes the greatest part of the stone; but the mixture is sometimes of another kind. This stone is now got in great quantities in the country, is easily cut, and has the good quality of not attracting the moisture in a wet season. Very good lime is burnt every where hereabouts, for masonry.

The town is now quite filled with inhabitants, which in regard to their country, religion, and trade, are very different from each other. You meet with excellent masters in all trades, and many things are made here full as well as in *England*. Yet no manufactures, especially for making fine cloth, are established. Perhaps the reason is, that it can be got with so little difficulty from *England*, and that the breed of sheep which is brought over, degenerates in process of time, and affords but a coarse wool.

Here is great plenty of provisions, and their prices are very moderate. There are no examples of an extraordinary dearth.

Every one who acknowledges God to be the Creator, preserver, and ruler of all things, and teaches or undertakes nothing against the state, or against the common peace, is at liberty to settle, stay, and carry on his trade here, be his religious principles ever so strange. No one is here molested on account of the erroneous principles of the doctrine which he follows, if he does not exceed the above-mentioned bounds. And he is so well secured by the laws in his person and property, and enjoys such liberties, that a citizen of *Philadelphia* may in a manner be said to live in his house like a king.

On a careful consideration of what I have already said, it will be easy to conceive how this city should rise so suddenly from nothing, into such grandeur and perfection, without supposing any powerful monarch's contributing to it, either by punishing the wicked, or by giving great supplies in money. And yet its fine appearance, good regulations, agreeable situation, natural advantages, trade, riches and power, are by no means inferior to those of any, even of the most ancient towns in *Europe*. It has not been necessary to force people to come and settle here; on the contrary, foreigners of different languages have left their country, houses, property, and relations, and ventured over wide and stormy seas, in order to come hither. Other countries, which have been peopled for a long space of time, complain of the small number of their inhabitants. But *Pennsylvania*, which was no better than a desert in the year 1681, and hardly contained five hundred people, now vies with several kingdoms in *Europe* in number of inhabitants. It has received numbers of people, which other countries, to their infinite loss, have either neglected or expelled.

* * * * * *

1.   Keeping in mind the two decades separating each travelogue, how does Kalm's account of Philadelphia compare with Sarah Kemble Knight's trip from Boston to New York? With William Byrd's tour of the rural mid-Atlantic?

2.   Despite its brevity, do you think Kalm is giving a complete picture of Philadelphia? What might he be overlooking? With the clarity of hindsight, what would we want to know about the socioeconomic and ethnic structures?

5–6   An Older Businessman Advises a Young One in 1748

Benjamin Franklin was one of our more colorful and eclectic colonial figures. His career ranged from diplomacy to printing, business to government, writing to science. Already retired in his early forties with a comfortable income from his printing business, in this piece, Franklin advanced his views on what made a man successful in business.

SOURCE: Benjamin Franklin, *The Works of Benjamin Franklin* (Boston: Hilliard, Gray and Company, 1836–40), 10 volumes.

Remember that TIME is Money. He that can earn Ten Shillings a Day by his Labour, and goes abroad, or sits idle one half of that Day, tho' he spends but Sixpence during his Diversion or Idleness, ought not to reckon That the only Expence; he has really spent or rather thrown away Five Shillings besides.

Remember that CREDIT is Money. If a Man lets his Money lie in my Hands after it is due, he gives me the Interest, or so much as I can make of it during that Time. This amounts to a considerable Sum where a Man has good and large Credit, and makes good Use of it.

Remember that Money is of a prolific generating Nature. Money can beget Money, and its Offspring can beget more, and so on. Five Shillings turn'd, is Six: Turn'd again, 'tis Seven and Three Pence; and so on 'til it becomes an Hundred Pound. The more there is of it, the more it produces every Turning, so that the Profits rise quicker and quicker. He that kills a breeding Sow, destroys all her Offspring to the thousandth Generation. He that murders a Crown, destroys all it might have produc'd, even Scores of Pounds.

Remember that Six Pounds a Year is but a Groat a Day. For this little Sum (which may be daily wasted either in Time or Expence unperceiv'd) a Man of Credit may on his own Security have the constant Possession and Use of an Hundred Pounds. So much in Stock briskly turn'd by an industrious Man, produces great Advantage.

Remember this Saying, 'That the good Paymaster is Lord of another Man's Purse. He that is known to pay punctually and exactly to the Time he promises, may at any Time, and on any Occasion, raise all the Money his Friends can spare. This is sometimes of great Use: Therefore never keep borrow'd Money an Hour beyond the Time you promis'd, lest a Disappointment shuts up your Friends Purse forever.

The most trifling Actions that affect a Man's Credit, are to be regarded. The Sound of your Hammer at Five in the Morning or Nine at Night, heard by a Creditor, makes him easy Six Months longer. But if he sees you at a Billiard Table, or hears your Voice in a Tavern, when you should be at Work, he sends for his Money the next Day. Finer Cloaths than he or his Wife wears, or greater Expence in any particular than he affords himself, shocks his Pride, and he duns you to humble you. Creditors are a kind of People, that have the sharpest Eyes and Ears, as well as the best Memories of any in the World.

Good-natur'd Creditors (and such one would always chuse to deal with if one could) feel Pain when they are oblig'd to ask for Money. Spare 'em that Pain, and they will love you. When you receive a Sum of Money, divide it among 'em in Proportion to your Debts. Don't be asham'd of paying a small Sum because you owe a greater. Money, more or less, is always welcome; and your Creditor had rather be at the Trouble of receiving Ten Pounds voluntarily brought him, tho' at ten different Times or Payments, than be oblig'd to go ten Times to demand it before he can receive it in a Lump. It shews, besides, that you are mindful of what you owe; it makes you appear a careful as well as an honest Man; and that still encreases your Credit.

Beware of thinking all your own that you possess, and of living accordingly. 'Tis a Mistake that many People who have Credit fall into. To prevent this, keep an exact Account for some Time of both your Expences and your Incomes. If you take the Pains at first to mention Particulars, it will have this good Effect; you will discover how wonderfully small trifling Expences mount up to large Sums, and will discern what might have been, and may for the future be saved, without occasioning any great Inconvenience.

In short, the Way to Wealth, if you desire it, is as plain as the Way to Market. It depends chiefly on two Words, INDUSTRY and FRUGALITY; i.e. Waste neither Time nor Money, but make the best Use of both. He that gets all he can honestly, and saves all he gets (necessary Expences excepted) will certainly become RICH; If that Being who governs the World, to whom all should look for a Blessing on their honest Endeavours, doth not in his wise Providence otherwise determine.

* * * * * *

1. In this short article, Benjamin Franklin outlines the basis for modern capitalism, from credit to the importance of credit ratings, from double entry bookkeeping to leveraging. Is his advice still practical today?

2. How do Benjamin Franklin's concerns, as presented in his writings, mark him compared to John Woolman, William Byrd, or Jonathan Edwards? What would you say are the primary concerns of each man?

5-7 A Witch Confesses Her Crimes in 1692

The Salem Witchcraft Trials are one of the more infamous moments in American history. Several hundred persons were arrested, scores were put in prison, and at least 19 were actually hung. The trials started because of convulsions and accusations by several young girls, inspired perhaps by the voodoo tales of a West Indian slave woman named Tituba, and Cotton Mather's recounting of four girls who had been bewitched in Boston a few years earlier. It is hard for us to understand today, but belief in witchcraft and witches would have been widespread at the time of the trials. Normal court procedures were suspended throughout the trials, but outside intervention eventually put an end to the episode, and reparations were paid to the victims. The following is the confession of one young girl.

SOURCE: Paul S. Boyer and Stephen Nissenvaum, eds., Salem Village Witchcraft: A Documentary Record of Local Conflict in Colonial New England (Belmont, CA: Wadsworth, 1972).

The Examination and Confession of Ann Foster at Salem Village, 15 July, 1692

After a while Ann ffoster confessed that the devil apered to her in the shape of a bird at several Times, such a bird as she neuer saw the like before; & that she had had this gift (viz. of striking ye afflicted downe with her eye euer since) & being askt why she thought yt bird was the diuill she answered because he came white & vanished away black & yt the diuill told her yt she should haue this gift & yt she must beliue him & told her she should haue prosperity & she said yt he had appeared to her three times & was always as a bird, and the last time was about half a year since, & sat upon a table had two legs & great eyes & yt it was the second time of his apearance that he promised her prosperity & yt it was Carriers wife about three weeks agoe yt came & perswaded her to hurt these people.

16 July 1692. Ann ffoster Examined confessed yt it was Goody Carrier yt made her a witch yt she came to her in person about Six yeares agoe & told her it she would not be a witch ye diuill should tare her in peices & carry her away at which time she promised to Serve the diuill yt she had bewitched a hog of John Loujoys to death & that she had hurt some persons in Salem Vilige, yt goody Carier came to her & would have her bewitch two children of Andrew Allins & that she had then two popets made & stuck pins in them to bewitch ye said children by which one of them dyed ye other very sick, that she was at the meeting of the witches at Salem Vilige, yt Goody Carier came & told her of the meeting and would haue her goe, so they got upon Sticks & went said Jorny & being there did see Mr. Buroughs ye minister who spake to them all, & this was about two months agoe that there was then twenty five persons meet together, that she tyed a knot in

a Rage & threw it into the fire to hurt Tim. Swan & that she did hurt the rest yt complayned of her by Squesing popets like them & so almost choked them.

18 July 1692. Ann ffoster Examined confessed yt ye diuill in shape of a man apeared to her wth Goody carier about six yeare since when they made her a witch & that she promised to serve the diuill two years, upon which the diuill promised her prosperity and many things but neuer performed it, that she & Martha Carier did both ride on a stick or pole when they went to the itch meeting at Salem Village & that the stick broak: as they were caried in the aire aboue the tops of the trees, & they fell but she did hang fast about the neck of Goody Carier & ware presently at the village, that she was then much hurt of her Leg, she further saith that she heard some of the witches say there was three hundred & fiue in the whole Country & that they would ruin that place ye Vilige, also said there was present at that meeting two men besides Mr. Burroughs ye minister & one of them had gray haire, she saith yt she formerly frequented the publique metting to worship god, but the diuill had such power ouer her yt she could not profit there & yt was her undoeing: she saith yt about three or foure yeares agoe Martha Carier told her she would bewitch James Hobbs child to death & the child dyed in twenty four hours.

21 July 92. Ann ffoster Examined Owned her former confesion being read to her and further confesed that the discourse amongst ye witches at ye meeting at Salem village was that they would afflict there to set up the Diuills Kingdome. This confesion is true as witness my hand.

Ann ffoster Signed & Owned the aboue Examination & Confession before me

Salem 10th September 1692.
John Higginson, Just Peace.

* * * * * *

1. *Why would the girls have started such a debacle? Why would Ann Foster have confessed?*

2. *What similar events have occurred in American history?*

5–8 A Puritan Preacher Admonishes His Flocks in 1741

Widely regarded as one of the greatest thinkers and most highly learned men of Puritan America, Jonathan Edwards was a preacher of considerable renown. About 1740, Edwards was largely responsible for the first great religious revival in America, which became known as the Great Awakening. The following excerpt, from his "Sinners in the Hands of an Angry God," is one of his most famous sermons, but doesn't reflect the wide breadth of his free-ranging philosophical ponderings. This sermon is a direct response to the outbursts of speaking in tongues and thrashing about on the floor that was happening in revival meetings of the Great Awakening at the time.

SOURCE: Jonathan Edwards, *Edwards on Revivals* (New York: Dunning & Spaulding, 1832).

[I preach] to unconverted persons in this congregation...every one of you that are out of Christ. That world of misery, that lake of burning brimstone, is extended abroad under you. There is the dreadful pit of the glowing flames of the wrath of God; there is hell's wide gaping mouth open; and you have nothing to stand upon, nor any thing to take hold of. There is nothing between you and hell but the air; it is only the power and mere pleasure of God that holds you up.

You probably are not sensible of this; you find you are kept out of hell, but do not see the hand of God in it; but look at other things, as the good state of your bodily constitution, your care of your own life, and the means you use for your own preservation. But indeed these things are nothing; if God should withdraw his hand, they would avail no more to keep you from falling, than the thin air to hold up a person that is suspended in it.

Your wickedness makes you as it were heavy as lead, and to tend downwards with great weight and pressure towards hell; and if God should let you go, you would immediately sink and swiftly descend and plunge into the bottomless gulf, and your healthy constitution, and your own care and prudence, and best contrivance, and all your righteousness, would have no more influence to uphold you and keep you out of hell, than a spider's web would have to stop a falling rock. Were it not that so is the sovereign pleasure of God, the earth would not bear you one moment; for you are a burden to it; the creation groans with you; the creature is made subject to the bondage of your corruption, not willingly; the sun does not willingly shine upon you to give you light to serve sin and Satan; the earth does not willingly yield her increase to satisfy your lusts; nor is it willingly a stage for your wickedness to be acted upon; the air does not willingly serve you for breath to maintain the flame of life in your vitals, while you spend your life in the service of God's enemies. God's creatures are good, and were made for men to serve God with, and do not willingly subserve to any other purpose, and groan when they are abused to purposes so directly contrary to their nature and end. And the world would spew you out, were it not for the sovereign hand of him who hath subjected it in hope. There are the black clouds of God's wrath now hanging directly over your heads, full of the dreadful storm, and big with thunder; and were it not for the restraining hand of God, it would immediately burst forth upon you. The sovereign pleasure of God, for the present, stays his rough wind; otherwise it would come with fury, and your destruction would come like a whirlwind, and you would be like the chaff of the summer threshing floor....

The God that holds you over the pit of hell, much as one holds a spider, or some loathsome insect, over the fire, abhors you, and is dreadfully provoked; his wrath towards you burns like fire; he looks upon you as worthy of nothing else, but to be cast into the fire; he is of purer eyes than to bear to have you in his sight; you are ten thousand times so abominable in his eyes, as the most hateful and venomous serpent is in ours. You have offended him infinitely more than ever a stubborn rebel did his prince: and yet it is nothing but his hand that holds you from falling into the fire every moment: it is ascribed to nothing else, that you did not go to hell the last night; that you was suffered to awake again in this world, after you closed your eyes to sleep; and there is no other reason to be given, why you have not dropped into hell since you arose in the morning, but that God's hand has held you up: there is no other reason to be given why you have not gone to hell, since you have sat here in the house of God, provoking his pure eyes by your sinful wicked manner of attending his solemn worship: yea, there is nothing else that is to be given as a reason why you do not this very moment drop down into hell.

O sinner! consider the fearful danger you are in: it is a great furnace of wrath, a wide and bottomless pit, full of the fire of wrath, that you are held over in the hand of that God, whose wrath is provoked and incensed as much against you, as against many of the damned in hell: you hang by a slender thread, with the flames of divine wrath flashing about it, and ready every moment to singe it, and burn it asunder; and you have no interest in any Mediator, and nothing to lay hold of to save yourself, nothing to keep off the flames of wrath, nothing of your own, nothing that you ever have done, nothing that you can do, to induce God to spare you one moment....

How dreadful is the state of those that are daily and hourly in danger of this great wrath and infinite misery! But this is the dismal case of every soul in this congregation that has not been born again, however moral and strict, sober and religious, they may otherwise be. Oh that you would consider it, whether you be young or old! There is reason to think, that there are many in this congregation now hearing this discourse, that will actually be the subjects of this very misery to all eternity. We know not who they are, or in what seats they sit, or what thoughts they now have. It may be they are now at ease, and hear all these things without much disturbance, and are now flattering themselves that they are not the persons; promising themselves that they shall escape. If we knew that there was one person, and but one, in the whole congregation, that was to be the subject of this misery, what an awful thing it would be to think of! If we knew who it was, what an awful sight would it be to see such a person! How all the rest of the congregation lift up a lamentable and bitter cry over him! But alas! Instead of one, how many is it likely will remember this discourse in hell! And it would be a wonder, if some that are now present should not be in hell in a very short time, before this year is out. And it would be no wonder if some persons, that now sit here in some seats of this meeting-house in health, and quiet and secure, should be there before tomorrow morning.

* * * * * *

1. *Does the Puritan God of wrath come to pervade American Christianity? Is this the same God you may have seen portrayed on American television or in a modern church? How would you compare a modern televangelist to someone like Jonathan Edwards?*

2. *How might Edwards's sermon have motivated the people of his day?*

From Empire to Independence, 1750–1776

6–1 Britian Forbids Americans Western Settlement, 1763

The Proclamation of 1763 only heightened strained relations between the American Colonists and Britain. The proclamation forbid Americans from settling west of the Appalachian Mountains, ordered settlers already there to move, and outlawed purchase of land from the Indians. The proclamation was largely in response to Pontiac's War, and attempted to pacify the Indians in the Northwest Territory. Settlers continued to stream into Tennessee and Kentucky and the boundaries of the act were later revised. The following are excerpts from the proclamation.

SOURCE: Henry Steele Commager, *Documents of American History* (New York: Appelton–Century–Crofts, 1948)

The Proclamation of 1763

Whereas we have taken into our royal consideration the extensive and valuable acquisitions in America secured to our Crown by the late definitive treaty of peace concluded at Paris the 10th day of February last; and being desirous that all our loving subjects, as well of our kingdom as of our colonies in America, may avail themselves, and with all convenient speed, of the great benefits and advantages which must accrue therefrom to their commerce, manufactures, and navigation: we have thought fit, with the advice of our Privy Council, to issue this our Royal Proclamation, hereby to publish and declare to all our loving subjects that we have, with the advice of our said Privy Council, granted our letters patent under our Great Seal of Great Britain, to erect within the countries and islands ceded and confirmed to us by the said treaty, four distinct and separate governments, styled and called by the names of Quebec, East West Florida, and Grenada....

And...we have...given express power and direction to our governors of our said colonies respectively, that so soon as the state and circumstances of the said colonies will admit thereof, they shall, with the advice and consent of the members of our council, summon and call general assemblies within the said governments respectively, in such manner and form as used and directed in those colonies and provinces in America, which are under our immediate government; and we have also given power to the said governors, with the consent of our said councils, and the representatives of the people, so to be summoned as aforesaid, to make, constitute, and ordain laws, statutes, and ordinances for the public peace, welfare, and good government of our said colonies, and of the people and inhabitants thereof, as near as may be, agreeable to the laws of England, and under such regulations and restrictions as are used in other colonies; and in the mean time, and until such assemblies can be called as aforesaid, all persons inhabiting in, or resorting to, our said colonies, may confide in our royal protection for the enjoyment of the benefit of the laws of our realm of England: for which purpose we have given power under our great seal to the governors of our said colonies respectively, to erect and constitute, with the advice of our said councils respectively, courts of judicature and public justice within our said colonies, for the hearing and determining all causes as well criminal as civil. according to law and equity, and as near as may be, agreeable to the laws of England, with liberty to all persons who may think themselves aggrieved by the sentence of such courts, in all civil cases, to appeal, under the usual limitations and restrictions, to us, in our privy council.

And whereas it is just and reasonable, and essential to our interest and the security of our colonies, that the several nations or tribes of Indians with whom we are connected, and who live under our protection, should not be molested or disturbed in the possession of such parts of our dominions and territories as, not having been ceded to or purchased by us, are reserved to them, or any of them, as their hunting-grounds; we do therefore, with the advice of our Privy Council, declare it to be our royal will and pleasure, that no Governor or commander in chief, in any of our colonies of Quebec, East Florida or West Florida, do presume, upon any pretence whatever, to grant warrants of survey, or pass any patents for lands beyond the bounds of their respective governments, as described in their commissions; as also that no Governor or commander in chief of our other colonies or plantations in America do presume for the present, and until our further pleasure be known, to grant warrants of survey or pass patents for any lands beyond the heads or sources of any of the rivers which fall into the Atlantic Ocean from the west or northwest; or upon any lands whatever, which, not having been ceded to or purchased by us, as aforesaid, are reserved to the said Indians, or any of them.

And we do further declare it to be our royal will and pleasure, for the present as aforesaid, to reserve under our sovereignty, protection, and dominion, for the use of the said Indians, all the land and territories not included within the limits of our said three new governments, or within the limits of the territory granted to the Hudson's Bay Company; as also all the land and territories lying to the westward of the sources of the rivers which fall into the sea from the west and northwest as aforesaid; and we do hereby strictly forbid, on pain of our displeasure, all our loving subjects from making any purchases or settlements whatever, or taking possession of any of the lands above reserved, without our special leave and license for that purpose first obtained.

And we do further strictly enjoin and require all persons whatever, who have either wilfully or inadvertantly seated themselves upon any lands within the countries above described, or upon any other lands which, not having been ceded to or purchased by us, are still reserved to the said Indians as aforesaid, forthwith to remove themselves from such settlements.

* * * * *

1. Looking at an historical almanac, what are the physical boundaries of East and West Florida, Quebec and Granada, as they are declared in the Proclamation of 1763?

2. What do you think England's motivation was in making this proclamation? Why would they want to formalize their control over the American colonists?

6-2 An American Colonist Opposes New Taxes and Asserts the Rights of the Colonists, 1764

One of the American colonists who advocated reconciliation with the British rather than independence, James Otis, a lawyer and Harvard graduate, strongly argued for the rights of the colonists. Otis resigned a position as a king's advocate general in America because he refused to issue writs of assistance, unspecified warrants allowing search of colonial citizen's property without cause. The following is an excerpt from Otis's pamphlet, The Rights of the British Colonies Asserted and Proved, in which he argues against the Sugar Act of 1764, as well as further taxation by the British to finance their government of America.

SOURCE: James Otis, The Rights of the British Colonies Asserted and Proved (Boston, 1764).

A plantation or colony, is a settlement of subjects, in a territory disjoined or remote from the mother country, and may be made by private adventurers or the public; but in both cases the Colonists are entitled to as ample rights, liberties and privileges as the subjects of the mother country are, and in some respects to more...

[Otis then defines these rights:]

3dly. No legislative, supreme or subordinate, has a right to make itself arbitrary...

4thly. The supreme legislative cannot justly assume a power of ruling by extempore arbitrary decrees, but is bound to dispense justice by known settled rules, and by duly authorized independent judges.

5thly. The supreme power cannot take from any man any part of his property, without his consent in person, or by representation.

6thly. The legislature cannot transfer the power of making laws to any other hands.

These are their bounds, which by God and nature are fixed, hitherto have they a right to come, and no further.

1. To govern by stated laws.

2. Those laws should have no other end ultimately, but the good of the people.

3. Taxes are not to be laid on the people, but by their consent in person, or by deputation.

4. Their whole power is not transferable.

These are the first principles of law and justice, and the great barriers of a free state, and of the British constitution in particular. I ask, I want no more—Now let it be shown how 'tis reconcileable with these principles, or to many other fundamental maxims of the British constitution, as well as the natural and civil rights, which by the laws of their country, all British subjects are intitled to, as their best inheritance and birth-right, that all the northern colonies, who are without one representative in the House of Commons, should be taxed by the British parliament.

That the colonists, black and white, born here, are free born British subjects, and entitled to all the essential civil rights of such, is a truth not only manifest from the provincial charters, from the principles of the common law, and acts of parliament; but from the British constitution... with a professed design to lecture the liberties of all the subjects to all generations.

In the 12 and 13 of Wm. cited above, the liberties of the subject are spoken of as their best birth-rights—No one ever dreamed, surely, that these liberties were confined to the realm. At that rate, no British subjects in the dominions could, without a manifest contradiction, be declared entitled to all the priviledges of subjects born within the realm, to all intents and purposes, which are rightly given foreigners, by parliament, after residing seven years.

These expressions of parliament, as well as of the charters, must be vain and empty sounds, unless we are allowed the essential rights of our fellow-subjects in Great-Britain....

I cannot but observe here, that if the parliament have an equitable right to tax our trade, 'tis indisputable that they have as good an one to tax the lands, and every thing else. The taxing trade furnishes one reason why the province other should be unequally born, upon a supposition that a tax on trade is not a tax on the whole. But take it either way, there is no foundation for the distinction some make in England, between an internal and an external tax on the colonies. By the first is meant a tax on trade, by the latter a tax on land, and the things on it. A tax on trade is either a tax of every man in the province, or 'tis not. If 'tis not a tax on the whole, 'tis unequal and unjust, that a heavy burden, should be laid on the trade of the colonies, to maintain an army of soldiers, custom-house officers, and fleets of guard-ships; all which, the incomes of both trade and land would not furnish means to support so lately as the last war, when all was at stake, and the colonies were reimbursed in part by parliament. How can it be supposed that all of a sudden the trade of the colonies alone can bear all this terrible burden. The late acquisitions in America, as glorious as they have been, and as beneficial as they are to Great-Britain, are only a security to these colonies against the ravages of the French and Indians. Our trade upon the whole is not, I believe, benefited by them one groat. All the time the French Islands were in our hands, the fine sugars, &c. were all shipped home. None as I have been informed were allowed to be bro't to the colonies. They were too delicious a morsel for a North American palate. If it be said that a tax on the trade of the colonies is an equal and just tax on the whole of the inhabitants: What then becomes of the notable distinction between external and internal taxes? Why may not the parliament lay stamps, land taxes, establish tythes to the church of England, and so indefinitely? I know of no bounds. I do not mention the tythes out of any disrespect to the church of England, which I esteem by far the best *national* church, and to have had as ornaments of it many of the greatest and best men in the world. But to those colonies who in general dissent from a principle of conscience, it would seem a little hard to pay towards the support of a worship, whose modes they cannot conform to.

If an army must be kept in America, at the expence of the colonies, it would not seem quite so hard if after the parliament had determined the sum to be raised, and apportioned it, to have allowed each colony to assess its quota, and raise it as easily to themselves as might be. But to have the whole levied and collected without our consent is extraordinary. 'Tis allowed even to *tributaries*, and those laid under *military* contribution, to assess and collect the sums demanded. The case of the provinces is certainly likely to he the hardest that can be instanced in story. Will it not equal any thing but down right military execution? Was there ever a tribute imposed even on the conquered? A fleet, an army of soldiers, and another of taxgatherers kept up, and not a single office either for securing or collecting the duty in the gift of the tributary state....

The sum of my argument is, That civil government is of God: That the administrators of it were originally the whole people: That they might have devolved it on whom they pleased: That this devolution is fiduciary, for the good of the whole: That by the British constitution, this devolution is on the King, lords and commons, the supreme, sacred and uncontrollable legislative power, not only in the realm, but thro' the dominions: That by the abdication, the original compact was broken to pieces: That by the revolution, it was renewed, and more firmly established, and the rights and liberties of the subject in all parts of the dominions, more fully explained and confirmed: That in consequence of this establishment, and the acts of succession and union his Majesty GEORGE III is rightful king and sovereign, and with his parliament, the supreme legislative of Great Britain; France and Ireland, and the dominions thereto belonging: That this constitution is the most free one, and by far the best, now existing on earth: That by this constitution, every man in the dominion is a free man: That no parts of his Majesty's dominions can be taxed without their consent: That every part has a right to be represented in the supreme or some subordinate legislature: That the refusal of this, would seem to be a contradiction in practice to the theory of the constitution: That the colonies are subordinate dominions, and are now in such a state, as to make it best for the good of the whole, that they should not only be continued in the enjoyment of subordinate legislation, but be also represented in some proportion to their number and estates, in the grand legislature of the nation: That this would firmly unite all parts of the British empire, in the greatest peace and prosperity; and render it invulnerable and perpetual.

* * * * *

1. *Reviewing Locke's philosophy of "Natural Rights," what do you think Otis takes from Locke? How does Otis modify these natural rights into constitutional and legal rights?*

2. *Do you think Otis was advocating American independence from England? Or was he asserting a better British governing of her American colonies?*

6-3 An American Moderate Speaks Against the Stamp Act, 1767

Like many American colonists, James Dickinson was a moderate who opposed separating from Britain. Refusing to sign the Declaration of Independence, Dickinson went on to serve in the revolutionary army, rising to the rank of brigadier general. Despite his moderate stance, Dickinson was active in the Constitutional Convention and wrote several important revolutionary pamphlets, the following selection taken from his Letters from a Pennsylvania Farmer to the Inhabitants of the British Colonies.

SOURCE: Forrest McDonald, *Empire and Nation* (Englewood Cliffs, NJ: Prentice Hall, 1962).

My dear Countrymen,

There is another late act of parliament, which appears to me to be unconstitutional, and as destructive to the liberty of these colonies, as that mentioned in my last letter; that is, the act for granting the duties on paper, glass, etc.

The parliament unquestionably possesses a legal authority to *regulate* the trade of *Great Britain*, and all her colonies. Such an authority is essential to the relation between a mother country and her colonies; and necessary for the common good of all. He who considers these provinces as states distinct from the *British Empire*, has very slender notions of *justice*, or of their *interests*. We are but parts of a *whole*; and therefore there must exist a power somewhere, to preside, and preserve the connection in due order. This power is lodged in the parliament; and we are as much dependent on *Great Britain*, as a perfectly free people can be on another.

I have looked over *every statute* relating to these colonies, from their first settlement to this time; and I find every one of them founded on this principle, till the *Stamp Act* administration. *All before*, are calculated to regulate trade, and preserve or promote a mutually beneficial intercourse between the several constituent parts of the empire; and though many of them imposed duties on trade, yet those duties were always imposed *with design* to restrain the commerce of one part, that was injurious to another, and thus to promote the general welfare. The raising of a revenue thereby was never intended. Thus the King, by his judges in his courts of justice, imposes fines, which all together amount to a very considerable sum, and contribute to the support of government: But this is merely a consequence arising from restrictions that only meant to keep peace and prevent confusion; and surely a man would argue very loosely, who should conclude from hence, that the King has a right to levy money in general upon his subjects. Never did the *British* parliament, till the period above mentioned, think of imposing duties in *America* FOR THE PURPOSE OF RAISING A REVENUE. Mr. *Greenville* first introduced this language, in the preamble to the 4th of GEO. III Chap. 15, which has these words—"And whereas it is just and necessary, that provision be made FOR RAISING A FURTHER REVENUE WITHIN YOUR MAJESTY'S DOMINIONS IN AMERICA, *towards defraying the said expences*, we your Majesty's most dutiful and loyal subjects, the COMMONS OF GREAT BRITAIN," etc. as before.

A few months after came the *Stamp Act*, which reciting this, proceeds in the same strange mode of expression, thus—"And whereas it is just and necessary, that provision be made FOR RAISING A FURTHER REVENUE WITHIN YOUR MAJESTY'S DOMINIONS IN AMERICA, *towards defraying the said expences*, we your Majesty's most dutiful and loyal subjects, the COMMONS OF GREAT BRITAIN, in parliament assembled, being desirous to make some provision in this present session of parliament, TOWARD RAISING THE SAID REVENUE IN AMERICA, have resolved to GIVE and GRANT unto your Majesty the several rates and duties herein after mentioned." etc.

The last act, granting duties upon paper, etc. carefully pursues these modern precedents. The preamble is, "Whereas it is expedient THAT A REVENUE SHOULD BE RAISED IN YOUR MAJESTY'S DOMINIONS IN AMERICA, *for making a more certain and adequate provision for defraying the charge of the administration of justice, and the support of civil government in such provinces, where it shall be found necessary; and towards further defraying the expences of defending, protecting and securing the said dominions, we your Majesty's most dutiful and loyal subjects, the* COMMONS OF GREAT BRITAIN, etc. GIVE and GRANT," etc. as before.

Here we may observe an authority *expressly* claimed and exerted to impose duties on these colonies; not for the regulation of trade; not for the preservation or promotion of a mutually beneficial intercourse between the several constituent parts of the empire, heretofore the sole objects of parliamentary institutions; *but for the single purpose of levying money upon us.*

This I call an innovation; and a most dangerous innovation....

Our great advocate, Mr. *Pitt*, in his speeches on the debate concerning the repeal of the *Stamp Act* acknowledged, that Great Britain could restrain our manufactures. His words are these—"This kingdom, as the supreme governing and legislative power, has ALWAYS bound the colonies by her regulations and RESTRICTIONS in trade, in navigation, in MANUFACTURES—in everything, *except that of taking their money out of their pockets WITHOUT THEIR CONSENT.* Again he says, "We may bind their trade CONFINE THEIR MANUFACTURES, and exercise every power whatever, *except that of taking their money out of their pockets WITHOUT THEIR CONSENT.*"...

From what has been said, I think this uncontrovertible conclusion may be deduced, that when a ruling state obliges a dependent state to take certain commodities from her alone, it is implied in the nature of that obligation; is essentially requisite to give it the least degree of justice; and is inseparably united with it, in order to preserve any share of freedom to the dependent state; *that those commodities should never be loaded with duties,* FOR THE SOLE PURPOSE OF LEVYING MONEY ON THE DEPENDENT STATE.

Upon the whole, the single question is, whether the parliament can legally impose duties to be paid *by the people of these colonies only,* FOR THE SOLE PURPOSE OF RAISING A REVENUE, on *commodities which she obliges us to take from her alone,* or, in other words, whether the parliament can legally take money out of our pockets WITHOUT our consent. If they can, our boasted liberty is but

> *Vox et praeterea nihil.*
> A sound and nothing else.
> A Farmer

* * * * *

1. *To what legislation is John Dickinson responding? What were the provisions of this British legislation?*

2. *Do you think Dickinson's argument reflects constitutional concerns rather than moral or humanitarian interests? Do you think these concerns were later incorporated into the U.S. constitution?*

6-4 The First American Congress Meets, 1774

Meeting in Philadelphia in 1774, the First Continental Congress was formed. It was an extralegal body at the time, as the colonies were still very much under the control of Britain. The Continental Congress, protested the British Coercive acts, as well as sought economic measures against Britain. The following "Declaration and Resolves of the First Continental Congress, October 14, 1774," outlines the rights the colonists felt they were entitled to as part of the natural rights of all men everywhere.

SOURCE: Henry Steele Commager, *Documents of American History* (New York: Appleton-Century-Crofts, 1948).

Whereas, since the close of the last war, the British parliament, claiming a power of right to bind the people of America by statute in all cases whatsoever hath, in some acts expressly imposed taxes on them, and in others, under various pretences, but in fact for the purpose of raising a revenue, hath imposed rates and duties payable in these colonies, established a board of commissioners with unconstitutional powers, and extended the jurisdiction of courts of Admiralty not only for collecting the said duties, but for the trial of causes merely arising within the body of a county.

And whereas, in consequence of other statutes, judges who before held only estates at will in their offices, have been made dependent on the Crown alon for their salaries, and standing armies kept in times of peace. And it has lately been resolved in Parliament, that by force of a statute made in the thirty-fifth year of the reign of king Henry the Eighth, colonists may be transported to England, and tried there upon accusations for treasons committed and misprisions, or concealments of treasons committed in the colonies; and by a late statute, such trials have been directed in cases therein mentioned.

And whereas, in the last session of Parliament, three statutes were made...[the Boston Port Act, the Massachusetts Government Act, the Administration of Justice Act], and another statute was then made [the Quebec Act]...All which statutes are impolitic, unjust, and cruel, as well as unconstitutional, and most dangerous and destructive of American rights.

And whereas, Assemblies have been frequently dissolved, contrary to the rights of the people, when they attempted to deliberate on grievances; and their dutiful, humble, loyal & reasonable petitions to the crown for redress have been repeatedly treated with contempt, by His Majesty's ministers of state.

The good people of the several Colonies of New-hampshire, Massachusetts-bay, Rhode-Island and Providence plantations, Connecticut, New-York, New-Jersey, Pennsylvania, Newcastle Kent and Sussex on Delaware, Maryland, Virginia, North-Carolina, and South-Carolina, justly alarmed at these arbitrary proceedings of parliament and administration, have severally elected, constituted, and appointed deputies to meet, and sit in general Congress, in the city of Philadelphia, in order to obtain such establishment, as that their religion, laws, and liberties, may not be subverted:

Whereupon the deputies so appointed being now assembled, in a full and free representation of these Colonies, taking into their most serious consideration the best means of attaining the ends aforesaid, do in the first place, as Englishmen their ancestors in like cases have usually done, for asserting and vindicating their rights and liberties, declare,

That the inhabitants of the English Colonies in North America, by the immutable laws of nature, the principles of the English constitution, and the several charters or compacts, have the following Rights:

Resolved, N. C. D.

1. That they are entitled to life, liberty, and property, & they have never ceded to any sovereign power whatever, a right to dispose of either without their consent.

2. That our ancestors, who first settled these colonies, were at the time of their emigration from the mother country, entitled to all the rights, liberties, and immunities of free and natural-born subjects within the realm of England.

3. That by such emigration they by no means forfeited, surrendered, or lost any of those rights, but that they were, and their descendants now are entitled to the exercise and enjoyment of all such of them, as their local and other circumstances enable them to exercise and enjoy.

4. That the foundation of English liberty, and of all free government, is a right in the people to participate in *their legislative council:* and as the English colonists are not represented, and from their local and other circumstances, cannot properly be represented in the British parliament, they are entitled to a free and exclusive power of legislation in their several provincial legislatures, where their right of representation can alone be preserved, in all cases of taxation and internal polity, subject only to the negative of their sovereign, in such manner as has been heretofore used and accustomed. But, from the necessity of the case, and a regard to the mutual interest of both countries, we cheerfully consent to the operation of such acts of the British parliament, as are bona fide restrained to the regulation of our external commerce, for the purpose of securing the commercial advantages of the whole empire to the mother country, and the commercial benefits of its respective members excluding every idea of taxation, internal or external, for raising a revenue on the subjects in America without their consent.

5. That the respective colonies are entitled to the common law of England, and more especially to the great and inestimable privilege of being tried by their peers of the vicinage, according to the course of that law.

6. That they are entitled to the benefit of such of the English statutes, as existed at the time of their colonization; tion; and which they have, by experience, respectively found to be applicable to their several local and other circumstances.

7. That these, his majesty's colonies, are likewise entitled to all the immunities and privileges granted and confirmed to them by royal charters, or secured by their several codes of provincial laws.

8. That they have right peaceably to assemble, consider of their grievances, and petition the King; and that all prosecutions, prohibitory proclamations, and commitments for the same, are illegal.

9. That the keeping a Standing army in these colonies, in times of peace, without the consent of the legislature of that colony in which such army is kept, is against law.

10. It is indispensably necessary to good government, and rendered essential by the English constitution, that the constituent branches of the legislature be independent of each other; that, therefore, the exercise of legislative power in several colonies, by a council appointed during pleasure, by the crown, is unconstitutional, dangerous, and destructive to the freedom of American legislation.

All and each of which the aforesaid deputies, in behalf of themselves, and their constituents, do claim, demand, and insist on, as their indubitable rights and liberties; which cannot be legally taken from them, altered or abridged by any power whatever, without their own consent, by their representatives in their several provincial legislatures.

In the course of our inquiry, we find many infringements and violations of the foregoing rights, which, from an ardent desire that harmony and mutual intercourse of affection and interest may be restored, we pass over for the present, and proceed to state such acts and measures as have been adopted since the last war, which demonstrate a system formed to enslave America.

Resolved, That the following acts of Parliament are infringements and violations of the rights of the colonists; and that the repeal of them is essentially necessary, in order to restore harmony between Great Britain and the American colonies,...viz.:

The several Acts of 4 Geo. 3, ch. 15 & ch. 34; 5 Geo. 3, ch. 25; 6 Geo. 3, ch. 52; 7 Geo. 3, ch. 41 & 46; 8 Geo. 3, ch. 22; which impose duties for the purpose of raising a revenue in America, extend the powers of the admiralty courts beyond their ancient limits, deprive the American subject of trial by jury, authorize the judges' certificate to indemnify the prosecutor from damages that he might otherwise be liable to, requiring oppressive security from a claimant of ships and goods seized before he shall be allowed to defend his property; and are subversive of American rights.

Also the 12 Geo. 3, ch. 24; entitled "An act for the

better preserving his Majesty's dockyards, magazines, ships, ammunition, and stores," which declares a new offense in America, and deprives the American subject of a constitutional trial by jury of the vicinage, by authorizing the trial of any person charged with the committing any offense described in the said act, out of the realm, to be indicted and tried for the same in any shire or county within the realm.

Also the three acts passed in the last session of parliament, for stopping the port and blocking up the harbour of Boston, for altering the charter & government of the Massachusetts-bay, and that which is entitled "An Act for the better administration of Justice," &c.

Also the act passed the same session for establishing the Roman Catholick Religion in the province of Quebec, abolishing the equitable system of English laws, and erecting a tyranny there, to the great danger, from so great a dissimilarity of Religion, law, and government, of the neighbouring British colonies....

Also the act passed the same session for the better providing suitable quarters for officers and soldiers in his Majesty's service in North America.

Also, that the keeping a standing army in several of these colonies, in time of peace, without the consent of the legislature of that colony in which the army is kept, is against law.

To these grievous acts and measures Americans cannot submit, but in hopes that their fellow subjects in Great-Britain will, on a revision of them, restore us to that state in which both countries found happiness and prosperity, we have for the present only resolved to pursue the following peaceable measures: 1st. To enter into a non-importation, non-consumption, and non-exportation agreement or association. 2. To prepare an address to the people of Great-Britain, and a memorial to the inhabitants of British America, & 3. To prepare a loyal address to his Majesty, agreeable to resolutions already entered into.

* * * * *

1.   How does this document become the basis of the U.S. constitution?

2.   What parts of this document have you already seen in James Otis, James Dickinson, and Patrick Henry? How much have all of these men borrowed from Locke?

6–5   A Colonist Makes an Impassioned Call to Arms, 1775

Patrick Henry gave what would become one of the most famous speeches of the American Revolution, the widely quoted "Speech to the Second Virginia Convention," whose famous "Give me liberty or give me death," included here, was to be a rallying cry for the colonists. Part of the growing number of Americans set on armed resistance as the course of action against the British, Henry was an impassioned orator who stirred the crowds. Successful as a lawyer and a member of the Virginia House of Burgesses, Henry lost his position at the national level after the revolution because he favored political treaties with Spain and France before America broke with England. Henry went on to become Governor of Virginia several times and opposed the ratification of the Constitution because it did not sufficiently protect state's rights. Henry's opposition led to the formation of the Bill of Rights.

SOURCE: William Wirt, *Sketches of the Life and Character of Patrick Henry* (Philadelphia: James Webster, 1818).

Speech to the Second Virginia Convention

We are apt to shut our eyes against a painful truth, and listen to the song of that siren, till she transforms us into beasts. Is this the part of wise men, engaged in a great and arduous struggle for liberty? Are we disposed to be of the number of those who, having eyes, see not, and having ears, hear not, the things which so nearly concern their temporal salvation? For my part, whatever anguish of spirit it may cost, I am willing to know the whole truth; to know the worst and to provide for it.

I have but one lamp by which my feet are guided; and that is the lamp of experience. I know of no way of judging of the future but by the past. And judging by the past, I wish to know what there has been in the conduct of the British ministry for the last ten years to justify those hopes with which gentlemen have been pleased to solace themselves and the House? Is it that insidious smile with which our petition has been lately received? Trust it not, sir; it will prove a snare to your feet. Suffer not yourselves to be betrayed with a kiss. Ask yourselves how this gracious reception of our petition comports with these warlike preparations which cover our waters and darken our land. Are fleets and armies necessary to a work of love and reconciliation? Have we shown ourselves so unwilling to be reconciled, that force must be called in to win back our love? Let us not deceive ourselves, sir. These are the implements of war and subjugation; the last arguments to which kings resort. I ask gentlemen, sir, what means this martial array, if its purpose be not to force us to submission? Can gentlemen assign any other possible

...It is natural for man to indulge in the illusions of hope.

motives for it? Has Great Britain any enemy, in this quarter of the world, to call for all this accumulation of navies and armies? No, sir, she has none. They are meant for us; they can be meant for no other. They are sent over to bind and rivet upon us those chains which the British ministry have been so long forging. And what have we to oppose to them? Shall we try argument? Sir, we have been trying that for the last ten years. Have we anything new to offer upon the subject? Nothing. We have held the subject up in every light of which it is capable; but it has been all in vain. Shall we resort to entreaty and humble supplication? What terms shall we find which have not been already exhausted? Let us not, I beseech you, sir, deceive ourselves longer.

Sir, we have done everything that could be done to avert the storm which is now coming on. We have petitioned—we have remonstrated—we have supplicated—we have prostrated ourselves before the throne, and have implored its interposition to arrest the tyrannical hands of the ministry and parliament. Our petitions have been slighted; our remonstrances have produced additional violence and insult; our supplications have been disregarded; and we have been spurned, with contempt, from the foot of the throne. In vain, after these things, may we indulge the fond hope of peace and reconciliation. There is no longer any room for hope. If we wish to be free—if we mean to preserve inviolate those inestimable privileges for which we have been so long contending—if we mean not basely to abandon the noble struggle in which we have been so long engaged, and which we have pledged ourselves never to abandon until the glorious object of our contest shall be obtained—we must fight! I repeat it, sir, we must fight! An appeal to arms and to the God of Hosts is all that is left us!

They tell us, sir, that we are weak—unable to cope with so formidable an adversary. But when shall we be stronger? Will it be the next week or the next year? Will it be when we are totally disarmed, and when a British guard shall be stationed in every house? Shall we gather strength by irresolution and inaction? Shall we acquire the means of effectual resistance by lying supinely on our backs, and hugging the delusive phantom of hope, until our enemies shall have bound us hand and foot? Sir, we are not weak, if we make a proper use of those means which the God of nature hath placed in our power. Three millions of people, armed in the holy cause of liberty, and in such a country as that which we possess, are invincible by any force which our enemy can send against us. Besides, sir, we shall not fight our battles alone. There is a just God who presides over the destinies of nations; and who will raise up friends to fight our battles for us. The battle, sir, is not to the strong alone; it is to the vigilant, the active, the brave. Besides, sir, we have no election. If we were base enough to desire it, it is now too late to retire from the contest. There is no retreat but in submission and slavery! Our chains are forged! Their clanking may be heard on the plains of Boston! The war is inevitable—and let it come! I repeat it, sir, let it come!

It is in vain, sir, to extenuate the matter. Gentlemen may cry, "Peace! peace !"—but there is no peace. The war is actually begun! The next gale that sweeps from the north will bring to our ears the clash of resounding arms! Our brethren are already in the field! Why stand we here idle? What is it that gentlemen wish? What would they have? Is life so dear, or peace so sweet, as to be purchased at the price of chains and slavery? Forbid it, Almighty God! I know not what course others may take; but as for me, give me liberty or give me death!

* * * * * *

1. *The American Revolution was not always the sure thing we now think it to be in retrospect. At the time, not everyone was in agreement to break away from England. How does Patrick Henry's speech reflect this growing movement towards a break with England? What rhetoric does he use to stir up those that listened to the speech?*

2. *What about the claims Henry makes within his speech against the British? Would we stand for this sort of thing today? Think of some countries where this same speech might be made now.*

3. *Henry was famous as an orator rather than a writer. The exact words of his speeches are not always known. What effect does this have on history? What does this mean for historians trying to recreate his speeches?*

6-6   An Anglican Preacher Denounces the American Rebels, 1775

Jonathan Boucher was an Anglican minister, born in England, who had little sympathy for the American revolutionaries. Living in Virginia, Boucher tutored George Washington's stepson and was a friend to the general, but was decidedly against Washington's cause. Boucher frequently used his pulpit to preach against the growing unrest in the British colonies. The following sermon excerpt comes front Boucher's book, A View of the Causes and Consequences of the American Revolution.

SOURCE: Jonathan Boucher, *A View of the Causes and Consequences of the American Revolution* (London: G.G. & J. Robinson, 1797).

On Civil Liberty, Passive Obedience, and Nonresistance

Obedience to government is every man's duty, because it is every man's interest; but it is particularly incumbent on Christians, because (in addition to its moral fitness) it is enjoined by the positive commands of God; and, therefore, when Christians are disobedient to human ordinances, they are also disobedient to God. If the form of government under which the good providence of God has been pleased to place us be mild and free, it is our duty to enjoy it with gratitude and with thankfulness and, in particular, to be careful not to abuse it by licentiousness. If it be less indulgent and less liberal than in reason it ought to be, still it is our duty not to disturb and destroy the peace of the community by becoming refractory and rebellious subjects and *resisting the ordinances of God.* However humiliating such acquiescence may seem to men of warm and eager minds, the wisdom of God in having made it our duty is manifest. For, as it is the natural temper and bias of the human mind to be impatient under restraint, it was wise and merciful in the blessed Author of our religion not to add any new impulse to the natural force of this prevailing propensity but, with the whole weight of his authority, altogether to discountenance every tendency to disobedience....

The mere man of nature (if such a one there ever was) has no freedom: *all his lifetime he is subject to bondage.* It is by being included within the pale of civil polity and government that he takes his rank in society as a free man.

Hence it follows that we are free, or otherwise, as we are governed by law, or by the mere arbitrary will, or wills, of any individual, or any number of individuals. And liberty is not the setting at nought and despising established laws—much less the making our own wills the rule of our own actions, or the actions of others—and not bearing (whilst yet we dictate to others) the being dictated to, even by the laws of the land; but it is the being governed by law and by law only. The Greeks described Eleutheria, or Liberty, as the daughter of Jupiter, the supreme fountain of power and law. And the Romans, in like manner, always drew her with the pretor's wand (the emblem of legal power and authority), as well as with the cap. Their idea, no doubt, was that liberty was the fair fruit of just authority and that it consisted in men's being subjected to law. The more carefully well-devised restraints of law are enacted, and the more rigorously they are executed in any country, the greater degree of civil liberty does that country enjoy. To pursue liberty, then, in a manner not warranted by law, whatever the pretense may be, is clearly to be hostile to liberty; and those persons who thus *promise you liberty are themselves the servants of corruption.*

"Civil liberty (says an excellent writer) is a severe and a restrained thing; implies, in the notion of it, authority, settled subordinations, subjection, and obedience; and is altogether as much hurt by too little of this kind, as by too much of it. And the love of liberty, when it is indeed the love of liberty, which carries us to withstand tyranny, will as much carry us to reverence authority, and to support it; for this most obvious reason, that one is as necessary to the being of liberty, as the other is destructive of it. And, therefore, the love of liberty which does not produce this effect, the love of liberty which is not a real principle of dutiful behavior toward authority, is as hypocritical as the religion which is not productive of a good life. Licentiousness is, in truth, such an excess of liberty as is of the same nature with tyranny. For, what is the difference betwixt them, but that one is lawless power exercised under pretense of authority, or by persons vested with it; the other, lawless power exercised under pretense of liberty, or without any pretense at all? A people, then, must always be less free in proportion as they are more licentious, licentiousness being not only different from liberty but directly contrary to it—a direct breach upon it."

True liberty, then, is a liberty to do everything that is right, and the being restrained from doing anything that is wrong.... The popular notion, that government was originally formed by the consent or by a compact of the people, rests on, and is supported by, another similar notion, not less popular, not better founded. This other notion is that the whole human race is born equal; and that no man is naturally inferior, or, in any respect, subjected to another; and that he can be made subject to another only by his own consent. The position is equally ill-founded and false both in its premises and conclusions. In hardly any sense that can be imagined is the position strictly true; but, as applied to the case under considera-tion, it is demonstrably not true. Man differs from man in everything that can be supposed to lead to supremacy and subjection, *as one star differs from another star in glory.* It was the purpose of the Creator that man should be social; but, without government, there can be no society; nor, without some relative inferiority and superiority, can there be any government. A musical instrument composed of chords, keys, or pipes, all perfectly equal in size and power, might as well be expected to produce harmony, as a society composed of members all perfectly equal to be productive of order and peace. If (according to the idea of the advocates of this chimerical scheme of equality) no man could rightfully *be compelled to come in* and be a member even of a government to be formed by a regular compact, but by his own individual consent, it clearly fol-lows, from the same principles, that neither could he rightfully be made or compelled to submit to the ordi-nances of any government already formed, to which he has not individually or actually consented. On the princi-ple of equality, neither his parents, nor even the vote of a majority of the society (however virtuously and honor-ably that vote might be obtained), can have any such authority over any man. Neither can it be maintained that acquiescence implies consent; because acquiescence may have been extorted from impotence or incapacity. Even an explicit consent can bind a man no longer than he choos-es to be bound. The same principle of equality that exempts him from being governed without his own con-sent clearly entitles him to recall and resume that consent whenever he sees fit; and he alone has a right to judge when and for what reasons it may be resumed.

Any attempt, therefore, to introduce this fantastic system into practice would reduce the whole business of social life to the wearisome, confused, and useless task of mankind's first expressing, and then withdrawing, their consent to an endless succession of schemes of govern-ment. Governments, though always forming, would never be completely formed; for the majority today might be the minority tomorrow, and, of course, that which is now fixed might and would be soon unfixed. Mr. Locke indeed says that, "by consenting with others to make one body-politic under government, a man puts himself under an obligation to every one of that society to submit to the determination of the majority, and to be concluded by it." For the sake of the peace of society, it is undoubtedly rea-sonable and necessary that this should be the case; but, on the principles of the system now under consideration, before Mr. Locke or any of his followers can have author-ity to say that it actually is the case, it must be stated and proved that every individual man, on entering into the social compact, did first consent, and declare his consent, to be concluded and bound in all cases by the vote of the majority. In making such a declaration, he would certain-ly consult both his interest and his duty; but at the same time he would also completely relinquish the principle of equality, and eventually subject himself to the possibility of being governed by ignorant and corrupt tyrants. Mr. Locke himself afterward disproves his own position respecting this supposed obligation to submit to the "determination of the majority," when he argues that a right of resistance still exists in the governed; for, what is resistance but a recalling and resuming the consent heretofore supposed to have been given, and in fact refus-ing to submit to the "determination of the majority"? It does not clearly appear what Mr. Locke exactly meant by what he calls "the determination of the majority"; but the only rational and practical public manner of declaring "the determination of the majority" is by law: the laws, therefore, in all countries, even in those that are despoti-cally governed, are to be regarded as the declared "deter-mination of a majority" of the members of that communi-ty; because, in such cases, even acquiescence only must be looked upon as equivalent to a declaration. A right of resistance, therefore, for which Mr. Locke contends, is incompatible with the duty of submitting to the determi-nation of "the majority," for which he also contends....

* * * * *

1. *What was a "Tory?" Was Boucher one?*

2. *Do you think arguments such as Boucher's led to the separation of church and state in the American governmental system? Why or why not?*

3. *What is Boucher's argument regarding the "will of the majority?" Compare and contrast it to the view of majority rule in the U.S. Constitution.*

6-7 An American Patriot Denounces the King, 1775

Born in England, Thomas Paine tried several careers before migrating to America and becoming a writer. Paine's pamphlet, Common Sense, *from which the following selection is taken, sold more than 100,000 copies in its early printings, emphasizing the importance of the pamphlet as a form of political communication in the colonial period. Paine's* Common Sense *advocated a new American government based on a philosophy of man's natural rights. Paine's ideas became crucial to independence movements worldwide, especially in Latin America.*

SOURCE: Thomas Paine, *Common Sense: Addressed to the Inhabitants of America* (Philadelphia: W. & T. Bradford, 1776).

Absolute governments, (tho' the disgrace of human nature) have this advantage with them, they are simple; if the people suffer, they know the head from which their suffering springs; know likewise the remedy; and are not bewildered by a variety of causes and cures. But the constitution of England is so exceedingly complex, that the nation may suffer for years together without being able to discover in which part the fault lies; some will say in one, and some in another, and every political physician will advise a different medicine.

I know it is difficult to get over local or long standing prejudices, yet if we will suffer ourselves to examine the component parts of the English constitution, we shall find them to be the base remains of two ancient tyrannies, compounded with some new Republican materials.

First.—The remains of Monarchical tyranny in the person of the King.

Secondly.—The remains of Aristocratical tyranny in the persons of the Peers.

Thirdly.—The new Republican materials, in the persons of the Commons, on whose virtue depends the freedom of England.

The two first, by being hereditary, are independent of the People; wherefore in a *constitutional sense* they contribute nothing towards the freedom of the State.

To say that the constitution of England is an *union* of three powers, reciprocally *checking* each other, is farcical; either the words have no meaning, or they are flat contradictions.

To say that the Commons is a check upon the King, presupposes two things.

First.—That the King is not to be trusted without being looked after; or in other words, that a thirst for

absolute power is the natural disease of monarchy.

Secondly.—That the Commons, by being appointed for that purpose, are either wiser or more worthy of confidence than the Crown.

But as the same constitution which gives the Commons a power to check the King by withholding the supplies, gives afterwards the King a power to check the Commons, by empowering him to reject their other bills; it again supposes that the King is wiser than those whom it has already supposed to be wiser than him. A mere absurdity!

There is something exceedingly ridiculous in the composition of Monarchy; it first excludes a man from the means of information, yet empowers him to act in cases where the highest judgment is required. The state of a king shuts him from the World, yet the business of a king requires him to know it thoroughly; wherefore the different parts, by unnaturally opposing and destroying each other, prove the whole character to be absurd and useless.

Some writers have explained the English constitution thus: the King, say they, is one, the people another; the Peers are a house in behalf of the King, the commons in behalf of the people; but this hath all the distinctions of a house divided against itself; and though the expressions be pleasantly arranged, yet when examined they appear idle and ambiguous; and it will always happen, that the nicest construction that words are capable of, when applied to the description of something which either can not exist, or is too incomprehensible to be within the compass of description, will be words of sound only, and though they may amuse the ear, they cannot inform the mind: for this explanation includes a previous question, viz. *how came the king by a power which the people are afraid to trust, and always obliged to check?* Such a power could not be the gift of a wise people, neither can any power, *which needs checking,* be from God; yet the provision which the constitution makes supposes such a power to exist.

But the provision is unequal to the task; the means either cannot or will not accomplish the end, and the whole affair is a *Felo de se:* for as the greater weight will always carry up the less, and as all the wheels of a machine are put in motion by one, it only remains to know which power in the constitution has the most weight, for that will govern: and tho' the others, or a part of them, may clog, or, as the phrase is, check the rapidity of its motion, yet so long as they cannot stop it, their endeavours will be ineffectual: The first moving power will at last have its way, and what it wants in speed is supplied by time.

That the crown is this overbearing part in the English constitution needs not be mentioned, and that it derives its whole consequence merely from being the giver of places and pensions is self-evident; wherefore, though we have been wise enough to shut and lock a door against absolute Monarchy, we at the same time have been foolish enough to put the Crown in possession of the key.

The prejudice of Englishmen, in favour of their own government, by King, Lords and Commons, arises as much or more from national pride than reason. Individuals are undoubtedly safer in England than in some other countries: but the will of the king is as much the law of the land in Britain as in France, with this difference, that instead of proceeding directly from his mouth, it is handed to the people under the formidable shape of an act of parliament. For the fate of Charles the First hath only made kings more subtle—not more just.

Wherefore, laying aside all national pride and prejudice in favour of modes and forms, the plain truth is that it is wholly owing to the constitution of the people, and not to the constitution of the government that the crown is not as oppressive in England as in Turkey.

An inquiry into the constitutional errors in the English form of government, is at this time highly necessary; for as we are never in a proper condition of doing

justice to others, while we continue under the influence of some leading partiality, so neither are we capable of doing it to ourselves while we remain lettered by any obstinate prejudice. And as a man who is attached to a prostitute is unfitted to choose or judge of a wife, so any prepossession in favour of a rotten constitution of government will disable us from discerning a good one....

* * * * *

1. We are all familiar with the three branches of American government. Review these for yourself. What are their English counterparts that Thomas Paine is addressing in this pamphlet? How does the American government grow out of this English system? How is it different?

2. What do you think was Thomas Paine's purpose in writing this essay? Does Paine represent the radical independence movement or does he council reconciliation? How would Paine's pamphlet have been used by the movement for American independence? Reconciliation?

6–8 The Colonists Declare Their Independence, 1776

Chosen by the Continental Congress to draft the Declaration of Independence, Thomas Jefferson expressed not only the views of his fellow congressmen, but his own as well. Jefferson's Declaration became an important philosophical basis for the formation of the American governmental ideal, namely that all men should have equal rights, regardless of their birth, in direct opposition to the English system of government at the time. Jefferson was a well educated lawyer, who made most of his money from his plantation, but spent his entire life in public service, becoming the third president of the United States. Jefferson also made important architectural and scientific contributions, but he is best know in this country for the following piece.

The Declaration of Independence

In Congress, July 4, 1776
THE UNANIMOUS DECLARATION
OF THE THIRTEEN UNITED STATES OF AMERICA

WHEN, in the course of human events, it becomes nec-

essary for one people to dissolve the political bands which have connected them with another, and to assume, among the powers of the earth, the separate and equal station to which the laws of nature and of nature's God entitle them, a decent respect to the opinions of mankind requires that they should declare the causes which impel them to the separation.

We hold these truths to be self-evident, that all men are created equal; that they are endowed by their Creator with certain unalienable rights; that among these, are life, liberty, and the pursuit of happiness. That, to secure these rights, governments are instituted among men, deriving their just powers from the consent of the governed; that, whenever any form of government becomes destructive of these ends, it is the right of the people to alter or to abolish it, and to institute a new government, laying its foundation on such principles, and organizing its powers in such form, as to them shall seem most likely to effect their safety and happiness. Prudence, indeed, will dictate that governments long established, should not be changed for light and transient causes; and, accordingly, all experience hath shown, that mankind are more disposed to suffer, while evils are sufferable, than to right themselves by abolishing the forms to which they are accustomed. But, when a long train of abuses and usurpations, pursuing invariably the same object, evinces a design to reduce them under absolute despotism, it is their right, it is their duty, to throw off such government and to provide new guards for their future security. Such has been the patient sufferance of these colonies, and such is now the necessity which constrains them to alter their former systems of government. The history of the present King of Great Britain is a history of repeated injuries and usurpations, all having, in direct object, the establishment of an absolute tyranny over these States. To prove this, let facts be submitted to a candid world:—

He has refused his assent to laws the most wholesome and necessary for the public good.

He has forbidden his governors to pass laws of immediate and pressing importance, unless suspended in their operation till his assent should be obtained; and, when so suspended, he has utterly neglected to attend to them.

He has refused to pass other laws for the accommodation of large districts of people, unless those people would relinquish the right of representation in the legislature; a right inestimable to them, and formidable to tyrants only.

He has called together legislative bodies at places unusual, uncomfortable, and distant from the depository of their public records, for the sole purpose of fatiguing them into compliance with his measures.

He has dissolved representative houses repeatedly, for opposing, with manly firmness, his invasions on the rights of the people.

He had refused, for a long time after such dissolutions, to cause others to be elected; whereby the legislative powers, incapable of annihilation, have returned to the people at large for their exercise; the state remaining, in the meantime, exposed to all the danger of invasion from without, and convulsions within.

He has endeavored to prevent the population of these States; for that purpose, obstructing the laws for naturalization of foreigners, refusing to pass others to encourage their migration hither, and raising the conditions of new appropriations of lands.

He has obstructed the administration of justice, by refusing his assent to laws for establishing judiciary powers.

He has made judges dependent on his will alone, for the tenure of their offices, and the amount and payment of their salaries.

He has erected a multitude of new offices, and sent hither swarms of officers to harass our people, and eat out their substance.

He has kept among us, in time of peace, standing armies, without the consent of our legislatures.

He has affected to render the military independent of, and superior to, the civil power.

He has combined, with others, to subject us to a jurisdiction foreign to our Constitution, and unacknowledged by our laws; giving his assent to their acts of pretended legislation:

For quartering large bodies of armed troops among us:

For protecting them by a mock trial, from punishment, for any murders which they should commit on the inhabitants of these States:

For cutting off our trade with all parts of the world:

For imposing taxes on us without our consent:

For depriving us, in many cases, of the benefit of trial by jury:

For transporting us beyond seas to be tried for pretended offences:

For abolishing the free system of English laws in a neighboring province, establishing therein an arbitrary government, and enlarging its boundaries, so as to render it at once an example and fit instrument for introducing the same absolute rule into these colonies:

For taking away our charters, abolishing our most valuable laws, and altering, fundamentally, the powers of our governments:

For suspending our own legislatures, and declaring themselves invested with power to legislate for us in all cases whatsoever.

He has abdicated government here, by declaring us out of his protection, and waging war against us.

He has plundered our seas, ravaged our coasts, burnt our towns, and destroyed the lives of our people.

He is, at this time, transporting large armies of foreign mercenaries to complete the works of death, desolation, and tyranny, already begun, with circumstances of cruelty and perfidy scarcely paralleled in the most barbarous ages, and totally unworthy the head of a civilized nation.

He has constrained our fellow citizens, taken captive on the high seas, to bear arms against their country, to become the executioners of their friends, and brethren, or to fall themselves by their hands.

He has excited domestic insurrections amongst us, and has endeavored to bring on the inhabitants of our frontiers, the merciless Indian savages, whose known rule of warfare is an undistinguished destruction of all ages, sexes, and conditions.

In every stage of these oppressions, we have petitioned for redress, in the most humble terms; our repeated petitions have been answered only by repeated injury. A prince, whose character is thus marked by every act which may define a tyrant, is unfit to be the ruler of a free people.

Nor have we been wanting in attention to our British brethren. We have warned them, from time to time, of attempts made by their legislature to extend an unwarrantable jurisdiction over us. We have reminded them of the circumstances of our emigration and settlement here. We have appealed to their native justice and magnanimity, and we have conjured them, by the ties of our common kindred, to disavow these usurpations, which would inevitably interrupt our connections and correspondence. They, too, have been deaf to the voice of justice and consanguinity. We must, therefore, acquiesce in the necessity which denounces our separation, and hold them, as we hold the rest of mankind, enemies in war, in peace, friends.

We, therefore, the representatives of the United States of America, in general Congress assembled, appealing to the Supreme Judge of the world for the rectitude of our intentions, do, in the name, and by the authority of the good people of these colonies, solemnly publish and declare, that these united colonies are, and of right ought to be, free and independent states: that they are absolved from all allegiance to the British Crown, and that all political connection between them and the state of Great Britain is, and ought to be, totally dissolved; and that, as free and independent states, they have full power to levy war, conclude peace, contract alliances, establish commerce, and to do all other acts and things which independent states may of right do. And, for the support of this

declaration, with a firm reliance on the protection of Divine Providence, we mutually pledge to each other our lives, our fortunes, and our sacred honor.

* * * * * *

1.   *What do you know about Thomas Jefferson and his views on the equality of men? What is the notion of equality of men as expressed in the constitution? Does it really mean all men are equal? Or does it mean that they have equal rights, that they should all have an equal chance at "life, liberty, and the pursuit of happiness?"*

2.   *What do you see as the connection between the philosophical and moral underpinnings expressed in the Declaration of Independence and the other documents you have read such as Paine's Common Sense and Henry's "Give me liberty speech?" How do they stand in opposition to Boucher's sermon?*

chapter 7

The Creation of the United States, 1776–1786

7-1 An American Patriot Tries to Stir Up the Soldiers of the American Revolution, 1776

Washington's Army spent a bleak winter camped at Valley Forge, near the confluence of Valley Creek and the Schuylkill River in Pennsylvania. Ill-equipped and underfed, largely due to political bickering and profiteering by their suppliers, thousands of soldiers deserted, reducing Washington's force from 9,000 to 6,000. The following is Thomas Paine's "These are the Times That Try Men's Souls" essay from his sixteen pamphlet series, The American Crisis, which was read to the troops in an attempt to bolster their flagging spirits.

SOURCE: Thomas Paine, *The American Crisis* (Williamsburg: Alexander Purdie, 1776).

The American Crisis

These are the times that try men's souls. The summer soldier and the sunshine patriot will, in this crisis, shrink from the service of his country; but he that stands it NOW, deserves the love and thanks of man and woman. Tyranny, like hell, is not easily conquered; yet we have this consolation with us, that the harder the conflict, the more glorious the triumph. What we obtain too cheap, we esteem too lightly; 'tis dearness only that gives every thing its value. Heaven knows how to put a proper price upon its goods; and it would be strange indeed, if so celestial an article as FREEDOM should not be highly rated. Britain, with an army to enforce her tyranny, has declared that she has a right (*not only to* TAX) but "to BIND *us in* ALL CASES WHATSOEVER," and if being *bound in that manner,* is not slavery, then is there no such a thing as slavery upon earth. Even the expression is impious, for so unlimited a power can belong only to God....

I have as little superstition in me as any man living, but my secret opinion has ever been, and still is, that God Almighty will not give up a people to military destruction, or leave them unsupportedly to perish, who have so earnestly and so repeatedly sought to avoid the calamities of war, by every decent method which wisdom could invent. Neither have I so much of the infidel in me, as to suppose that He has relinquished the government of the world, and given us up to the care of devils; and as I do not. I cannot see on what grounds the king of Britain can look up to Heaven for help against us: a common murderer, a highwayman, or a house-breaker, has as good a pretence as he.

'Tis surprising to see how rapidly a panic will sometimes run through a country. All nations and ages have been subject to them: Britain has trembled like an ague at the report of a French fleet of flat bottomed boats; and in the fourteenth century the whole English army, after ravaging the kingdom of France, was driven back like men petrified with fear; and this brave exploit was performed by a few broken forces collected and headed by a woman, Joan of Arc. Would that heaven might inspire some Jersey maid to spirit up her countrymen, and save her fair fellow sufferers from ravage and ravishment!...

...I call not upon a few, but upon all: not on *this* state or *that* state, but on *every* state; up and help us; lay your shoulders to the wheel; better have too much force than too little, when so great an object is at stake. Let it be told to the future world, that in the depth of winter, when nothing but hope and virtue could survive, that the city and the country, alarmed at one common danger, came forth to meet and to repulse it. Say not that thousands are gone, turn out your tens of thousands; throw not the burden of the day upon Providence, but "*show your faith by your works,*" that God may bless you. It matters not where you live, or what rank of life you hold, the evil or the blessing will reach you all. The far and the near, the home counties and the back, the rich and the poor, will suffer or rejoice alike. The heart that feels not now, is dead: the blood of his children will curse his cowardice, who shrinks back at a time when a little might have saved the whole, and made *them* happy. I love the man that can smile in trouble, that can gather strength from distress, and grow brave by reflection. 'Tis the business of little minds to shrink; but he whose heart is firm, and whose conscience approves his conduct, will pursue his principles unto death. My own line of reasoning is to myself as straight and clear as a ray of light. Not all the treasures of the world, so far as I believe, could have induced me to support an offensive war, for I think it murder; but if a thief breaks into my house, burns and destroys my property, and kills or threatens to kill me, or those that are in it, and to "*bind me in all cases whatsoever,*" to his absolute will, am I to suffer it? What signifies it to me, whether he who does it is a king or a common man; my countryman or not my countryman: whether it be done by an individual villain, or an army of them? If we reason to the root of things we shall find no difference; neither can any just cause be assigned why we should punish in the one case and pardon in the other. Let them call me rebel, and welcome, I feel no concern from it; but I should suffer the misery of devils, were I to make a whore of my soul by swearing allegiance to one whose character is that of a sottish, stupid, stubborn, worthless, brutish man. I conceive likewise a horrid idea in receiving mercy from a being, who at the last day shall be shrieking to the rocks and mountains to cover him, and fleeing with terror from the orphan, the widow, and the slain of America.

There are cases which cannot be overdone by language, and this is one. There are persons too who see not the full extent of the evil which threatens them, they solace themselves with hopes that the enemy, if they succeed, will be merciful. It is the madness of folly, to expect mercy from those who have refused to do justice; and even mercy, where conquest is the object, is only a trick of war; the cunning of the fox is as murderous as the violence of the wolf; and we ought to guard equally against both....

I thank God that I fear not. I see no real cause for fear. I know our situation well, and can see the way out of it....By perseverance and fortitude we have the prospect of a glorious issue; by cowardice and submission, the sad choice of a variety of evils—a ravaged country—a depopulated city—habitations without safety, and slavery without hope—our homes turned into barracks and bawdy-houses for Hessians, and a future race to provide for, whose fathers we shall doubt of. Look on this picture and weep over it! and if there yet remains one thoughtless wretch who believes it not, let him suffer it unlamented....

* * * * *

1. What is Paine calling for in this essay?

2. What does Paine use to refute the British right to govern America? How does this fit into the separation of church and state?

3. What effect do you think this essay would have had on Washington's demoralized troops when it was read to them at Valley Forge?

7-2 *A Colonial Woman Argues for Equal Rights, 1776*

Abigail Adams was one of the more prominent advocates for women's rights in colonial America. Abigail's letters to her husband, John Adams, reveal the sort of philosophical basis by which she argued for the equality of women under a new American government. The following excerpt is from a letter Abigail wrote to her husband, and his response, while John was at the Continental Congress in 1776.

SOURCE: *Charles Francis Adams, Familiar Letters of John Adams and his wife Abigail Adams (Boston: Houghton, Mifflin & Co., 1875).*

Abigail to John

...I long to hear that you have declared an independancy—and by the way in the new Code of Laws which I suppose it will be necessary for you to make I desire you would Remember the Ladies, and be more generous and favourable to them than your ancestors. Do not put such unlimited power into the hands of the Husbands. Remember all Men would be tyrants if they could. If perticular care and attention is not paid to the Laidies we are determined to foment a Rebelion, and will not hold ourselves bound by any Laws in which we have no voice, or Representation.

That your Sex are Naturally Tyrannical is a Truth so thoroughly established as to admit of no dispute, but such of you as wish to be happy willingly give up the harsh title of Master for the more tender and endearing one of Friend. Why then, not put it out of the power of the vicious and the Lawless to use us with cruelty and indignity with impunity. Men of Sense in all Ages abhor those customs which treat us only as the vassals of your Sex. Regard us then as Beings placed by providence under your protection and in immitation of the Supreem Being make use of that power only for our happiness.

John to Abigail

...As to your extraordinary Code of Laws, I cannot but laugh. We have been told that our Struggle has loosened the bands of Government every where. That Children and Apprentices were disobedient—that schools and Colleges were grown turbulent—that Indians slighted their Guardians and Negroes grew insolent to their Masters. But your Letter was the first Intimation that another Tribe more numerous and powerfull than all the rest were grown discontented.—This is rather too coarse a Compliment but you are so saucy, I wont blot it out.

Depend upon it, We know better than to repeal our Masculine systems. Altho they are in full Force, you know they are little more than Theory. We dare not exert our Power in its full Latitude. We are obliged to go fair, and softly, and in Practice you know We are the subjects. We have only the Name of Masters, and rather than give up this, which would compleatly subject Us to the Despotism of the Petticoat, I hope General Washington, and all our brave Heroes would fight. I am sure every good Politician would plot, as long as he would against Despotism. Empire, Monarchy, Aristocracy, Oligarchy, or Ochlocracy.—A fine Story indeed. I begin to think the Ministry as deep as they are wicked. After stirring up Tories, Landjobbers, Trimmers, Bigots, Canadians, Indians, Negroes, Hanoverians, Hessians, Russians, Irish Roman Catholicks, Scotch Renegadoes, at last they have stimulated the [Ladies] to demand Priviledges and threaten to rebel.

* * * * * *

1. *What do you think of Abigail Adams's assertions in her letter? What do you think of John Adams's reply to his wife's letter? Is he making fun of her?*

2. *What do these pair of letters tell us about attitudes towards women in colonial America?*

7-3   A Free African American Petitions the Government for Emancipation of All Slaves, 1777

Prince Hall was a black slave freed in 1770. Making a living for himself working with leather and as a caterer, Hall went on to found the first Black Mason's Lodge, an organization that still plays a prominent role in many black communities. Hall was active in organizing African American citizens and trying to free slaves the rest of his life. The following is Hall's petition to the Massachusetts legislature for the freedom of slaves within the state.

SOURCE: *Massachusetts Historical Collections, Fifth Series, No. 3* (Boston, 1788)

To the Honorable Council & House of
Representatives for the State of Massachusetts-Bay in General Court assembled January 13th 1777.

The Petition of a great number of Negroes who are detained in a state of Slavery in the Bowels of a free & Christian Country Humbly Shewing

That your Petitioners apprehend that they have, in common with all other Men, a natural & unalienable right to that freedom, which the great Parent of the Universe hath bestowed equally on all Mankind, & which they have never forfeited by any compact or agreement whatever—But they were unjustly dragged, by the cruel hand of Power, from their dearest friends, & some of them even torn from the embraces of their tender Parents. From a populous, pleasant and plentiful Country—& in Violation of the Laws of Nature & of Nation & in defiance of all the tender feelings of humanity, brought hither to be sold like Beasts of Burden, & like them condemned to slavery for Life—Among a People professing the mild Religion of Jesus—A People not insensible of the sweets of rational freedom—Nor without spirit to resent the unjust endeav-

ours of others to reduce them to a State of Bondage & Subjection—Your Honors need not be informed that a Life of Slavery, like that of your petitioners, deprived of every social privilege, of every thing requisite to render Life even tolerable, is far worse than Non-Existence—In imitation of the laudable example of the good People of these States, your Petitioners have long & patiently waited the event of Petition after Petition by them presented to the legislative Body of this State, & can not but with grief reflect that their success has been but too similar—They can not but express their astonishment, that it has never been considered, that every principle from which America has acted in the course of her unhappy difficulties with Great-Britain, pleads stronger than a thousand arguments in favor of your Petitioners. They therefore humbly beseech your Honors, to give this Petition its due weight & consideration, & cause an Act of the Legislature to be passed, whereby they may be restored to the enjoyment of that freedom which is the natural right of all Men—& their Children (who were born in this Land of Liberty) may not be held as Slaves after they arrive at the age of twenty one years—So may the Inhabitants of this State (no longer chargeable with the inconsistency of acting, themselves, the part which they condemn & oppose in others) be prospered in their present glorious struggles for Liberty; & have those blessings secured to them by Heaven, of which benevolent minds can not wish to deprive their fellow Men.

And your Petitioners, as in Duty Bound shall ever pray.

Lancaster Hill	
Peter Bess	Negroes Petition to the Hon'ble
Brister Slenten	Gen Assembly—Mass.
Prince Hall	March 18
Jack Purpont *his mark*	Judge Sargeant
	M. Balton
Nero Suneto *his mark*	M. Appleton
	Coll. Brooks
Newport Symner *his mark*	M. Stony
	W. Lowell
Job Lock	Matter Atlege
	W. Davis

1. What does Prince Hall's petition reveal about slavery in 18th century Massachusetts?

2. How does Hall foreshadow the abolitionist movement?

3. Compare the impact of this document to the narrative of Venture Smith or Olaudah Equiano which you have read in previous chapters. Which writings had the greater impact on you?

* * * * *

7-4 A Common Soldier Tells About the Battle of Yorktown, 1781

Joseph Plumb Martin was just an ordinary soldier in the American revolutionary army, but his book, A Narrative of Some of the Adventures, Dangers and Sufferings of a Revolutionary Soldier, provides us with a valuable record of the colonial soldier's life. Martin makes clear that many soldiers were more concerned with their next meal than notions of political philosophy; Martin's account also illustrates some of the hardships endured by the ill-equipped and under supplied soldiers under Washington's command. The following excerpt from Martin's book is about the battle of Yorktown.

SOURCE: Joseph Plumb Martin, *Private Yankee Doodle*, edited by George F. Scheer, (Boston: Little, Brown. 1962).

...We now began to make preparations for laying close siege to the enemy. We had holed him and nothing remained but to dig him out. Accordingly, after taking every precaution to prevent his escape, [we] settled our guards, provided fascines and gabions, made platforms for the batteries, to be laid down when needed, brought on our battering pieces, ammunition, &c. On the fifth of October we began to put our plans into execution.

One-third part of all the troops were put in requisition to be employed in opening the trenches. We had holed of our Sappers and Miners were ordered out this night to assist the engineers in laying out the works. It was a very dark and rainy night. However, we repaired to the place and began by following the engineers and laying laths of pine wood end-to-end upon the line marked out by the officers for the trenches. We had not proceeded far in this business before the engineers ordered us to desist and remain where we were and be sure not to straggle a foot from the spot while they were absent from us. In a few minutes after their departure, there came a man alone to us, having on a surtout, as we conjectured, it being exceeding dark, and inquired for the engineers. We now began to be a little jealous for our safety, being alone and without arms, and within forty rods of the British trenches. The stranger inquired what troops we were, talked familiarly with us a few minutes, when, being informed

which way the officers had gone, he went off in the same direction, after strictly charging us, in case we should be taken prisoners, not to discover to the enemy what troops we were. We were obliged to him for his kind advice, but we considered ourselves as standing in no great need of it, for we knew as well as he did that Sappers and Miners were allowed no quarters, at least, are entitled to none, by the laws of warfare, and of course should take care, if taken, and the enemy did not find us out, not to betray our own secret.

In a short time the engineers returned and the aforementioned stranger with them. They discoursed together some time when, by the officers often calling him "Your Excellency," we discovered that it was General Washington. Had we dared, we might have cautioned him for exposing himself too carelessly to danger at such a time, and doubtless he would have taken it in good part if we had. But nothing ill happened to either him or ourselves.

It coming on to rain hard, we were ordered back to our tents, and nothing more was done that night. The next night, which was the sixth of October, the same men were ordered to the lines that had been there the night before. We this night completed laying out the works. The troops of the line were there ready with entrenching tools and began to entrench, after General Washington had struck a few blows with a pickax, a mere ceremony, that it might be said "General Washington with his own hands first broke ground at the siege of Yorktown." The ground was sandy and soft, and the men employed that night eat no "idle bread" (and I question if they eat any other), so that by daylight they had covered themselves from danger from the enemy's shot, who, it appeared, never mistrusted that we were so near them the whole night, their attention being directed to another quarter. Our people had sent to the western side of this marsh a detachment to make a number of fires, by which, and our men often passing before the fires, the British were led to imagine that we were about some secret mischief there, and consequently directed their whole fire to that quarter, while we were entrenching literally under their noses.

As soon as it was day they perceived their mistake and began to fire where they ought to have done sooner. They brought out a fieldpiece or two without their trenches, and discharged several shots at the men who were at work erecting a bomb battery, but their shot had no effect and they soon gave it over. They had a large bulldog and every time they fired he would follow their shots across our trenches. Our officers wished to catch him and oblige him to carry a message from them into the town to his masters, but he looked too formidable for any of us to encounter.

I do not remember, exactly, the number of days we were employed before we got our batteries in readiness to open upon the enemy, but think it was not more than two or three. The French, who were upon our left, had completed their batteries a few hours before us, but were not allowed to discharge their pieces till the American batteries were ready. Our commanding battery was on the near bank of the [York] river and contained ten heavy guns; the next was a bomb battery of three large mortars; and so on through the whole line. The whole number, American and French, was ninety-two cannon, mortars and howitzers. Our flagstaff was in the ten-gun battery, upon the right of the whole. I was in the trenches the day that the batteries were to be opened. All were upon the tiptoe of expectation and impatience to see the signal given to open the whole line of batteries, which was to be the hoisting of the American flag in the ten-gun battery. About noon the much-wished-for signal went up. I confess I felt a secret pride swell my heart when I saw the "star-spangled banner" waving majestically in the very faces of our implacable adversaries. It appeared like an omen of success to our enterprise, and so it proved in reality. A simultaneous discharge of all the guns in the line followed, the French troops accompanying it with "Huzza for the Americans!" It was said that the first shell sent from our batteries entered an elegant house formerly owned or occupied by the Secretary of State under the British government, and burned directly over a table surrounded by a large party of British officers at dinner, killing and wounding a number of them. This was a warm day to the British.

The siege was carted on warmly for several days, when most of the guns in the enemy's works were silenced. We now began our second parallel, about halfway between our works and theirs. There were two strong redoubts held by the British, on their left. It was necessary for us to possess those redoubts before we could complete our trenches. One afternoon, I, with the rest of our corps that had been on duty in the trenches the night but one before, were ordered to the lines. I mistrusted something extraordinary, serious or comical, was going forward, but what I could not easily conjecture.

We arrived at the trenches a little before sunset. I saw several officers fixing bayonets on long staves. I then concluded we were about to make a general assault upon the enemy's works, but before dark I was informed of the whole plan, which was to storm the redoubts, the one by the Americans and the other by the French. The Sappers and Miners were furnished with axes and were to proceed in front and cut a passage for the troops through the abatis, which are composed of the tops of trees, the small branches cut off with a slanting stroke which renders them as sharp as spikes. These trees are then laid at a small distance from the trench or ditch, pointing outwards, and the butts fastened to the ground in such a manner that they cannot be removed by those on the outside of them. It is almost impossible to get through them. Through these we were to cut a passage before we or the other assailants could enter.

At dark the detachment was formed and advanced beyond the trenches and lay down on the ground to await the signal for advancing to the attack, which was to be three shells from a certain battery near where we were lying. All the batteries in our line were silent, and we lay anxiously waiting for the signal. The two brilliant planets, Jupiter and Venus, were in close contact in the western hemisphere, the same direction that the signal was to be made in. When I happened to cast my eyes to that quarter, which was often, and I caught a glance of them, I was ready to spring on my feet, thinking they were the signal for starting. Our watchword was "Rochambeau," the commander of the French forces' name, a good watchword, for being pronounced Ro-sham-bow, it sounded, when pronounced quick, like rush-on-boys.

We had not lain here before the expected signal was given, for us and the French, who were to storm the other redoubt, by the three shells with their fiery trains mounting the air in quick succession. The word up, up, was then reiterated through the detachment. We immediately moved silently on toward the redoubt we were to attack, with unloaded muskets. Just as we arrived at the abatis, the enemy discovered us and directly opened a sharp fire upon us. We were now at a place where many of our large shells had burst in the ground, making holes sufficient to bury an ox in. The men, having their eyes fixed upon what was transacting before them, were every now and then falling into these holes. I thought the British were killing us off at a great rate. At length, one of the holes happening to pick me up, I found out the mystery of the huge slaughter.

As soon as the firing began, our people began to cry, "The fort's our own!" and it was "Rush on boys." The Sappers and Miners soon cleared a passage for the infantry, who entered it rapidly. Our Miners were ordered not to enter the fort, but there was no stopping them. "We will go," said they. "Then go to the d-l," said the commanding officer of our corps, "if you will." I could not pass at the entrance we had made, it was so crowded. I therefore forced a passage at a place where I saw our shot had cut away some of the abatis; several others entered at the same place. While passing, a man at my side received a ball in his head and fell under my feet, crying out bitterly.

While crossing the trench, the enemy threw hand grenades (small shells) into it. They were so thick that I at first thought them cartridge papers on fire, but was soon undeceived by their cracking. As I mounted the breast-work, I met an old associate hitching himself down into the trench. I knew him by the light of the enemy's musketry, it was so vivid. The fort was taken and all quiet in a very short time. Immediately after the firing ceased, I went out to see what had become of my wounded friend and the other that fell in the passage. They were both dead. In the heat of the action I saw a British soldier jump over the walls of the fort next the river and go down the bank, which was almost perpendicular and twenty or thirty feet high. When he came to the beach he made off for the town, and if he did not make good use of his legs I never saw a man that did.

All that were in the action of storming the redoubt were exempted from further duty that night. We laid down upon the ground and rested the remainder of the night as well as a constant discharge of grape and canister shot would permit us to do, while those who were on duty for the day completed the second parallel by including the captured redoubts within it. We returned to camp early in the morning, all safe and sound, except one of our lieutenants, who had received a slight wound on the top of the shoulder by a musket shot. Seven or eight men belonging to the infantry were killed, and a number wounded....

We were on duty in the trenches twenty-four hours, and forty-eight hours in camp. The invalids did the camp duty, and we had nothing else to do but to attend morning and evening roll calls and recreate ourselves as we pleased the rest of the time, till we were called upon to take our turns on duty in the trenches again. The greatest inconvenience we felt was the want of good water, there being none near our camp but nasty frog ponds where all the horses in the neighborhood were watered, and we were forced to wade through the water in the skins of the ponds, thick with mud and filth, to get at water in any wise fit for use, and that full of frogs. All the springs about the country, although they looked well, tasted like copperas water or like water that had been standing in iron or copper vessels....

After we had finished our second line of trenches there was but little firing on either side. After Lord Cornwallis had failed to get off, upon the seventeenth day of October (a rather unlucky day for the British) he requested a cessation of hostilities for, I think, twenty-four hours, when commissioners from both armies met at a house between the lines to agree upon articles of capitulation. We waited with anxiety the termination of the armistice and as the time drew nearer our anxiety increased. The time at length arrived—it passed, and all remained quiet. And now we concluded that we had obtained what we had taken so much pains for, for which we had encountered so many dangers, and had so anxiously wished. Before night we were informed that the British had surrendered and that the siege was ended....

* * * * *

1. What does Joseph Plumb Martin's account tell you about the plight of the colonial soldier? How does this compare to the abstract notions of freedom and liberty for which the war was fought?

2. What was the battle of Yorktown? What was its significance in the revolutionary war?

SOURCE: B. B. Thacher, Indian Biography (New York: Harper & Brothers, 1834).

7-5   A Delaware Chief Speaks to the British, 1781

The Delaware Indians were largely an agricultural people who had occupied the Delaware Basin in the 17th and 18th centuries. The Delaware had long established a slash and burn farming, whereby the land belonged to whoever was on it for as long as they needed it. Having made a treaty with William Penn in 1682, the Pennsylvania government later cheated the Delaware out of half a million acres in 1737 with the Walker Purchase. Many of the Delaware fought with the French in the French and Indian war and later sided with the British in the American Revolution. The following is a speech by Captain Pipe, a Delaware chief to the British at Detroit.

Speech to the British at a Council in Detroit, November, 1781

Captain Pipe (Delaware)

"Father!"—he began; and here he paused, turned round to the audience with a most sarcastic look, and then proceeded in a lower tone, as addressing them—"I have said father, though indeed I do not know why I should call him so—I have never known any father but the French—I have considered the English only as brothers. But as this name is imposed upon us, I shall make use of it and say—"

"Father"—fixing his eyes again on the Commandant—

"Some time ago you put a war-hatchet into my hands, saying, 'take this weapon and try it on the heads of my enemies, the Long-Knives, and let me know afterwards if it was sharp and good.'"

"Father!—At the time when you gave me this weapon, I had neither cause nor wish to go to war against a foe who had done me no injury. But you say you are my father—and call me your child—and in obedience to you I received the hatchet. I knew that if I did not obey you, you would withhold from me the necessaries of life, which I could procure nowhere but here.

"Father! You may perhaps think me a fool, for risking my life at your bidding—and that in a cause in which I have no prospect of gaining any thing. For it is your cause, and not mine—you have raised a quarrel among yourselves—and you ought to fight it out—It is *your* concern to fight the Long-Knives—You should not compel your children, the Indians, to expose themselves to danger for your sake.

"Father!—Many lives have already been lost on *your account*—The tribes have suffered, and been weakened—Children have lost parents and brothers—Wives have lost husbands—It is not known how many more may perish before *your* war will be at an end.

"Father!—I have said, you may perhaps think me a fool, for thus thoughtlessly rushing on your enemy! Do not believe this, Father: Think not that I want sense to convince me, that although you now pretend to keep up a perpetual enmity to the Long-Knives, you may, before long, conclude a peace with them.

"Father! You say you love your children, the Indians.—This you have often told them; and indeed it is your interest to say so to them, that you may have them at your service.

"But, Father! Who of us can believe that you can love a people of a different colour from your own, better than those who have a white skin, like yourselves?

"Father! Pay attention to what I am going to say.

While you, Father, are setting me on your enemy, much in the same manner as a hunter sets his dog on the game; while I am in the act of rushing on that enemy of yours, with the bloody destructive weapon you gave me, I may, perchance, happen to look back to the place from whence you started me, and what shall I see? Perhaps I may see my father shaking hands with the Long-Knives; yes, with those very people he now calls his enemies. I may *then* see him laugh at my folly for having obeyed his orders; and yet I am now risking my life at his command!—Father! keep what I have said in remembrance.

"Now, Father! here is what has been done with the hatchet you gave me" [handing the stick with the scalps on it]. "I have done with the hatchet what you ordered me to do, and found it sharp. Nevertheless, I did not do all that I might have done. No, I did not. My heart failed within me. I felt compassion for your enemy. Innocence had no part in your quarrels; therefore I distinguished—I spared. I took some live flesh, which, while I was bringing to you, I spied one of your large canoes, on which I put it for you. In a few days you will receive this flesh, and find that the skin is of the same color with your own.

"Father! I hope you will not destroy what I have saved. You, Father, have the means of preserving that which would perish with us from want. The warrior is poor, and his cabin is always empty; but your house, Father, is always full."

* * * * *

1. *What does Captain Pipe's speech tell you about the Delaware Indian's role in the Revolutionary War?*

2. *How does the Delaware's view of war seem to vary from that of the British as revealed in Pipe's speech? What about differing views of land ownership?*

SOURCE: Henry Steele Commager, *Documents of American History* (NewYork: Appleton-Century-Crofts, 1948).

7-6   *Britian Signs Treaty Ending Revolutionary War, 1783*

The Treaty of Paris, 1783, brought an official end to the American Revolutionary War. It is sometimes erroneously called the Treaty of Versailles. The treaty was signed by Britain, America, France, Spain, and the Netherlands, all of whom had a stake in America. The treaty provided for fishing rights, land boundaries, as well as free passage to all on the Mississippi. The treaty is reproduced here.

Treaty of Peace with Great Britain
September 3, 1783

...ART, 1.—His Britannic Majesty acknowledges the said United States, viz. New Hampshire, Massachusetts Bay, Rhode Island, and Providence Plantations, Connecticut, New York, New Jersey, Pennsylvania, Delaware, Maryland, Virginia, North Carolina, South Carolina, and Georgia, to be free, sovereign and independent States;

that he treats with them as such, and for himself, his heirs and successors, relinquishes all claims to the Government, proprietary and territorial rights of the same, and every part thereof.

ART. II.—And that all disputes which might arise in future, on the subject of the boundaries of the said United States may be prevented, it is hereby agreed and declared, that the following are, and shall be their boundaries, viz.: From the northwest angle of Nova Scotia, viz.: that angle which is formed by a line drawn due north from the source of Saint Croix River to the Highlands; along the said Highlands which divide those rivers that empty themselves into the river St. Lawrence, from those which fall into the Atlantic Ocean, to the northwesternmost head of Connecticut River; thence down along the middle of that river, to the forty-fifth degree of north latitude; thence, by a line due west on said latitude, until it strikes the river Iroquois or Cataraquy; thence along the middle of said river into Lake Ontario, through the middle of said lake until it strikes the communication by water between that lake and Lake Erie; thence along the middle of said communication into Lake Erie, through the middle of said lake until it arrives at the water communication between that lake and Lake Huron; thence along the middle of said water communication into the Lake Huron; thence through the middle of said lake to the water communication between that lake and Lake Superior; thence through Lake Superior northward of the Isles Royal and Phelipeaux, to the Long Lake; thence through the middle of said Long Lake, and the water communication between it and the Lake of the Woods, to the said Lake of the Woods; thence through the said lake to the most northwestern point thereof, and from thence on a due west course to the river Mississippi; thence by a line to be drawn along the middle of the said river Mississippi until it shall intersect the northernmost part of the thirty-first degree of north latitude. South, by a line to be drawn due east from the determination of the line last mentioned, in the latitude of thirty-one degrees north of the Equator, to the middle of the river Appalachicola or Catahouche; thence along the middle thereof to its junction with the Flint River; thence straight to the head of St. Mary's River; and thence down along the middle of St. Mary's River to the Atlantic Ocean. East, by a line to be drawn along the middle of the river St. Croix, from its mouth in the Bay of Fundy to its source, and from its source directly north to the aforesaid Highlands, which divide the rivers that fall into the Atlantic Ocean from those which fall into the river St. Lawrence; comprehending all islands within twenty leagues of any part of the shores of the United States, and lying between lines to be drawn due east from the points where the aforesaid boundaries between Nova Scotia on the one part, and East Florida on the other, shall respectively touch the Bay of Fundy and the Atlantic Ocean; excepting such islands as now are, or heretofore have been, within the limits of the said province of Nova Scotia.

ART. III.—It is agreed that the people of the United States shall continue to enjoy unmolested the right to take fish of every kind on the Grand Bank, and on all the other banks of Newfoundland; also in the Gulph of Saint Lawrence, and at all other places in the sea where the inhabitants of both countries used at any time heretofore to fish. And also that the inhabitants of the United States shall have liberty to take fish of every kind on such part of the coast of Newfoundland as British fishermen shall use (but not to dry or cure the same on that island) and also on the coasts, bays and creeks of all other of His Britannic Majesty's dominions in America; and that the American fishermen shall have liberty to dry and cure fish in any of the unsettled bays, harbours and creeks of Nova Scotia, Magdalen Islands, and Labrador, so long as the same shall remain unsettled; but so soon as the same or either of them shall be settled, it shall not be lawful for the said fishermen to dry or cure fish at such settlements, without a previous agreement for that purpose with the inhabitants, proprietors or possessors of the ground.

ART. IV.—It is agreed that creditors on either side shall meet with no lawful impediment to the recovery of the full value in sterling money, of all *bona fide* debts heretofore contracted.

ART. V.—It is agreed that the Congress shall earnestly recommend it to the legislatures of the respective States, to provide for the restitution of all estates, rights and properties which have been confiscated, belonging to real British subjects, and also of the estates, rights and properties of persons resident in districts in the possession of His Majesty's arms, and who have not borne arms against the said United States. And that persons of any other description shall have free liberty to go to any part or parts of any of the thirteen United States, and therein to remain twelve months, unmolested in their endeavours to obtain the restitution of such of their estates, rights and properties as may have been confiscated; and that Congress shall also earnestly recommend to the several States a reconsideration and revision of all acts or laws regarding the premises, so as to render the said laws or acts perfectly consistent, not only with justice and equity, but with that spirit of conciliation which, on the return of the blessings of peace, should universally prevail. And that Congress shall also earnestly recommend to the several States, that the estates, rights and properties of such last mentioned persons, shall be restored to them, they refunding to any persons who may be now in possession, the *bona fide* price (where any has been given) which such persons may have paid on purchasing any of the said lands, rights or properties, since the confiscation. And it is agreed, that all persons who have any interest in confiscated lands, either by debts, marriage settlements or otherwise, shall meet with no lawful impediment in the prosecution of their just rights.

ART. VI.—That there shall be no future confiscations made, nor any prosecutions commenced against any person or persons for, or by reason of the part which he or they may have taken in the present war; and that no person shall, on that account, suffer any future loss or damage, either in his person, liberty or property; and that those who may be in confinement on such charges, at the time of the ratification of the treaty in America, shall be immediately set at liberty, and the prosecutions so commenced be discontinued.

ART. VII.—There shall be a firm and perpetual peace between His Britannic Majesty and the said States, and between the subjects of the one and the citizens of the other, wherefore all hostilities, both by sea and land, shall from henceforth cease; All prisoners on both sides shall be set at liberty, and His Britannic Majesty shall, with all convenient speed, and without causing any destruction, or carrying away any negroes or other property of the American inhabitants, withdraw all his armies, garrisons and fleets from the said United States, and from every post, place and harbour within the same; leaving in all fortifications the American artillery that may be therein; And shall also order and cause all archives, records, deeds and papers, belonging to any of the said States, or their citizens, which, in the course of the war, may have fallen into the hands of his officers, to be forthwith restored and deliver'd to the proper States and persons to whom they belong.

ART. VIII.—The navigation of the river Mississippi, from its source to the ocean, shall forever remain free and open to the subjects of Great Britain, and the citizens of the United States.

ART. IX.—In case it should so happen that any place or territory belonging to Great Britain or to the United States, should have been conquer'd by the arms of either from the other, before the arrival of the said provisional articles in America, it is agreed, that the same shall be restored without difficulty, and without requiring any compensation....

* * * * *

1.   *What does the Treaty of Paris accede to the Americans? The British?*

2.   *Review an historical atlas. What were the physical boundaries of America in 1783?*

3.   *Why do you think fishing rights were such an important fixture in the treaty?*

7-7 *Congress Decides What to do with the Western Lands, 1785*

Congress passed the Land Ordinance of 1785 as a means of administering the Old Northwest Territory. They hoped the sale of the western lands would bring money into a cash starved government. Several factors, including corruption, prevented this from coming to pass. The ordinance set aside a certain amount of land in each township for public schools as well as retaining land for public universities, forming the foundation for public education in America. The entire law is attached.

SOURCE: Henry Steele Commager, *Documents of American History* (New York: Appleton-Century-Crofts, 1948).

Land Ordinance of 1785
May 20, 1785

An Ordinance for ascertaining the mode of disposing of Lands in the Western Territory.

BE it ordained by the United States in Congress assembled,

that the territory ceded by individual States to the United States, which has been purchased of the Indian inhabitants, shall be disposed of in the following manner:

A surveyor from each state shall be appointed by Congress or a Committee of the States, who shall take an oath for the faithful discharge of his duty, before the Geographer of the United States....

The Surveyors, as they are respectively qualified shall proceed to divide the said territory into townships of six miles square, by lines running due north and south, and others crossing these at right angles, as near as may be, unless where the boundaries of the late Indian purchases may render the same impracticable....

The first line, running due north and south as aforesaid, shall begin on the river Ohio, at a point that shall be found to be due north from the western termination of a line, which has been run as the southern boundary of the State of Pennsylvania; and the first line, running east and west, shall begin at the same point, and shall extend throughout the whole territory. Provided, that nothing herein shall be construed, as fixing the western boundary of the State of Pennsylvania. The geographer shall designate the townships, or fractional parts of townships, by numbers progressively from south to north; always beginning each range with No. 1; and the ranges shall he distinguished by their progressive numbers to the westward. The first range, extending from the Ohio to the lake Erie, being marked No. 1. The Geographer shall personally attend to the running of the first east and west line; and shall take the latitude of the extremes of the first north and south line, and of the mouths of the principal rivers.

The lines shall be measured with a chain; shall be plainly marked by chaps on the trees, and exactly described on a plat; whereon shall be noted by the surveyor, at their proper distances, all mines, salt-springs, salt-licks and mill-seats, that shall come to his knowledge, and all water-courses, mountains and other remarkable and permanent things, over and near which such lines shall pass, and also the quality of the lands.

The plats of the townships respectively, shall be marked by subdivisions into lots of one mile square, or 640 acres, in the same direction as the external lines, and numbered from 1 to 36; always beginning the succeeding range of the lots with the number next to that with which the preceding one concluded....

...And the geographer shall make...returns, from time to time, of every seven ranges as they may be surveyed. The Secretary of War shall have recourse thereto, and shall take by lot therefrom, a number of townships...as will be equal to one seventh pan of the whole of such seven ranges for the use of the late Continental army....

The board of treasury shall transmit a copy of the original plats, previously noting thereon the township and fractional parts of townships, which shall have fallen to the several states, by the distribution aforesaid, to the commissioners of the loan-office of the several states, who, after giving notice...shall proceed to sell the townships or fractional parts of townships, at public vendue, in the following manner, viz.: The township or fractional part of a township No. 1, in the first range, shall be sold entire; and No. 2, in the same range, by lots; and thus in alternate order through the whole of the first range...provided, that none of the lands, within the said territory, be sold under the price of one dollar the acre, to be paid in specie, or loan-office certificates, reduced to specie value, by the scale of depreciation, or certificates of liquidated debts of the United States, including interest, besides the expense of the survey and other charges thereon, which are hereby rated at thirty six dollars the township...on failure of which payment, the said lands shall again be offered for sale.

There shall be reserved for the United States out of every township the four lots, being numbered 8, 11, 26, 29, and out of every fractional part of a township, so many lots of the same numbers as shall be found thereon, for future sale. There shall be reserved the lot No. 16, of every township, for the maintenance of public schools within the said township; also one-third part of all gold, silver, lead and copper mines, to be sold, or otherwise disposed of as Congress shall hereafter direct....

And Whereas Congress...stipulated grants of land to certain officers and soldiers of the late Continental army...for complying with such engagements, Be it ordained, That the secretary of war...determine who are the objects of the above resolutions and engagements...and cause the townships, or fractional parts of townships, hereinbefore reserved for the use of the late Continental army, to be drawn for in such manner as he shall deem expedient....

1. How does the Land Ordinance of 1785 come to affect the American landscape, particularly the built environment?

* * * * * *

2. How does this ordinance form the monetary, land, and tax base for public education in America?

SOURCE: Francis Newton Thorpe, *The Federal and State Constitutions* (Washington, D.C.: Government Printing Office, 1909).

7-8 Territorial Governments are Established by Congress, 1787

With the Northwest Ordinance of 1787, Congress instituted what was to be the territorial model of government for the western United States until 1862. The Northwest Ordinance created a procedure for governing the territories and bringing them into statehood. Most importantly, the ordinance established the equality of new states with the original thirteen. The following is the act in its entirety.

The Northwest Ordinance

Be it ordained by the authority aforesaid, That there shall be appointed from time to time by Congress, a governor, whose commission shall continue in force for the term of three years, unless sooner revoked by Congress; he shall reside in the district, and have a freehold estate therein in 1,000 acres of land, while in the exercise of his office.

There shall be appointed from time to time by Congress, a secretary, whose commission shall continue in force for four years unless sooner revoked; he shall reside in the district, and have a freehold estate therein in 500 acres of land, while in the exercise of his office. It shall be his duty to keep and preserve the acts and laws passed by the legislature, and the public records of the district, and the proceedings of the governor in his executive department, and transmit authentic copies of such acts and proceedings, every six months, to the Secretary of Congress: There shall also be appointed a court to consist of three judges, any two of whom to form a court, who shall have a common law jurisdiction, and reside in the district, and have each therein a freehold estate in 500 acres of land while in the exercise of their offices; and their commissions shall continue in force during good behavior.

The governor and judges, or a majority of them, shall adopt and publish in the district such laws of the original States, criminal and civil, as may be necessary and best suited to the circumstances of the district, and report them to Congress from time to time: which laws shall be in force in the district until the organization of the General Assembly therein, unless disapproved of by Congress; but afterwards the Legislature shall have authority to alter them as they shall think fit.

The governor, for the time being, shall be commander-in-chief of the militia, appoint and commission all officers in the same below the rank of general officers; all general officers shall be appointed and commissioned by Congress.

Previous to the organization of the general assembly, the governor shall appoint such magistrates and other civil officers in each county or township, as he shall find necessary for the preservation of the peace and good order in the same: After the general assembly shall be organized, the powers and duties of the magistrates and other civil officers shall be regulated and defined by the said assembly; but all magistrates and other civil officers not herein otherwise directed, shall, during the continuance of this temporary government, be appointed by the governor.

For the prevention of crimes and injuries, the laws to be adopted or made shall have force in all parts of the district, and for the execution of process, criminal and civil, the governor shall make proper divisions thereof; and he shall proceed from time to time as circumstances may require, to lay out the parts of the district in which the Indian titles shall have been extinguished, into counties and townships, subject however to such alterations as may thereafter be made by the legislature.

So soon as there shall be five thousand free male inhabitants of full age in the district, upon giving proof thereof to the governor, they shall receive authority, with time and place, to elect representatives from their counties or townships to represent them in the general assem-

bly: *Provided*. That, for every five hundred free male inhabitants, there shall be one representative, and so on progressively with the number of free male inhabitants shall the right of representation increase, until the number of representatives shall amount to twenty-five; after which, the number and proportion of representatives shall be regulated by the legislature: *Provided*. That no person be eligible or qualified to act as a representative unless he shall have been a citizen of one of the United States three years, and be a resident in the district, or unless he shall have resided in the district three years; and, in either case, shall likewise hold in his own right, in fee simple, two hundred acres of land within the same: *Provided, also, That* a freehold in fifty acres of land in the district, having been a citizen of one of the states, and being resident in the district, or the like freehold and two years residence in the district, shall be necessary to qualify a man as an elector of a representative.

The representatives thus elected, shall serve for the term of two years; and, in case of the death of a representative, or removal from office, the governor shall issue a writ to the county or township for which he was a member, to elect another in his stead, to serve for the residue of the term.

The general assembly or legislature shall consist of the governor, legislative council, and a house of representatives. The Legislative Council shall consist of five members, to continue in office five years, unless sooner removed by Congress; any three of whom to be a quorum: and the members of the Council shall be nominated and appointed in the following manner, to wit: As soon as representatives shall be elected, the Governor shall appoint a time and place for them to meet together; and, when met, they shall nominate ten persons, residents in the district, and each possessed of a freehold in five hundred acres of land, and return their names to Congress; five of whom Congress shall appoint and commission to serve as aforesaid; and, whenever a vacancy shall happen in the council, by death or removal from office, the house of representatives shall nominate two persons, qualified as aforesaid, for each vacancy, and return their names to Congress; one of whom Congress shall appoint and commission for the residue of the term. And every five years, four months at least before the expiration of the time of service of the members of council, the said house shall nominate ten persons, qualified as aforesaid, and return their names to Congress; five of whom Congress shall appoint and commission to serve as members of the council five years, unless sooner removed. And the governor, legislative council, and house of representatives, shall have authority to make laws in all cases, for the good government of the district, not repugnant to the principles and articles in this ordinance established and declared. And all bills, having passed by a majority in the house, and by a majority in the council, shall be referred to the governor for his assent; but no bill, or legislative act whatever, shall be of any force without his assent. The governor shall have power to convene, prorogue, and dissolve the general assembly, when, in his opinion, it shall be expedient.

The governor, judges, legislative council, secretary, and such other officers as Congress shall appoint in the district, shall take an oath or affirmation of fidelity and of office; the governor before the president of congress, and all other officers before the Governor. As soon as a legislature shall be formed in the district, the council and house assembled in one room, shall have authority, by joint ballot, to elect a delegate to Congress, who shall have a seat in Congress, with a right of debating but not of voting during this temporary government.

And, for extending the fundamental principles of civil and religious liberty, which form the basis whereon these republics, their laws and constitutions are erected; to fix and establish those principles as the basis of all laws, constitutions, and governments, which forever hereafter shall be formed in the said territory: to provide also for the establishment of States, and permanent government therein, and for their admission to a share in the federal councils on an equal footing with the original States, at as early periods as may be consistent with the general interest:

It is hereby ordained and declared by the authority aforesaid, That the following articles shall be considered as articles of compact between the original States and the people and States in the said territory and forever remain unalterable, unless by common consent, to wit:

ART. I. No person, demeaning himself in a peaceable and orderly manner, shall ever be molested on account of his mode of worship or religious sentiments, in the said territory.

ART. 2. The inhabitants of the said territory shall always be entitled to the benefits of the writ of *habeas corpus*, and of the trial by jury; of a proportionate representation of the people in the legislature; and of judicial proceedings according to the course of the common law. All persons shall be bailable, unless for capital offences, where the proof shall be evident or the presumption great. All fines shall be moderate; and no cruel or unusual punishments shall be inflicted. No man shall be deprived of his liberty or property, but by the judgment of his peers or the law of the land; and, should the public exigencies make it necessary, for the common preservation, to take any person's property, or to demand his particular services, full compensation shall be made for the same. And, in the just preservation of rights and property, it is understood and declared, that no law ought ever to be made, or have force in the said territory, that shall, in any manner whatever, interfere with or affect private contracts or engagements, *bona fide*, and without fraud, previously formed.

ART. 3. Religion, morality, and knowledge, being necessary to good government and the happiness of mankind, schools and the means of education shall forever be encouraged. The utmost good faith shall always be observed towards the Indians; their lands and property shall never be taken from them without their consent; and, in their property, rights, and liberty, they shall never be invaded or disturbed, unless in just and lawful wars authorized by Congress; but laws founded in justice and humanity, shall from time to time be made for preventing wrongs being done to them, and for preserving peace and friendship with them....

ART. 5. There shall be formed in the said territory, not less than three nor more than five States.... And, whenever any of the said States shall have sixty thousand free inhabitants therein, such State shall be admitted, by its delegates, into the Congress of the United States, on an equal footing with the original States in all respects whatever, and shall be at liberty to form a permanent constitution and State government: *Provided*, the constitution and government so to be formed, shall be republican, and in conformity to the principles contained in these articles; and, so far as it can be consistent with the general interest of the confederacy, such admission shall be allowed at an earlier period, and when there may be a less number of free inhabitants in the State than sixty thousand.

ART. 6. There shall be neither slavery nor involuntary servitude in the said territory, otherwise than in the punishment of crimes whereof the party shall have been duly convicted: *Provided, always*, That any person escaping into the same, from whom labor or service is lawfully claimed in any one of the original States, such fugitive may be lawfully reclaimed and conveyed to the person claiming his or her labor or service as aforesaid.

* * * * * *

1. *What were the geographical boundaries of the Northwest Territory in 1787? Consult an historical atlas.*

2. *How did the ownership of property as a qualification for suffrage affect the political process? How did it affect women? Poor people? People of color? How long did this regulation continue in America?*

3. *How is the legislative system of the Northwest Ordinance different from today's legislative bodies?*

⭐

7–9   Massachusetts Farmers Take Up Arms in Revolt Against Taxes, 1786

The years of 1785–1786 saw economic depression in America. Massachusetts farmers were angered by high taxes and declining farm prices. The farmers also disagreed with a law which required payment of all debts in specie, which was difficult to obtain. Finally, as their properties were being auctioned off to cover debts, the farmers revolted. Led by Daniel Shays, an officer in the revolutionary war, the farmers disrupted court proceedings and attacked the armory at Springfield, but were thwarted. Shays' Rebellion, as it came to be known, was short lived and the legislature passed several measures to relieve the farmer's economic pressure, though it was not everything the Shaysites had hoped for. The following letters by Daniel Gray and Thomas Grover outline many of the problems surrounding the Rebellion and express public sentiment at the time.

SOURCE: Henry Steele Commager, *Documents of American History* (New York: Appleton-Century-Crofts, 1948).

1. An ADDRESS to the People of the several towns in the county of Hampshire, now at arms.

GENTLEMEN,

We have thought proper to inform you of some of the principal causes of the late risings of the people, and also of their present movement, viz.

1st. The present expensive mode of collecting debts, which by reason of the great scarcity of cash, will of necessity fill our gaols with unhappy debtors; and thereby a reputable body of people rendered incapable of being serviceable either to themselves or the community.

2d. The monies raised by impost and excise being appropriated to discharge the interest of governmental securities, and not the foreign debt, when these securities are not subject to taxation.

3d. A suspension of the writ of Habeas Corpus, by which those persons who have stepped forth to assert and maintain the rights of the people, are liable to be taken and conveyed even to the most distant part of the Commonwealth, and thereby subjected to an unjust punishment.

4th. The unlimited power granted to Justices of the Peace and Sheriffs, Deputy Sheriffs, and Constables, by the Riot Act, indemnifying them to the prosecution thereof; when perhaps, wholly actuated from a principle of revenge, hatred, and envy.

Furthermore, Be assured, that this body, now at

arms, despise the idea of being instigated by British emissaries, which is so strenuously propagated by the enemies of our liberties: And also wish the most proper and speedy measures may be taken, to discharge both our foreign and domestick debt.

Per Order,

DANIEL GRAY, Chairman
of the Committee.

2. To the Printer of the Hampshire Herald.
SIR,

It has some how or other fallen to my lot to be employed in a more conspicuous manner than some others of my fellow citizens, in stepping forth on defence of the rights and privileges of the people, more especially of the county of Hampshire.

Therefore, upon the desire of the people now at arms, I take this method to publish to the world of mankind in general, particularly the people of this Commonwealth, some of the principal grievances we complain of,…

In the first place, I must refer you to a draught of grievances drawn up by a committee of the people, now at arms, under the signature of Daniel Gray, chairman, which is heartily approved of; some others also are here added, viz.

1st. The General Court, for certain obvious reasons, must be removed out of the town of Boston.

2d. A revision of the constitution is absolutely necessary.

3d. All kinds of governmental securities, now on interest, that have been bought of the original owners for two shillings, and the highest for six shillings and eight pence on the pound, and have received more interest than the principal cost the speculator who purchased them—that if justice was done, we verily believe, nay positively know, it would save this Commonwealth thousands of pounds.

4th. Let the lands belonging to this Commonwealth, at the eastward, be sold at the best advantage to pay the remainder of our domestick debt.

5th. Let the monies arising from impost and excise be appropriated to discharge the foreign debt.

6th. Let that act, passed by the General Court last June by a small majority of only seven, called the Supplementary Act, for twenty-five years to come, be repealed.

7th. The total abolition of the Inferiour Court of Common Pleas and General Sessions of the Peace.

8th. Deputy Sheriffs totally set aside, as a useless set of officers in the community; and Constables who are really necessary, be empowered to do the duty, by which means a large swarm of lawyers will be banished from their wonted haunts, who have been more damage to the people at large, especially the common farmers, than the savage beasts of prey.

To this I boldly sign my proper name, as a hearty wellwisher to the real rights of the people.

THOMAS GROVER

Worcester, December 7, 1786.

* * * * * *

1. *Do you think Shays' Rebellion helped to strengthen the centralization of the federal government in America? Why or why not?*

2. *What were the economic problems as outlined in Gray's letter? How do they compare to our current economic problems, especially for farmers?*

chapter 8

The United States of North America, 1787–1800

8–1 Constitutional Convention Delegate Blasts Federal Government, 1787

Like many delegates to the Constitutional Convention in Philadelphia in 1787, Luther Martin was concerned over states losing their individual rights and the federal government taking too strong a centralist role. A lawyer, and member of the Continental Congress, Martin later refused to sign the Constitution because he thought it gave to much power to the federal level. Having successfully defended many famous cases, including Aaron Burr for treason and Samuel Chase for impeachment, Martin died in poverty. The following passage illustrates his opposition to a strong central government.

SOURCE: Morton Borden, ed., *The Antifederalist Papers* (East Lansing, Mich.: Michigan State University Press, 1965), pp. 200–202.

THE favorers of monarchy, and those who wished the total abolition of state governments—well knowing that a government founded on truly federal principles... would be destructive of their views; and knowing they were too weak in numbers openly to bring forward their system; conscious also that the people of America would reject it if proposed to them—joined their interest with that party who wished a system giving particular states the power and influence over the others, procuring in return mutual sacrifices from them, in giving the government great and undefined powers as to its legislative and executive; well knowing that, by departing from a federal system they paved the way for their favorite object—the destruction of the state governments, and the introduction of monarchy....

The thirteen states are thirteen distinct, political individual existences, as to each other; the federal government is, or ought to be, a government over these thirteen political, individual existences, which form the members of that government; and as the largest state is only a single individual of the government, it ought to have only one vote; the smallest state, being also an individual member of the government, ought also to have one vote. By giving one state, or one or two states, more votes

than the others, the others thereby are enslaved to such state or states, having the greater number of votes.

In a federal government over states equally free, sovereign, and independent, every state ought to have an equal share in making the federal laws or regulations, and in carrying them into execution, neither of which is the case in this system, but the reverse, the states not having an equal voice in the legislature, nor in the appointment of the executive, the judges, and the officers of government. In this whole system there is but one federal feature—the appointment of the senators by the states, and the equality of suffrage in that branch; but this feature is only federal in appearance. For six years the senators are rendered totally and absolutely independent of their state. During that time they may join in measures ruinous and destructive to their states, even such as should totally annihilate their state governments; and their state cannot recall them, nor exercise any control over them.

Viewing it [the Constitution] as a national government, calculated and designed to abolish the state governments—it was opposed for the following reasons: It was said that this continent was too extensive for one national government, which should have sufficient power and energy to persuade and hold in obedience, all its parts, consistently with the enjoyment and preservation of liberty. It was insisted that governments of a republican nature are those best calculated to preserve the freedom and happiness of the citizen—that governments of this kind are only calculated for a territory but small in extent—that the only method by which an extensive continent like America could be united together, consistently with the principles of freedom, must be by having a number of strong and energetic state governments.

By the power to lay and collect taxes the government has the power to lay what indirect taxes they please; afterwards to impose on the people direct taxes to what amount they choose, and thus to sluice them at every vein as long as they have a drop of blood, without any control or restraint; while all the officers for collecting those taxes are to be appointed by the federal government, and are not accountable to the states.

I voted against the section putting it out of the power of a state to pass any law impairing the obligation of contracts. I considered that there might be times of such great public distress as should render it the duty of a government in some measure to interfere, by passing laws totally or partially stopping courts of justice; or authorizing the debtor to pay by installments, or by delivering up his property to his creditor at a reasonable valuation. The times have been such as to render regulations of this kind necessary to prevent the wealthy creditor and the moneyed man from totally destroying the poor and industrious debtor.

[From] the best judgment I could form while in

Convention, I then was, and yet remained, decidedly of the opinion that ambition and interest had so far blinded the understanding of some of the principal framers of the Constitution that, while they were labouring to erect a fabrick by which they themselves might be exalted and benefited, they were rendered insensible to the sacrifice of the freedom and happiness of the states and their citizens, which must, inevitably be the consequence....

I most sacredly believe their object is the total abolition and destruction of all state governments, and the erection on their ruins of one great and extensive empire, calculated to aggrandize and elevate its rulers and chief officers far above the common herd of mankind, to enrich them with wealth, and to encircle them with honours and glory, and which according to my judgment on the maturest reflection, must inevitably be attended with the most humiliating and abject slavery of their fellow citizens, by the sweat of whose brows, and by the toil of whose bodies, it can only be effected.

* * * * * *

1.   *What is Luther Martin arguing against in this essay? Why would he oppose a strong centralized government?*

2.   *How centralized is our government today compared to the federal authority that Martin is opposing?*

⭐

8-2   *The Father of the Constitution Defends Republicanism, 1787*

James Madison is best known as the "Father of the Constitution." More than a simple governing document, the Constitution was intended as a moral and philosophical statement as well. Madison had a keen sense of governmental structure and how to frame these ideals in a workable statute that would maintain its intended efficacy. Madison wrote a series of Federalist Papers which help to explain the reasoning and rationale behind the Constitution. The following selection reveals the intricate thought and purpose that went into drafting the Constitution.

SOURCE: *The Federalist* (Washington, D.C.: J. Gideon, 1818).

The Federalist No. 10 (Madison)

Among the numerous advantages promised by a well constructed Union, none deserves to be more accurately developed than its tendency to break and control the violence of faction. The friend of popular governments, never finds himself so much alarmed for their character and fate, as when he contemplates their propensity to this dangerous vice. He will not fail therefore to set a due value on any plan which, without violating the principles to which he is attached, provides a proper cure for it. The instability, injustice and confusion introduced into the public councils, have in truth been the mortal diseases under which popular governments have every where perished; as they continue to be the favorite and fruitful topics from which the adversaries to liberty derive their most specious declamations. The valuable improvements made by the American Constitutions on the popular models, both ancient and modern, cannot certainly be too much admired; but it would be an unwarrantable partiality, to contend that they have as effectually obviated the danger on this side as was wished and expected. Complaints are every where heard from our most considerate and virtuous citizens, usually the friends of public and private faith, and of public and personal liberty; that our governments are too unstable; that the public good is disregarded in the conflicts of rival parties; and that measures are too often decided, not according to the rules of justice, and the rights of the minor party; but by the superior force of an interested and over-bearing majority. However anxiously we may wish that these complaints had no foundation, the evidence of known facts will not permit us to deny that they are in some degree true.... These must be chiefly, if not wholly, effects of the unsteadiness and injustice, with which a factious spirit has tainted our public administrations.

By a faction I understand a number of citizens, whether amounting to a majority or minority of the whole, who are united and actuated by some common impulse of passion, or of interest, adverse to the rights of other citizens, or to the permanent and aggregate interests of the community.

There are two methods of curing the mischiefs of faction: the one, by removing its causes; the other, by controlling its effects.

There are again two methods of removing the causes of faction: the one by destroying the liberty which is essential to its existence; the other, by giving to every citizen the same opinions, the same passions, and the same interests....

The two great points of difference between a Democracy and a Republic are, first, the delegation of the Government, in the latter, to a small number of citizens elected by the rest: secondly, the greater number of citizens, and greater sphere of country, over which the latter may be extended.

The effect of the first difference is, on the one hand to refine and enlarge the public views, by passing them through the medium of a chosen body of citizens, whose wisdom may best discern the true interest of their country, and whose patriotism and love of justice, will be least likely to sacrifice it to temporary or partial considerations. Under such a regulation, it may well happen that the public voice pronounced by the representatives of the people, will be more consonant to the public good, than if pronounced by the people themselves convened for the purpose. On the other hand, the effect may be inverted. Men of factious tempers, of local prejudices, or of sinister designs, may by intrigue, by corruption or by other means, first obtain the suffrages, and then betray the interests of the people. The question resulting is, whether small or extensive Republics are most favorable to the election of proper guardians of the public weal; and it is clearly decided in favor of the latter by two obvious considerations.

In the first place it is to be remarked that however small the Republic may be, the Representatives must be raised to a certain number, in order to guard against the cabals of a few; and that however large it may be, they must be limited to a certain number, in order to guard against the confusion of a multitude. Hence the number of Representatives in the two cases, not being in proportion to that of the Constituents, and being proportionally greatest in the small Republic, it follows, that if the proportion of fit characters, be not less, in the large than in the small Republic, the former will present a greater option, and consequently a greater probability of a fit choice.

In the next place, as each Representative will be chosen by a greater number of citizens in the large than in the small Republic, it will be more difficult for unworthy candidates to practise with success the vicious arts, by which elections are too often carried; and the suffrages of the people being more free, will be more likely to centre on men who possess the most attractive merit, and the most diffusive and established characters.

It must be confessed, that in this, as in most other cases, there is a mean, on both sides of which inconveniences will be found to lie. By enlarging too much the number of electors, you render the representative too little acquainted with all their local circumstances and lesser interests; as by reducing it too much, you render him unduly attached to these, and too little fit to comprehend and pursue great and national objects. The Federal Constitution forms a happy combination in this respect; the great and aggregate interests being referred to the national, the local and particular, to the state legislatures.

The other point of difference is, the greater number of citizens and extent of territory which may be brought within the compass of Republican, than of Democratic Government; and it is this circumstance principally which renders factious combinations less to be dreaded in the former, than in the latter. The smaller the society, the fewer probably will be the distinct parties and interests composing it; the fewer the distinct parties and interests, the more frequently will a majority be found of the same party; and the smaller the number of individuals composing a majority, and the smaller the compass within which they are placed, the more easily will they concert and execute their plans of oppression. Extend the sphere, and you take in a greater variety of parties and interests; you make it less probable that a majority of the whole will have a common motive to invade the rights of other citizens; or if such a common motive exists, it will be more difficult for all who feel it to discover their own strength, and to act in unison with each other. Besides other impediments, it may be remarked, that where there is a consciousness of unjust or dishonorable purposes, a communication is always checked by distrust, in proportion to the number whose concurrence is necessary....

The influence of factious leaders may kindle a flame within their particular States, but will be unable to spread a general conflagration through the other States: a religious sect, may degenerate into a political faction in a part of the Confederacy; but the variety of sects dispersed over the entire face of it, must secure the national Councils against any danger from that source: a rage for paper money, for an abolition of debts, for an equal division of property, or for any other improper or wicked project, will be less apt to pervade the whole body of the Union, than a particular member of it; in the same proportion as such a malady is more likely to taint a particular county or district, than an entire State.

In the extent and proper structure of the Union, therefore, we behold a Republican remedy for the diseases most incident to Republican Government. And according to the degree of pleasure and pride, we feel in being Republicans, ought to be our zeal in cherishing the spirit, and supporting the character of Federalists.

****

1. *What specific constitutional questions is James Madison addressing in this essay? What sorts of larger governmental philosophical issues is he grappling with?*

2. *Explain for yourself the differences between a Republic and Democracy. Do you agree with Madison's argument for a republican governmental structure?*

8-3 Seneca Chiefs' Petition Washington for Return of Their Land, 1790

The Seneca, a part of the Six Nations League of the Iroquois, had allied with the British during the revolutionary war. As part of westward expansion, and also possibly as retribution, much of their land was taken after the war. The following letter, by three Seneca chiefs, Big Tree, Corn-Planter, and Half-Town, implores the great father, George Washington, to return their land to them.

SOURCE: Samuel Gardner Drake, *Biography and History of the Indians of North America* (Boston: O.L. Perkins, 1834).

Letter to President Washington, 1790
Big Tree, Cornplanter, and Half-Town (Seneca)

Father: The voice of the Seneca nations speaks to you; the great counsellor, in whose heart the wise men of all the *thirteen fires* [13 U.S.] have placed their wisdom. It may be very small in your ears, and we, therefore, entreat you to hearken with attention; for we are able to speak of things which are to us very great.

When your army entered the country of the Six Nations, we called you the *town destroyer*; to this day, when your name is heard, our women look behind them and turn pale, and our children cling close to the necks of their mothers.

When our chiefs returned from Fort Stanwix, and laid before our council what had been done there, our nation was surprised to hear how great a country you had compelled them to give up to you, without your paying to us any thing for it. Every one said, that your hearts were yet swelled with resentment against us for what had happened during the war, but that one day you would consider it with more kindness. We asked each other, *What have we done to deserve such severe chastisement?*

Father: when you kindled your 13 fires separately, the wise men assembled at them told us that you were all brothers; the children of one great father, who regarded the red people as his children. They called us brothers, and invited us to his protection. They told us that he resided beyond the great water where the sun first rises; and that he was a king whose power no people could resist, and that his goodness was as bright as the sun. We accepted the invitation, and promised to obey him. What the Seneca nation promises, they faithfully perform. When you refused obedience to that king, he commanded us to assist his beloved men in making you sober. In obeying him, we did no more than yourselves had led us to promise. We were deceived; but your people teaching us to confide in that king, had helped to deceive us; and we now appeal to your breast, *Is all the blame ours?*

Father: when we saw that we had been deceived, and heard the invitation which you gave us to draw near to the fire you had kindled, and talk with you concerning peace, we made haste towards it. You told us you could crush us to nothing; and you demanded from us a great country, as the price of that peace which you had offered to us: *as if our want of strength had destroyed our rights.* Our chiefs had felt your power, and were unable to contend against you, and they therefore gave up that country. What they agreed to has bound our nation, but your anger against us must by this time be cooled, and although our strength is not increased, nor your power become less, we ask you to consider calmly—*Were the terms dictated to us by your commissioners reasonable and just?...*

Father: you have said that we were in your hand, and that by closing it you could crush us to nothing. Are you determined to crush us? If you are, tell us so; that those of our nation who have become your children, and have determined to die so, may know what to do. In this case, one chief has said, he would ask you to put him out of his pain. Another, who will not think of dying by the hand of his father, or his brother, has said he will retire to the Chataughque, eat of the fatal root, and sleep with his fathers in peace.

All the land we have been speaking of belonged to the Six Nations. No part of it ever belonged to the king of England, and he could not give it to you.

Hear us once more. At Fort Stanwix we agreed to deliver up those of our people who should do you any wrong, and that you might try them and punish them according to your law. We delivered up two men accordingly. But instead of trying them according to your law, the lowest of your people took them from your magistrate, and put them immediately to death. It is just to punish the murder with death; but the Senecas will not deliver up their people to men who disregard the treaties of their own nation.

* * * * * *

1. What role did the Seneca play in the revolutionary war? Why was their land taken? How much of it was taken?

2. What do you think of Big Tree, Corn-Planter, and Half-Town's Letter? How effective do you think it was? What does it tell you about the Seneca's condition following the Revolution?

8–4   The Secretary of State and the Secretary of the Treasury Battle about the Constitution, 1791

Political and personal enemies, Thomas Jefferson and Alexander Hamilton were often at odds, both philosophically and on a more practical plane. Hamilton favored the formation of a national bank, and Jefferson opposed it. Both men claimed constitutional grounds as the foundation of their arguments. Jefferson favored a more literal interpretation of the constitution, while Hamilton argued for a broader reading of implied powers. The following excerpts outline some of their respective arguments.

SOURCE: Melvin J. Wrofsky, ed., *Documents of American Constitutional and Legal History* (Philadelphia: Temple University Press, 1989).

Thomas Jefferson

I consider the foundation of the Constitution as laid on this ground that 'all powers not delegated to the U.S. by the Constitution, not prohibited by it to the states, are reserved to the states or to the people.' To take a single step beyond the boundaries thus specially drawn around the powers of Congress, is to take possession of a boundless field of power, no longer susceptible of any definition.

The incorporation of a bank, and other powers assumed by this bill have not, in my opinion, been delegated to the U.S. by the Constitution.

I.   They are not among the powers specially enumerated, for these are

1.   A power to lay taxes for the purpose of paying the debts of the U.S. But no debt is paid by this bill, nor any tax laid. Were it a bill to raise money, it's origination in the Senate would condemn it by the constitution.

2.   'to borrow money.' But this bill neither borrows money, nor ensures the borrowing it. The proprietors of the bank will be just as free as any other money holders, to lend or not to lend their money to the public. The operation proposed in the bill, first to lend them two millions, and then borrow them back again, cannot change the nature of the latter act, which will still be a payment, and not a loan, call it by what name you please.

3.   'to regulate commerce with foreign nations, and among the states, and with the Indian tribes.' To erect a bank, and to regulate commerce, are very different acts. He who erects a bank creates a subject of commerce in its bills: so does he who makes a bushel of wheat, or digs a dollar out of the mines. Yet neither of these persons regulates commerce thereby. To erect a thing which may be bought and sold, is not to prescribe regulations for buying and selling. Besides; if this was an exercise of the power of regulating commerce, it would be void, as extending as much to the internal commerce of every state, as to its external. For the power given to Congress by the Constitution, does not extend to the internal regulation of the commerce of a state (that is to say of the commerce between citizen and citizen) which remains exclusively with its own legislature; but to its external commerce only, that is to say, its commerce with another state, or with foreign nations or with the Indian tribes. Accordingly the bill does not propose the measure as a 'regulation of trade,' but as 'productive of considerable advantage to trade.'

Still less are these powers covered by any other of the special enumerations.

II.   Nor are they within either of the general phrases, which are the two following.

1.   'To lay taxes to provide for the general welfare of the U.S.' that is to say 'to lay taxes for the purpose of providing for the general welfare'. For the laying of taxes is the power and the general welfare the purpose for which the power is to be exercised. They are not to lay taxes ad libitum for any purpose they please; but only to pay the debts or provide for the welfare of the Union. In like manner they are not to do anything they please to provide for the general welfare, but only to lay taxes for that purpose....

2.   The second general phrase is 'to make all laws necessary and proper for carrying into execution the enumerated powers.' But they can all be carried into execution without a bank. A bank therefore is not necessary, and consequently not authorised by this phrase...

...It must be added however, that unless the President's mind on a view of every thing which is urged for and against this bill, is tolerably clear that it is unauthorised by the constitution, if the pro and the con hang so even as to balance his judgment, a just respect for the wisdom of the legislature would naturally decide the balance in favour of their opinion. It is chiefly for cases where they are clearly misled by error, ambition, or interest, that the constitution has placed a check in the negative of the President.

Alexander Hamilton

The Secretary of the Treasury having perused with attention the papers containing the opinions of the Secretary of State and the Attorney-General, concerning the constitutionality of the bill for establishing a national bank, proceeds, according to the order of the President, to submit the reasons which have induced him to entertain a different opinion....

In entering upon the argument, it ought to be premised that the objections of the Secretary of State and the Attorney-General are founded on a general denial of the authority of the United States to erect corporations. The latter, indeed, expressly admits, that if there be anything in the bill which is not warranted by the Constitution, it is the clause of incorporation.

Now it appears to the Secretary of the Treasury that this *general principle* is *inherent* in the very *definition* of government, and *essential* to every step of the progress to be made by that of the United States, namely: That every power vested in a government is in its nature *sovereign*, and includes, by *force of the term*, a right to employ all the *means* requisite and fairly applicable to the attainment of the *ends* of such power, and which are not precluded by restrictions and exceptions specified in the Constitution, or not immoral, or not contrary to the *essential ends* of political society.

This principle, in its application to government in general, would be admitted as an axiom; and it will be incumbent upon those who may incline to deny it, to prove a distinction, and to show that a rule which, in the general system of things, is essential to the preservation of the social order, is inapplicable to the United States.

The circumstance that the powers of sovereignty are in this country divided between the National and State governments, does not afford the distinction required. It does not follow from this, that each of the portion of *powers* delegated to the one or to the other, is not sovereign with *regard to its proper objects*. It will only *follow* from it, that each has sovereign power as to *certain things*, and not as to *"other things."* To deny that the Government of the United States has sovereign power, as to its declared purposes and trusts, because its power does not extend to all cases, would be equally to deny that the State governments have sovereign power in any case, because their power does not extend to every case. The tenth section of the first article of the Constitution exhibits a long list of very important things which they may not do. And thus the United States would furnish the singular spectacle of a *political society* without government, without government.

If it would be necessary to bring proof to a proposition so clear, as that which affirms that the powers of the Federal Government, as to *its objects*, were sovereign, there is a clause of its Constitution which would be decisive. It is that which declares that the Constitution, and the laws of the United States made in pursuance of it, and all treaties made, or which shall be made, under their authority, shall be the *supreme law of the land*. The power which can create the *supreme law of the land* in *any case*, is doubtless *sovereign* as to such case.

This general and indisputable principle puts at once an end to the *abstract* question, whether the United States have power to erect a corporation; that is to say, to give a *legal* or *artificial capacity* to one or more persons, distinct from the *natural*. For it is unquestionably incident to *sovereign power* to erect corporations, and consequently to *that* of the United States, in *relation* to the *objects* intrusted to the management of the government. The difference is this: where the authority of the government is general, it can create corporations in *all cases*; where it is confined to certain branches of legislation, it can create corporations *only* in those cases....

...A hope is entertained that it has, by this time, been made to appear, to the satisfaction of the President, that a bank has a natural relation to the power of collecting taxes—to that of regulating trade—to that of providing for the common defence—and that, as the bill under consideration contemplates the government in the light in of a joint proprietor of the stock of the bank, it brings the case within the provision of the clause of the Constitution which immediately respects the property of the United States.

Under a conviction that such a relation subsists, the Secretary of the Treasury, with all deference, conceives that it will result as a necessary consequence from the position, that all the specified powers of government are sovereign, as to the proper objects; that the incorporation of a bank is a constitutional measure; and that the objections taken to the bill, in this respect, are ill-founded.

* * * * * *

1. What constitutional issues are at stake in this essay? What are Hamilton and Jefferson arguing about? What is Jefferson's central argument? What is Hamilton's rebuttal?

2. Why would a central federal bank have been needed at the time? Why was it necessary and desirable? What would the arguments against its existence be?

8-5   Farmers Protest the New Whiskey Tax, 1790

The powers of the central federal government were put to the test in 1790 when a new tax was placed on whiskey. The farmers of western Pennsylvania made whiskey out of their excess corn as it was easier to transport than corn and readily traded, used as currency in many areas. The tax brought a refusal from the farmers and talk of seceding from the United States. At the behest of Alexander Hamilton, President Washington sent 13,000 troops to the area in 1794, at which point the rebellion dissipated. The rebellion was an important step in the ascendancy of the federal government as the supreme power in America. The following is the farmer's petition to the Pennsylvania General Assembly.

SOURCE: *Pennsylvania Archives,* First Series, II (1855).

To the Honorable the Representatives of the Freemen of Pennsylvania, in General Assembly met.

The Petition of the Inhabitants of Westmoreland County—Humbly Sheweth.

That your petitioners are greatly aggrieved by the present operation of an Excise Law, passed on the 19th day of March, 1783, by which we are made subject to a duty of four pence per gallon on all spirituous liquors distilled and consumed amongst us from the productions of our farms, even for private and domestic uses. It is generally believed that excise laws, in all nations and at all periods, have given greater disgust, and created greater tumults amongst the people, than any other species of taxation ever adopted for the raising of revenue; we do not hesitate to declare, that this law has already been productive of all those and many other evils, and that it is the only one passed since our revolution that has been treated with general disapprobation, and reflected upon with universal abhorrence and detestation: and such has been the resentment of many of our fellow citizens, which we are sorry to have occasion to confess, that they have, upon several occasions, proceeded to unwarrantable lengths in opposing its operations.

We do not deny that we are as strongly rooted in the habits, and as much addicted to the use of spirituous liquors as our brethren in the eastern part of the state: having emigrated from among them, we cannot be condemned for carrying their customs along with us. But independent of habit, we find that the moderate use of spirits is essentially necessary in several branches of our agriculture.

In this new country, labourers are exceedingly

scarce, and their hire excessively high, and we find that liquor proves a necessary means of engaging their service and securing their continuance through the several important seasons of the year, when the pressing calls of labour must be attended to, let the conditions be what they may. For these reasons we have found it absolutely necessary to introduce a number of small distilleries into our settlements, and in every circle of twenty or thirty neighbours, one of these are generally erected, merely for the accommodation of such neighbourhood and without any commercial views whatever. The proprietor thereof receives the grain (rye only) from the people, and returns the stipulated quantity of liquor, after retaining the toll agreed upon. In this manner we are supplied with this necessary article, much upon the same conditions that our mills furnish us with flour; and why we should be made subject to a duty for drinking our grain more than eating it, seems a matter of astonishment to every reflecting mind.

These distilleries, small and insignificant as they are, have always been classed among the first objects of taxation, and have been highly estimated in the valuation of property. This, we conceive, might fully suffice, without extending revenue to the mean and humble manufacture produced by them.

With as much propriety a duty might be laid on the rye we feed to our horses; the bread we eat ourselves, or any other article manufactured from the products of our own farms.

Our remote situation from the channels of commerce, has long ago prohibited the use of all imported liquors amongst us, and as we are aiming at independence in our manner of living, we have neither the abilities or inclination to aspire to their use. We freely resign them to our eastern neighbours, whom Providence has placed under the meridian rays of commercial affluence, and whose local situation confer on them many enjoyments which nature has denied to us; and whilst they are revelling in the luxuries of the most bountiful foreign climes, we are perfectly content with the humble produce of our own farms, and it is our only wish to be permitted to enjoy them in freedom.

We beg that we may not be considered as unfriendly to the supporting of a government, which we so highly approve, as that of Pennsylvania. We have too exalted ideas of the blessings deriving from it, to ever suffer such thoughts to harbour in our breasts. The payment of the state tax has always been submitted to with cheerfulness, and paid to the utmost of our abilities. And here we cannot forbear expressing our astonishment at the suspension of a tax so just and equitable in its nature, whilst the excise complained of is continued to be exacted with rigor. We have reason to believe that the produce of this excise will amount to the same, or perhaps exceed that of our state tax, and if we had any security for the net produce thereof getting into the treasury, it would afford some consolation; but from the flagrant delinquency which we have experienced from many of our revenue officers in this county, as well as from a want of confidence in the present excise officer and his security, our fears are greatly awakened upon the present occasion.

We find that the security required by law from this county, is fixed at the low rate of one hundred and fifty pounds only, when it is probable that the sum to be collected, may amount to one thousand. On this circumstance we shall only remark, that there are few men in the present day, who would not readily forfeit and pay a penalty of one hundred and fifty pounds, provided they could put a thousand in their pockets by so doing.

It is with pleasure that we reflect upon the many instances of liberality and general encouragement which the legislature, as well as many respectable societies, have given through the course of some years past, for rendering ourselves still more independent of foreign nations, by promoting and improving every branch of our own manufacture; we therefore flatter ourselves that the present assembly will no longer suffer a law to remain in existence which is so evidently calculated to counteract the virtuous designs of those respectable bodies, and which proves so universally obnoxious to the people of this western world....

* * * * * *

1. *What do the farmers claim to be their reason for opposing the Whiskey Tax in their petition? How valid do you think their argument is?*

2. *How did the Whiskey Rebellion help establish the strength of the central federal government? How would it have weakened it?*

8–6 *A Frenchman Comments on the American Character, 1782*

Michel-Guillaume John De Crevecoeur was a French essayist and farmer who lived in America before, during, and after the American Revolution. De Crevecoeur originally supported the British loyalists in the early days of the war, but became good friends with Franklin, Jefferson, and other prominent American leaders, serving as the French consul. De Crevecoeur wrote a series of essays called Letters From An American Farmer, which were published in 1782. De Crevecoeur's insight to the American character is revealed in the following essay.

SOURCE: J. Hector St., John De Crevecoeur: Letters from an American Farmer (Philadelphia: Mathew Carey, 1793).

Letters from an American Farmer

I wish I could be acquainted with the feelings and thoughts which must agitate the heart and present themselves to the mind of an enlightened Englishman, when he first lands on this continent. He must greatly rejoice that he lived at a time to see this fair country discovered and settled; he must necessarily feel a share of national pride, when he views the chain of settlements which embellishes these extended shores. When he says to himself, this is the work of my countrymen, who, when convulsed by factions, afflicted by a variety of miseries and wants, restless and impatient, took refuge here. They brought along with them their national genius, to which they principally owe what liberty they enjoy, and what substance they possess. Here he sees the industry of his native country displayed in a new manner, and traces in their works the embryos of all the arts, sciences, and ingenuity which flourish in Europe. Here he beholds fair cities, substantial villages, extensive fields, an immense country filled with decent houses, good roads, orchards, meadows, and bridges, where an hundred years ago all was wild, woody, and uncultivated! What a train of pleasing ideas this fair spectacle must suggest; it is a prospect which must inspire a good citizen with the most heartfelt pleasure. The difficulty consists in the manner of viewing so extensive a scene. He is arrived on a new continent; a modern society offers itself to his contemplation, different from what he had hitherto seen. It is not composed, as in Europe, of great lords who possess everything, and of a herd of people who have nothing. Here are no aristocratical families, no courts, no kings, no bishops, no ecclesiastical dominion, no invisible power giving to a few a very visible one; no great manufacturers employing thousands, no great refinements of luxury. The rich and the poor are not so far removed from each other as they are in Europe. Some few towns excepted, we are all tillers of the earth, from Nova Scotia to West Florida. We are a people of cultivators, scattered over an immense territory, communicating with each other by means of good roads and navigable rivers, united by the silken bands of mild government, all respecting the laws, without dreading their power, because they are equitable. We are all animated with the spirit of an industry which is unfettered and unrestrained, because each person works for himself. If he travels through our rural districts he views not the hostile castle, and the haughty mansion, contrasted with the clay-built hut and miserable cabin, where cattle and men help to keep each other warm, and dwell in meanness, smoke, and indigence. A pleasing uniformity of decent competence appears throughout our habitations. The meanest of our log-houses is a dry and comfortable habitation. Lawyer or merchant are the fairest titles our towns afford; that of a farmer is the only appellation of the rural inhabitants of our country. It must take some time ere he can reconcile himself to our dictionary, which is but short in words of dignity, and names of honour. There, on a Sunday, he sees a congregation of respectable farmers and their wives, all clad in neat homespun, well mounted, or riding in their own humble waggons. There is not among them an esquire, saving the unlettered magistrate. There he sees a parson as simple as his flock, a farmer who does not riot on the labour of others. We have no princes, for whom we toil, starve, and bleed: we are the most perfect society now existing in the world....

The next wish of this traveller will be to know whence came all these people. They are a mixture of English, Scotch, Irish, French, Dutch, Germans, and Swedes. From this promiscuous breed, that race now called Americans have arisen. The eastern provinces must indeed be excepted, as being the unmixed descendants of Englishmen. I have heard many wish that they had been more intermixed also: for my part, I am no wisher, and think it much better as it has happened. They exhibit a most conspicuous figure in this great and variegated picture; they too enter for a great share in the pleasing perspective displayed in these thirteen provinces. I know it is fashion able to reflect on them, but I respect them for what they have done; for the accuracy and wisdom with which they have settled their territory; for the decency of their manners; for their early love of letters; their ancient college, the first in this hemisphere; for their industry; which to me who am but a farmer, is the criterion of everything. There never was a people, situated as they are, who with so ungrateful a soil have done more in so short a time. Do you think that the monarchical ingredients which are more prevalent in other governments, have purged them from all foul stains? Their histories assert the contrary.

In this great American asylum, the poor of Europe have by some means met together, and in consequence of various causes; to what purpose would they ask one another what countrymen they are? Alas, two thirds of them had no country. Can a wretch who wanders about, who works and starves, whose life is a continual scene of sore affliction or pinching penury; can that man call England or any other kingdom his country? A country that had no bread for him, whose fields procured him no harvest, who met with nothing but the frowns of the rich, the severity of the laws, with jails and punishments; who owned not a single foot of the extensive surface of this planet? No! Urged by a variety of motives, here they came. Every thing has tended to regenerate them; new laws, a new mode of living, a new

social system; here they are become men; in Europe they were as so many useless plants, wanting vegetative mould, and refreshing showers; they withered, and were mowed down by want, hunger, and war: but now by the power of transplantation, like all other plants they have taken root and flourished! Formerly they were not numbered in any civil lists of their country, except in those of the poor; here they rank as citizens. By what invisible power has this surprising metamorphosis been performed? By that of the laws and that of their industry. The laws, the indulgent laws, protect them as they arrive, stamping on them the symbol of adoption; they receive ample rewards for their labours; these accumulated rewards procure them lands; those lands confer on them the title of freemen, and to that title every benefit is affixed which men can possibly require. This is the great operation daily performed by our laws....

What attachment can a poor European emigrant have for a country where he had nothing? The knowledge of the language, the love of a few kindred as poor as himself, were the only cords that tied him: his country is now that which gives him land, bread, protection, and consequence. *Ubi panis ibi patria*, is the motto of all emigrants. What then is the American, this new man? He is either an European, or the descendant of an European, hence that strange mixture of blood, which you will find in no other country. I could point out to you a family whose grandfather was an Englishman, whose wife was Dutch, whose son married a French woman, and whose present four sons have now four wives of different nations. *He* is an American, who, leaving behind him all his ancient prejudices and manners, receives new ones from the new mode of life he has embraced, the new government he obeys, and the new rank he holds. He becomes an American by being received in the broad lap of our great *Alma Mater*. Here individuals of all nations are melted into a new race of men, whose labours and posterity will one day cause great changes in the world. Americans are the western pilgrims, who are carrying along with them the great mass of arts, sciences, vigour, and industry which began long since in the east; they will finish the great circle. The Americans were once scattered all over Europe; here they are incorporated into one of the finest systems of population which has ever appeared, and which will hereafter become distinct by the power of the different climates they inhabit. The American ought therefore to love this country much better than that wherein either he or his forefathers were born. Here the rewards of his industry follow with equal steps the progress of his labour; his labour is founded on the basis of nature, *self-interest*; can it want a stronger allurement? Wives and children, who before in vain demanded of him a morsel of bread, now, fat and frolicsome, gladly help their father to clear those fields whence exuberant crops are to arise to feed and to clothe them all; without any part being claimed, either by a despotic prince, a rich abbot, or a mighty lord. Here religion demands but little of him; a small voluntary salary to the minister, and gratitude to God; can he refuse these? The American is a new man, who acts upon new principles; he must therefore entertain new ideas, and form new opinions. From involuntary idleness, servile dependence, penury, and useless labour, he has passed to toils of a very different nature, rewarded by ample subsistence.—This is an American....

* * * * * *

1. What do you think of the picture John De Crevecoeur paints of America as a great melting pot of immigrants? Is it accurate? Who is left out of De Crevecoeur's picture?

2. The French have been great commentators on America, De Crevecoeur and Alexis De Tocqueville being two of the more well known. Why do you think the French had such an interest in the United States?

3. De Crevecoeur asserts that there is a new, uniquely American people with their own distinct character. Do you agree or disagree?

8-7 A Post-Revolutionary Woman Argues for Women's Equality, 1790

Judith Sargent Murray was an outspoken feminist in post-revolutionary America, frequently writing under the pen name of "Constantia." Murray argued fervently for the equality of women, especially for the parity of their minds and intellect with those of men, which would have been particularly important in the age of Enlightenment. Murray uses God and the bible as the basis for her argument in the following excerpt from an essay by Constantia.

SOURCE: *The Massachusetts Magazine* 2 (April and May, 1790).

...Yes, ye lordly, ye haughty sex, our souls are by nature *equal* to yours; the same breath of God animates, enlivens, and invigorates us; and that we are not fallen lower than yourselves, let those witness who have greatly towered above the various discouragements by which they have been so heavily oppressed; and though I am unacquainted with the list of celebrated characters on either side, yet from the observations I have made in the contracted circle in which I have moved, I dare confidently believe, that from the commencement of time to the present day, there hath been as many females, as males, who, by the *mere force of natural powers*, have merited the crown of applause; who, *thus unassisted*, have seized the wreath of fame. I know there are who assert, that as the animal powers of the one sex are superiour, of course their mental faculties also must be stronger; thus attributing strength of mind to the transient organization of this earth born tenement. But if this reasoning is just, man must be content to yield the palm to many of the brute creation, since by not a few of his brethren of the field, he is far surpassed in bodily strength. Moreover, was this argument admitted, it would prove too much, for occular demonstration evinceth, that there are many robust masculine ladies, and effeminate gentlemen. Yet I fancy that Mr. Pope, though clogged with an enervated body, and distinguished by a diminutive stature, could nevertheless lay claim to greatness of soul; and perhaps there are many other instances which might be adduced to combat so unphilosophical an opinion. Do we not often see, that when the clay built tabernacle is well nigh dissolved, when it is just ready to mingle with the parent soil, the immortal inhabitant aspires to, and even attaineth heights the most sublime, and which were before wholly unexplored. Besides, were we to grant that animal strength proved any thing, taking into consideration the accustomed impartiality of nature, we should be induced to imagine, that she had invested the female mind with superiour strength as an equivalent for the bodily powers of man. But waving this however palpable advantage, for *equality only*, we wish to contend.

I am aware that there are many passages in the sacred oracles which seem to give the advantage to the other sex; but I consider all these as wholly metaphorical. Thus David was a man after God's own heart, yet see him enervated by his licentious passions! behold him following Uriah to the death, and show me wherein could consist the immaculate Being's complacency. Listen to the curses which Job bestoweth upon the day of his nativity, and tell me where is his perfection, where his patience—literally it existed not. David and Job were types of him who was to come; and the superiority of man, as exhibited in scripture, being also emblematical, all arguments deduced from thence, of course fall to the ground. The exquisite delicacy of the female mind proclaimeth the exactness of its texture, while its nice sense of honour announceth its innate, its native grandeur. And indeed, in one respect, the preeminence seems to be tacitly allowed us, for after an education which limits and confines, and employments and recreations which naturally tend to enervate the body, and debilitate the mind; after we have from early youth been adorned with ribbons, and other gewgaws, dressed out like the ancient victims previous to a sacrifice, being taught by the care of our parents in collecting the most showy materials that the ornamenting our exteriour ought to be the principal object of our attention; after, I say, fifteen years thus spent, we are introduced into the world, amid the united adulation of every beholder. Praise is sweet to the soul; we are immediately intoxicated by large draughts of flattery, which being plentifully administered, is to the pride of our hearts the most acceptable incense. It is expected that with the other sex we should commence immediate war, and that we should triumph over the machinations of the most artful. We must be constantly upon our guard; prudence and discretion must be our characteristicks; and we must rise superior to, and obtain a complete victory over those who have been long adding to the native strength of their minds, by an unremitted study of men and books, and who have, moreover, conceived from the loose characters which they have been portrayed in the extensive variety of their reading, a most contemptible opinion of the sex. Thus unequal, we are, notwithstanding, forced to the combat, and the infamy which is consequent upon the smallest deviation in our conduct, proclaims the high idea which was formed of our native strength; and thus, indirectly at least, is the preference acknowledged to be our due. And if we are allowed an equality of acquirement, let serious studies equally employ our minds, and we will bid our souls arise to equal strength. We will meet upon even ground, the despot man; we will rush with alacrity to the combat, and, crowned by success, we shall then answer the exalted expectations which are formed. Though sensibility, soft compassion, and gentle commiseration, are inmates in the female bosom, yet against every deep laid art, altogether fearless of the event, we will set them in array; for assuredly the wreath of victory will encircle the spotless brow. If we meet an equal, a sensible friend, we will reward him with the hand of amity, and through life we will be assiduous to promote his happiness; but from every deep laid scheme for our ruin, retiring into ourselves, amid the flowery paths of science, we will indulge in all the refined and sentimental pleasures of contemplation. And should it still be urged, that the studies thus inlisted upon would interfere with our more peculiar department, I must further reply, that *early hours*, and close application, will do wonders; and to her who is from the first dawn of reason taught to fill up time rationally, both the requisites will be easy. I grant that niggard fortune is too generally unfriendly to the mind; and that much of that valuable treasure, time, is necessarily expended upon the wants of the body; but it should be remembered, that in embarrassed circumstances our companions have as little leisure for literary improvement, as is afforded to us; for most certainly their provident care is at least as requisite as our exertions. Nay, we have even more leisure for sedentary pleasures, as our avocations are more retired, much less laborious, and, as hath been observed, by no means require that avidity of attention which is proper to the employments of the other sex. In high life, or, in other words, where the parties are in possession of affluence, the objection respecting time is wholly obviated, and of course falls to the ground; and it may also be repeated, that many of those hours which are at present swallowed up in fashion and scandal, might be redeemed, were we habituated to useful reflections. But in one respect, O ye arbiters of our fate! we confess that the superiority is indubitably yours; you are by nature formed for our protectors; we pretend not to vie with you in bodily strength; upon this point we will never contend for victory. Shield us then, we beseech you, from external evils, and in return we will transact *your* domestick affairs. Yes, *your,* for are you not equally interested in those matters with ourselves? Is not the elegancy of neatness as agreeable to your sight as to ours; is not the well favoured viand equally delightful to your taste; and doth not your sense of hearing suffer as much, from the discordant sounds prevalent in an ill regulated family, produced by the voices of children and many *et ceteras?*

CONSTANTIA.

* * * * * *

1. What is the basis of Judith Sargent Murray's argument? Do you agree?

2. What does Murray's essay reveal about women's roles in post-revolutionary New England? What do you think was the role of feminists in post-revolutionary New England?

8–8 An American School Teacher Calls for an American Language, 1789

More famous for his 19th century dictionaries, Noah Webster had already risen to prominence in the late 1700s as a school teacher and author of The American Spelling Book. Webster delivered a series of lectures in the 1780s which addressed the formation of an American English. The following essay outlines reforms which Webster thought would simplify spelling and writing, as well as give America a unique language all her own.

SOURCE: Noah Webster, *Dissertations on The English Language* (Boston: Isaiah Thomas and Company, 1789).

The Reforming of Spelling (1789)

IT HAS been observed by all writers on the English language, that the orthography or spelling of words is very irregular; the same letters often representing different sounds, and the same sounds often expressed by different letters. For this irregularity, two principal causes may be assigned:

1. The changes to which the pronunciation of a language is liable, from the progress of science and civilization.

2. The mixture of different languages, occasioned by revolutions in England, or by a predilection of the learned, for words of foreign growth and ancient origin.…

The question now occurs: ought the Americans to retain these faults which produce innumerable inconveniences in the acquisition and use of the language, or ought they at once reform these abuses, and introduce order and regularity into the orthography of the AMERICAN TONGUE?

Let us consider this subject with some attention.

Several attempts were formerly made in England to rectify the orthography of the language. But I apprehend their schemes failed of success, rather on account of their intrinsic difficulties than on account of any necessary impracticability of a reform. It was proposed, in most of these schemes, not merely to throw out superfluous and silent letters, but to introduce a number of new characters. Any attempt on such a plan must undoubtedly prove unsuccessful. It is not to be expected that an orthography, perfectly regular and simple, such as would be formed by a "Synod of Grammarians on principles of science," will

ever be substituted for that confused mode of spelling which is now established. But it is apprehended that great improvements may be made, and an orthography almost regular, or such as shall obviate most of the present difficulties which occur in learning our language, may be introduced and established with little trouble and opposition.

The principal alterations necessary to render our orthography sufficiently regular and easy, are these:

1. The omission of all superfluous or silent letters; as in *bread*. Thus *bread, head, give, breast, built, meant, realm, friend,* would be spelt *bred, hed, giv, brest, bilt, ment, relm, frend*. Would this alteration produce any inconvenience, any embarrassment or expense? By no means. On the other hand, it would lessen the trouble of writing, and much more, of learning the language; it would reduce the true pronunciation to a certainty; and while it would assist foreigners and our own children in acquiring the language, it would render the pronunciation uniform, in different parts of the country, and almost prevent the possibility of changes.

2. A substitution of a character that has a certain definite sound for one that is more vague and indeterminate. Thus by putting *ee* instead of *ea* or *ie*, the words *mean, near, speak, grieve, zeal,* would become *meen, neer, speek, greev, zeel*. This alteration would not occasion a moment's trouble; at the same time it would prevent a doubt respecting the pronunciation; whereas the *ea* and *ie* having different sounds, may give a learner much difficulty. Thus *greef* should be substituted for *grief; kee* for *key; beleev* for *believe; laf* for *laugh; dawter* for *daughter; plow* for *plough; tuf* for *tough; proov* for *prove; blud* for *blood;* and *draft* for *draught*. In this manner *ch* in Greek derivatives should be changed into *k;* for the English *ch* has a soft sound, as in *cherish;* but *k* always a hard sound. Therefore *character, chorus, cholic, architecture,* should be written *karacter, korus, kolic, arkitecture;* and were they thus written, no person could mistake their true pronunciation.

Thus *ch* in French derivatives should be changed into *sh; machine, chaise, chevalier,* should be written *masheen, chaze, shevaleer;* and *pique, tour, oblique,* should be written *peek, toor, obleek*.

3. A trifling alteration in a character or the addition of a point would distinguish different sounds, with the substitution of a new character. Thus a very small stroke across *th* would distinguish its two sounds. A point over a vowel, in this manner, ȧ, or ȯ, or ʈ, might answer all the purposes of different letters. And for the dipthong *ow,* let the two letters be united by a small stroke, or both engraven on the same piece of metal, with the left hand line of the *w* united to the *o*.

These, with a few other inconsiderable alterations,

would answer every purpose, and render the orthography sufficiently correct and regular.

The advantages to be derived from these alterations are numerous, great and permanent.

1. The simplicity of the orthography would facilitate the learning of the language. It is now the work of years for children to learn to spell; and after all, the business is rarely accomplished. A few men, who are bred to some business that requires constant exercise in writing, finally learn to spell most words without hesitation; but most people remain, all their lives, imperfect masters of spelling, and liable to make mistakes, whenever they take up a pen to write a short note. Nay, many people, even of education and fashion, never attempt to write a letter, without frequently consulting a dictionary.

But with the proposed orthography, a child would learn to spell, without trouble, in a very short time, and the orthography being very regular, hc would ever afterwards find it difficult to make a mistake. It would, in that case, be as difficult to spell *wrong* as it is now to spell *right.*

Besides this advantage, foreigners would be able to acquire the pronunciation of English, which is now so difficult and embarrassing that they are either wholly discouraged on the first attempt, or obliged, after many years' labor, to rest contented with an imperfect knowledge of the subjcct.

2. A correct orthography would render the pronunciation of the language as uniform as the spelling in books. A general uniformity thro the United States would be the event of such a reformation as I am here recommending. All persons, of every rank, would speak with some degree of precision and uniformity. Such a uniformity in these states is very desirable; it would remove prejudice, and conciliate mutual affection and respect.

3. Such a reform would diminish the number of letters about one sixteenth or eighteenth. This would save a page in eighteen; and a saving of an eighteenth in the expense of books, is an advantagc that should not be overlooked.

4. But a capital advantage of this reform in these states would be, that it would make a difference between the English orthography and the American. This will startle those who have not attended to the subject; but I am confident that such an event is an object of vast political consequence. For the alteration, however small, would encourage the publication of books in our own country. It would render it, in some measure, necessary that all books should be printed in America. The English would never copy our orthography for their own use; and consequently the same impressions of books would not answer for both countries. The inhabitants of the present generation would read the English impressions; but posterity, being taught a different spelling, would prefer the

American orthography.

Besides this, a *national language* is a band of *national union.* Every engine should be employed to render the people of this country *national;* to call their attachments home to their own country; and to inspire them with the pride of national character. However they may boast of independence, and the freedom of their government, yet their *opinions* are not sufficiently independent; an astonishing respect for the arts and literature of their parent country, and a blind imitation of its manners, are still prevalent among the Americans. Thus an habitual respect for another country, deserved indeed and once laudable, turns their attention from their own interests, and prevents their respecting themselves....

Sensible I am how much easier it is to propose improvements than to *introduce* them. Everything *new* starts the idea of difficulty; and yet it is often mere novelty that excites the appearance; for on a slight examination of the proposal, the difficulty vanishes. When we firmly believe a scheme to be practicable, the work is *half* accomplished. We are more frequently deterred by fear from making an attack than repulsed in the encounter.

Habit also is opposed to changes; for it renders even our errors dear to us. Having surmounted all difficulties in childhood, we forget the labor, the fatigue, and the perplexity we suffered in the attempt, and imagine the progress of our studies to have been smooth and easy. What seems intrinsically right is so merely thro habit.

Indolence is another obstacle to improvements. The most arduous task a reformer has to execute, is to make people *think;* to rouse them from that lcthargy which, like the mantle of sleep, covers them in repose and contentment.

But America is in a situation the most favorable for great reformations; and the present time is, in a singular degree, auspicious. The minds of men in this country have been awakened. New scenes have been, for many years, presenting new occasions for exertion; unexpected distresses have called forth the powers of invention; and the application of new expedients has demanded every possible exercise of wisdom and talents. Attention is roused; the mind expanded; and the intellectual faculties invigorated. Here men are prepared to receive improvements, which would be rejected by nations whose habits have not been shaken by similar events.

Now is the time, and *this* the country, in which we may expect success, in attempting changes favorable to language, science and government. Delay, in the plan here proposed, may be fatal; under a tranquil general government, the minds of men may again sink into indolence; a national acquiescence in error will follow; and posterity be doomed to struggle with difficulties, which time and accident will perpetually multiply.

Let us then seize the present moment, and establish

a *national language*, as well as a national government. Let us remember that there is a certain respect due to the opinions of other nations. As an independent people, our reputation abroad demands that in all things we should be federal; be *national*; for if we do not respect *ourselves*, we may be assured that *other nations* will not respect us. In short, let it be impressed upon the mind of every American that to neglect the means of commanding respect abroad is treason against the character and dignity of a brave independent people....

* * * * * *

1.   *What do you think of Noah Webster's suggestions for simplifying the English language? Would they have made it easier for you to learn to read and write?*

2.   *Webster asserts forming an American language. Does America have a unique language? What power does a language hold for a people?*

chapter 9

The Agrarian Republic, 1800–1824

9–1 Two Explorers Meet the Shoshone, 1805

Thomas Jefferson had wanted to send an exploration party to the Pacific Coast for quite some time before the purchase of the Louisiana Territory in 1803. Meriwether Lewis and William Clark were the two adventurers selected for the task. Gone from 1804 until 1806, Lewis and Clark and their band of about 47 men had an arduous journey, but discovered new animals and plants and started relations with many Indian tribes as they made their way from St. Louis up the Missouri to the Columbia to the Pacific Coast and back. Their journals were not widely published until the early 1900s, but have been used extensively since then by historians. In the following excerpt they describe the Shoshone and a portion of their trip.

SOURCE: Nicholas Biddle, ed., *History of the Expedition Under the Command of Captain Lewis and Clark* (Philadelphia: Bradford & Inskeep, 1814).

MONDAY AUGUST 19TH 1805.—

...[This Band of] The Shoshonees may be estimated at about 100 warriors, and about three times that number of women and children. they have more children among them than I expected to have seen among a people who procure subsistence with such difficulty, there are but few very old persons, nor did they appear to treat those with much tenderness or respect. The man is the sole propryetor of his wives and daughters, and can barter or dispose of either as he thinks proper a plurality of wives is common among them, but these are not generally sisters as with the Minnetares & Mandans but are purchased of different fathers. The father frequently disposes of his infant daughters in marriage to men who are grown or to men who have sons for whom they think proper to provide wives, the compensation given in such cases usually consists of horses or mules which the father receives at the time of contract and converts to his own use, the girl remains with her parents until she is conceived to have obtained the age of puberty which with them is considered to be about the age of 13 or 14 years, the female at this age is surrendered to her sovereign lord and husband agreeably to contract, and with her is frequently restored by the father quite as much as he received in the first instance in payment for his daughter; but this is discretionary with the father. Sah-car-gar-we-ah had been thus disposed of before she was taken by the Minnetares, or had arrived to the years of puberty, the husband was yet living with this band, he was more than double her age and had two other wives, he claimed her as his wife but said that as she had had a child by another man, who was Charbono, that he did not want her.

They seldom correct their children particularly the boys who soon become masters of their own acts. They give as a reason that it cows and breaks the spirit of the boy to whip him, and that he never recovers his independence of mind after he is grown. They treat their women but with little respect, and compel them to perform every species of drudgery. they collect the wild fruits and roots, attend to the horses or assist in that duty, cook, dress the skins and make all their apparel, collect wood and make their fires, arrange and form their lodges, and when they travel pack the horses and take charge of all the baggage; in short the man does little else except attend his horses hunt and fish. the man considers himself degraded if he is compelled to walk any distance; and if he is so unfortunately poor as only to possess two horses he rides the best himself and leaves the woman or women if he has more than one, to transport their baggage and children on the other, and to walk if the horse is unable to carry the additional weight of their persons. the chastity of their women is not held in high estimation, and the husband will for a trifle barter the companion of his bead for a night or longer if he conceives the reward adiquate; tho' they are not so importunate that we should caress their women as the sioux were. and some of their women appear to be held more sacred than in any nation we have seen. I have requested the men to give them no cause of jealousy by having connection with their women without their knowledge, which with them, strange as it may seem is considered as disgraceful to the husband as clandestine connections of a similar kind are among civilized nations. to prevent this mutual exchange of good offices altogether I know it impossible to effect, particularly on the pan of our young men whom some months abstanence have made very polite to those tawney damsels. no evil has yet resulted and I hope will not from these connections.

notwithstanding the late loss of horses which this people sustained by the Minnetares the stock of the band may be very safely estimated at seven hundred of which they are perhaps about 40 coalts and half that number of mules. their arms offensive and defensive consist in the bow and arrows shield, some, lances, and a weapon called by the Cippeways who formerly used it, the pog-gar'-mag-gon' [war club]. in fishing they employ wairs, gigs, and fishing hooks. the salmon is the principal object of their pursuit. They snair wolves and foxes.

I was anxious to learn whether these people had the

105

veneral, and made the enquiry through the interpreter and his wife; the information was that they sometimes had it but I could not learn their remedy; they most usually die with it's effects. this seems a strong proof that these disorders bothe ganaraehah and Louis Venerae [syphilis] are imported and perhaps those other disorders might have been contracted from other indian tribes who by a round of communications might have obtained from the Europeans since it was introduced into that quarter of the globe. but so much detached on the other ha[n]d from all communication with the whites that I think it most probable that those disorders are original with them.

from the middle of May to the first of September these people reside on the waters of the Columbia where they consider themselves in perfect security from their enimies as they have not as yet ever found their way to this retreat; during this season the salmon furnish the principal part of their subsistence and as this fish either perishes or returns about the 1st of September they are compelled at this season in surch of subsistence to resort to the Missouri, in the vallies of which, there is more game even [than] within the mountains. here they move slowly down the river in order to collect and join other bands either of their own nation or the Flatheads, and having become sufficiently strong as they conceive venture on the Eastern side of the Rocky mountains into the plains, where the buffaloe abound. but they never leave the interior of the mountains while they can obtain a scanty subsistence, and always return as soon as they have acquired a good stock of dryed meat in the plains; thus alternately obtaining their food at the risk of their lives and retiring to the mountains, while they consume it. These people are now on the eve of their departure for the Missouri, and inform us that they expect to be joined at or about the three forks by several bands of their own nation, and a band of the Flatheads.

[Clark]

AUGUST 19TH MONDAY 1805.—

A very cold morning Forst to be seen we set out a 7 oClock and proceeded on thro a wide level Vallie this Vallie Continues 5 miles & then becomes narrow, we proceeded on up the main branch with a gradial assent to the head and passed over a low mountain and Decended a Steep Decent to a butifull Stream, passed over a Second hill of a verry Steep assent & thro' a hilley Countrey for 8 miles an[d] Encamped on a Small Stream, the Indians with us we wer oblige[d] to feed. one man met me with a mule & Spanish Saddle to ride, I gave him a westcoat a mule is considered of great value among those people we proceeded on over a verry mountainous Countrey across the head & hollows & Springs.

[Lewis]

TUESDAY AUGUST 20TH 1805.—

I walked down the river about 3/4 of a mile and selected a place near the river bank unperceived by the Indians for a cash [cache], which I set three men to make, and directed the centinel to discharge his gun if he perceived any of the Indians going down in that direction which was to be the signal for the men at work on the cash to desist and seperate, least these people should discover our deposit and rob us of the baggage we intend leaving here. by evening the cash was completed unperceived by the Indians, and all our packages made up, the Pack-saddles and harness is not yet complete. in this operation we find ourselves at a loss for nails and boards; for the first we substitute throngs of raw hide which answer verry well, and for the last [had] to cut off the blades of our oars and use the plank of some boxes which have heretofore held other articles and put those articles into sacks of raw hide which I have had made for the purpose. by this means I have obtained as many boards as will make 20 saddles which I suppose will be sufficient for our present exegencies. I made up a small assortment of medicines, together with the specemines of plants, minerals, seeds &c, which, I have collected between this place and the falls of the Missouri which I shall deposit here.

I now prevailed on the Chief to instruct me with respect to the geography of his country. this he undertook very cheerfully, by delineating the rivers on the ground. but I soon found that his information fell far short of my expectation or wishes. he drew the river on which we now are [the Lemhi] to which he placed two branches just above us, which he shewed me from the openings of the mountains were in view; he next made it discharge itself into a large river which flowed from the S.W. about ten miles below us [the Salmon], then continued this joint stream in the same direction of this valley or N.W. for 2 more days march and then enclined it to the West for 2 more days march. here we placed a number of heaps of sand on each side which he informed me represented the vast mountains of rock eternally covered with snow through which the river passed. that the perpendicular and even juting rocks so closely hemmed in the river that there was no possibil[it]y of passing along the shore; that the bed of the river was obstructed by sharp pointed rocks and the rapidity of the stream such that the whole surface of the river was beat into perfect foam as far as the eye could reach. that the mountains were also inaccessible to man or horse. he said that this being the state of the country in that direction that himself nor none of his nation had ever been further down the river than these mountains.

I then enquired the state of the country on either side of the river but he could not inform me... I now asked Cameahwait by what rout the Pierced nosed [Nez Percé] indians, who he informed me inhabited this river below the mountains, came over to the Missouri; this he informed me was to the north, but added that the road was a very bad one as he had been informed by them and that they had suffered excessively with hunger on the rout being obliged to subsist for many days on berries alone as there was no game in that part of the mountains which were broken rockey and so thickly covered with timber that they could scarcely pass. however knowing that Indians had passed, and did pass, at this season on that side of this river to the same below the mountains, my rout was instantly settled in my own mind, p[r]ovided the account of this river should prove true on an investigation of it, which I was determined should be made before we would undertake the rout by land in any direction. I felt perfectly satisfyed, that if the Indians could pass these mountains with their women and Children, that we could also pass them; and that if the nations on this river below the mountains were as numerous as they were stated to be that they must have some means of subsistence which it would be equally in our power to procure in the same country. they informed me that there was no buffaloe on the West side of the mountains; that the game consisted of a few Elk deer and Antelopes, and that the natives subsisted on fish and roots principally.

in this manner I spend the day smoking with them and acquiring what information I could with respect to their country. they informed me that they could pass to the Spaniards by the way of the yellow-stone river in 10 days. I can discover that these people are by no means friendly to the Spaniards. their complaint is, that the Spaniards will not let them have fire arms and ammunition, that they put them off by telling them that if they suffer them to have guns they will kill each other, thus leaving them defenceless and an easy prey to their bloodthirsty neighbours to the East of them, who being in possession of fire arms hunt them up and murder them without respect to sex or age and plunder them of their horses on all occasions. they told me that to avoid their enemies who were eternally harrassing them that they were obliged to remain in the interior of these mountains at least two thirds of the year where the[y] suffered as we then saw great heardships for the want of food sometimes living for

weeks without meat and only a little fish roots and berries. but this added Cámeahwait, with his ferce eyes and lank jaws grown meager for the want of food, would not be the case if we had guns, we could then live in the country of buffaloe and eat as our enimies do and not be compelled to hide ourselves in these mountains and live on roots and berries as the bear do. we do not fear our enimies when placed on an equal footing with them. I told them that the Minnetares Mandans...had promised us to desist from making war on them & that we would indevour to find the means of making the Minnetares of fort d[e] Prarie or as they call them Pahkees desist from waging war against them also. that after our finally returning to our homes towards the rising sun whitemen would come to them with an abundance of guns and every other article necessary to their defence and comfort, and that they would be enabled to supply themselves with these articles on reasonable terms in exchange for the skins of the beaver Otter and Ermin so abundant in their country. they expressed great pleasure at this information and said they had been long anxious to see the whitemen that traded guns; and that we might rest assured of their friendship and that they would do whatever we wished them.

* * * * * *

1. Jefferson had long wanted to send an expedition to the west coast to discover a route to the Pacific, make friends with the Indians, and make a scientific record of the plants, animals, and geography. What other motivations might Jefferson have had?

2. From this entry, what can you discern about Lewis's attitude towards the Indians? What can you glean about the Indians themselves?

3. Although this is just one part of the trip, what can you say about the difficulties of the trip for Lewis and Clark and their men?

9-2   Supreme Court Retains Right to Overrule Legislation, 1803

The Marbury versus Madison case revolved around William Marbury, who had been appointed a justice of the peace by President John Adams two days before Adams ended his term. The new President, Thomas Jefferson, denied Marbury the position by directing Secretary of State James Madison not to deliver the commission. Marbury filed a lawsuit, asking the Supreme Court to issue a writ of mandamus, forcing Madison to deliver the commission. Chief Justice John Marshall ruled that the court was not authorized to issue writs of mandamus, and, more importantly, in the following excerpt from the decision, made it clear that the Supreme Court did, however, have the power to declare legislation unconstitutional, thereby maintaining the balance of power in government. This is one of the landmark decisions of the Supreme Court, giving them more authority than they had previously held.

...The authority, therefore, given to the Supreme Court, by the act establishing the judicial courts of the United States, to issue writs of mandamus to public officers, appears not to be warranted by the constitution; and it becomes necessary to enquire whether a jurisdiction, so conferred, can be exercised.

The question, whether an act, repugnant to the constitution, can become the law of the land, is a question deeply interesting to the United States; but, happily, not of an intricacy proportioned to its interest. It seems only necessary to recognize certain principles, supposed to have been long and well established, to decide it.

That the people have an original right to establish, for their future government, such principles as, in their opinion, shall most conduce to their own happiness, is the basis on which the whole American fabric has been erected. The exercise of this original right is a very great exertion; nor can it, nor ought it, to be frequently repeated. The principles, therefore, so established, are deemed fundamental. And as the authority from which they proceed is supreme, and can seldom act, they are designed to be permanent.

This original and supreme will organizes the government, and assigns to different departments their respective powers. It may either stop here, or establish certain limits not to be transcended by those departments.

The government of the United States is of the latter description. The powers of the legislature are defined and limited; and that those limits may not be mistaken, or forgotten, the constitution is written. To what purpose are powers limited, and to what purpose is that limitation committed to writing, if these limits may, at any time, be passed by those intended to be restrained? The distinction between a government with limited and unlimited powers is abolished, if those limits do not confine the persons on whom they are imposed, and if acts prohibited and acts allowed, are of equal obligation. It is a proposition too plain to be contested, that the constitution controls any legislative act repugnant to it; or, that the legislature may alter the constitution by an ordinary act.

Between these alternatives there is no middle ground. The constitution is either a superior, paramount law, unchangeable by ordinary means, or it is on a level with ordinary legislative acts, and, like other acts, is alterable when the legislature shall please to alter it.

If the former part of the alternative be true, then a legislative act contrary to the constitution is not law; if the latter part be true, then written constitutions are absurd attempts, on the part of the people, to limit a power in its own nature illimitable.

Certainly all those who have framed written constitutions contemplate them as forming the fundamental and paramount law of the nation, and consequently, the theory of every such government must be, that an act of the legislature, repugnant to the constitution, is void.

This theory is essentially attached to a written constitution, and is, consequently, to be considered, by this court, as one of the fundamental principles of our society. It is not therefore to be lost sight of in the further consideration of this subject.

If an act of the legislature, repugnant to the constitution, is void, does it, notwithstanding its invalidity, bind the courts, and oblige them to give it effect? Or, in other words, though it be not law, does it constitute a rule as operative as if it was a law? This would be to overthrow in fact what was established in theory; and would seem, at first view, an absurdity too gross to be insisted on. It shall, however, receive a more attentive consideration.

It is emphatically the province and duty of the judicial department to say what the law is. Those who apply the rule to particular cases, must of necessity expound and interpret that rule. If two laws conflict with each other, the courts must decide on the operation of each.

So if a law be in opposition to the constitution; if both the law and the constitution apply to a particular case, so that the court must either decide that case conformably to the law, disregarding the constitution; or conformably to the constitution, disregarding the law; the court must determine which of these conflicting rules governs the case. This is of the very essence of judicial duty.

If, then, the courts are to regard the constitution, and the constitution is superior to any ordinary act of the legislature, the constitution, and not such ordinary act, must govern the case to which they both apply.

Those then who controvert the principle that the constitution is to be considered, in court, as a paramount law, are reduced to the necessity of maintaining that courts must close their eyes on the constitution, and see only the law.

This doctrine would subvert the very foundation of all written constitutions. It would declare that an act which, according to the principles and theory of our government, is entirely void, is yet, in practice, completely obligatory. It would declare that if the legislature shall do what is expressly forbidden, such act, notwithstanding the express prohibition, is in reality effectual. It would be giving to the legislature a practical and real omnipotence, with the same breath which professes to restrict their powers within narrow limits. It is prescribing limits, and declaring that those limits may be passed at pleasure.

That it thus reduces to nothing what we have deemed the greatest improvement on political institutions—

SOURCE: William Cranch, Reports of Cases Argued and Adjudged in the Supreme Court of the United States (Washington, D.C.: John Conrad & Co., 1804).

a written constitution—would of itself be sufficient, in America, where written constitutions have been viewed with so much reverence, for rejecting the construction. But the peculiar expressions of the constitution of the United States furnish additional arguments in favour of its rejection.

The judicial power of the United States is extended to all cases arising under the constitution.

Could it be the intention of those who gave this power, to say that in using it the constitution should not be looked into? That a case arising under the constitution should be decided without examining the instrument under which it arises?

This is too extravagant to be maintained.

In some cases, then, the constitution must be looked into by the judges. And if they can open it at all, what part of it are they forbidden to read or to obey?

There are many other parts of the constitution which serve to illustrate this subject. It is declared that "no tax or duty shall be laid on articles exported from any state." Suppose a duty on the export of cotton, of tobacco, or of flour; and a suit instituted to recover it. Ought judgment to be rendered in such a case? Ought the judges to close their eyes on the constitution, and only see the law?

The constitution declares that "no bill of attainder or ex post facto law shall be passed."

If, however, such a bill should be passed, and a person should be prosecuted under it; must the court condemn to death those victims whom the constitution endeavors to preserve?

"No person," says the constitution, "shall be convicted of treason unless on the testimony of two witnesses to the same overt act, or on confession in open court."

Here the language of the constitution is addressed especially to the courts. It prescribes, directly for them, a rule of evidence not to be departed from. If the legislature should change that rule, and declare one witness, or a confession out of court, sufficient for conviction, must the constitutional principle yield to the legislative act?

From these, and many other selections which might be made, it is apparent, that the framers of the constitution contemplated that instrument as a rule for the government of courts, as well as of the legislature.

Why otherwise does it direct the judges to take an oath to

support it? This oath certainly applies, in an especial manner, to their conduct in their official character. How immoral to impose it on them, if they were to be used as the instruments, and the knowing instruments, for violating what they swear to support!

The oath of office, too, imposed by the legislature, is completely demonstrative of the legislative opinion on this subject. It is in these words: "I do solemnly swear that I will administer justice without respect to persons, and do equal right to the poor and to the rich; and that I will faithfully and impartially discharge all the duties incumbent on me as _____, according to the best of my abilities and understanding, agreeably to the constitution, and laws of the United States."

Why does a judge swear to discharge his duties agreeably to the constitution of the United States, if that constitution forms no rule for his government? If it is closed upon him, and cannot be inspected by him?

If such be the real state of things, this is worse than solemn mockery. To prescribe, or to take this oath, becomes equally a crime.

It is also not entirely unworthy of observation that in declaring what shall be the supreme law of the land, the constitution itself is first mentioned; and not the laws of the United States generally, but those only which shall be made in pursuance of the constitution, have that rank.

Thus, the particular phraseology of the constitution of the United States confirms and strengthens the principle, supposed to be essential to all written constitutions, that a law repugnant to the constitution is void; and that courts, as well as other departments, are bound by that instrument.

The rule must be discharged.

* * * * * *

1. *What is the crux of Chief Justice John Marshall's argument? How does he base it in the constitution?*

2. *What would have been the implications of the court's decision if the decision had gone the other way? What would it have done to the "checks and balances" of the American governmental system?*

9–3 A Shawnee Argues for a United Indian Resistance, 1810

After mistreatment of the Native Americans by Presidents Jefferson and Madison, Tecumseh, a Shawnee, tried to organize the Midwestern Indian tribes into a united political alliance to thwart the steady advance of the white settlers. Tecumseh argued that the land belonged to all Indians and hence, no individual tribe could strike a treaty or sell their land because of this common ownership. Indians led by Tecumseh's brother, "The Prophet," were defeated in the Battle of Tippecanoe in 1811, largely putting an end to the Indian confederacy. The British made Tecumseh a general in the War of 1812 where he recruited Indians for the British and died fighting in the Battle of the Thames in Canada in 1813. The following is a speech by Tecumseh to Governor William Henry Harrison.

SOURCE: Samuel G. Drake, *Biography and History of the Indians of North America* (Boston: O.L Perkin, 1834).

Speech to Governor William Henry Harrison at Vincennes, August 12, 1810

Tecumseh (Shawnee)

It is true I am a Shawanee. My forefathers were warriors. Their son is a warrior. From them I only take my existence; from my tribe I take nothing. I am the maker of my own fortune; and oh! that I could make that of my red people, and of my country, as great as the conceptions of my mind, when I think of the Spirit that rules the universe. I would not then come to Governor Harrison, to ask him to tear the treaty, and to obliterate the landmark; but I would say to him, Sir, you have liberty to return to your own country. The being within, communing with past ages, tells me, that once, nor until lately, there was no white man on this continent. That it then all belonged to red men, children of the same parents, placed on it by the Great Spirit that made them, to keep it, to traverse it, to enjoy its productions, and to fill it with the same race. Once a happy race. Since made miserable by the white people, who are never contented, but always encroaching. The way, and the only way to check and stop this evil, is, for all the red men to unite in claiming a common and equal right in the land, as it was at first, and should be yet; for it never was divided, but belongs to all, for the use of each. That no part has a right to sell, even to each other, much less to strangers; those who want all, and will not do with less. The white people have no right to take the land from the Indians, because they had it first; it is theirs. They may sell, but all must join. Any sale not made by all is not valid. The late sale is bad. It was made by a part only. Part do not know how to sell. It requires all to make a bargain for all. All red men have equal rights to the unoccupied land. The right of occupancy is as good in one place as in another. There cannot be two occupations in the same place. The first excludes all others. It is not so in hunting or travelling; for there the same ground will serve many, as they may follow each other all day; but the camp is stationary, and that is occupancy. It belongs to the first who sits down on his blanket or skins, which he has thrown upon the ground, and till he leaves it no other has a right.

* * * * * *

1. *Different views of land ownership were a constant source of conflict between Native Americans and the government. What is Tecumseh's view of land ownership? Do you agree with it?*

2. *Pretend you were Governor Harrison. What response would you make to Tecumseh?*

9–4 A War Hawk Speaks About the British, 1811

As a newly elected speaker of the house, and congressman from Kentucky, Henry Clay was a staunch advocate of war against the British in 1811. Clay was also an Indian hater and strongly in favor of American expansionism. Widely renowned as a powerful orator, an important political skill in his day, Clay lent his full voice to the "War Hawks" who favored war, pushing a reluctant Madison into the War of 1812. The following speech illustrates Clay's talent for speaking, as well as the fervor with which he plead his case.

SOURCE: Henry Clay, *The Life and Speeches of Henry Clay* (New York: Greeley & M'Elrath, 1843).

…What are we to gain by war, has been emphatically asked? In reply, he would ask, what are we not to lose by peace?—commerce, character, a nation's best treasure, honor! If pecuniary considerations alone are to govern, there is sufficient motive for the war. Our revenue is reduced, by the operation of the belligerent edicts, to about six million of dollars, according to the Secretary of the Treasury's report. The year preceding the embargo, it was sixteen. Take away the Orders in Council, it will again mount up to sixteen millions. By continuing, therefore, in peace, if the mongrel state in which we are deserve that denomination, we lose annually, in revenue only, ten millions of dollars. Gentlemen will say, repeal the law of nonimportation. He contended that, if the United States were capable of that perfidy, the revenue would not be restored to its former state, the Orders in Council continuing. Without an export trade, which those orders prevent, inevitable ruin would ensue, if we imported as freely as we did prior to the embargo. A nation that carries on an import trade without an export trade to support it, must, in the end, be as certainly bankrupt, as the individual would be, who incurred an annual expenditure, without an income.

He had no disposition to swell, or dwell upon the catalogue of injuries from England. He could not, however, overlook the impressment of our seamen; an aggression upon which he never reflected without feelings of indignation, which would not allow him appropriate language to describe its enormity. Not content with seizing upon all our property, which falls within her rapacious grasp, the personal rights of our countrymen—rights which forever ought to be sacred, are trampled upon and violated. The Orders in Council were pretended to have been reluctantly adopted as a measure of retaliation. The French decrees, their alleged basis, are revoked. England resorts to the expedient of denying the fact of the revocation, and Sir William Scott, in the celebrated case of the Fox and others, suspends judgment that proof may be adduced of it. And, at the moment when the British Ministry through that judge, is thus affecting to controvert that fact, and to place the release of our property upon its establishment, instructions are prepared for Mr. Foster to meet at Washington the very revocation which they were contesting. And how does he meet it? By fulfilling the engagement solemnly made to rescind the orders? No, sir, but by demanding that we a shall secure the introduction into the Continent of British manufactures. England is said to be fighting for the world, and shall we, it is asked, attempt to weaken her exertions? If, indeed, the aim of the French Emperor be universal dominion (and he was willing to allow it to the argument,) what a noble cause it presented to British valor. But, how is her philanthropic purpose to be achieved? By scrupulous observance of the rights of others, by respecting that code of public law, which she professes to vindicate, and by abstaining from self aggrandizement. Then would she command the sympathies of the world. What are we required to do by those who would engage our feelings and wishes in her behalf? To bear the actual cuffs of her arrogance, that we may escape a chimerical French subjugation! We are invited, conjured to drink the potion of British poison actually

presented to our lips, that we may avoid the imperial dose prepared by perturbed imaginations. We are called upon to submit to debasement, dishonor, and disgrace to bow the neck to royal insolence, as a course of preparation for manly resistance to Gallic invasion! What nation, what individual was ever taught, in the schools of ignominious submission, the patriotic lessons of freedom and independence? Let those who contend for this humiliating doctrine, read its refutation in the history of the very man against whose insatiable thirst of dominion we are warned. The experience of desolated Spain, for the last fifteen years, is worth volumes. Did she find her repose and safety in subserviency to the will of that man? Had she boldly stood forth and repelled the first attempt to dictate to her Councils, her Monarch would not now be a miserable captive at Marseilles. Let us come home to our own history. It was not by submission that our fathers achieved our independence. The patriotic wisdom that placed you, Mr. Chairman, said Mr. C., under that canopy, penetrated the designs of a corrupt Ministry, and nobly fronted encroachment on its first appearance. It saw beyond the petty taxes, with which it commenced, a long train of oppressive measures terminating in the total annihilation of liberty; and, contemptible as they were, did not hesitate to resist them. Take the experience of the last four or five years, and which, he was sorry to say, exhibited in appearance, at least, a different kind of spirit. He did not wish to view the past further than to guide us for the future. We were but yesterday contending for the indirect trade—the right to export to Europe the coffee and sugar of the West Indies. To-day we are asserting our claim to the direct trade—the right to export our cotton, tobacco, and other domestic produce to market. Yield this point, and tomorrow intercourse between New Orleans and New York—between the planters on James river and Richmond, will be interdicted. For, sir, the career of encroachment is never arrested by submission. It will advance while there remains a single privilege on which it can operate. Gentlemen say that this Government is unfit for any war, but a war of invasion. What, is it not equivalent to invasion, if the mouths of our harbors and outlets are blocked up, and we are denied egress from our own waters? Or, when the burglar is at our door, shall we bravely sally forth and repel his felonious entrance, or meanly skulk within the cells of the castle?

He contended that the real cause of British aggression was not to distress an enemy but to destroy a rival. A comparative view of our commerce with England and the continent would satisfy any one of the truth of this remark. Prior to the embargo, the balance of trade between this country and England was between eleven and fifteen millions of dollars in favor of England. Our consumption of her manufactures was annually increasing, and had risen to nearly $50,000,000. We exported to her what she most wanted, provisions and raw materials for her manufactures, and received in return what she was most desirous to sell. Our exports to France, Holland, Spain, and Italy, taking an average of the years 1802, 3, and 4, amounted to about $12,000,000 of domestic, and about $18,000,000 of foreign produce. Our imports from the same countries amounted to about $25,000,000. The foreign produce exported consisted chiefly of luxuries from the West Indies. It is apparent that this trade, the balance of which was in favor, not of France, but of the United States, was not of very vital consequence to the enemy of England. Would she, therefore, for the sole purpose of depriving her adversary of this commerce, relinquish her valuable trade with this country, exhibiting the essential balance in her favor—nay, more; hazard the peace of the country? No, sir, you must look for an explanation of her conduct in the jealousies of a rival. She sickens at your prosperity, and beholds in your growth—your sails spread on every ocean, and your numerous seamen—the foundations of a Power which, at no very dis-

tant day, is to make her tremble for naval superiority. He had omitted before to notice the loss of our seamen, if we continued in our present situation. What would become of the one hundred thousand (for he understood there was about that number) in the American service? Would they not leave us and seek employment abroad, perhaps in the very country that injures us?

* * * * * *

1. Henry Clay uses an economic argument as the basis for declaring war on Britain. Do you think it is a valid reason for starting a war? What other arguments does Clay give for entering a war with Britain?

2. What do you think about Clay's oratorical style? Is it inflammatory? Do you think it would have been influential in its day?

9–5   The President Asks Congress for a Declaration of War, 1812

By June of 1812, the British seizure of American sailors had reached a point that could no longer be ignored by President James Madison. Although it is thought Madison was pushed into war by certain congressmen in exchange for reassurance of re-election, Madison's speech, which follows, leaves little room for doubt as to the need for action on the part of America. What Madison hoped would be a quick victory saw Washington invaded, although America did eventually win the War of 1812.

SOURCE: Henry Steele Commager, *Documents of American History* (New York: Appleton-Century-Crofts, 1948).

Madison's War Message June 1, 1812

WASHINGTON, June 1, 1812.

To the Senate and House of Representatives of the United States:

I communicate to Congress certain documents, being a continuation of those heretofore laid before them on the subject of our affairs with Great Britain.

Without going back beyond the renewal in 1803 of the war in which Great Britain is engaged, and omitting unrepaired wrongs of inferior magnitude, the conduct of her Government presents a series of acts hostile to the United States as an independent and neutral nation.

British cruisers have been in the continued practice of violating the American flag on the great highway of nations, and of seizing and carrying off persons sailing under it, not in the exercise of a belligerent right founded on the law of nations against an enemy, but of a municipal prerogative over British subjects. British jurisdiction is thus extended to neutral vessels in a situation where no laws can operate but the law of nations and the laws of the country to which the vessels belong, and a self-redress is assumed which, if British subjects were wrongfully detained and alone concerned, is that substitution of force for a resort to the responsible sovereign which falls within the definition of war....

The practice, hence, is so far from affecting British subjects alone that, under the pretext of searching for these, thousands of American citizens, under the safeguard of public law and of their national flag, have been torn from their country and from everything dear to them; have been dragged on board ships of war of a foreign nation and exposed, under the severities of their discipline, to be exiled to the most distant and deadly climes, to risk their lives in the battles of their oppressors, and to be the melancholy instruments of taking away those of their own brethren.

Against this crying enormity, which Great Britain would be so prompt to avenge if committed against herself the United States have in vain exhausted remonstrances and expostulations, and that no proof might be wanting of their conciliatory dispositions, and no pretext left for a continuance of the practice, the British Government was formally assured of the readiness of the

United States to enter into arrangements such as could not be rejected if the recovery of British subjects were the real and the sole object. The communication passed without effect.

British cruisers have been in the practice also of violating the rights and the peace of our coasts. They hover over and harass our entering and departing commerce. To the most insulting pretensions they have added the most lawless proceedings in our very harbors, and have wantonly spilt American blood within the sanctuary of our territorial jurisdiction....

Under pretended blockades, without the presence of an adequate force and sometimes without the practicability of applying one, our commerce has been plundered in every sea, the great staples of our country have been cut off from their legitimate markets, and a destructive blow aimed at our agricultural and maritime interests. In aggravation of these predatory measures they have been considered as in force from the dates of their notification, a retrospective effect being thus added, as has been done in other important cases, to the unlawfulness of the course pursued. And to render the outrage the more signal these mock blockades have been reiterated and enforced in the face of official communications from the British Government declaring as the true definition of a legal blockade "that particular ports must be actually invested and previous warning given to vessels bound to them not to enter."

Not content with these occasional expedients for laying waste our neutral trade, the cabinet of Britain resorted at length to the sweeping system of blockades, under the name of orders in council, which has been molded and managed as might best suit its political views, its commercial jealousies, or the avidity of British cruisers....

Abandoning still more all respect for the neutral rights of the United States and for its own consistency, the British Government now demands as prerequisites to a repeal of its orders as they relate to the United States that a formality should be observed in the repeal of the French decrees nowise necessary to their termination nor exemplified by British usage, and that the French repeal, besides including that portion of the decrees which operates within a territorial jurisdiction, as well as that which operates on the high seas, against the commerce of the United States should not be a single and special repeal in relation to the United States, but should be extended to whatever other neutral nations unconnected with them may be affected by those decrees/...

It has become, indeed, sufficiently certain that the commerce of the United States is to be sacrificed, not as interfering with the belligerent rights of Great Britain; not as supplying the wants of her enemies, which she herself supplies; but as interfering with the monopoly which she

covets for her own commerce and navigation. She carries on a war against the lawful commerce of a friend that she may the better carry on a commerce with an enemy—a commerce polluted by the forgeries and perjuries which are for the most part the only passports by which it can succeed.....

In reviewing the conduct of Great Britain toward the United States our attention is necessarily drawn to the warfare just renewed by the savages on one of our extensive frontiers—a warfare which is known to spare neither age nor sex and to be distinguished by features peculiarly shocking to humanity. It is difficult to account for the activity and combinations which have for some time been developing themselves among tribes in constant intercourse with British traders and garrisons without connecting their hostility with that influence and without recollecting the authenticated examples of such interpositions heretofore furnished by the officers and agents of that Government.

Such is the spectacle of injuries and indignities which have been heaped on our country, and such the crisis which its unexampled forbearance and conciliatory efforts have not been able to avert....

Our moderation and conciliation have had no other effect than to encourage perseverance and to enlarge pretensions. We behold our seafaring citizens still the daily victims of lawless violence, committed on the great common and highway of nations, even within sight of the country which owes them protection. We behold our vessels, freighted with the products of our soil and industry, or returning with the honest proceeds of them, wrested from their lawful destinations, confiscated by prize courts no longer the organs of public law but the instruments of arbitrary edicts, and their unfortunate crews dispersed and lost, or forced or inveigled in British ports into British fleets, whilst arguments are employed in support of these aggressions which have no foundation but in a principle equally supporting a claim to regulate our external commerce in all cases whatsoever.

We behold, in fine, on the side of Great Britain a state of war against the United States, and on the side of the United States a state of peace toward Great Britain.

Whether the United States shall continue passive under these progressive usurpations and these accumulating wrongs, or, opposing force to force in defense of their national rights, shall commit a just cause into the hands of the Almighty Disposer of Events, avoiding all connections which might entangle it in the contest or views of other powers, and preserving a constant readiness to concur in an honorable reestablishment of peace and friendship, is a solemn question which the Constitution wisely confides to the legislative department of the Government. In recommending it to their early deliberations I am happy in the assurance that the decision will be worthy the enlightened and patriotic councils of a virtuous, a free, and a powerful nation....

* * * * * *

1. What charges is James Madison leveling against Britain? Do you believe all of these charges? What would you have done about them?

2. Madison faced problems within his own government. How might a disunited front from Washington have affected his speech? What might Madison be trying to accomplish with this speech?

3. Compare Madison's speech with that of Henry Clay regarding the War of 1812. What can you discern about the two men from their respective speeches?

9–6 Supreme Court Bolsters Federal Power, 1819

In McCulloch versus Maryland, McCulloch, the cashier of the Baltimore branch of the Bank of the United States, refused to pay the state tax on the bank in Maryland. The states were largely unhappy with the federal bank, and were trying to force them out of business with high taxes. Chief Justice John Marshall, who served on the Supreme Court for thirty five years (1801–1835), used the case to not only uphold the rights of the national bank, but to further assert the power of the federal government and bolster the role of the Supreme Court. The following section from the decision outlines the power of the federal government over the states.

SOURCE: Henry Wheaton, *Reports of Cases Argued and Adjudged in the Supreme Court of the United States* (Washington, D.C.: John Conrad & Co., 1819).

McCulloch v. Maryland

The first question made in this cause is, has Congress power to incorporate a bank?

It has been truly said, that this can scarcely be considered as an open question, entirely unprejudiced by the former proceedings of the nation respecting it. The principle now and contested was introduced at a very early period of our history, has been recognized by many successive legislatures, and has been acted upon by the judicial department, in cases of peculiar delicacy, as a law of undoubted obligation....

In discussing this question, the counsel for the State of Maryland have deemed it of some importance, in the construction of the constitution, to consider that instrument not as emanating from the people, but as the act of sovereign and independent States. The powers of the general government, it has been said, are delegated by the States, who alone are truly sovereign; and must be exercised in subordination to the States, who alone possess supreme dominion.

It would be difficult to sustain this proposition. The convention which framed the constitution was, indeed, elected by the State legislatures. But the instrument, when it came from their hands, was a mere proposal, without obligation, or pretensions to it. It was reported to the then existing Congress of the United States, with a request that it might "be submitted to a convention of Delegates, chosen in each State, by the people thereof, under the recommendation of its legislature, for their assent and ratification." This mode of proceeding was adopted; and by the Convention, by Congress, and by the State Legislatures, the instrument was submitted to the people. They acted upon it, in the only manner in which they can act safely, effectively, and wisely, on such a subject, by assembling in Convention. It is true, they assembled in their several States; and where else should they have assembled? No political dreamer was ever wild enough to think of breaking down the lines which separate the States, and of compounding the American people into one common mass. Of consequence, when they act, they act in their States. But the measures they adopt do not, on that account cease to be the measures of the people themselves, or become the measures of the state governments.

From these Conventions the constitution derives its whole authority. The government proceeds directly from the people; is "ordained and established" in the name of the people; and is declared to be ordained, "in order to form a more perfect union, establish justice, insure domestic tranquility, and secure the blessings of liberty to themselves and to their posterity." The assent of the States, in their sovereign capacity, is implied in calling a Convention, and thus submitting that instrument to the people. But the people were at perfect liberty to accept or reject it; and their act was final. It required not the affirmance, and could not be negatived, by the State governments. The constitution, when thus adopted, was of complete obligation, and bound the State sovereignties....

...The government of the Union, then (whatever may be the influence of this fact on the case), is emphatically and truly a government of the people. In form and in substance it emanates from them, its powers are granted by them, and are to be exercised directly on them, and for their benefit.

This government is acknowledged by all to be one of enumerated powers. The principle, that it can exercise only the powers granted to it, would seem too apparent to have required to be enforced by all those arguments which its enlightened friends, while it was depending before the people, found it necessary to urge. That principle is now universally admitted. But the question respecting the extent of the powers actually granted, is perpetually arising, and will probably continue to arise, as long as our system shall exist. In discussing these questions, the conflicting powers of the State and general governments must be brought into view, and the supremacy of their respective laws, when they are in opposition, must be settled.

If any one proposition could command the universal assent of mankind, we might expect it would be this: that the government of the Union, though limited in its powers, is supreme within its sphere of action. This would seem to result necessarily from its nature. It is the government of all; its powers are delegated by all; it represents all, and acts for all. Though any one State may be willing to control its operations, no State is willing to allow others to control them. The nation, on those subjects on which it can act, must necessarily bind its component parts. But this question is not left to mere reason: the people have, in express terms, decided it, by saying, "this constitution, and the laws of the United States, which shall be made in pursuance thereof," "shall be the supreme law of the land," and by requiring that the members of the State legislatures, and the officers of the executive and judicial departments of the States, shall take the oath of fidelity to it.

The government of the United States, then, though limited in its powers, is supreme; and its laws, when made in pursuance of the constitution, form the supreme law of the land, "anything in the constitution or laws of any State, to the contrary, notwithstanding."

Among the enumerated powers, we do not find that of establishing a bank or creating a corporation. But there is no phrase in the instrument which, like the articles of confederation, excludes incidental or implied powers; and which requires that everything granted shall be expressly and minutely described. Even the 10th amendment, which was framed for the purpose of quieting the excessive jealousies which had been excited, omits the word "expressly," and declares only that the powers "not delegated to the United States, nor prohibited to the States, are reserved to the States or to the people"; thus leaving the question, whether the particular power which may become the subject of contest, has been delegated to the one government, or prohibited to the other, to depend on a fair construction of the whole instrument. The men who drew and adopted this amendment, had experienced the embarrassments resulting from the insertion of this word in the articles of confederation, and probably omitted it to avoid those embarrassments. A constitution, to contain an accurate detail of all the subdivisions of which its great powers will admit, and of all the means by which they may be carried into execution, would partake of the prolixity of a legal code, and could scarcely be embraced by the human mind. It would probably never be understood by the public. Its nature, therefore, requires that only its great outlines should be marked, its important objects designated, and the minor ingredients which compose those objects be deduced from the nature of the objects themselves. That this idea was entertained by the framers of the American constitution, is not only to be inferred from the nature of the instrument, but from the language. Why else were some of the limitations, found in the 9th section of the first article, introduced? It is also, in some degree, warranted by their having omitted to use any restrictive term which might prevent its receiving a fair and just interpretation. In considering this question, then, we must never forget, that it is *a constitution* we are expounding…

* * * * * *

1. *What is the central argument to Chief Justice Marshall's decision? Do you agree with it?*

2. *State's rights were a big issue in the early 19th century. What was the position of Jefferson on state's rights? John Adams? Washington? Hamilton?*

9–7 *Missouri Admitted to Statehood, Slavery at Issue, 1820*

When Missouri applied for statehood in 1819, several northern congressmen wanted her admitted only on the condition that an antislavery amendment within the state be attached to the bill. Not only slavery, but the balance of power within congress between northern and southern states was at stake. Finally, a compromise was reached when Maine also applied for statehood. The Missouri compromise, as this bill came to be known, was moved through congress by Speaker of the House, Henry Clay. Slavery would be prohibited north of a line drawn at 36 degrees, 30 minutes latitude. The following sections from the bill admitting Missouri to statehood outline the relevant parts pertaining to slavery.

SOURCE: Henry Steele Commager, *Documents of American History* (New York: Appleton-Century-Crofts, 1948).

Missouri Enabling Act March 6, 1820

An Act to authorize the people of the Missouri territory to

form a constitution and state government, and for the admission of such state into the Union on an equal footing with the original states, and to prohibit slavery, in certain territories.

Be it enacted That the inhabitants of that portion of the Missouri territory included within the boundaries hereinafter designated, be, and they are hereby, authorized to form for themselves a constitution and state government, and to assume such name as they shall deem proper; and the said state, when formed, shall be admitted into the Union, upon an equal footing with the original states, in all respects whatsoever.

SEC. 2. That the said state shall consist of all the territory included within the following boundaries, to wit: Beginning in the middle of the Mississippi river, on the parallel of thirty-six degrees of north latitude; thence west, along that parallel of latitude, to the St. Francois river; thence up, and following the course of that river, in the middle of the main channel thereof, to the parallel of latitude of thirty-six degrees and thirty minutes; thence west, along the same, to a point where the said parallel is intersected by a meridian line passing through the middle of the mouth of the Kansas river, where the same empties into the Missouri river, thence, from the point aforesaid north, along the said meridian line, to the intersection of the parallel of latitude which passes through the rapids of the river Des Moines, making the said line to correspond with the Indian boundary line; thence east, from the point of intersection last aforesaid, along the said parallel of latitude, to the middle of the channel of the main fork of the said river Des Moines; thence down and along the middle of the main channel of the said river Des Moines, to the mouth of the same, where it empties into the Mississippi river; thence, due east, to the middle of the main channel of the Mississippi river; thence down, and following the course of the Mississippi river, in the middle of the main channel thereof, to the place of beginning:...

SEC. 3. That all free white male citizens of the United States, who shall have arrived at the age of twenty-one years, and have resided in said territory three months previous to the day of election, and all other persons qualified to vote for representatives to the general assembly of the said territory, shall be qualified to be elected, and they are hereby qualified and authorized to vote, and choose representatives to form a convention....

SEC. 8. That in all that territory ceded by France to the United States, under the name of Louisiana, which lies north of thirty-six degrees and thirty minutes north latitude, not included within the limits of the state, contemplated by this act, slavery and involuntary servitude, otherwise than in the punishment of crimes, whereof the parties shall have been duly convicted, shall be, and is hereby, forever prohibited: *Provided always*, That any person escaping into the same, from whom labour or service is lawfully claimed, in any state or territory of the United States, such fugitive may be lawfully reclaimed and conveyed to the person claiming his or her labour or service as aforesaid.

* * * * * *

1. *How many states were pro-slavery at the time of Missouri's statehood? How many were antislavery?*

2. *Why would the control of slavery in the newly acquired Louisiana Purchase have been so important at this time?*

9–8 The President Addresses the Union, 1823

Presidential State of the Union addresses are rarely given the status of great documents. But James Monroe's 1823 State of the Union speech became known as The Monroe Doctrine, one of the most famous pieces of policy of our time. Faced with numerous domestic problems ranging from North/South antagonisms to economic depressions brought on by the Panic of 1819, America was also threatened by Russian activity in the Northwest, British designs on Cuba, and Spain's desire to re-acquire her lost colonies. The Monroe Doctrine firmly established American intentions to stop outside intervention in the Western Hemisphere and is printed here complete.

SOURCE: James D. Richardson, ed., *A Compilation of Messages and Papers of the Presidents, 1789-1897* (Washington, D.C.: Government Printing Office, 1869-99).

Fellow citizens of the Senate and the House of Representatives:

...At the proposal of the Russian Imperial Government, made through the minister of the Emperor residing here, a full power and instructions have been transmitted to the minister of the United States at St. Petersburg to arrange by amicable negotiation the respective rights and interests of the two nations on the northwest coast of this continent. A similar proposal had been made by His Imperial Majesty to the government of Great Britain, which has likewise been acceded to. The government of the United States has been desirous, by this friendly proceeding, of manifesting the great value which they have invariably attached to the friendship of the Emperor and their solicitude to cultivate the best understanding with his government. In the discussions to which this interest has given rise and in the arrangements by which they may terminate, the occasion has been judged proper for asserting, as a principle in which the rights and interests of the United States are involved, that the American continents, by the free and independent condition which they have assumed and maintain, are henceforth not to be considered as subjects for future colonization by any European powers....

It was stated at the commencement of the last session that a great effort was then making in Spain and Portugal to improve the condition of the people of those countries, and that it appeared to be conducted with extraordinary moderation. It need scarcely be remarked that the result has been so far very different from what was then anticipated. Of events in that quarter of the globe, with which we have so much intercourse and from which we derive our origin, we have always been anxious and interested spectators. The citizens of the United States cherish sentiments the most friendly in favor of the liberty and happiness of their fellow men on that side of the Atlantic. In the wars of the European powers in matters relating to themselves we have never taken any part, nor does it comport with our policy so to do. It is only when our rights are invaded or seriously menaced that we resent injuries or make preparation for our defense. With the movements in this hemisphere we are of necessity more immediately connected, and by causes which must be obvious to all enlightened and impartial observers. The political system of the allied powers is essentially different in this respect from that of America. This difference proceeds from that which exists in their respective governments: and to the defense of our own, which has been achieved by the loss of so much blood and treasure, and matured by the wisdom of their most enlightened citizens, and under which we have enjoyed unexampled felicity, this whole nation is devoted. We owe it, therefore, to candor and to the amicable relations existing between the United States and those powers to declare that we should consider any attempt on their part to extend their system to any portion of this hemisphere as dangerous to our peace and safety. With the existing colonies or dependencies of any European power we have not interfered and shall not interfere. But with the governments who have declared their independence and maintained it, and whose independence we have, on great consideration and on just principles, acknowledged, we could not view any interposition for the purpose of oppressing them, or controlling in any other manner their destiny, by any European power in any other light than as the manifestation of an unfriendly disposition toward the United States. In the

war between those new Governments and Spain we declared our neutrality at the time of their recognition, and to this we have adhered, and shall continue to adhere, provided no change shall occur which, in the judgment of the competent authorities of this Government, shall make a corresponding change on the part of the United States indispensable to their security.

The late events in Spain and Portugal shew that Europe is still unsettled. Of this important fact no stronger proof can be adduced than that that the allied powers should have thought it proper, on any principle satisfactory to themselves, to have interposed by force in the internal concerns of Spain. To what extent such interposition may be carried, on the same principle, is a question in which all independent powers whose governments differ from theirs are interested, even those most remote, and surely none more so than the United States. Our policy in regard to Europe, which was adopted at an early stage of the wars which have so long agitated that quarter of the globe, nevertheless remains the same, which is, not to interfere in the internal concerns of any of its powers; to consider the government de facto as the legitimate government for us; to cultivate friendly relations with it, and to preserve those relations by a frank, firm, and manly policy, meeting in all instances the just claims of every power, submitting to injuries from none. But in regard to those continents circumstances are eminently and conspicuously different. It is impossible that the allied powers should extend their political system to any portion of either continent without endangering our peace and happiness; nor can anyone believe that our southern brethren, if left to themselves, would adopt it of their own accord. It is equally impossible, therefore, that we should behold such interposition in any form with indifference. If we look to the comparative strength and resources of Spain and those new Governments, and their distance from each other, it must be obvious that she can never subdue them. It is still the true policy of the United States to leave the parties to themselves, in the hope that other powers will pursue the same course.

* * * * * *

1. *Why would President Monroe have shifted the national focus to matters of foreign policy? What events were taking place in America at this time?*

2. *America has been widely criticized for her intervention in other governments in this hemisphere, particularly in Latin America. How does the Monroe Doctrine set up this interference? What do you know about America's interference in Latin America? What do you think about it?*

9–9 A Seneca Chief Addresses Missionaries, 1805

Red Jacket, a Seneca chief, was strongly opposed to the introduction of foreign customs to his people. Originally allied with the British in the Revolutionary War, Red Jacket made peace with the Americans, although he frequently opposed the American government, especially over land treaties. A gifted orator, one of Red Jacket's speeches to the missionaries who were trying to convert his people is reproduced here.

SOURCE: Benjamin B. Thatcher, *Indian Biography* (New York: Harper and Brothers, 1834).

Friend and Brother!

It was the will of the Great Spirit that we should meet together this day. He orders all things, and he has given us a fine day for our council. He has taken his garment from before the sun, and caused it to shine with brightness upon us. Our eyes are opened that we see clearly. Our ears are unstopped that we have been able to hear distinctly the words you have spoken. For all these favors we thank the Great Spirit, and him only.

Brother!—This council fire was kindled by you. It was at your request that we came together at this time. We have listened with attention to what you have said. You requested us to speak our minds freely. This gives us great joy, for we now consider that we stand upright before you, and can speak what we think. All have heard your voice, and all speak to you as one man. Our minds are agreed.

Brother!—You say you want an answer to your talk before you leave this place. It is right you should have one, as you are a great distance from home, and we do not wish to detain you. But we will first look back a little, and tell you what our fathers have told us, and what we have heard from the white people.

Brother!—Listen to what we say. There was a time when our forefathers owned this great island. Their seats extended from the rising to the setting sun. The Great Spirit had made it for the use of Indians. He had created the buffalo, the deer, and other animals for food. He made the bear and the beaver, and their skins served us for clothing. He had scattered them over the country, and taught us how to take them. He had caused the earth to produce corn for bread. All this he had done for his red children because he loved them. If we had any disputes about hunting-grounds, they were generally settled without the shedding of much blood. But an evil day came upon us. Your forefathers crossed the great waters, and landed on this island. Their numbers were small. They

found friends and not enemies. They told us they had fled from their own country for fear of wicked men, and come here to enjoy their religion. They asked for a small seat. We took pity on them, granted their request, and they sat down amongst us. We gave them corn and meat. They gave us poison in return. The white people had now found our country. Tidings were carried back, and more came amongst us. Yet we did not fear them. We took them to be friends. They called us brothers. We believed them, and gave them a larger seat. At length their numbers had greatly increased. They wanted more land. They wanted our country. Our eyes were opened, and our minds became uneasy. Wars took place. Indians were hired to fight against Indians, and many of our people were destroyed. They also brought strong liquors among us. It was strong and powerful, and has slain thousands.

Brother!—Our seats were once large, and yours were very small. You have now become a great people, and we have scarcely a place left to spread our blankets. You have got our country, but are not satisfied. You want to force your religion upon us.

Brother!—Continue to listen. You say that you are sent to instruct us how to worship the Great Spirit agreeably to his mind; and if we do not take hold of the religion which you white people teach, we shall be unhappy hereafter. You say that you are right and we are lost. How do we know this to be true? We understand that your religion is written in a book. If it was intended for us as well as for you, why has not the Great Spirit given it to us; and not only to us, but why did he not give to our forefathers the knowledge of that book, with the means of understanding it rightly? We only know what you tell us about it. How shall we know when to believe, being so often deceived by the white people.

Brother!—You say there is but one way to worship and serve the Great Spirit. If there is but one religion, why do you white people differ so much about it? Why not all agree, as you can all read the book?

Brother!—We do not understand these things. We are told that your religion was given to your forefathers, and has been handed down from father to son. We also have a religion which was given to our forefathers, and has been handed down to us their children. We worship that way. It teaches us to be thankful for all the favors we receive, to love each other, and to be united. We never quarrel about religion.

Brother!—The Great Spirit has made us all. But he has made a great difference between his white and red children. He has given us a different complexion and different customs. To you he has given the arts; to these he has not opened our eyes. We know these things to be true. Since he has made so great a difference between us in other things, why may we not conclude that he has given us a different religion, according to our understanding? The Great Spirit does right. He knows what is best for his children. We are satisfied.

Brother!—We do not wish to destroy your religion, or take it from you. We only want to enjoy our own.

Brother!—You say you have not come to get our land or our money, but to enlighten our minds. I will now tell you that I have been at your meetings and saw you collecting money from the meeting. I cannot tell what this money was intended for, but suppose it was for your minister; and if we should conform to your way of thinking, perhaps you may want some from us.

Brother!—We are told that you have been preaching to white people in this place. These people are our neighbors. We are acquainted with them. We will wait a little while, and see what effect your preaching has upon them. If we find it does them good and makes them honest and less disposed to cheat Indians, we will then consider again what you have said.

Brother!—You have now heard our answer to your talk, and this is all we have to say at present. As we are going to part, we will come and take you by the hand, and hope the Great Spirit will protect you on your journey, and return you safe to your friends.

* * * * * *

1. *What can we learn about Seneca cosmology from Red Jacket's speech?*

2. *What can we tell abut Red Jacket's view of white men from this speech? Do you agree with him?*

3. *Red Jacket makes some strong arguments regarding the freedom of religion for all people. What are they?*

9-10   A Camp Meeting Heats Up, 1829

Francis Trollope, an English novelist of modest success, left us a valuable social history of early 19th century America in her book, Domestic Manners of Americans. *The book formed the opinion of Americans for many Europeans at the time and is still useful to historians. The following excerpt tells the story of a camp meeting, a religious revival that had gained popularity after the second "Great Awakening" in the early 1800s. The camp meetings were not only scenes of religious renewal, they provided what might be the only social contact for isolated settlers.*

SOURCE: Frances Trollope, Domestic Manners of Americans (London: Whittaker, Treacher & Co., 1832).

A Camp Meeting, 1829

It was in the course of this summer that I found the opportunity I had long wished for, of attending a camp-meeting, and I gladly accepted the invitation of an English lady and gentleman to accompany them in their carriage to the spot where it is held; this was in a wild district on the confines of Indiana.

The prospect of passing a night in the back woods of Indiana was by no means agreeable, but I screwed my courage to the proper pitch, and set forth determined to see with my own eyes, and hear with my own ears, what a camp-meeting really was. I had heard it said that being at a camp-meeting was like standing at the gate of heaven, and seeing it opening before you; I had heard it said, that being at a camp-meeting was like finding yourself within the gates of hell; in either case there must be something to gratify curiosity, and compensate one for the fatigue of a long rumbling ride and a sleepless night.

We reached the ground about an hour before midnight, and the approach to it was highly picturesque. The spot chosen was the verge of an unbroken forest, where a space of about twenty acres appeared to have been partially cleared for the purpose. Tents of different sizes were pitched very near together in a circle round the cleared space; behind them were ranged an exterior circle of carriages of every description, and at the back of each were fastened the horses which had drawn them thither. Through this triple circle of defence we distinguished numerous fires burning brightly within it; and still more numerous lights flickering from the trees that were left in the enclosure. The moon was in meridian splendour above our heads....

When we arrived, the preachers were silent; but we heard issuing from nearly every tent mingled sounds of praying, preaching, singing, and lamentation....

We made the circuit of the tents, pausing where attention was particularly excited by sounds more vehement than ordinary. We contrived to look into many; all were strewed with straw, and the distorted figures that we saw kneeling, sitting, and lying amongst it, joined to the woeful and convulsive cries, gave to each, the air of a cell in Bedlam [Bethlehem Hospital, an insane asylum in London]....

At midnight a horn sounded through the camp, which, we were told, was to call the people from private to public worship; and we presently saw them flocking from all sides to the front of the preachers' stand. Mrs. B. and I contrived to place ourselves with our backs supported against the lower part of this structure, and we were thus enabled to witness the scene which followed without personal danger. There were about two thousand persons assembled.

One of the preachers began in a low nasal tone, and, like all other Methodist preachers, assured us of the enormous depravity of man as he comes from the hands of his Maker, and of his perfect sanctification after he had wrestled sufficiently with the Lord to get hold of him, *et caetera*. The admiration of the crowd was evinced by almost constant cries of "Amen! Amen!" "Jesus! Jesus!" "Glory! Glory!" and the like. But this comparative tranquility did not last long: the preacher told them that "this night was the time fixed upon for anxious sinners to wrestle with the Lord;" that he and his brethren "were at hand to help them," and that such as needed their help were to come forward into "the pen."... "The pen" was the space immediately below the preachers' stand; we were therefore placed on the edge of it, and were enabled to see and hear all that took place in the very centre of this extraordinary exhibition.

The crowd fell back at the mention of the *pen*, and for some minutes there was a vacant space before us. The preachers came down from their stand and placed themselves in the midst of it, beginning to sing a hymn, calling upon the penitents to come forth. As they sung they kept turning themselves round to every part of the crowd, and, by degrees, the voices of the whole multitude joined in chorus. This was the only moment at which I perceived any thing like the solemn and beautiful effect, which I had heard ascribed to this woodland worship. It is certain that the combined voices of such a multitude, heard at dead of night, from the depths of their eternal forests, the many fair young faces turned upward, and looking paler and lovelier as they met the moon-beams, the dark figures of the officials in the middle of the circle, the lurid glare thrown by the altar-fires on the woods beyond, did altogether produce a fine and solemn effect, that I shall not easily forget; but ere I had well enjoyed it, the scene changed, and sublimity gave place to horror and disgust....

...Above a hundred persons, nearly all females, came forward, uttering howlings and groans, so terrible that I shall never cease to shudder when I recall them. They appeared to drag each other forward, and on the word being given, "let us pray," they all fell on their knees; but this posture was soon changed for others that permitted greater scope for the convulsive movements of their limbs; and they were soon all lying on the ground in an indescribable confusion of heads and legs. They threw about their limbs with such incessant and violent motion, that I was every instant expecting some serious accident to occur.

But how am I to describe the sounds that proceeded from this strange mass of human beings? I know no words which can convey an idea of it. Hysterical sobbings, convulsive groans, shrieks and screams the most appalling, burst forth on all sides. I felt sick with horror. As if their hoarse and overstrained voices failed to make noise enough, they soon began to clap their hands violently....

One woman near us continued to "call on the Lord," as it is termed, in the loudest possible tone, and without a moment's interval, for the two hours that we kept our dreadful station. She became frightfully hoarse, and her face so red as to make me expect she would burst a blood-vessel. Among the rest of her rant, she said, "I will hold fast to Jesus, I never will let him go; if they take me to hell, I will still hold him fast, fast, fast!" ...

* * * * *

1. *What value do documents such as Trollope's Domestic Manners of Americans have for historians? What can you extract about early 19th-century life from this excerpt?*

2. *What seems to be the role of women at the camp meetings? Speculate as to why they might find the camp meetings to be a place of self expression.*

chapter 10

The Growth of Democracy, 1824–1840

10–1 A Legal Scholar Opposes Spreading the Vote, 1821

One of the foremost legal scholars of his day, James Kent was the first professor of law at Columbia College in 1794, and often referred to as "the American Blackstone." As America struggled with the issue of who could vote in the early 19th century, Kent, like many, opposed broadening voting rights and desired to restrict the electoral rights to property holders. Kent opposed universal suffrage at the 1821 New York constitutional convention, his tenet is reproduced here.

SOURCE: *Reports of the Proceedings and Debates of the Convention of 1821, Assembled for the Purpose of Amending the Constitution of the State of New York* (Albany: E. and E. Hosford, 1821).

These are some of the fruits of our present government; and yet we seem to be dissatisfied with our present condition, and we are engaged in the bold and hazardous experiment of remodelling the constitution. Is it not fit and discreet; I speak as to wise men; is it not fit and proper that we should pause in our career, and reflect well on the immensity of the innovation in contemplation? Discontent in the midst of so much prosperity, and with such abundant means of happiness, looks like ingratitude, and as if we were disposed to arraign the goodness of Providence. Do we not expose ourselves to the danger of being deprived of the blessings we have enjoyed?....

The senate has hitherto been elected by the farmers of the state—by the free and independent lords of the soil, worth at least $250 in freehold estate, over and above all debts charged thereon. The governor has been chosen by the same electors, and we have hitherto elected citizens of elevated rank and character. Our assembly has been chosen by freeholders, possessing a freehold of the value of $50, or by persons renting a tenement of the yearly value of $5, and who have been rated and actually paid taxes to the state. By the report before us, we propose to annihilate, at one stroke, all those property distinctions and to bow before the idol of universal suffrage. That extreme democratic principle, when applied to the legislative and executive departments of the government, has been regarded with terror, by the wise men of every age,

because in every European republic, ancient and modern, in which it has been tried, it has terminated disastrously, and been productive of corruption, injustice, violence, and tyranny. And dare we flatter ourselves that we are a peculiar people, who can run the career of history, exempted from the passions which have disturbed and corrupted the rest of mankind. If we are like other races of men, with similar follies and vices, then I greatly fear that our posterity will have reason to deplore in sackcloth and ashes, the delusion of the day....

Now, sir, I wish to preserve our senate as the representative of the landed interest. I wish those who have an interest in the soil, to retain the exclusive possession of a branch in the legislature, as a strong hold in which they may find safety through all the vicissitudes which the state may be destined, in the course of Providence, to experience. I wish them to be always enabled to say that their freeholds cannot be taxed without their consent. The men of no property, together with the crowds of dependents connected with great manufacturing and commercial establishments, and the motley and undefinable population of crowded ports, may, perhaps, at some future day, under skilful management predominate in the assembly, and yet we should be perfectly safe if no laws could pass without the free consent of the owners of the soil. That security we at present enjoy; and it is that security which I wish to retain.

The apprehended danger from the experiment of universal suffrage applied to the whole legislative department, is no dream of the imagination. It is too mighty an excitement for the moral constitution of men to endure. The tendency of universal suffrage, is to jeopardize the rights of property, and the principles of liberty. There is a constant tendency in human society, and the history of every age proves it; there is a tendency in the poor to cover a share in the plunder of the rich; in the debtor to relax or avoid the obligation of contracts; in the majority to tyrannize over the minority, and trample down their rights; in the indolent and profligate, to cast the whole burthens of society upon the industrious and the virtuous; and *there is a tendency in ambitious and wicked men, to inflame these combustible materials*. It requires a vigilant government, and a firm administration of justice, to counteract that tendency. Thou shalt not covet; thou shalt not steal; are divine injunctions induced by this miserable depravity of our nature. Who can undertake to calculate with any precision, how many millions of people, this great state will contain in the course of this and the next century, and who can estimate the future extent and magnitude of our commercial ports? The disproportion between the men of property, and the men of no property, will be in every society in a ratio to its commerce, wealth, and population. We are no longer to remain plain and simple republics of farmers, like the New-England colonists, or the Dutch settlements on the Hudson. We are fast becoming a great nation, with great commerce, manufactures, population, wealth, luxuries, and with the vices and miseries that they engender. One seventh of the population of the city of Paris at this day subsists on charity, and one third of the inhabitants of that city die in the hospitals; what would become of such a city with universal suffrage? France has upwards of four, and England upwards of five millions of manufacturing and commercial labourers without property. Could these Kingdoms sustain the weight of universal suffrage? The radicals in England, with the force of that mighty engine, would at once sweep away the property, the laws, and the liberties of that island like a deluge.

The growth of the city of New-York is enough to startle and awaken those who are pursuing the IGNUS FATUUS of universal suffrage.

* * * * * *

1. *What is Kent's central argument against universal suffrage? Do you agree with it?*

2. *What might men like Kent have stood to gain by limiting the vote? What groups are left completely out of his discussion?*

10-2   *What Shall be the Role of Government, 1834*

The role of state versus federal rights and individual versus state rights was still being hotly contested in the early 19th century. The debate was carried on not only in the courts and congress, but by common people in the street and in newspapers. The following editorial by William Leggett, editor of the Evening Post, taken from Nov. 21, 1834, explores just these issues. Leggett wrote on a broad variety of topics, but was most often critical of the government, and fought for the rights of the individual.

SOURCE: Theodore Sedgwick, Jr., ed., *A Collection of the Political Writings of William Leggett* (New York: Taylor & Dodd, 1840).

True Functions of Government

"There are no necessary evils in Government. Its evils exist only in its abuses. If it would confine itself to *equal protection*, and, as heaven does its rains, shower its favours alike on the high and the low, the rich and the poor, it would be an unqualified blessing."

This is the language of our venerated President, and the passage deserves to be written in letters of gold, for neither in truth of sentiment or beauty of expression can it be surpassed. We choose it as our text for a few remarks on the true functions of Government.

The fundamental principle of all governments is the protection of person and property from domestic and foreign enemies; in other words, to defend the weak against the strong. By establishing the social feeling in a community, it was intended to counteract that selfish feeling, which, in its proper exercise, is the parent of all worldly good, and, in its excesses, the root of all evil. The functions of Government, when confined to their proper sphere of action, are therefore restricted to the making of general laws, uniform and universal in their operation, for these purposes, and for no other.

Governments have no right to interfere with the pursuits of individuals, as guaranteed by those general laws, by offering encouragements and granting privileges to any particular class of industry, or any select bodies of men, inasmuch as all classes of industry and all men are equally important to the general welfare, and equally entitled to protection.

Whenever a Government assumes the power of discriminating between the different classes of the community, it becomes, in effect, the arbiter of their prosperity, and exercises a power not contemplated by any intelligent people in delegating their sovereignty to their rulers. It then becomes the great regulator of the profits of every species of industry, and reduces men from a dependence on their own exertions, to a dependence on the caprices of their Government. Governments possess no delegated right to tamper with individual industry a single hair's-breadth beyond what is essential to protect the rights of person and property.

In the exercise of this power of intermeddling with the private pursuits and individual occupations of the citizen, a Government may at pleasure elevate one class and depress another; it may one day legislate exclusively for the farmer, the next for the mechanic, and the third for the manufacturer, who all thus become the mere puppets of legislative cobbling and tinkering, instead of independent citizens, relying on their own resources for their prosperity. It assumes the functions which belong alone to an overruling Providence, and affects to become the universal dispenser of good and evil.

This power of regulating—of increasing or diminishing the profits of labour and the value of property of all kinds and degrees, by direct legislation, in a great measure destroys the essential object of all civil compacts, which, as we said before, is to make the social a counterpoise to the selfish feeling. By thus operating directly on the latter, by offering one class a bounty and another a discouragement, they involve the selfish feeling in every struggle of party for the ascendancy, and give to the force of political rivalry all the bitterest excitement of personal interests conflicting with each other. Why is it that parties now exhibit excitement aggravated to a degree dangerous to the existence of the Union and to the peace of society? Is it not that by frequent exercises of partial legislation, almost every man's personal interests have become deeply involved in the result of the contest? In common times, the strife of parties is the mere struggle of ambitious leaders for power; now they are deadly contests of the whole mass of the people, whose pecuniary interests are implicated in the event, because the Government has usurped and exercised the power of legislating on their private affairs. The selfish feeling has been so strongly called into action by this abuse of authority as almost to overpower the social feeling, which it should be the object of a good Government to foster by every means in its power.

No nation, knowingly and voluntarily, with its eyes open, ever delegated to its Government this enormous power, which places at its disposal the property, the industry, and the fruits of the industry, of the whole people. As a general rule, the prosperity of rational men depends on themselves. Their talents and their virtues shape their fortunes. They are therefore the best judges of their own affairs, and should be permitted to seek their own happiness in their own way, untrammelled by the capricious interference of legislative bungling, so long as they do not violate the equal rights of others, nor transgress the general laws for the security of person and property.

But modern refinements have introduced new principle in the science of Government. Our own Government, most especially, has assumed and exercised an authority over the people, not unlike that of weak and vacillating parents over their children, and with about the same degree of impartiality. One child becomes a favourite because he has made a fortune, and another because he has failed in the pursuit of that object; one because of its beauty, and another because of its deformity. Our Government has thus exercised the right of dispensing favours to one or another class of citizens at will; of directing its patronage first here and then there; of bestowing one day and taking back the next; of giving to the few and denying to the many; of investing wealth with new and exclusive privileges, and distributing, as it were at random, and with a capricous policy, in unequal portions, what it ought not to bestow, or what, if given away, should be equally the portion of all.

A government administered on such a system of policy may be called a Government of Equal Rights, but it is in its nature and essence a disguised despotism. It is the capricious dispenser of good and evil, without any restraint, except its own sovereign will. It holds in its hand the distribution of the goods of this world, and is consequently the uncontrolled master of the people.

Such was not the object of the Government of the United States, nor such the powers delegated to it by the people. The object was beyond doubt to protect the weak against the strong, by giving them an equal voice and equal rights in the state; not to make one portion stronger, the other weaker at pleasure, by crippling one or more classes of the community, or making them tributary to one alone. This is too great a power to entrust to Government. It was never given away by the people, and is not a right, but a usurpation.

Experience will show that this power has always been exercised under the influence and for the exclusive benefit of wealth. It was never wielded in behalf of the community. Whenever an exception is made to the general law of the land, founded on the principle of equal rights, it will always be found to be in favour of wealth.

These immunities are never bestowed on the poor. They have no claim to a dispensation of exclusive benefits, and their only business is to *"take care of the rich that the rich may take care of the poor."*

Thus it will be seen that the sole reliance of the labouring classes, who constitute a vast majority of every people on the earth, is the great principle of Equal Rights; that their only safeguard against oppression is a system of legislation which leaves all to the free exercise of their talents and industry, within the limits of the GENERAL LAW, and which, on no pretence of public good, bestows on any particular class of industry, or any particular body of men, rights or privileges not equally enjoyed by the great aggregate of the body politic.

Time will remedy the departures which have already been made from this sound republican system, if the people but jealously watch and indignantly frown on any future attempts to invade their equal rights, or appropriate to the few what belongs to all alike. To quote, in conclusion, the language of the great man, with whose admirable sentiment we commenced these remarks, "it is time to pause in our career—if we cannot—at once, in justice to the interests vested under improvident legislation, make our government what it ought to be, we can at least take a stand against all new grants of monopolies and exclusive privileges, and against any prostitution of our Government to the advancement of the few at the expense of the many."

* * * * * *

1. *What is Leggett's central argument? Do you agree? Who does he seem to be supporting?*

2. *Is Leggett saying that government has too much power in individual lives? Cite examples to either agree or disagree.*

3. *How is Leggett using the press to create the "Fourth Estate?"*

10-3 The Cherokee are Sent to the Indian Territory, 1835

Discovery of gold on Cherokee lands marked the end of their struggle to save their cultural homes in the South. Going so far as to sue the state of Georgia in the Supreme Court in 1831, the Cherokees lost. In Cherokee Nation v. Georgia, Chief Justice Marshall ruled that the Cherokee were under the jurisdiction of Georgia and must move. The Treaty of New Echota, signed by a very small number of Cherokee in 1835, fraudulently gave all their land to white settlers. Finally, President Jackson proposed removing all of the Southern Indians to the Indian Territory, west of the Mississippi. The "trail of tears," where thousands died during their relocation in 1838, is only a part of the devastation wrecked on the Cherokee. In the following 1835 address to Congress, Jackson outlines his rationale for moving the Indians.

SOURCE: James Richardson, ed., *A Compilation of the Messages and Papers of the Presidents* (Washington, D.C.: Government Printing Office, 1896–99).

…The plan of removing the aboriginal people who yet remain within the settled portions of the United States to the country west of the Mississippi River approaches its consummation. It was adopted on the most mature consideration of the condition of this race, and ought to be persisted in till the object is accomplished, and prosecuted with as much vigor as a just regard to their circumstances will permit, and as fast as their consent can be obtained. All preceding experiments for the improvement of the Indians have failed. It seems now to be an established fact that they can not live in contact with a civilized community and prosper. Ages of fruitless endeavors have at length brought us to a knowledge of this principle of intercommunication with them. The past we can not recall, but the future we can provide for. Independently of the treaty stipulations into which we have entered with the various tribes for the usufructuary rights they have ceded to us, no one can doubt the moral duty of the Government of the United States to protect and if possible to preserve and perpetuate the scattered remnants of this race which are left within our borders. In the discharge of this duty an extensive region in the West has been assigned for their permanent residence. It has been divided into districts and allotted among them. Many have already removed and others are preparing to go, and with the exception of two small bands living in Ohio and Indiana, not exceeding 1,500 persons, and of the Cherokees, all the tribes on the east side of the Mississippi, and extending from Lake Michigan to Florida, have entered into engagements which will lead to their transplantation.

The plan for their removal and reëstablishment is founded upon the knowledge we have gained of their character and habits, and has been dictated by a spirit of enlarged liberality. A territory exceeding in extent that relinquished has been granted to each tribe. Of its climate, fertility, and capacity to support an Indian population the representations are highly favorable. To these districts the Indians are removed at the expense of the United States, and with certain supplies of clothing, arms, ammunition, and other indispensable articles; they are also furnished gratuitously with provisions for the period of a year after their arrival at their new homes. In that time, from the nature of the country and of the products raised by them, they can subsist themselves by agricultural labor, if they choose to resort to that mode of life; if they do not they are upon the skirts of the great prairies, where countless herds of buffalo roam, and a short time suffices to adapt their own habits to the changes which a change of the animals destined for their food may require. Ample arrangements have also been made for the support of schools; in some instances council houses and churches are to be erected, dwellings constructed for the chiefs, and mills for common use. Funds have been set apart for the maintenance of the poor; the most necessary mechanical arts have been introduced, and blacksmiths, gunsmiths, wheelwrights, millwrights, etc., are supported among them. Steel and iron, and sometimes salt, are purchased for them, and plows and other farming utensils, domestic animals, looms, spinning wheels, cards, etc., are presented to them. And besides these beneficial arrangements, annuities are in all cases paid, amounting in some instances to more than $30 for each individual of the tribe, and in all cases sufficiently great, if justly divided and prudently expended, to enable them, in addition to their own exertions, to live comfortably. And as a stimulus for exertion, it is now provided by law that "in all cases of the appointment of interpreters or other persons employed for the benefit of the Indians a preference shall be given to persons of Indian descent, if such can be found who are properly qualified for the discharge of the duties."

Such are the arrangements for the physical comfort and for the moral improvement of the Indians. The necessary measures for their political advancement and for their separation from our citizens have not been neglected. The pledge of the United States has been given by Congress that the country destined for the residence of this people shall be forever "secured and guaranteed to them." A country west of Missouri and Arkansas has been assigned to them, into which the white settlements are not to be pushed. No political communities can be formed in that extensive region, except those which are established by the Indians themselves or by the United States for them and with their concurrence. A barrier has thus been raised for their protection against the encroachment of our citizens, and guarding the Indians as far as possible from those evils which have brought them to their present condition. Summary authority has been given by law to destroy all ardent spirits found in their country, without waiting the doubtful result and slow process of a legal seizure. I consider the absolute and unconditional interdiction of this article among these people as the first and great step in their melioration. Halfway measures will answer no purpose. These can not successfully contend against the cupidity of the seller and the overpowering appetite of the buyer. And the destructive effects of the traffic are marked in every page of the history of our Indian intercourse....

* * * * * *

1. *Why were the Cherokee unable to "live in contact with a civilized community and prosper" as Jackson asserts in his speech? What is Jackson's rationale?*

2. *Do you think Jackson was sincerely acting in what he thought were the Indians' best interests? Why or why not? What other agendas might Jackson and others have had for relocating the Indians?*

3. *What are the economic measures Jackson proposes for the Indians?*

10-4   A Cherokee Speaks for His Tribe, 1826

Elias Boudinot was a Cherokee educated in a mission school in Cornwall, Connecticut. As the editor of the first national Cherokee paper, the Cherokee Phoenix, in 1828, using their own syllabury, Boudinot was widely read. Boudinot also published a book, Poor Sarah: or the Indian Woman. Boudinot was one of the signers of the Treaty of Echota and favored Cherokee relocation to the Indian Territory, a view for which he was murdered in 1839. The following is from "An Address to the Whites," in which Boudinot lists some of the accomplishments of his tribe.

SOURCE: Theda Perdue, ed., *Cherokee Editor: The Writings of Elias Boudinot* (Knoxville: University of Tennessee Press, 1983).

...In many places the word of God is regularly preached and explained, both by missionaries and natives; and there are numbers who have publicly professed their belief and interest in the merits of the great Saviour of the world. It is worthy of remark, that in no ignorant country have the missionaries undergone less trouble and difficulty, in spreading a knowledge of the Bible, than in this. Here, they have been welcomed and encouraged by the proper authorities of the nation, their persons have been protected, and in very few instances have some individual vagabonds threatened violence to them. Indeed it may be said with truth, that among no heathen people has the faithful minister of God experienced greater success, greater reward for his labour, than in this. He is surrounded by attentive hearers, the words which flow from his lips are not spent in vain. The Cherokees have had no established religion of their own, and perhaps to this circumstance we may attribute, in part, the facilities with which

missionaries have pursued their ends. They cannot be called idolators; for they never worshipped Images. They believed in a Supreme Being, the Creator of all, the God of the white, the red, and the black man. They also believed in the existence of an evil spirit who resided, as they thought, in the setting sun, the future place of all who in their life time had done iniquitously. Their prayers were addressed alone to the Supreme Being, and which if written would fill a large volume, and display much sincerity, beauty and sublimity. When the ancient customs of the Cherokees were in their full force, no warrior thought himself secure, unless he had addressed his guardian angel; no hunter could hope for success, unless before the rising sun he had asked the assistance of his God, and on his return at eve had offered his sacrifice to him.

There are three things of late occurance, which must certainly place the Cherokee Nation in a fair light, and act as a powerful argument in favor of Indian improvement.

First. The invention of letters.

Second. The translation of the New Testament into Cherokee.

And Third. The organization of a Government.

The Cherokee mode of writing lately invented by George Guest, who could not read any language nor speak any other than his own, consists of eighty-six characters, principally syllabic, the combinations of which form all the words of the language. Their terms may be greatly simplified, yet they answer all the purposes of writing, and already many natives use them.

The translation of the New Testament, together with Guest's mode of writing, has swept away that barrier which has long existed, and opened a spacious channel for the instruction of adult Cherokees. Persons of all ages and classes may now read the precepts of the Almighty in their own language. Before it is long, there will scarcely be an individual in the nation who can say, "I know not

God neither understand I what thou sayest," for all shall know him from the greatest to the least. The aged warrior over whom has rolled three score and ten years of savage life, will grace the temple of God with his hoary head; and the little child yet on the breast of its pious mother shall learn to lisp its Maker's name.

The shrill sound of the Savage yell shall die away as the roaring of far distant thunder; and Heaven wrought music will gladden the affrighted wilderness. "The solitary places will be glad for them, and the desert shall rejoice and blossom as a rose." Already do we see the morning star, forerunner of approaching dawn, rising over the tops of those deep forests in which for ages have echoed the warrior's whoop. But has not God said it, and will he not do it? The Almighty decrees his purposes, and man cannot with all his ingenuity and device countervail them. They are more fixed in their course than the rolling sun—more durable than the everlasting mountains.

The Government, though defective in many respects, is well suited to the condition of the inhabitants. As they rise in information and refinement, changes in it must follow, until they arrive at that state of advancement, when I trust they will be admitted into all the privileges of the American family.

The Cherokee Nation is divided into eight districts, in each of which are established courts of justice, where all disputed cases are decided by a Jury, under the direction of a circuit Judge, who has jurisdiction over two districts. Sheriffs and other public officers are appointed to execute the decisions of the courts, collect debts, and arrest thieves and other criminals. Appeals may be taken to the Superior Court, held annually at the seat of Government. The Legislative authority is vested in a General Court, which consists of the National Committee and Council. The National Committee consists of thirteen members, who are generally men of sound sense and fine talents. The National Council consists of thirty-two members, who act as the representatives of the people. Every bill passing these two bodies, becomes the law of the land. Clerks are appointed to do the writings, and record the proceedings of the Council. The executive power is vested in two principal chiefs, who hold their office during good behaviour, and sanction all the decisions of the legislative council. Many of the laws display some degree of civilization, and establish the respectability of the nation.

Polygamy is abolished. Female chastity and honor are protected by law. The Sabbath is respected by the Council during session. Mechanics are encouraged by law. The practice of putting aged persons to death for witchcraft is abolished and murder has now become a governmental crime.

From what I have said, you will form but a faint opinion of the true state and prospects of the Cherokees. You will, however, be convinced of three important truths.

First, that the means which have been employed for the christianization and civilization of this tribe, have been greatly blessed. Second, that the increase of these means will meet with final success. Third, that it has now become necessary, that efficient and more than ordinary means should be employed.

Sensible of this last point, and wishing to do something for themselves, the Cherokees have thought it advisable that there should be established, a Printing Press and a Seminary of respectable character; and for these purposes your aid and patronage are now solicited. They wish the types, as expressed in their resolution, to be composed of English letters and Cherokee characters. These characters have now become extensively used in the nation; their religious songs are written in them; there is an astonishing eagerness in people of all classes and ages to acquire a knowledge of them; and the New Testament has been translated into their language. All this impresses on them the immediate necessity of procuring types. The most informed and judicious of our nation, believe that such a press would go further to remove ignorance, and her offspring superstition and prejudice, than all other means. The adult part of the nation will probably grovel on in ignorance and die in ignorance, without any fair trial upon them, unless the proposed means are carried into effect. The simplicity of this method of writing, and the eagerness to obtain a knowledge of it, are evinced by the astonishing rapidity with which it is acquired, and by the numbers who do so. It is about two years since its introduction, and already there are a great many who can read it. In the neighbourhood in which I live, I do not recollect a male Cherokee, between the ages of fifteen and twenty five, who is ignorant of this mode of writing. But in connexion with those for Cherokee characters, it is necessary to have types for English letters. There are many who already speak and read the English language, and can appreciate the advantages which would result from the publication of their laws and transactions in a well conducted newspaper. Such a paper, comprising a summary of religious and political events, etc. on the one hand; and on the other, exhibiting the feelings, disposition, improvements, and prospects of the Indians; their traditions, their true character, as it once was and as it now is; the ways and means most likely to throw the mantle of civilization over all tribes; and such other matter as will tend to diffuse proper and correct impressions in regard to their condition—such a paper could not fail to create much interest in the American community, favourable to the aborigines, and to have a powerful influence on the advancement of the Indians themselves. How can the patriot or the philanthropist devise efficient means, without full and correct information as to the subjects of his labour. And I am inclined to think, after all that has been written in narratives, professedly to elucidate the leading traits of their character, that the public knows little of that character. To obtain a correct and complete knowledge of these people, there must exist a vehicle of Indian Intelligence, altogether different from those which have heretofore been employed. Will not a paper published in an Indian country, under proper and judicious regulations, have the desired effect? I do not say that Indians will produce learned and elaborate dissertations in explanation and vindication of their own character; but they may exhibit specimens of their intellectual efforts, of their eloquence of their moral, civil and physical advancement, which will do quite as much to remove prejudice and to give profitable information....

* * * * * *

1. *Do you agree with Boudinot's statement that "the Cherokees have had no organized religion?" Is this plausible? Did they have a governmental system before centralization?*

2. *What do you think about the standards by which Boudinot measures the civilization of his tribe?*

10–5   A Choctaw Chief Bids Farewell, 1832

The Choctaw lived in central and southern Mississippi at the time of first European contact. Enemies of their more warlike neighbors, the Chickasaws, the Choctaw relied on slash and burn agriculture for their sustenance. As more and more Indians were removed from land desired by white settlers, the Choctaw were no exception. Having ceded the last of their lands to the American government by 1830, they, like the Cherokee, were moved to the Indian Territory in what is now Oklahoma. George W. Harkins, a chief of the Choctaws, wrote this "Farewell Letter to the American People," in 1832.

SOURCE: *The American Indian, December, 1926.*

To the American People.

It is with considerable diffidence that I attempt to address the American people, knowing and feeling sensibly my incompetency; and believing that your highly and well improved minds could not be well entertained by the address of a Choctaw. But having determined to emigrate west of the Mississippi river this fall, I have thought proper in bidding you farewell, to make a few remarks of my views and the feelings that actuate me on the subject of our removal.

Believing that our all is at stake and knowing that you readily sympathize with the distressed of every country, I confidently throw myself on your indulgence and ask you to listen patiently. I do not arrogate to myself the prerogative of deciding upon the expediency of the late treaty, yet I feel bound as a Choctaw, to give a distinct expression of my feelings on that interesting (and to the Choctaws) all important subject.

We were hedged in by two evils, and we chose that which we thought least. Yet we could not recognize the right that the state of Mississippi had assumed to legislate for us. Although the legislature of the state were qualified to make laws for their own citizens, that did not qualify them to become law makers to a people who were so dissimilar in manners and customs as the Choctaws are to the Mississippians. Admitting that they understood the people, could they remove that mountain of prejudice that has ever obstructed the streams of justice, and prevented their salutary influence from reaching my devoted countrymen? We as Choctaws rather chose to suffer and be free, than live under the degrading influence of laws, where our voice could not be heard in their formation.

Much as the state of Mississippi has wronged us, I cannot find in my heart any other sentiment than an ardent wish for her prosperity and happiness.

I could cheerfully hope that those of another age and generation may not feel the effects of those oppressive measures that have been so illiberally dealt out to us; and that peace and happiness may be their reward. Amid the gloom and honors of the present separation, we are cheered with a hope that ere long we shall reach our destined home, and that nothing short of the basest acts of treachery will ever be able to wrest it from us, and that we may live free. Although your ancestors won freedom on the fields of danger and glory, our ancestors owned it as their birthright, and we have had to purchase it from you as the vilest slaves buy their freedom.

Yet it is said that our present movements are our own voluntary acts—such is not the case. We found ourselves like a benighted stranger, following false guides, until he was surrounded on every side, with fire or water. The fire was certain destruction, and feeble hope was left him of escaping by water. A distant view of the opposite shore encourages the hope; to remain would be utter annihilation. Who would hesitate, or would say that his plunging into the water was his own voluntary act? Painful in the extreme is the mandate of our expulsion. We regret that it should proceed from the mouth of our professed friend, and for whom our blood was commingled with that of his bravest warriors, on the field of danger and death.

But such is the instability of professions. The man who said that he would plant a stake and draw a line around us, that never should be passed, was the first to say he could not guard the lines, and drew up the stake and wiped out all traces of the line. I will not conceal from you my fears, that the present grounds may be removed—I have my forebodings—who of us can tell after witnessing what has already been done, what the next force may be.

I ask you in the name of justice, for repose for myself and my injured people. Let us alone—we will not harm you, we want rest. We hope, in the name of justice, that another outrage may never be committed against us, and that we may for the future be cared for as children, and not driven about as beasts, which are benefitted by a change of pasture.

Taking an example from the American government, and knowing the happiness which its citizens enjoy, under the influence of mild republican institutions, it is the intention of our countrymen to form a government assimilated to that of our white brethren in the United States, as nearly as their condition will permit.

We know that in order to protect the rights and secure the liberties of the people, no government approximates so nearly to perfection as the one to which we have alluded. As east of the Mississippi we have been friends, so west we will cherish the same feelings, with additional fervor; and although we may be removed to the desert, still we shall look with fine regard, upon those who have promised us their protection. Let that feeling be reciprocated.

Friends, my attachment to my native land is strong—that cord is now broken; and we must go forth as wanderers in a strange land! I must go—let me entreat you to regard us with feelings of kindness, and when the hand of oppression is stretched against us, let me hope that every part of the United States, filling the mountains and valleys, will echo and say stop, you have no power, we are the sovereign people, and our friends shall no more be disturbed. We ask you for nothing that is incompatible with your other duties.

We go forth sorrowful, knowing that wrong has been done. Will you extend to us your sympathizing regards until all traces of disagreeable oppositions are obliterated, and we again shall have confidence in the professions of our white brethren.

Here is the land of our progenitors, and here are their bones; they left them as a sacred deposit, and we have been compelled to venerate its trust; it is dear to us yet we cannot stay, my people are dear to me, with them I must go. Could I stay and forget them and leave them to struggle alone, unaided, unfriended, and forgotten by our great father? I should then be unworthy the name of a Choctaw, and be a disgrace to my blood. I must go with them; my destiny is cast among the Choctaw people. If they suffer, so will I; if they prosper, then I will rejoice. Let me again ask you to regard us with feelings of kindness.

* * * * *

1. What do you think about Harkins's assertion that America "readily" sympathize[s] with the distressed of every country"? How did this relate to the fate of the Choctaws?

2. What is the overall tone of Harkins's letter? What does this imply?

SOURCE: Edwin P. Whipple, The Great Speeches and Orations of Daniel Webster (Boston: Little, Brown, 1889).

10–6 American Senator Opposes Nullification, 1830

Daniel Webster has been marked as one of the greatest orators of all time, compared to Cicero and Demosthenes. Educated as a lawyer, Webster served in congress and dominated it for many years, along with Henry Clay and John C. Calhoun. As a senator, one of Webster's more famous speeches was against Senator Robert Hayne over the rights of states to nullification, the ability to declare a federal law invalid within their state. Webster's "Liberty and Union, now and forever, one and inseparable" speech was one of the great congressional defenses of the federal government's overriding power.

...If anything be found in the national constitution, either by original provision or subsequent interpretation, which ought not to be in it, the people know how to get rid of it. If any construction be established unacceptable to them, so as to become practically a part of the constitution, they will amend it, at their own sovereign pleasure. But while the people choose to maintain it as it is, while they are satisfied with it, and refuse to change it, who has given, or who can give, to the state legislatures a right to alter it, either by interference, construction, or otherwise? Gentlemen do not seem to recollect that the people have any power to do anything for themselves. They imagine there is no safety for them any longer than they are under the close guardianship of the state legislatures. Sir, the people have not trusted their safety, in regard to the general constitution, to these hands. They have required other security, and taken other bonds. They have chosen to trust themselves, first, to the plain words of the instrument, and to such construction as the government itself, in doubtful cases, should put on its own powers, and under their oaths of office and subject to their responsibility to them; just as the people of a state trust their own state government with similar power. Secondly, they have reposed their trust in the efficacy of frequent elections, and in their own power to remove their own servants and agents whenever they see cause. Thirdly, they have reposed their trust in the judicial power, which, in order that it might be trustworthy, they have made as respectable, as disinterested, and as independent as was practicable. Fourthly, they have seen fit to rely, in case of necessity, or high expediency on their known and admitted power to alter or amend the constitution, peaceably and quietly, whenever experience shall point out defects or imperfections. And, finally, the people of the United States have at no time, in no way, directly or indirectly, authorized any state legislature to construe or interpret *their* high instrument of government; much less, to interfere, by their own power, to arrest its course and operation.

If, sir, the people in these respects had done otherwise than they have done, their constitution could neither have been preserved, nor would it have been word preserving. And if its plain provisions shall now be disregarded, and these new doctrines interpolated in it, it will become as feeble and helpless a being as its enemies, whether early or more recent, could possibly desire. It will exist in every state but as a poor dependent on state permission. It must borrow leave to be and will be, no longer than state pleasure, or state discretion, sees fit to grant the indulgence, and prolong its poor existence.

But, sir, although there are fears, there are hopes also. The people have preserved this, their own chosen constitution, for forty years, and have seen their happiness, prosperity, and renown grow with its growth, and strengthen with its strength. They are now, generally, strongly attached to it. Overthrown by direct assault, it cannot be; evaded, undermined, NULLIFIED, it will not be, if we, and those who shall succeed us here, as agents and representatives of the people, shall conscientiously and vigilantly discharge the two great branches of our public trust, faithfully to preserve, and wisely to administer it....

I have not allowed myself, sir, to look beyond the Union, to see what might lie hidden in the dark recess, behind. I have not coolly weighed the chances of preserving liberty when the bonds that unite us together shall be broken asunder. I have not accustomed myself to hang over the precipice of disunion, to see whether, with my short sight, I can fathom the depth of the abyss below; nor could I regard him as a safe counselor in the affairs of this government, whose thoughts should be mainly bent on considering, not how the Union should be best preserved, but how tolerable might be the condition of the people when it shall be broken up and destroyed. While the Union lasts, we have high, exciting gratifying prospects spread out before us, for us and our children. Beyond that I seek not to penetrate the vail. God grant that in my day, at least, that curtain may not rise! God grant that on my vision never may be opened what lies behind! When my eyes shall be turned to behold for the last time the sun in heaven, may I not see him shining on the broken and dishonored fragments of once glorious Union; on states dissevered, discordant belligerent; on a land rent with civil feuds, or drenched it may be, in fraternal blood! Let their last feeble and lingering glance rather behold the gorgeous ensign of the republic, now known and honored throughout the earth still full high advanced, its arms and trophies streaming in their original luster, not a stripe erased or polluted, not a single star obscured, bearing for its motto, no such miserable interrogatory as "What is all this worth?" nor those other words of delusion and folly, "Liberty first and Union afterwards;" but everywhere, spread all over in characters of living light, blazing on all its ample folds, as they float over the sea and over the land, and in every wind under the whole heavens, that other sentiment, dear to every true American heart—Liberty and Union, now and forever, one and inseparable!

* * * * *

1. Webster argues that the people have the power to remove anything from the constitution which they do not approve of. Is this true? How does it connect with his argument that states do not have the same power? What is at stake here?

2. Webster's speech stretched, extemporaneously, to over 100 pages. What do you think of his oratory skills? Do we have such orators today? How has television and the media affected the oratorical tradition?

10-7 *South Carolina Refuses the Tariff, 1832*

The battle over export and import tariffs reached a head in 1832 when South Carolina declared the federal tariff of July 12, 1832 "null, void, and...not binding on this state." At stake was much more than just the tariff, also the ongoing battle between state's rights and federal jurisdiction, which would eventually escalate into the Civil War. The following is a section of the act declaring South Carolina's Ordinance of Nullification in which they state that the tariffs are unconstitutional and therefore not binding on South Carolina.

SOURCE: Henry Steele Commager, *Documents of American History* (N.Y.: Appleton-Century-Crofts, 1948).

An Ordinance to Nullify certain acts of the Congress of the United States, purporting to be laws laying duties and imposts on the importation of foreign commodities.

Whereas the Congress of the United States, by various acts, purporting to be acts laying duties and imposts on foreign imports, but in reality intended for the protection of domestic manufactures, and the giving of bounties to classes and individuals engaged in particular employments, at the expense and to the injury and oppression of other classes and individuals, and by wholly exempting from taxation certain foreign commodities, such as are not produced or manufactured in the United States, to afford a pretext for imposing higher and excessive duties on articles similar to those intended to be protected, hath exceeded its just powers under the Constitution, which confers on it no authority to afford such protection, and hath violated the true meaning and intent of the Constitution, which provides for equality in imposing the burthens of taxation upon the several States and portions of the Confederacy: *And whereas* the said Congress, exceeding its just power to impose taxes and collect revenue for the purpose of effecting and accomplishing the specific objects and purposes which the Constitution of the United States authorizes it to effect and accomplish, hath raised and collected unnecessary revenue for objects unauthorized by the Constitution:—

We, therefore, the people of the State of South Carolina in Convention assembled, do declare and ordain,...That the several acts and parts of acts of the Congress of the United States, purporting to be laws for the imposing of duties and imposts on the importation of foreign commodities,...and, more especially,...[the tariff acts of 1828 and 1832],...are unauthorized by the Constitution of the United States, and violate the true meaning and intent thereof, and are null, void, and no law, nor binding upon this State, its officers or citizens; and all promises, contracts, and obligations, made or entered into, or to be made or entered into, with purpose to secure the duties imposed by the said acts, and all judicial proceedings which shall be hereafter had in affirmance thereof, are and shall be held utterly null and void.

And it is further Ordained, That it shall not be lawful for any of the constituted authorities, whether of this State or of the United States, to enforce the payment of duties imposed by the said acts within the limits of this State; but it shall be the duty of the Legislature to adopt such measures and pass such acts as may be necessary to give full effect to this Ordinance, and to prevent the enforcement and arrest the operation of the said acts and parts of acts of the Congress of the United States within the limits of this State, from and after the 1st day of February next,...

And it is further Ordained, That in no case of law or equity, decided in the courts of this State, wherein shall be drawn in question the authority of this ordinance, or the validity of such act or acts of the Legislature as may be passed for the purpose of giving effect thereto, or the validity of the aforesaid acts of Congress, imposing duties, shall any appeal be taken or allowed to the Supreme Court of the United States, nor shall any copy of the record be printed or allowed for that purpose; and if any such appeal shall be attempted to be taken, the courts of this State shall proceed to execute and enforce their judgments, according to the laws and usages of the State, without reference to such attempted appeal, and the person or persons attempting to take such appeal may be dealt with as for a contempt of the court.

And it is further Ordained, That all persons now holding any office of honor, profit, or trust, civil or military, under this State, (members of the Legislature excepted), shall, within such time, and in such manner as the Legislature shall prescribe, take an oath well and truly to obey, execute, and enforce, this Ordinance, and such act or acts of the Legislature as may be passed in pursuance thereof, according to the true intent and meaning of the same; and on the neglect or omission of any such person or persons so to do, his or their office or offices shall be forthwith vacated....and no person hereafter elected to any office of honor, profit, or trust, civil or military, (members of the Legislature excepted), shall, until the Legislature shall otherwise provide and direct, enter on the execution of this office,...until he shall, in like manner, have taken a similar oath; and no juror shall be empannelled in any of the courts of this State, in any cause in which shall be in question this Ordinance, or any act of the Legislature passed in pursuance thereof, unless he shall first, in addition to the usual oath, have taken an oath that he will well and truly obey, execute, and enforce this Ordinance, and such act or acts of the Legislature as may be passed to carry the same into operation and effect, according to the true intent and meaning thereof.

And we, the People of South Carolina, to the end that it may be fully understood by the Government of the United States, and the people of the co-States, that we are determined to maintain this, our Ordinance and Declaration, at every hazard, *Do further Declare* that we will not submit to the application of force, on the part of the Federal Government, to reduce this State to obedience; but that we will consider the passage, by Congress, of any act...to coerce the State, shut up her ports, destroy or harass her commerce, or to enforce the acts hereby declared to be null and void, otherwise than through the civil tribunals of the country, as inconsistent with the longer continuance of South Carolina in the Union: and that the people of this State will thenceforth hold themselves absolved from all further obligation to maintain or preserve their political connexion with the people of the other States, and will forthwith proceed to organize a separate Government, and do all other acts and things which sovereign and independent States may of right to do.

* * * * *

1.   *What is South Carolina's legal argument for nullification? Summarize it.*

2.   *How does this act reconcile itself against Daniel Webster's speech against state's rights to nullification? How do states challenge congressional law today? Then?*

10-8   A Staunch Feminist Advocates Equality, 1843

One of the transcendentalists, an important 19th-century American literary and intellectual movement, Margaret Fuller was also an ardent feminist. One of the first professional newspaper women, she edited the Transcendental journal the Dial as well as working as an assistant editor on Horace Greeley's New York Tribune. In addition, she published several books. The following selection from her essay "The Great Lawsuit: Man versus Men, Woman versus Women," illustrates her struggle with the concept of gender roles.
SOURCE: Mason Wade, ed., *The Writings of Margaret Fuller* (N.Y.: The Viking Press, 1941).

...Though the national independence be blurred by the servility of individuals; though freedom and equality have been proclaimed only to leave room for a monstrous display of slave dealing, and slave keeping; though the free American so often feels himself free, like the Roman, only to pamper his appetites and his indolence through the misery of his fellow beings, still it is not in vain, that the verbal statement has been made, "All men are born free and equal." There it stands, a golden certainty, wherewith to encourage the good, to shame the bad. The new world may be called clearly to perceive that it incurs the utmost penalty, if it reject the sorrowful brother. And if men are deaf, the angels hear. But men cannot be deaf. It is inevitable that an external freedom, such as has been achieved for the nation, should be so also for every member of it. That, which has once been clearly conceived in the intelligence, must be acted out....

We sicken no less at the pomp than the strife of words. We feel that never were lungs so puffed with the wind of declamation, on moral and religious subjects, as now. We are tempted to implore these "word-heroes," these word-Catos, word-Christs, to beware of cant above all things; to remember that hypocrisy is the most hopeless as well as the meanest of crimes, and that those must surely be polluted by it, who do not keep a little of all this morality and religion for private use. We feel that the mind may "grow black and rancid in the smoke" even of altars. We start up from the harangue to go into our closet and shut the door. But, when it has been shut long enough, we remember that where there is so much smoke, there must be some fire; with so much talk about virtue and freedom must be mingled some desire for them; that it cannot be in vain that such have become the common topics of conversation among men; that the very newspapers should proclaim themselves Pilgrims, Puritans, Heralds of Holiness. The king that maintains so costly a retinue cannot be a mere Count of Carabbas fiction. We have waited here long in the dust; we are tired and hungry, but the triumphal procession must appear at last.

Of all its banners, none has been more steadily upheld, and under none has more valor and willingness for real sacrifices been shown, than that of the champions of the enslaved African. And this band it is, which, partly in consequence of a natural following out of principles, partly because many women have been prominent in that cause, makes, just now, the warmest appeal in behalf of woman.

Though there has been a growing liberality on this point, yet society at large is not so prepared for the demands of this party, but that they are, and will be for some time, coldly regarded as the Jacobins of their day.

"Is it not enough," cries the sorrowful trader, "that you have done all you could to break up the national Union, and thus destroy the prosperity of our country, but now you must be trying to break up family union, to take my wife away from the cradle, and the kitchen hearth, to vote at polls, and preach from a pulpit? Of course, if she does such things, she cannot attend to those of her own sphere. She is happy enough as she is. She has more leisure than I have, every means of improvement, every indulgence."

"Have you asked her whether she was satisfied with these indulgences?"

"No, but I know she is. She is too amiable to wish what would make me unhappy, and too judicious to wish to step beyond the sphere of her sex. I will never consent to have our peace disturbed by any such discussions."

"'Consent'—you? it is not consent from you that is in question, it is assent from your wife."

"I am the head and she the heart."

"You are not the head of your wife. God has given her a mind of her own."

"I am the head and she the heart."

"God grant you play true to one another then. If the head represses no natural pulse of the heart, there can be no question as to your giving your consent. Both will be of one accord, and there needs but to present any question to get a full and true answer. There is no need of precaution, of indulgence, or consent. But our doubt is whether the heart consents with the head, or only acquiesces in its decree; and it is to ascertain the truth on this point, that we propose some liberating measures."

Thus vaguely are these questions proposed and discussed at present. But their being proposed at all implies much thought, and suggests more. Many women are considering within themselves what they need that they have not, and what they can have, if they find they need it. Many men are considering whether women are capable of being and having more than they are and have, and whether, if they are, it will be best to consent to improvement in their condition.

The numerous party, whose opinions are already labelled and adjusted too much to their mind to admit of any new light, strive, by lectures on some model-woman of bridal-like beauty and gentleness, by writing or lending little treatises, to mark out with due precision the limits of woman's sphere, and woman's mission, and to prevent other than the rightful shepherd from climbing the wall, or the flock from using any chance gap to run astray.

Without enrolling ourselves at once on either side, let us look upon the subject from that point of view which to-day offers. No better, it is to be feared, than a high house-top. A high hill-top, or at least a cathedral spire, would be desirable.

It is not surprising that it should be the Anti-Slavery party that pleads for woman, when we consider merely that she does not hold property on equal terms with men; so that, if a husband dies without a will, the wife, instead of stepping at once into his place as head of the family, inherits only a part of his fortune, as if she were a child, or ward only, not an equal partner.

We will not speak of the innumerable instances, in which profligate or idle men live upon the earnings of industrious wives; or if the wives leave them and take with them the children, to perform the double duty of mother and father, follow from place to place, and threaten to rob them of the children, if deprived of the rights of a husband, as they call them, planting themselves in their poor lodgings, frightening them into paying tribute by taking from them the children, running into debt at the expense of these otherwise so overtasked helots. Though such instances abound, the public opinion of his own sex is against the man, and when cases of extreme tyranny are made known, there is private action in the wife's favor. But if woman be, indeed, the weaker party, she ought to have legal protection, which would make such oppression impossible.

And knowing that there exists, in the world of men, a tone of feeling towards women as towards slaves, such as is expressed in the common phrase, "Tell that to women and children;" that the infinite soul can only work through them in already ascertained limits; that the prerogative of reason, man's highest portion, is allotted to them in a much lower degree; that it is better for them to be engaged in active labor, which is to be furnished and directed by those better able to think, &c. &c.; we need not go further, for who can review the experience of last week, without recalling words which imply, whether in jest or earnest, these views, and views like these? Knowing this, can we wonder that many reformers think that measures are not likely to be taken in behalf of women, unless their wishes could be publicly represented by women?

That can never be necessary, cry the other side. All men are privately influenced by women; each has his wife, sister, or female friends, and is too much biassed by these relations to fail of representing their interests.

And if this is not enough, let them propose and enforce their wishes with the pen. The beauty of home would be destroyed, the delicacy of the sex be violated, the dignity of halls of legislation destroyed, by an attempt to introduce them there. Such duties are inconsistent with those of a mother; and then we have ludicrous pictures of *ladies* in hysterics at the polls, and senate chambers filled with cradles.

But if, in reply, we admit as truth that woman seems destined by nature rather to the inner circle, we much add that the arrangements of civilized life have not been as yet such as to secure it to her. Her circle, if the duller, is not the quieter. If kept from excitement, she is not from drudgery. Not only the Indian carries the burdens of the camp, but the favorites of Louis the Fourteenth accompany him in his journeys, and the washerwoman stands at her tub and carries home her work at all seasons, and in all states of health.

As to the use of the pen, there was quite as much opposition to woman's possessing herself of that help to free-agency as there is now to her seizing on the rostrum or the desk; and she is likely to draw, from a permission to plead her cause that way, opposite inferences to what might be wished by those who now grant it.

As to the possibility of her filling, with grace and dignity, any such position, we should think those who had seen the great actresses, and heard the Quaker preachers of modern times, would not doubt, that woman can express publicly the fulness of thought and emotion, without losing any of the peculiar beauty of her sex....

* * * * * *

1. *Compare Margaret Fuller's writings to earlier American women you have read about in other chapters. What can you surmise about the changing roles of women? What about the roles of feminists?*

2. *Fuller parallels the role of women to that of slaves in her argument. What do you think of this? Is this valid? Why or why not? How so?*

10–9   *Transcendentalist Promotes Individualism, 1841*

Ralph Waldo Emerson is probably the best known of all the transcendentalists. Educated at Harvard, Emerson also graduated from Harvard's Divinity School and served as a preacher for a number of years before turning to writing and public lecturing full time. Emerson's essays and public lectures remain an important record of American intellectual thought. Emerson's home in Concord, Massachusetts was an central gathering point for such thinkers as the Channings, Henry David Thoreau, and Margaret Fuller. In the following piece, "Self Reliance," from his first volume of essays, Emerson glorifies the role of the individual as the true hero.

SOURCE: Ralph Waldo Emerson, *Emerson's Complete Works* (Cambridge, Mass: The Riverside Press, 1883–93).

I read the other day some verses written by an eminent painter which were original and not conventional. Always the soul hears an admonition in such lines, let the subject be what it may. The sentiment they instil is of more value than any thought they may contain. To believe your own thought, to believe that what is true for you in your private heart is true for all men,—that is genius. Speak your latent conviction, and it shall be universal sense; for always the inmost becomes the outmost—and our first thought is rendered back to us by the trumpets of the Last Judgment. Familiar as the voice of the mind is to each, the highest merit we ascribe to Moses, Plato and Milton is that they set at naught books and traditions, and spoke not what men, but what they thought. A man should learn to detect and watch that gleam of light which flashes across his mind from within, more than the lustre of the firmament of bards and sages. Yet he dismisses without notice his thought, because it is his. In every work of genius we recognize our own rejected thoughts; they come back to us with a certain alienated majesty. Great works of art have no more affecting lesson for us than this. They teach us to abide by our spontaneous impression with good-humored inflexibility then most when the whole cry of voices is on the other side. Else to-morrow a stranger will say with masterly good sense precisely what we have thought and felt all the time, and we shall be forced to take with shame our own opinion from another.

There is a time in every man's education when he arrives at the conviction that envy is ignorance; that imitation is suicide; that he must take himself for better for worse as his portion; that though the wide universe is full of good, no kernel of nourishing corn can come to him but through his toil bestowed on that plot of ground which is given to him to till. The power which resides in him is new in nature, and none but he knows what that is which he can do, nor does he know until he has tried.

Not for nothing one face, one character, one fact, makes much impression on him, and another none. It is not without preëstablished harmony, this sculpture in the memory. The eye was placed where one ray should fall, that it might testify of that particular ray. Bravely let him speak the utmost syllable of his confession. We but half express ourselves, and are ashamed of that divine idea which each of us represents. It may be safely trusted as proportionate and of good issues, so it be faithfully imparted, but God will not have his work made manifest by cowards. It needs a divine man to exhibit anything divine. A man is relieved and gay when he has put his heart into his work and done his best; but what he has said or done otherwise shall give him no peace. It is a deliverance which does not deliver. In the attempt his genius deserts him; no muse befriends; no invention, no hope.

Trust thyself: every heart vibrates to that iron string.

Accept the place the divine providence has found for you, the society of your contemporaries, the connexion of events. Great men have always done so, and confided themselves childlike to the genius of their age, betraying their perception that the Eternal was stirring at their heart, working through their hands, predominating in all their being. And we are now men, and must accept in the highest mind the same transcendent destiny; and not pinched in a corner, not cowards fleeing before a revolution, but redeemers and benefactors, pious aspirants to be noble clay under the Almighty effort let us advance on Chaos and the Dark....

These are the voices which we hear in solitude, but they grow faint and inaudible as we enter into the world. Society everywhere is in conspiracy against the manhood of every one of its members. Society is a joint-stock company, in which the members agree, for the better securing of his bread to each shareholder, to surrender the liberty and culture of the eater. The virtue in most request is conformity. Self-reliance is its aversion. It loves not realities and creators, but names and customs.

Whoso would be a man, must be a nonconformist. He who would gather immortal palms must not be hindered by the name of goodness, but must explore if it be goodness. Nothing is at last sacred but the integrity of your own mind. Absolve you to yourself, and you shall have the suffrage of the world. I remember an answer which when quite young I was prompted to make to a valued adviser who was wont to importune me with the dear old doctrines of the church. On my saying, What have I to do with the sacredness of traditions, if I live wholly from within? My friend suggested,—"But these impulses may be from below, not from above." I replied, "They do not seem to me to be such; but if I am the devil's child, I will live then from the devil." No law can be sacred to me but that of my nature. Good and bad are but names very readily transferable to that or this; the only right is what is after my constitution; the only wrong what is against it. A man is to carry himself in the presence of all opposition as if every thing were titular and ephemeral but he. I am ashamed to think how easily we capitulate to badges and names, to large societies and dead institutions. Every decent and well-spoken individual affects and sways me more than is right. I ought to go upright and vital, and speak the rude truth in all ways....

What I must do is all that concerns me, not what the people think. This rule, equally arduous in actual and in intellectual life, may serve for the whole distinction between greatness and meanness. It is the harder because you will always find those who think they know what is your duty better than you know it. It is easy in the world to live after the world's opinion; it is easy in solitude to live after our own; but the great man is he who in the midst of the crowd keeps with perfect sweetness the independence of solitude.

The objection to conforming to usages that have become dead to you is that it scatters your force. It loses your time and blurs the impression of your character. If you maintain a dead church, contribute to a dead Bible Society, vote with a great party either for the Government or against it, spread your table like base house-keepers,—under all these screens I have difficulty to detect the precise man you are. And of course so much force is withdrawn from your proper life. But do your thing, and I shall know you. Do your work, and you shall reinforce yourself. A man must consider what a blindman's-buff is this game of conformity. If I know your sect I anticipate your argument. I hear a preacher announce for his text and topic the expediency of one of the institutions of his church. Do I not know beforehand that not possibly can he say a new and spontaneous word?... Well, most men have bound their eyes with one or another handkerchief, and attached themselves to some one of these communities of opinion. This conformity makes them not false in a few particulars, authors of a few lies, but false in all particulars. Their every truth is not quite true. Their two is not the real two, their four not the real four: so that every word they say chagrins us and we know not where to begin to set them right. Meantime nature is not slow to equip us in the prison-uniform of the party to which we adhere. We come to wear one cut of face and figure, and acquire by degrees the gentlest asinine expression. There is a mortifying experience in particular, which does not fail to wreak itself also in the general history; I mean "the foolish face of praise," the forced smile which we put on in company where we do not feel at ease, in answer to conversation which does not interest us. The muscles, not spontaneously moved but moved by a low usurping wilfulness, grow tight about the outline of the face, and make the most disagreeable sensation; a sensation of rebuke and warning which no brave young man will suffer twice.

For nonconformity the world whips you with its displeasure....It is easy enough for a firm man who knows the world to brook the rage of the cultivated classes. Their rage is decorous and prudent, for they are timid, as being very vulnerable themselves. But when to their feminine rage the indignation of the people is added, when the ignorant and the poor are aroused, when the unintelligent brute force that lies at the bottom of society is made to growl and mow, it needs the habit of magnanimity and religion to treat it godlike as a trifle of no concern.

The other terror that scares us from self-trust is our consistency; a reverence for our past act or word because the eyes of others have no other data for computing our orbit than our past acts, and we are loath to disappoint them.

But why should you keep your head over your shoulder? Why drag about this monstrous corpse of your memory, lest you contradict somewhat you have stated in this or that public place? Suppose you should contradict yourself; what then?...

A foolish consistency is the hobgoblin of little minds, adored by little statesmen and philosophers and divines. With consistency a great soul has simply nothing to do. He may as well concern himself with his shadow on the wall. Out upon your guarded lips! Sew them up with packthread, do. Else if you would be a man speak what you think to-day in words as hard as cannon balls, and to-morrow speak what to-morrow thinks in hard words again, though it contradict everything you said to-day. Ah, then exclaim the aged ladies, you shall be sure to be misunderstood! Misunderstood! It is a right fool's word. Is it so bad then to be misunderstood? Pythagoras was misunderstood, and Socrates, and Jesus, and Luther, and Copernicus, and Galileo, and Newton, and every pure and wise spirit that ever took flesh. To be great is to be misunderstood....

* * * * * *

1.   *The cult of the individual is a central American tenet. How does Emerson support this? Cite specific quotations.*

2.   *Emerson frequently presented his work in the Lyceum circuit, a sort of popular public adult education. What does this tell you about social conditions at the time?*

3.   *Emerson advocates non-conformity. But is this itself a conformation? What conformity is he rebelling against?*

chapter 11

The South and Slavery, 1780s–1850s

11-1 Congress Prohibits Importation of Slaves, 1807

President Thomas Jefferson strongly supported the congressional bills to prohibit the importation of slaves. Ironically, Jefferson himself was a slave owner. The bills were an outgrowth of the section of the Constitution that stated "The importation of persons as any of the States shall think proper to admit, shall not be prohibited by the Congress prior to the year 1808...." At Jefferson's behest, both the House of Representatives and the Senate introduced bills outlawing the importation of slaves. The following excerpt outlines the law and the penalties regarding the importation of slaves.

SOURCE: Henry Steele Commager, *Documents of American History* (New York: Appleton-Century-Crofts, 1948).

An Act to prohibit the importation of Slaves into any port or place within the jurisdiction of the United States, from and after the first day of January, in the year of our Lord one thousand eight hundred and eight.

Be it enacted, That from and after the first day of January, one thousand eight hundred and eight, it shall not be lawful to import or bring into the United States or the territories thereof from any foreign kingdom, place, or country, any negro, mulatto, or person of colour, as a slave, or to be held to service or labour.

Sec. 2. That no citizen of the United States, or any other person, shall, from and after the first day of January, in the year of our Lord one thousand eight hundred and eight, for himself, or themselves, or any other person whatsoever, either as master, factor, or owner, build, fit, equip, load or to otherwise prepare any ship or vessel, in any port or place within the jurisdiction of the United States, nor shall cause any ship or vessel to sail from any port or place within the same, for the purpose of procuring any negro, mulatto, or person of colour, from any foreign kingdom, place, or country, to be transported to any port or place whatsoever within the jurisdiction of the United States, to be held, sold, or disposed of as slaves, or to be held to service or labour: and if any ship or vessel shall be so fitted out for the purpose aforesaid, or shall be caused to sail so as aforesaid, every such ship or vessel, her tackle, apparel, and furniture, shall be forfeited to the

United States, and shall be liable to be seized, prosecuted, and condemned in any of the circuit courts or district courts, for the district where the said ship or vessel may be found or seized....

Sec. 4. If any citizen or citizens of the United States, or any person resident within the jurisdiction of the same, shall, from and after the first day of January, one thousand eight hundred and eight, take on board, receive or transport from any of the coasts or kingdoms of Africa, or from any other foreign kingdom, place, or country, any negro, mulatto, or person of colour in any ship or vessel, for the purpose of selling them in any port or place within the jurisdiction of the United States as slaves, or to be held to service or labour, or shall be in any ways aiding or abetting therein, such citizen or citizens, or person, shall severally forfeit and pay five thousand dollars, one moiety thereof to the use of any person or persons who shall sue for and prosecute the same to effect....

Sec. 6. That if any person or persons whatsoever, shall, from and after the first day of January, one thousand eight hundred and eight, purchase or sell any negro, mulatto, or person of colour, was so brought within the jurisdiction of the United States, as aforesaid, such purchaser and seller shall severally forfeit and pay for every negro, mulatto, or person of colour, or brought from any foreign kingdom, place, or country, or from the dominions of any foreign state, immediately adjoining to the United States, after the last day of December, one thousand eight hundred and seven, knowing at the time of such purchase or sale, such negro, mulatto, or person of colour, was so brought within the jurisdiction of the United States, as aforesaid, such purchaser and seller shall severally forfeit and pay for every negro, mulatto, or person of colour, so purchased or sold as aforesaid, eight hundred dollars....

Sec. 7. That if any ship or vessel shall be found, from and after the first day of January, one thousand eight hundred and eight, in any river, port, bay, or harbor, or on the high seas, within the jurisdictional limits of the United States, or hovering on the coast thereof, having on board any negro, mulatto, or person of colour, for the purpose of selling them as slaves, or with intent to land the same, in any port or place within the jurisdiction of the United States, contrary to the prohibition of the act, every such ship or vessel, together with her tackle, apparel, and furniture, and the goods or effects which shall be found on board the same, shall be forfeited to the use of the United States, and may be seized, prosecuted, and condemned, in any court of the United States, having jurisdiction thereof. And it shall be lawful for the President of the United States, and he is hereby authorized, should he deem it expedient, to cause any of the armed vessels of the United States to be manned and employed to cruise on any part of the coast of the United States, or territories thereof, where he may judge attempts will be made to violate the provisions of this act, and to instruct and direct the commanders of armed vessels of the United States, to seize, take, and bring into any port of the United States all such ships or vessels; and moreover to seize, take, or bring into any port of the U.S. all ships or vessel of the U.S. wheresoever found on the high seas, contravening the provisions of this act, to be proceeded against according to law....

* * * * *

1. *This bill only outlaws the importation of slaves, not their use, sale, or possession within the United States. Why do you think this was?*

2. *What would this bill have done to the already existent tension between the northern and southern states in the Union?*

11-2   *State Laws Govern Slavery, 1824*

Southern states were free to draw up their own laws regarding the treatment of slaves within their borders, but they were more similar than different. The generally commonly held legal principles were that the slaves were under the complete control of their masters and had few legal rights. Slaves could not own property, file lawsuits, or make contracts, they were property. If the state wanted to execute a slave for a crime, the state must pay the master, as it was depriving the owner of property. The following section, taken from the Civil Code of Louisiana in 1824 serves as an example of slave laws throughout the South.

SOURCE: *Civil Code of the State of Louisiana* (Baton Rouge, La.: n.p., 1825).

ART. 172.—The rules prescribing the police and conduct to be observed with respect to slaves in this State, and the punishment of their crimes and offences, are fixed by special laws of the Legislature.

ART. 173.—The slave is entirely subject to the will of his master, who may correct and chastise him, though not with unusual rigor, nor so as to maim or mutilate him, or to expose him to the danger of loss of life, or to cause his death.

ART. 174.—The slave is incapable of making any kind of contract, except those which relate to his own emancipation.

ART. 175.—All that a slave possesses, belongs to his master; he possesses nothing of his own, except his *peculium*, that is to say, the sum of money, or moveable estate, which his master chooses he should possess.

ART. 176.—They can transmit nothing by succession or otherwise; but the succession of free persons related to them which they would have inherited had they been free, may pass through them to such of their descendants as may have acquired their liberty before the succession is opened.

ART. 177.—The slave is incapable of exercising any public office, or private trust; he cannot be tutor, curator, executor nor attorney; he cannot be a witness in either civil or criminal matters, except in cases provided for by particular laws. He cannot be a party in any civil action, either as plaintiff or defendant, except when he has to claim or prove his freedom.

ART. 178.—When slaves are prosecuted in the name of the State, for offences they have committed, notice must be given to their masters.

ART. 179.—Masters are bound by the acts of their slaves done by their command, as also by their transactions and dealings with respect to the business in which they have entrusted or employed them; but in case they should not have authorised or entrusted them, they shall be answerable only for so much as they have benefitted by the transaction.

ART. 180.—The master shall be answerable for all the damages occasioned by an offence or quasi-offence committed by his slave, independent of the punishment inflicted on the slave.

ART. 181.—The master however may discharge himself from such responsibility by abandoning his slave to the person injured; in which case such person shall sell such slave at public auction in the usual form, to obtain payment of the damages and costs; and the balance, if any, shall be returned to the master of the slave, who shall be completely discharged, although the price of the slave should not be sufficient to pay the whole amount of the damages and costs; provided that the master shall make the abandonment within three days after the judgment awarding such damages, shall have been rendered; provided also that it shall not be proved that the crime or offence was committed by his order; for in case of such proof the master shall be answerable for all damages resulting therefrom, whatever be the amount, without being admitted to the benefit of the abandonment.

ART. 182.—Slaves cannot marry without the consent of their masters, and their marriages do not produce any of the civil effects which result from such contract.

ART. 183.—Children born of a mother then in a state of slavery, whether married or not, follow the condition of their mother; they are consequently slaves and belong to the master of their mother.

ART. 184.—A master may manumit his slave in this State, either by an act *inter vivos* or by a disposition made in prospect of death, provided such manumission be made with the forms and under the conditions prescribed by law; but an enfranchisement, when made by a last will, must be express and formal, and shall not be implied by any other circumstances of heir, testamentary executorship or other dispositions of this nature, which, in such case, shall be considered as if they had not been made.

ART. 185.—No one can emancipate his slave, unless the slave has attained the age of thirty years, and has behaved well at least for four years preceding his emancipation.

ART. 186.—The slave who has saved the life of his master, his master's wife, or one of his children, may be emancipated at any age.

ART. 187.—The master who wishes to emancipate his slave, is bound to make a declaration of his intentions to the judge of the parish where he resides; the judge must order notice of it to be published during forty days by advertisement posted at the door of the court house; and if, at the expiration of this delay, no opposition be made that shall authorise the master to pass an act of emancipation.

ART. 188.   The act of emancipation imports an obligation on the part the person granting it, to provide the subsistence of the slave emancipated, if he should be unable to support himself.

ART. 189.—An emancipation or perfected, is irrevocable, on the part of the master or his heirs.

ART. 190.—Any enfranchisement made in fraud of creditors, or of the portion reserved by law to forced heirs is null and void; and such fraud shall be considered as proved, when it shall appear that at the moment of executing the enfranchisement, the person granting it had not sufficient property to pay his debs or to leave to his heir the portion to them reserved by law the same rule will apply if the slave thus manumitted, was specially mortgaged; but in this case the enfranchisement shall take effect, provided the slave or any one in his behalf shall pay the debt for which the mortgage was given.

ART. 191.—No master of slaves shall be compelled, either directly or indirectly, to enfranchise any of them, except only in cases where the enfranchisement shall be made for services rendered to the State, by virtue of an act of the Legislature of the same, and on the State satisfying to the master the appraised value of the manumitted slave....

* * * * *

1. *What legal rights does a slave have under these statutes? What legal rights does a slave owner retain?*

2. *What can we discern about the lives of slaves from reading these laws? How do they help the historian reconstruct the history of slavery?*

SOURCE: Benjamin Henry Latrobe, *Impression Respecting New Orleans*, edited by Samuel Wilson, Jr. (New York: Columbia University Press, 1951).

11–3   *An Architect Describes African American Music and Instruments in 1818*

Born in England, Benjamin Henry Latrobe was a gifted architect who designed many of the buildings in our nation's capitol. President Thomas Jefferson put Latrobe in charge of completing the U.S. Capitol, and Latrobe also rebuilt many of the structures after they were burnt in the war of 1812 by the British. Latrobe is largely responsible for the Greek revival style of the capitol's buildings as well as helping to elevate the status of architects to that of professionals. Latrobe is also responsible for drawing and describing the musical instruments he saw in New Orleans when he was there to build a waterworks for the city around 1818. Many of the instruments Latrobe saw are of African origin, as seen in the following passage.

This long dissertation has been suggested by my accidentally stumbling upon the assembly of negroes which I am told every Sunday afternoon meets on the Common in the rear of the city. My object was to take a walk with Mr. Coulter on the bank of the Canal Caron-delet as far as the Bayou St. John. In going up St. Peters Street & approaching the common I heard a most extraordinary noise, which I supposed to proceed from some horse mill, the horses trampling on a wooden floor. I found, however, on emerging from the houses onto the Common, that it proceeded from a crowd of 5 or 600 persons assembled in an open space or public square. I went to the spot & crowded near enough to see the performance. All those who were engaged in the business seemed to be *blacks*. I did not observe a dozen yellow faces. They were formed into circular groupes [*sic*] in the midst of four of which, which I examined (but there were more of them), was a ring, the largest not 10 feet in diameter. In the first were two women dancing. They held each a coarse handkerchief extended by the corners in their hands, & *set* to each other in a miserably dull & slow figure, hardly moving their feet or bodies. The music consisted of two drums and a stringed instrument. An old man sat astride of a cylindrical drum about a foot in diameter, & beat it with incredible quickness with the edge of his hand & fingers. The other drum was an open staved thing held between the knees & beaten in the same manner. They made an incredible noise. The most curious instrument, however, was a stringed instrument which no doubt was imported from Africa. On the top of the finger board was the rude figure of a man in a sitting posture, & two pegs behind him to which the strings were fastened. The body was a calabash. It was played upon by a very little old man, apparently 80 or 90 years old.

The women squalled out a burthen to the playing at intervals, consisting of two notes, as the negroes, working in our cities, respond to the song of their leader. Most of the circles contained the same sort of dancers. One was larger, in which a ring of a dozen women walked, by way of dancing, round the music in the center. But the instruments were of a different construction. One, which from the color of the wood seemed new, consisted of a block cut into something of the form of a cricket bat with a long & deep mortice down the center. This thing made a considerable noise, being beaten lustily on the side by a short stick. In the same orchestra was a square drum, looking like a stool, which made an abominably loud noise; also a calabash with a round hole in it, the hole studded with brass nails, which was beaten by a woman with two short sticks.

A man sung an uncouth song to the dancing which I suppose was in some African language, for it was not French, & the women screamed a detestable burthen on one single note. The allowed amusements of Sunday have, it seems, perpetuated here those of Africa among its inhabitants. I have never seen anything more brutally savage, and at the same time dull & stupid, than this whole exhibition. Continuing my walk about a mile along the canal, & returning after Sunset near the same spot, the noise was still heard. There was not the least disorder among the crowd, nor do I learn on enquiry, that these weekly meetings of the negroes have ever produced any mischief.

* * * * *

1.   What does Latrobe's account tell us about African American life in New Orleans?

2.   What value does material culture have for the historian in trying to recreate social history? How can the use of something like music help to complete the story?

11–4   Slave Culture Documented in Song, 1867

As early as 1867 writers were beginning to recognize the value of documenting slave folk culture as it was already beginning to disappear. Slave Songs of the United States appeared in 1867 and recorded many songs which were already being lost. However, many of the songs survive today as spirituals and hymns. Several selections from Slave Songs appear here.

SOURCE: William Francis Allen, Charles Pickard Ware, and Lucy McKim Garrison, *Slave Songs of the United States* (New York: A. Simpson & Co., 1867).

Nobody Knows the Trouble I've Had

Nobody knows de trouble I've had [or, I've seen],
Nobody knows but Jesus
Nobody knows de trouble I've had
    Glory hallelu.
One morning I was a-walking down,
    O yes, Lord!
I saw some berries a-hanging down,
    O yes, Lord!
    (Refrain)
I pick de berry and I suck de juice,
    O yes, Lord!
Just us sweet us the honey in de comb,
    O yes, Lord!
    (Refrain)
Sometimes I'm up, sometimes I'm down,
Sometimes I'm almost on de groun'.
    (Refrain)
What make ole Satan hate me so?
Cause he got me once and he let me go.
    (Refrain)

Deep River

Deep river, my home is over Jordan, Deep river,
Lord, I want to cross over into campground,
Lord, I want to cross over into campground,
Lord, I want to cross over into campground.
Oh, chillun, Oh, don't you want to go to that gospel feast,
That promised land, that land, where all is peace?
Walk into heaven, and take my seat,
And cast my crown at Jesus feet,
Lord, I want to cross over into campground.
Lord, I want to cross over into campground.
Deep river, my home is over Jordan, Deep river
Lord, I want to cross over into campground,
Lord, I want to cross over into campground,
Lord, I want to cross over into campground, Lord!

Roll, Jordan, Roll

My brudder [sister, or a name] sittin' on de tree of life,
An' he yearde when Jordan roll;
Roll, Jordan, Roll, Jordan, Roll, Jordan, roll!
O march de angel march, O march de angel march;
O my soul arise in Heaven, Lord,
For to year when Jordan roll.
Little chil'en, learn to fear de Lord,
And let your days be long;
Roll, Jordan, &c.
O, let no false nor spiteful word,
Be found upon your tongue;
Roll, Jordan, &c.

Go Down, Moses

When Israel was in Egypt's land,
Let my people go;
Oppressed so hard they could not stand,
Let my people go.
Chorus:
Go down, Moses, way down in Egypt's land;
Tell old Pharoah, to let my people go.
Thus saith the Lord, bold Moses said,
Let my people go;
If not I'll smite your first born dead,
Let my people go;
No more shall they in bondage toil,
Let my people go;
Let them come out with Egypt's spoil,
Let my people go.
O 'twas a dark and dismal night,
Let my people go;
When Moses led the Israelites,
Let my people go.
The Lord told Moses what to do,
Let my people go;
To lead the children of Israel through,
Let my people go.
O come along, Moses, you won't get lost,
Let my people go;
Stretch our your rod and come across,
Let my people go.
As Israel stood by the water side,
Let my people go;
At the command of God it did divide,
Let my people go.
And when they reached the other side,
Let my people go;
They sang a song of triumph o'er,
Let my people go.
You won't get lost in the wilderness,

Let my people go;
With a lighted candle in your breast,
Let my people go.
O let us all from bondage flee,
Let my people go;
And let us all in Christ be free,
Let my people go.
We need not always weep and moan,
Let my people go;
And wear these slavery chains forlorn,
Let my people go;
What a beautiful morning that will be,
Let my people go.
When time breaks up in eternity,
Let my people go.

Didn't My Lord Deliver Daniel

Didn't my Lord deliver Daniel, deliver Daniel, deliver
Daniel,
Didn't my Lord deliver Daniel,
An' why not every man.
He delivered Daniel from de lion's den,
Jonah from de belly of de whale,
An' de Hebrew chillun from de fiery furnace,
An' why not every man.
Didn't my Lord deliver Daniel, deliver Daniel, deliver
Daniel,
Didn't my Lord deliver Daniel,
An' why not every man.
De moon run down in a purple stream,
De sun forbear to shine,
An' every star disappear,
King Jesus shall-a be mine.
(Refrain)
De win' blow' eas' an' de win' blows wes',
It blows like de judgement day,
An' every po' soul dat never did pray
'll be glad to pray dat day.
(Refrain)
I set my foot on de Gospel ship,
An de ship begin to sail,
It landed me over on Canaan's shore,
An' I'll never come back no mo'.
(Refrain)

* * * * * *

1.   The Slave Songs often speak of deliverance from this
life in the hereafter. They also speak of God delivering
Daniel from the lion, or Jonah from the whale. How
would these have been used by slaves? Why might
these have been popular images?

2. *Many of these songs form the basis for Protestant hymns. How many of these do you recognize? Do you know of others?*

3. *What use do folk songs such as these have for the historian? What can we learn about a culture by studying its music?*

11–5   Southern Novel Depicts Slavery, 1832

As anti-slavery forces gained strength, slave owners sought philosophical positions from which to defend slavery. Many pro-slavery contingents in the south maintained that they treated their slaves well and that it was necessary to protect the slaves from themselves, that their masters had their best interests at heart. John P. Kennedy wrote a novel, Swallow Barn, which depicted an imaginary plantation with an exemplary slave owner. The following excerpt paints an idyllic picture of happy slaves and kind masters with little mention of the poverty and drudgery of plantation work by slaves.

SOURCE: John Pendleton Kennedy, *Swallow Barn* (Philadelphia: Carly & Lee, 1832).

...in Virginia, it will be seen, that on the score of accommodation, the inmates of these dwellings were furnished according to a very primitive notion of comfort. Still, however, there were little garden-patches attached to each, where cymblings, cucumbers, sweet potatoes, watermelons and cabbages flourished in unrestrained luxuriance. Add to this, that there was abundance of poultry domesticated about the premises, and it may be perceived that, whatever might be in the inconveniences of shelter, there was no want of what, in all countries, would be considered a reasonable supply of luxuries.

Nothing more attracted my observation than the swarms of little negroes that basked on the sunny sides of these cabins, and congregated to gaze at us as we surveyed their haunts. They were nearly all in that costume of the golden age which I have therefore described; and showed their slim shanks and long heels in all varieties of their grotesque natures. Their predominant love of sunshine, and their lazy, listless postures, and apparent content to be silently looking abroad, might well afford a comparison to a set of terrapins luxuriating in the genial warmth of summer, on the logs of a mill-pond.

And there, too, were the prolific mothers of this redundant brood,—a number of stout negro-women who thronged the doors of the huts, full of idle curiosity to see us. And, when to these are added a few reverend, wrinkled, decrepit old men, with faces shortened as if with drawing-strings, noses that seemed to have run all to nostril, and

with feet of the configuration of a mattock, my reader will have a tolerably correct idea of this negro-quarter, its population, buildings, external appearance, situation and extent.

Meriwether, I have said before, is a kind and considerate master. It is his custom frequently to visit his slaves, in order to inspect their condition, and, where it may be necessary, to add to their comforts or relieve their wants. His coming amongst them, therefore, is always hailed with pleasure. He has constituted himself into a high court of appeal, and makes it a rule to give all their petitions a patient hearing, and to do justice in the premises. This, he tells me, he considers as indispensably necessary;—he says, that no overseer is entirely to be trusted: that there are few men who have the temper to administer wholesome laws to any population, however small, without some omissions or irregularities; and that this is more emphatically true of those who administer them entirely at their own will. On the present occasion, in almost every house where Frank entered, there was some boon to be asked; and I observed, that in every case, the petitioner was either gratified or refused in such a tone as left no occasion or disposition to murmur. Most of the women had some bargains to offer, of fowls or eggs or other commodities of household use, and Meriwether generally referred them to his wife, who, I found, relied almost entirely on this resource, for the supply of such commodities; the negroes being regularly paid for whatever was offered in this way.

One old fellow had a special favour to ask,—a little money to get a new padding for his saddle, which, he said, "galled his cretur's back." Frank, after a few jocular passages with the veteran, gave him what he desired, and sent him off rejoicing.

"That, sir," said Meriwether, "is no less a personage than Jupiter. He is an old bachelor, and has his cabin here on the hill. He is now near seventy, and is a kind of King of the Quarter. He has a horse, which he extorted from me last Christmas; and I seldom come here without finding myself involved in some new demand, as a consequence of my donation. Now he wants a pair of spurs which, I suppose, I must give him. He is a preposterous coxcomb, and Ned has administered to his vanity by a present of a *chapeau de bras*—a relic of my military era, which he wears on Sundays with a conceit that has brought upon him as much envy as admiration—the usual condition of greatness."

The air of contentment and good humor and kind

family attachment, which was apparent throughout this lit-tle community, and the familiar relations existing between them and the proprietor struck me very pleasantly. I came here a stranger, in great degree, to the negro character, knowing but little of the domestic history of these people, their duties, habits or temper, and somewhat disposed, indeed, from prepossessions, to look upon them as severely dealt with, and expecting to have my sympathies excited towards them as objects of commiseration. I have had, therefore, rather a special interest in observing them. The contrast between my preconceptions of their condition and the reality which I have witnessed, has brought me a most agreeable surprise. I will not say that, in a high state of cul-tivation and of such self-dependence as they might possibly attain in a separate national existence, they might not become a more respectable people; but I am quite sure they never could become a happier people than I find them here. Perhaps they are destined, ultimately, to that national exis-tence, in the clime from which they derive their origin—that this is a transition state in which we see them in Virginia. If it be so, no tribe of people have ever passed from barbarism to civilization whose middle stage of progress has been more secure from harm, more genial to their character, or better supplied with mild and beneficient guardianship, adapted to the actual state of their intellectual feebleness, than the negroes of Swallow Barn. And, from what I can gather, it is pretty much the same on the other estates in this region. I hear of an unpleasant exception to this remark now and then; but under such conditions as warrant the opinion that the unfavorable case is not more common than that which may be found in a survey of any other department of society. The oppression of apprentices, of seamen, of sol-diers, of subordinates, indeed, in every relation, may furnish elements for a bead-roll of social grievances quite as strik-ing, if they were diligently noted and brought to view.

What the negro is finally capable of, in the way of civilization, I am not philosopher enough to determine. In the present stage of his existence, he presents himself to my mind as essentially parasitical in his nature. I mean that he is, in his moral constitution, a dependant upon the white race; dependant for guidance and direction even to the pro-curement of his most indispensable necessaries. Apart from this protection he has the helplessness of a child,—without foresight, without faculty of contrivance, without thrift of any kind. We have instances, in the neighborhood of this estate, of individuals of the tribe falling into the most deplorable destitution from the want of that constant super-vision which the race seems to require. This helplessness may be the due and natural impression which two centuries of servitude have stamped upon the tribe. But it is not the less a present and insurmountable impediment to that most cruel of all projects—the direct, broad emancipation of these people,—an act of legislation in comparison with which the revocation of the edict of Nantes would be enti-tled to be ranked among political benefactions. Taking instruction from history, all organized slavery is inevitably but a temporary phase of human condition. Interest, neces-sity and instinct, all work to give progression to the relations of mankind, and finally to elevate each tribe or race to its maximum of refinement and power. We have no reason to suppose that the negro will be an exception to this law.

At present, I have said, he is parasitical. He grows upward, only as the vine to which nature has supplied the sturdy tree as a support. He is extravagantly imitative. The older negroes here have—with some spice of comic mixture in it—that formal, grave and ostentatious style of manners, which belonged to the gentlemen of former days; they are profuse of bows and compliments, and very aristocratic in their way. The younger ones are equally to be remarked for aping the style of the present time, and especially for such tags of dandyism in dress as come within their reach. Their fondness for music and dancing is a predominant passion. I never meet a negro man—unless he is quite old—that he is not whistling and the women sing from morning till night. And as to dancing, the hardest day's work does not restrain their desire to indulge in such pastime. During the harvest, when their toil is pushed to its utmost—the time being one of recognized privileges—they dance almost the whole night. They are great sportsmen, too. They angle and haul the seine, and hunt and tend their traps, with a zest that never grows weary. Their gayety of heart is constitutional and perennial, and when they are together they are as volu-ble and noisy as so many blackbirds. In short, I think them the most good-natured, careless, light-hearted, and happily-constructed human beings I have ever seen. Having but few and simple wants, they seem to me to be provided with every comfort which falls within the ordinary compass of enjoyment,—as that word may be applied to express posi-tive pleasures scattered through the course of daily occupa-tion—than any other laboring people I am acquainted with....

* * * * * *

1. What do you think about Kennedy's description of slave life? Is it accurate? How does it compare to other accounts you have read?

2. Although Swallow Barn is a novel, it reveals what Kennedy though about African Americans. Kennedy uses these views to justify slavery. What are these views? How does Kennedy justify slavery? How can we use novels and works of fiction to elaborate our historical perspective?

11–6   A Slave Tells of His Sale at Auction, 1848

The auctioning of slaves, the separation of mothers from their children, men from their families, was perhaps one of the most inhumane aspects of slavery. As anti-slavery opinions continued to rise, slave narratives became more and more popular to account for the atrocities of southern slave owners. No one was seen as more villainous than the slave trader himself, even by slave owners. The account of one slave's auction is captured here in a passage from Henry Watson's Narrative of Henry Watson, A Fugitive Slave. Written by Himself, which was published in 1848.

SOURCE: Henry Watson, *Narrative of Henry Watson, A Fugitive Slave* (Boston: 1848).

…My mother was the cook at what slaves call the great house. I was allowed to remain with her at the house. The last time I saw her, she placed me on the bed, which was in a room adjoining the kitchen, and bid me go to sleep, saying that she would be back again in a few moments. I did so; and when I awoke in the morning I found myself in the great house, wrapped in a blanket, before the fire. I could not account for this change that had been made with me through the night. I asked for my mother, but no one spoke. I went out into the kitchen, where she used to work. She was not there, and it was evident to me, that she was gone; where, I knew not. I returned to the house, and implored my mistress, with tears in my eyes, to tell me where my mother had gone. She refused, though a mother herself, to give me any satisfaction whatever. Every exertion was made on my part to find her, or hear some tidings of her; but all my efforts were unsuccessful; and from that day I have never seen or heard from her. This cruel separation brought on a fit of sickness, from which they did not expect I would recover. The old slave-woman who took care of me during my sickness, by way of consolation, gave me as much information as she could about my mother's being taken away. She told me that a slave-dealer drove to the door in a buggy, and my mother was sent for to come into the house; when, getting inside, she was knocked down, tied, and thrown into the buggy, and carried away. As the old woman related these things to me, I felt as if all hope was gone; that I was forsaken and alone in this world. More forcibly did I then feel the galling chains of slavery, the cruelty and barbarism arising from it, than I ever have since. I resolved, however, to bear with all patiently, till I became large enough to run away, and search for my mother.

I had recovered from my sickness but a few months, when one day, looking up the road, I saw a man riding towards the house; I ran with the rest of the children to hide ourselves until the man had gone. When I had remained concealed some time, I ventured out again, and found Mr. Bibb, my master, looking for me, who ordered me into the house; and when I got there, to my astonishment, I found the man whom we had hid ourselves from, sitting in the room. After he had inspected me to his satisfaction, I was ordered out of the room, and went to play, and had forgotten the whole affair, when my master called me again, and ordered me to hold the stranger's horse. I did so, and in a few minutes he came forth and ordered me to mount behind him. This, with his assistance, I did; but rode only a short distance; when I jumped from the horse and ran for the house as fast as I could. He succeeded, however, in overtaking me, and I was again put on the horse, this time in front of him; and in this way was I carried to Fredericksburg. I was then placed in the possession of Mr. Janer, better known as Parson Janer; the man that had bought me being the son of Mr. Janer, who was one of those jolly, good-natured clergymen, who, while he feasted his numerous guests in the parlor, starved his slaves in the kitchen. After remaining there awhile, it was determined to send me to Richmond. The same man that brought me, came for me and ordered me to take a seat on the stage-coach, and the next day I found myself in Richmond, and stopped at the Eagle Hotel, kept by Mr. Holman, where I remained two or three days, and then was carried to the auction room; entering which, I found several slaves, seated around the room waiting for the hour of sale. Some were in tears; others were apparently cheerful. This brought to my mind my mother, and caused me to shed many tears; but they fell unheeded. The auctioneer was busy examining the slaves before the sale commenced. At last everything was ready, and the traffic in human flesh began. I will attempt to give as accurate an account of the language and ceremony of a slave auction as I possibly can. "Gentlemen, here is a likely boy; how much? He is sold for no fault; the owner wants money. His age is forty. Three hundred dollars is all that I am offered for him. Please to examine him; he is warranted sound. Boy, pull off your shirt roll up your pants—for we want to see if you have been whipped." If they discover any scars, they will not buy; saying that the nigger is a bad one. The auctioneer seeing this, cries, "Three hundred dollars, gentlemen, three hundred dollars. Shall I sell him for three hundred dollars? I have just been informed by his master, that he is an honest boy, and belongs to the same church that he does." This turns the tide frequently, and the bids go up fast; and he is knocked off for a good sum. After the men and women are sold, the children are put on the stand. I was the first put up. On my appearance, several voices cried, "How old is that little nigger?" On hearing this expression, I again burst into tears, and wept so that I have no distinct recollection of his answer. I was at length knocked down to a man whose name was Denton, a slave trader, then purchasing slaves for the Southern market. His first name I have forgotten. Each one of the traders has private jails, which are for the purpose of keeping slaves in; and they are generally kept by some confidential slave. Denton had one of these jails, to which I was conducted by his trusty slave; and on entering I found a great many slaves there, waiting to be sent off as soon as their numbers increased. These jails are enclosed by a wall about 16 feet high, and the yard-room is for the slaves to exercise in; and consists of but one room, in which all sexes and ages are huddled together in a mass. I stayed in this jail but two days, when the number was completed, and we were called out to form a line. Before we had proceeded far, Mr. Denton gave orders for us to stop, for the purpose of handcuffing some of the men, which, he said in a loud voice, "had the devil in them." The men belonging to this drove were all married men, and all leaving their wives and children behind; he, judging from their tears that they were unwilling to go, had them made secure. We started again on our journey, Mr. Denton taking the lead in his sulky; and the driver, Mr. Thornton, brought up the rear. I will not weary my readers with the particulars of our march to Tennessee, where we stopped several days for the purpose of arranging our clothes. While stopping, the men were hired out to pick cotton. While in Tennessee, we lost four of our number, who died from exposure on the road. After the lapse of three weeks, we started again on our journey, and in about four weeks arrived in Natchez, Miss., and went to our pen, which Mr. Denton had previously hired for us, and had our irons taken off and our clothes changed; for

Mr. Denton was expecting visitors to examine the flock, as he would sometimes term us. There was a sign-board in front of the house, which informed traders that he had on hand, blacksmiths, carpenters, field-hands; also several sickly ones, whom he would sell very cheap. In a short time purchasers became plenty, and our number diminished. I was not sold for several weeks, though I wished to be the first, not wishing to witness his cruelty to his slaves any longer; for if they displeased him in the least, he would order them to be stripped, and tied hand and foot together. He would then have his paddle brought, which was a board about two feet in length and one inch in thickness, having fourteen holes bored through it, about an inch in circumference. This instrument of torture he would apply, until the slave was exhausted, on parts which the purchaser would not be likely to examine. This mode of punishment is considered one of the most cruel ever invented, as the flesh protrudes through these holes at every blow, and forms bunches and blisters the size of each hole, causing much lameness and soreness to the person receiving them. This punishment is generally inflicted in the morning, before visitors come to examine the slaves…

* * * * *

1. *How would Henry Watson's narrative have been used by abolitionists? What do you think of the atrocities reported here? Do you think the story moved people to action?*

2. *Although the narrative is probably accurate, it is quite possibly written by northern abolitionists who are transcribing Watson's story. What evidence do you see of this? Does it diminish the impact of the story?*

11-7 A Farm Journal Reports on the Care and Feeding of Slaves, 1836

Slaves were seen as valuable property and their care and maintenance was of no less importance to slave owners than the management of their livestock or crops. Unfortunately, the slaves were frequently seen as having little more value than livestock, and were certainly treated as property, to be managed for best profitability. Articles in farm journals on how best to manage and exploit slaves were numerous, even in such relatively prestigious tomes as The Farmer's Register. Particularly noteworthy articles on slave management were reproduced in several different issues, such as this letter to The Southern Agriculturist which was reprinted in The Farmer's Register.

SOURCE: Willie Lee Rose, ed., *A Documentary History of Slavery in North America* (New York: Oxford University Press, 1976).

Notions on the Management of Negroes, &c.

1. *Cleanliness* is a matter which cannot be too closely attended to. Every owner should make it a rule to appoint a certain day in the week, for reviewing his negroes and their habitations, to see that both are clean and in good order. For myself, I select Sunday, as the best day for this

purpose. My mode of making such reviews, is the following:

I appoint a certain hour for attending to this matter on each Sabbath, say nine o'clock in the morning. Every negro distinctly understands, that at this hour he will be reviewed. An hour or so previous to the review, I make it the business of the driver to sound the horn, for the negroes to prepare themselves and houses for inspection. When the hour for review has arrived, it is also his business to attend upon me, and report the plantation ready for inspection. This being done, I repair to the negro houses. At the door of each house, the occupants thereof are seen standing with their children, if they have any. My business here is to call their respective names, and to see that every one has had his head well combed and cleaned, and their faces, hands, and feet well washed. The men are required, in addition to this, to have themselves shaved. That they may have no excuse for neglecting this requirement, those that need them are provided with combs and razors. I now see that their blankets, and all other body and bed clothing, have been hung out to air, if the weather be fine. Their pots are also examined. I particularly see that they have been well cleaned, and that nothing like "caked hominy," or potatoes is suffered to remain about them. I next enter their houses, and there see that every thing has been cleansed—that their pails, dressers, tables, &c. have all been washed down—that their chimneys have been swept and the ashes therefrom removed to one general heap in the yard, which serves me as an excellent manure for my lands. Being situated where my negroes procure many oysters, I make them save the shells, which they place in one pile, of which I burn lime enough each year, to white-wash my negro houses, both outside and inside. This not only gives a neat appearance to the houses, but preserves the boards of the same, and destroys all vermin which might infest them. From the inspection of the negro houses, I proceed to their *well*, and there see that the water is pure and healthy.

I should here state, that I repeat on Sunday what I do every time that I see any of my negroes viz. to examine that their clothes are not ragged or broken. Recollecting that a "stitch in time saves nine," I suffer none of them ever to appear with broken clothes. I give them the best clothes and I see that they do not suffer them to be ruined from carelessness. In all of my inspections I have a little book, in which I note down every thing that I see amiss. The negro who has been the cause, is called up on the morrow, and receives such reprimand or punishment as his case may require.

Having mentioned their own duties, it will, perhaps, not be amiss to state what I owe them also. Exacting as I do, the utmost *cleanliness* of them, I particularly observe *cleanliness* in my own person. For instance, I never appear before my negroes unshaved, or negligently dressed, and every thing that I have to do, I do with as much punctuality and exactness as I am capable of. Ignorant minds are ever apt to imitate their superiors, and upon this principle it will be found, that if the master is negligent in the observance of his duties, the slave will also become so.

2. *Diet.*—This is a matter of more importance than most planters are aware of. It is only necessary to inquire of the physician, or to consult any medical work, to be convinced that an improper attention to diet, is one of the most prolific causes of disease among our negroes, as well as whites. It is the almost universal custom in this state, to give out to each negro a weekly allowance of corn or potatoes, and to suffer them to cook it as they please. For many reasons, this plan is the most agreeable to the negroes. I shall show, however, that it is far from being the most advantageous either to their health, or comfort. Every planter knows that there are many negroes, who rather than be at the trouble of cooking their own victuals, will trade away their allowance with their more industrious fellow-workers, for one-half; and even where this is not the case, they are always found ready to barter away their whole weekly allowance to some neighboring dram shop, for a gallon of whiskey, or a pound or two of tobacco, or bread. Where negroes are permitted to cook their own food, they neither have the time, nor capability to do it properly. It cannot be expected that the slave who is all day at hard work, can pay a proper attention to preparing his food after the day's labor. He generally comes home tired, and before he has half cooked his meal, hunger induces him to devour it. It is true that some negroes cook their food in the field, while at work, but even this mode, must at once strike everyone as very improper. In nine cases out of ten, they cook with bad water, in dirty pots, and without salt. But I shall not enlarge upon the many ill effects arising from permitting negroes to have their allowance, and to cook it themselves. One of your correspondents, in a former number in an article on this subject, has pointed out many of the evils; I shall, therefore, detail a remedy which I have been applying for many years; and let me assure you, Mr. Editor, each year has caused me to be better pleased with its observance. First, then, when I give out corn as an allowance, I have it all ground into grist. And that this might be done with ease, I at first procured myself a corn mill worked by horse power, which, while it grinds and cracks all the corn on my plantation, only cost me a couple of hundred dollars. The corn being ground, I allow to each negro ten quarts of grist. Seven quarts of this I retain to be cooked for them, by a cook appointed for the purpose. The balance, three quarts, I give them to feed their poultry, or to do with, what they please. I have a person appointed to cook for all my negroes, who amount to about fifty in all. It is her business to prepare two meals

per day; and for each meal she cooks a pint of grist to each grown hand, and in a smaller proportion for the younger negroes. That the food may be well done, she is required to cook in two or three distinct pots. Both for breakfast and dinner, I allow a small portion of meat of some kind, to boil with their food. And here let me observe, that a bit of meat, which when divided among them all, would not afford a taste for anyone, will when cooked together, make soup enough to satisfy the whole plantation. In winter I require of the cook to have their breakfast ready at 8 o'clock, at which time the horn is sounded, and each negro comes with his piggin or bowl, and receives his portion, which is measured out to him by the driver. Dinner is required to be ready at 2 o'clock, and the same rules are observed as at breakfast. Since I have been cooking for the negroes of my plantation, I have never known one of them to complain of not having enough to eat. When I first adopted this rule, my negroes objected to it very much. But in a year or so they saw the utility of the practice, and now I am convinced, that they would not abandon it for a great deal, so much does it contribute to their comfort and health.

* * * * * *

1.   What does this account tell us about slave life? What does it tell us about the status of slaves on plantations?

2.   How might this account have been used by abolitionists? By pro-slavery factions?

11–8 A Slave Girl Tells of Her Life, 1861

Harriet Jacobs's Life of a Slave Girl, *first published in 1861, has become one of the classic narratives of slavery, told from a woman's view. Jacobs's tales of rape and sexual exploitation reveal a horror of slavery not sufficiently understood or discussed. The book's authenticity was under question for many years, as it was heavily edited by white abolitionists and published under a pen name. But its later authentication and compelling account mark it as one of the best slave narratives and necessary for comprehending the fear that was the life of slaves, particularly the women.*

SOURCE: Harriet Jacobs, *Incidents in the Life of a Slave Girl* (Boston: published for the author, 1861).

During the first years of my service in Dr. Flint's family, I was accustomed to share some indulgences with the children of my mistress. Though this seemed to me no more than right, I was grateful for it, and tried to merit the kindness by the faithful discharge of my duties. But I now entered on my fifteenth year—a sad epoch in the life of a slave girl. My master began to whisper foul words in my ear. Young as I was, I could not remain ignorant of their import. I tried to treat them with indifference or contempt. The master's age, my extreme youth, and the fear that his conduct would be reported to my grandmother, made me bear this treatment for many months. He was a crafty man, and resorted to many means to accomplish his purposes. Some times he had stormy, terrific ways, that made his victims tremble; sometimes he assumed a gentleness that he thought must surely subdue. Of the two, I preferred his stormy moods, although they left me trembling. He tried his utmost to corrupt the pure principles my grandmother had instilled. He peopled my young mind with unclean images, such as only a vile monster could think of. I turned from him with disgust and hatred. But he was my master. I was compelled to live under the same roof with him—where I saw a man forty years my senior daily violating the most sacred commandments of nature. He told me I was his property; that I must be subject to his will in all things. My soul revolted against the mean tyranny. But where could I turn for protection? No matter whether the slave girl be as black as ebony or as fair as her mistress. In either case, there is no shadow of law to protect her from insult, from violence, or even from death; all these are inflicted by fiends who bear the shape of men. The mistress, who ought to protect the helpless victim, has no other feelings towards her but those of jealousy and rage. The degradation, the wrongs, the vices, that grow out of slavery, are more than I can describe. They are greater than you would willingly believe. Surely, if you credited one half the truths that are told you concerning the helpless millions suffering in this cruel bondage, you at the north would not help to tighten the yoke. You surely would refuse to do for the master, on your own soil, the mean and cruel work which trained bloodhounds and the lowest class of whites do for him at the south.

Every where the years bring to all enough of sin and sorrow; but in slavery the very dawn of life is darkened by these shadows. Even the little child, who is accustomed to wait on her mistress and her children, will learn, before she is twelve years old, why it is that her mistress hates such and such a one among the slaves. Perhaps the child's own mother is among those hated ones. She listens to violent outbreaks of jealous passion, and cannot help understanding what is the cause. She will become prematurely knowing in evil things. Soon she will learn to tremble when she hears her master's footfall. She will be compelled to realize that she is no longer a child. If God has bestowed beauty upon her; it will prove her greatest curse. That which commands admiration in the white woman only hastens the degradation of the female slave. I know that some are too much brutalized by slavery to feel the humiliation of their position; but many slaves feel it most acutely, and shrink from the memory of it. I cannot tell how much I suffered in the presence of these wrongs, nor how I am still pained by the retrospect. My master met me at every turn, reminding me that I belonged to him, and swearing by heaven and earth that he would compel me to submit to him. If I went out for a breath of fresh air, after a day of unwearied toil, his footsteps dogged me. If I knelt by my mother's grave, his dark shadow fell on me even there. The light heart which nature had given me became heavy with sad forebodings. The other slaves in my master's house noticed the change. Many of them pitied me; but none dared to ask the cause. They had no need to inquire. They knew too well the guilty practices under that roof; and they were aware that to speak of them was an offence that never went unpunished.

I longed for some one to confide in. I would have given the world to have laid my head on my grandmother's faithful bosom, and told her all my troubles. But Dr. Flint swore he would kill me, if I was not as silent as the grave. Then, although my grandmother was all in all to me, I feared her as well as loved her. I had been accustomed to look up to her with a respect bordering upon awe. I was very young, and felt shamefaced about telling her such impure things, especially as I knew her to be very strict on such subjects. Moreover, she was a woman of a high spirit. She was usually very quiet in her demeanor; but if her indignation was once roused, it was not very easily quelled. I had been told that she once chased a white gentleman with a loaded pistol, because he insulted one of her daughters. I dreaded the consequences of a violent outbreak; and both pride and fear kept me silent. But though I did not confide in my grandmother, and even evaded her vigilant watchfulness and inquiry, her presence in the neighborhood was some protection to me. Though she had been a slave, Dr. Flint was afraid of her. He dreaded her scorching rebukes. Moreover, she was known and patronized by many people; and he did not wish to have his villany made public. It was lucky for me that I did not live on a distant plantation, but in a town not so large that the inhabitants were ignorant of each other's affairs. Bad as are the laws and customs in a slaveholding community, the doctor, as a professional man, deemed it prudent to keep up some outward show of decency....

I once saw two beautiful children playing together. One was a fair white child; the other was her slave; and also her sister. When I saw them embracing each other, and heard their joyous laughter, I turned sadly away from the lovely sight. I foresaw the inevitable blight that would fall on the little slave's heart. I knew how soon her laughter would be changed to sighs. The fair child grew up to be a still fairer woman. From childhood to womanhood her pathway was blooming with flowers, and overarched by a sunny sky. Scarcely one day of her life had been clouded when the sun rose on her happy bridal morning.

How had those years dealt with her slave sister, the little playmate of her childhood? She, also, was very beautiful; but the flowers and sunshine of love were not for her. She drank the cup of sin, and shame, and misery, whereof her persecuted race are compelled to drink.

In view of these things, why are ye silent, ye free men and women of the north? Why do your tongues falter in maintenance of the right? Would that I had more ability! But my heart is so full, and my pen is so weak! There are noble men and women who plead for us, striving to help those who cannot help themselves. God bless them! God give them strength and courage to go on! God bless those, every where, who are laboring to advance the cause of humanity!

* * * * * *

1. *Like Henry Watson's account of slave auctions, Harriet Jacobs's narrative was probably edited extensively by white abolitionists. Does this diminish its impact? Is all history somehow edited from the actual narrative?*

2. *Accounts of rape and sexual abuse within slavery are spread across time and location, from colonial America to the Civil War. How does Harriet Jacobs's account of sexual exploitation affect your view of slavery? Why do you think women, by and large, have received less attention than men in the tale of slavery?*

11–9 A Muslim Slave Speaks Out, 1831

Since the Moors had been in West Africa since 1100, it is no surprise that many of the Africans stolen into slavery and brought to the United States were followers of Islam. However, Islam and its role in slavery and the life of slaves has received considerably less emphasis than the importance of Protestant religions to slaves. The "Autobiography of Omar ibn Seid, Slave in North Carolina, 1831" is the tale of one Muslim slave, and makes for interesting reading. Seid was educated in mathematics, spoke Arabic, and was a cotton cloth merchant before being captured and sold into slavery. The following excerpt tells of his capture, escape, and servitude to General James Owen.

SOURCE: American Historical Review, 30 (1925).

You asked me to write my life. I am not able to do because I have much forgotten my own, as well as the Arabic language. Neither can I write very grammatically of according to the true idiom. And so, my brother, I beg you, in God's name, not to blame me, for I am a man of weak eyes, and of a weak body.

My name is Omar ibn Seid. My birthplace was Fut Tūr between the two rivers. I sought knowledge under the instruction of a Sheikh called Mohammed Seid, my own brother, and Sheikh Soleiman Kembeh, and Sheikh Gabriel Abdal. I continued my studies twenty-five years, and then returned to my home where I remained six years. Then there came to our place a large army, who killed many men, and took me, and brought me to the great sea, and sold me into the hands of the Christians, who bound me and sent me on board a great ship and we sailed upon the great sea a month and a half, when we came to a place called Charleston in the Christian language. There they sold me to a small, weak, and wicked man, called Johnson, a complete infidel, who had no fear of God at all. Now I am a small man, and unable to do hard work so I fled from the hand of Johnson and after a month came to a place called Fayd-il [Fayetteville]. There I saw some great houses (churches). On the new moon I went into a church to pray. A lad saw me and rode off to the place of his father and informed him that he had seen a black man in the church. A man named Handah (Hunter?) and another man with him on horseback, came attended by a troop of dogs. They took me and made me go with them twelve miles to a place called Fayd-il, where they put me into a great house from which I could not go out. I continued in the great house (which, in the Christian language, they called *jail*) six-teen days and nights. One Friday the jailor came and opened

the door of the house and I saw a great many men, all Christians, some of whom called out to me, "What is your name? Is it Omar or Seid?" I did not understand their Christian language. A man called Bob Mumford took me and led me out of the jail, and I was very well pleased to go with them to their place. I stayed at Mumford's four days and nights, and then a man named Jim Owen, son-in-law of Mumford, having married his daughter Betsey, asked me if I was willing to go to a place called Bladen. I said, Yes, I was willing. I went with them and have remained in the place of Jim Owen until now.

Before [after?] I came into the hand of Gen. Owen a man by the name of Mitchell came to buy me. He asked me if I were willing to go to Charleston City. I said "No, no, no, no, no, no, no, I not willing to go to Charleston. I stay in the hand of Jim Owen."

O ye people of North Carolina, O ye people of S. Carolina, O ye people of America all of you; have you, among you any two such men as Jim Owen and John Owen? These men are good men. What food they eat they give to me to eat. As they clothe themselves they clothe me. They permit me to read the gospel of God, our Lord, and Saviour, and King; who regulates all our circumstances, our health and wealth, and who bestows his mercies willingly, not by constraint. According to power I open my heart, as to a great light, to receive the true way, the way of the Lord Jesus the Messiah.

Before I came to the Christian country, my religion was the religion of "Mohammed, the Apostle of God—may God have mercy upon him and give him peace." I walked to the mosque before day-break, washed my face and head and hands and feet. I prayed at noon, prayed in the afternoon, prayed at sunset, prayed in the evening. I gave alms every year, gold, silver, seeds, cattle, sheep, goats, rice, wheat, and barley. I gave tithes of all the above-named things. I went every year to the holy war against the infidels. I went on pilgrimage to Mecca, as all did who were able.—My father had six sons and five daughters, and my mother had three sons and one daughter. When I left my country I was thirty-seven years old; I have been in the country of the Christians twenty-four years.

* * * * * *

1. The role of Islam within slavery is not as widely studied as that of Protestant religions. Why do you think this is?

2. What does Seid's narrative tell us about his treatment? Did different slave owners treat their slaves differently? Does this diminish the moral question of slavery? Why or why not?

chapter 12

Industry and the North, 1790s–1850s

12–1 A German Colonist Writes about the New American Settlements in Illinois in 1819

Ferdinand Ernst was the wealthy promoter of a colony of German settlers in frontier Illinois. In this account of his journey through this new state in western America, he describes the rural settlements recently planted by American farmers from Pennsylvania, Virginia, Kentucky, and Tennessee. Ernst's letters were so appealing that within a decade thousands of Germans flocked to the west to make a fresh start.

SOURCE: Ferdinand Ernst, "Travels in Illinois in 1819," *Transactions of the Illinois State Historical Society* 8 (1903).

According to the Constitution of the State of Illinois this town [Vandalia] is to be the seat of the government of the State, and the lots will be publicly sold on the 6th of September of this year. In the vicinity of this town is a large amount of fine lands; but everyone is full of praise for those which lie about 60 to 80 miles northward upon the river Sangamon. The Indians have concluded their treaty with Congress, and the latter is now in full possession of these so highly prized regions. In consideration of all this we regarded it more advisable to wait, and resolved for the present to settle in the town Vandalia, and then from here purchase land in time. In order to use the interval to as good advantage as possible, we began to build a little house here from logs, after the manner of the Americans—the logs are laid one upon another, the ends let down into grooves. As soon as the building was far enough advanced so that my companion was able to finish it alone, I started upon a journey to view the wonderful land upon the Sangamon before I returned to Europe. On the 27th of August I, accompanied by a guide, set out upon this little journey. We were both mounted, and had filled our portmanteaus as bountifully as possible with food for man and horse, because upon such a journey in those regions one can not count upon much.…

On Sugar creek, where we passed the second night, we found, right at the point of the timber, a family who had not yet finished their log cabin. Half a mile farther three families had settled near an excellent spring, and here we passed the night. Upon this little stream, which

about 15 miles to the north of its source empties into the Sangamon, about 60 farms have already been laid out and indeed all since this spring of 1819. They have only broken up the sod of the prairie with the plow and planted their corn, and now one sees these splendid fields covered almost without exception with corn from ten to 15 feet high. It is no wonder that such a high degree of fruitfulness attracts men to bid defiance to the various dangers and inconveniences that might, up to this time, present themselves to such a settlement. And one can therefore predict that possibly no region in all this broad America will be so quickly populated as this. Nevertheless, one must regard as venturesome daredevils all settlers who this early have located here for they trespassed upon the possessions of the Indians, and ran the risk of being driven out or killed during the great annual hunt of the Indians, if that treaty at Edwardsville had not fortunately been made. But now how many will migrate hither since everything is quiet and safe here! Let us consider these present farmers in respect to their property right upon these their plantations. How extremely dangerous is their position in this regard! The land is not even surveyed, and therefore cannot be offered for sale for three or four years. And then, when offered for sale, anyone is at liberty to outbid the present settler for his farm which is already in cultivation. If now all these considerations and actual dangers could not restrain men from migrating to this territory, this then is the most convincing proof of its value and that it is justly styled "the beautiful land on the Sangamon."

From Sugar creek we turned immediately westward with the intention of reaching the point where the Sangamon empties into the Illinois and there crossing the former to the north bank. We crossed Lake creek, then the two branches of Spring creek, both of which flow in the open prairie—a thing which I had never before seen here in America. On the other side of Spring creek is a camping ground of the Indians, whence the prairie rises to gentle hills where we found two fine springs shaded simply by a few trees. The water of these brooks flows swift and clear through the luxuriant prairie, the high grass of which often reaches above the head of the horseman. From these two little brooks rises a plain which extends to Richland creek.

Here we passed the night at the home of farmer Schaffer, who was just then employed in breaking up more prairie. It was a pleasure to me to see that this first plowing produced arable ground like the best clover field. I advised him to plant at least a small part to wheat which from appearances must undoubtedly be the best and most suitable grain for this soil. He, however, asserted that maize planted upon it the next spring would be more profitable. Nevertheless, he promised to make a trial with wheat; but he had already intended this year's corn field for the wheat. Maize, turnips and melons were the products which he expected this year upon the first breaking up of the prairie.

That this region leaves nothing to be desired with respect to health was sufficiently demonstrated to me by the healthy appearance of its inhabitants.

Further on in the prairie we again found some springs, and continuing westward, about noon reached another small river upon which we found three or four farms. The timber on this river bank consisted almost exclusively of sugar trees, and gave those people the most promising prospect of a harvest of sugar the coming spring. From all reports which we gathered it appeared to us that no one upon the bank of the Illinois river had ever been to the mouth of the Sangamon; prevented from doing so by the difficulty of penetrating the intervening woods and underbrush; but they estimated the distance at about 25 or 30 miles.

Since the heat was oppressive and the flies unendurable we were obliged to give up further progress to the Illinois river, we therefore turned again to the Sangamon, and toward noon reached its forest. Here, also, we found three farms, but we could not pass the river as it was very high. This river (the Sangamon) is rather large, and must be navigable the greater part of the year for medium sized vessels. It differs very advantageously from all the other rivers of western America in that its clear water even in this dry time maintains a moderate height, and it is uncommonly well stocked with fish.

We were now obliged to proceed farther up the river, and between the mouths of Sugar and Spring creeks we found a crossing where there was a canoe in which we crossed and let the horses swim alongside. The bank of the river is here about 50 feet high, measured from the surface of the Sangamon, where a broad plain is formed—a grand spot for the founding of a city. Below, upon the river bank, I found a very good clay for pottery and tile work. As soon as we had left the timber of the Sangamon, upon the other bank we came into another large prairie where a not insignificant hill covered with timber attracted our attention. It was the Elkhart (Grove.) This place is renowned on account of its agreeable and advantageous situation. A not too steep hill about two miles in circuit provided with two excellent springs, is the only piece of timbered land in a prairie from six to eight miles broad. Its forest trees show great fertility of the soil.

I found on it sugar trees from 3 to 4 feet in diameter, and the farmer settled here, Mr. Latham, had 30 acres enclosed by the wood of the ash. This hill is lost toward the Sangamon, as well as northward toward the Onaquispasipi in alternating hills without forest, which, to me, judging from the kinds of which grass they bore, seemed very well adapted to sheep grazing or vineyards. Eastward, at the foot of the hill, is a level, rich prairie.

Here Mr. Latham had planted 30 acres of corn this spring which thrived beyond all expectation. From this soil I took a small sample which seems to consist of loam and an insignificant admixture of sand. In the surrounding prairie the two springs reappear which were lost in the ground at the edge of the forest.

Towards the south there are several springs in the prairie, some which form little waterfalls often three or four feet high. All the circumstances make the Elkhart not only a beautiful, but—from an agricultural point of view—a very valuable possession. For whoever owns the woodlands of the Elkhart controls at the same time the greater part of the large and rich prairie surrounding it, where, on account of the scarcity of wood, it would be difficult to establish a farm. This farm is, up to the present time, the one situated farthest north in the whole State of Illinois—except, perhaps, in the military lands on the other side of the Illinois river. However, it will not remain so much longer, since 15 miles farther, where formerly stood the Kickapoo Indian capital, some corn fields have been laid out, and a farm will be established there towards spring.

We continued our journey northward and soon reached the charming banks of the Onaquispasipi (Satz). Alas! this river was likewise too high to be crossed on horseback. Here a rather passable road runs northward to Fort Clair, (Clark) on Lake Peoria. The soil northward on (of) the Sangamon has far more sand in it than in the remaining part of the State; and the only thing that might be feared would be that, on that account, its exceptional fertility in time might decrease. But this point of time is certainly very far off. The Onaquispasipi is still a more beautiful river than the Sangamon, for it has all the characteristics of the latter but in a higher degree. It is likewise navigable for medium sized vessels.

In this prairie I found many rattlesnakes; but all small, of gray color, and of one species. During my entire journey I have heard of no fatality produced by their bite. Unable to get across the river we were obliged to forego examination of the locality of Kickapoo town, and we started on our return journey. We had, however, seen enough to be able to assert that this region is one of the most important in the State of Illinois; or rather, will become such in a short time. One of the greatest obstacles that may retard the rapid population of this district is the scarcity of wood; yet, there is sufficient timber for a moderate population, and the stock of forest will soon greatly increase now that the destructive prairie fires will be stopped. Likewise the rivers Sangamon and Onaquispasipi can greatly facilitate the importation of this article. These two rivers will not only open up a market for all produce in the direction of St. Louis and New Orleans, but their proximity to the Illinois river will in time furnish this region with another very promising prospect by the lakes to New York City by means of the canal now in progress connecting that city and Lake Erie.

It is, also, a very easy thing to unite the Illinois with Lake Michigan by a 12-mile canal—even now, in the case of high water, the transit there is now made. By means of this canal then, inland navigation would be opened up from New York to New Orleans, a distance of 3,000 English miles. Such an internal waterway not only does not exist at the present time in the whole world, but, it will never exist anywhere else. Besides, this State enjoys the navigation of its boundary and internal rivers amounting to 3,094 miles, and all are placed in communication with each other through the Mississippi. In short, I do not believe that any one State in all America is so highly favored by nature, in every respect, as the State of Illinois.

The entire length of the Sangamon is still unknown; yet we know that it is navigable for at least 300 miles from its union with the Illinois. About 60 miles from its mouth it separates into two arms of which the southern one bears the name Mooqua, which, in the language of the Kickapoo Indians signifies "wolf's face." This arm is up to the present time the best known, and its borders are already rather well occupied with farms. Above the source of the Sangamon is found a rock 50 feet high which has a fissure in its middle. In this fissure the Indians placed tobacco, maize, honey and other products of the land as a thanks offering to the Great Spirit.

The Indians, for the most part, cultivate some maize, and are great reverers of this useful grain. As soon as the first ripe ears of maize are brought to the chief he institutes a grand feast where music and dance delight the company, and where the pipe of peace is industriously smoked. The benefits of the maize to the white settlers are manifold. As soon as the ears have attained some maturity it furnishes a good healthy food. The ears are either boiled in water, or roasted by the fire. From its meal, bread is prepared, and they make a porridge from it which with milk is an excellent dish. Besides this it is fed to all cattle, especially horses and pigs. Even its dry stalks are carefully preserved in stacks to serve as fodder for horses and cattle during the winter.

After an extremely tiresome day's journey we reached, about 11:00 o'clock at night the first farms on Shoal creek where we spent the night. Here the ague was raging, especially among those who had come here this year from the eastern states. This sickness is owing very much to the manner of life of these people; for they live in part upon dried venison, water melons, etc., and often expose themselves to wet weather. Such a manner of life must of necessity produce sickness. The wholesome effect of quinine is striking in the treatment of these fevers. I had brought a quantity of it with me from Baltimore, and this remedy very soon helped everyone to whom I administered it.

On the 5th of September I arrived at Vandalia. This place, in accordance with the Constitution, is to become the seat of government of the new State. It is 50 miles from Edwardsville, and about 60 from the Wabash; so that it is located about in the middle of the State. Its situation is well chosen, upon a bank of the Kaskaskia, 50 feet high, and richly provided with wood for building, and with good spring water, as well as with a vicinage of excellent land. The river, which is navigable to this point, here describes a sharp curve which amounts very nearly to a right-angle, coming from the east and going to the south.

The plan of the town is a square subdivided into 64 squares, and the space of two of these squares in the middle is intended for public use. Every square, having eight building lots, contains 320 square rods; each building lot is 80 feet wide 152 feet deep. Each square is cut from south to north by a 16-foot alley; and the large, regular and straight streets, 80 feet wide, intersect each other at right-angles.

Only four weeks ago the Commissioners advertised the sale of these lots (it will take place tomorrow), and there is already considerable activity manifested. Charles Reavise and I were the first who began to build. How difficult it was at that time to penetrate the dense forest which embraces the entire circuit of the future city. At present there are several passable roads leading hither. Now the most active preparations are being made for the construction of houses, and we are daily visited by travelers. But how it will have changed in 10 or 20 years! All these huge forests will have then disappeared and a flourishing city with fine buildings will stand in their place. A free people will then from this place rule itself through its representatives and watch over their freedom and well-being.

* * * * * *

1. *Ernst reports that Indians had recently vacated the country, leaving the land to the Americans. To what sequence of events was he referring?*

2. *Describe the ways in which these Illinois farmers made their living.*

12-2 The Treasury Secretary Reports on the Future of Industry in 1791

During his service as the first Secretary of the Treasury of the United States during the Washington Administration, Alexander Hamilton issued his famous "Report on Manufactures." Submitted to Congress in December, 1791, the Report served as the capstone of Hamilton's comprehensive economic program. It was an ambitious plan for the use of government securities as investment capital for infant industries, federal bounties to encourage innovation, and high protective tariffs, a system that he hoped would result in the development of an industrial economy. One of the most interesting features of Hamilton's report was his conviction that the United States could become a great power only if agriculture were balanced by industry.

SOURCE: H. C. Lodge, *The Works of Alexander Hamilton* (New York: G.P. Putnam's Sons, 1904).

The expediency of encouraging manufactures in the United States...appears at this time to be pretty generally admitted. The embarrassments which have obstructed the progress of our external trade, have led to serious reflections on the necessity of enlarging the sphere of our domestic commerce. The restrictive regulations, which, in foreign markets, abridge the vent of the increasing surplus of our agricultural produce...beget an earnest desire that a more extensive demand for that surplus may be created at home....

To affirm that the labor of the manufacturer is unproductive, because he consumes as much of the produce of land as he adds value to the raw material which he manufactures, is not better founded than it would be to affirm that the labor of the farmer, which furnishes materials to the manufacturer, is unproductive, because he consumes an equal value of manufactured articles. Each furnishes a certain portion of the produce of his labor to the other, and each destroys a corresponding portion of the produce of the labor of the other. In the meantime, the maintenance of two citizens, instead of one, is going on; the State has two members instead of one; and they, together, consume twice the value of what is produced from the land....

It is now proper to proceed a step further, and to enumerate the principal circumstances from which it may be inferred that manufacturing establishments not only occasion a positive augmentation of the produce and revenue of the society, but that they contribute essentially to rendering them greater than they could possibly be without such establishments. These circumstances are:

1. The division of labor.
2. An extension of the use of machinery.
3. Additional employment to classes of the community not ordinarily engaged in the business.
4. The promoting of emigration from foreign countries.
5. The furnishing greater scope for the diversity of talents and dispositions, which discriminate men from each other.
6. The affording a more ample and various field for enterprise.
7. The creating, in some instances, a new, and securing, in all, a more certain and steady demand for the surplus produce of the soil.

Each of these circumstances has a considerable influence upon the total mass of industrious effort in a community; together, they add to it a degree of energy and effect which is not easily conceived....

I. AS TO THE DIVISION OF LABOR

It has justly been observed, that there is scarcely any thing of greater moment in the economy of a nation than the proper division of labor. The separation of occupations causes each to be carried to a much greater perfection than it could possibly acquire if they were blended. This arises principally from three circumstances:

1st. The greater skill and dexterity naturally resulting from a constant and undivided application to a single object....

2d. The economy of time, by avoiding the loss of it, incident to a frequent transition from one operation to another of a different nature....

3d. An extension of the use of machinery. A man occupied on a single object will have it more in his power, and will be more naturally led to exert his imagination, in devising methods to facilitate and abridge labor, than if he were perplexed by a variety of independent and dissimilar operations....

2. AS TO AN EXTENSION OF THE USE OF MACHINERY, A POINT WHICH, THOUGH PARTLY ANTICIPATED, REQUIRES TO BE PLACED IN ONE OR TWO ADDITIONAL LIGHTS

The employment of machinery forms an item of great importance in the general mass of national industry. It is an artificial force brought in aid of the natural force of man; and, to all the purposes of labor, is an increase of hands, an accession of strength, unencumbered too by the expense of maintaining the laborer. May it not, therefore, be fairly inferred, that those occupations which give greatest scope to the use of this auxiliary, contribute most to the general stock of industrious effort, and, in consequence, to the general product of industry?....

3. *AS TO THE ADDITIONAL EMPLOYMENT OF CLASSES OF THE COMMUNITY NOT ORIGINALLY ENGAGED IN THE PARTICULAR BUSINESS*

This is not among the least valuable of the means by which manufacturing institutions contribute to augment the general stock of industry and production. In places where those institutions prevail, besides the persons regularly engaged in them, they afford occasional and extra employment to industrious individuals and families, who are willing to devote the leisure resulting from the intermissions of their ordinary pursuits to collateral labors, as a resource for multiplying their acquisitions or their enjoyments. The husbandman himself experiences a new source of profit and support from the increased industry of his wife and daughters, invited and stimulated by the demands of the neighboring manufactories.

It is worthy of particular remark that, in general, women and children are rendered more useful, and the latter more early useful, by manufacturing establishments, than they would otherwise be. Of the number of persons employed in the cotton manufactories of Great Britain, it is computed that four sevenths, nearly, are women and children, of whom the greatest proportion are children, and many of them of a very tender age....

4. *AS TO PROMOTING OF EMIGRATION FROM FOREIGN COUNTRIES*

Men reluctantly quit one course of occupation and livelihood for another, unless invited to it by very apparent and proximate advantages. Many who would go from one country to another, if they had a prospect of continuing with more benefit the callings to which they have been educated, will often not be tempted to change their situation by the hope of doing better in some other way. Manufacturers who, listening to the powerful invitations of a better price for their fabrics or their labor, of greater cheapness of provisions and raw materials, of an exemption from the chief part of the taxes, burthens, and restraints which they endure in the Old World, of greater personal independence and consequence, under the operation of a more equal government, and of what is far more precious than mere religious toleration, a perfect equality of religious privileges, would probably flock from Europe to the United States, to pursue their own trades or professions, if they were once made sensible of the advantages they would enjoy, and were inspired with an assurance of encouragement and employment, will, with difficulty, be induced to transplant themselves, with a view to becoming cultivators of land....

5. *AS TO THE FURNISHING GREATER SCOPE FOR THE DIVERSITY OF TALENTS AND DISPOSITIONS, WHICH DISCRIMINATE MEN FROM EACH OTHER*

If there be any thing in a remark often to be met with, namely, that there is, in the genius of the people of this country, a peculiar aptitude for mechanic improvements, it would operate as a forcible reason for giving opportunities to the exercise of that species of talent, by the propagation of manufactures.

6. *AS TO THE AFFORDING A MORE AMPLE AND VARIOUS FIELD FOR ENTERPRISE*

The spirit of enterprise, useful and prolific as it is, must necessarily be contracted or expanded, in proportion to the simplicity or variety of the occupations and productions which are to be found in a society. It must be less in a nation of mere cultivators, than in a nation of cultivators and merchants; less in a nation of cultivators and merchants, than in a nation of cultivators, artificers, and merchants.

7. *AS TO THE CREATING, IN SOME INSTANCES, A NEW, AND SECURING, IN ALL, A MORE CERTAIN AND STEADY DEMAND FOR THE SURPLUS PRODUCE OF THE SOIL*

This is among the most important of the circumstances which have been indicated. It is a principal means by which the establishment of manufactures contributes to an augmentation of the produce or revenue of a country, and has an immediate and direct relation to the prosperity of agriculture.

It is evident that the exertions of the husbandman will be steady or fluctuating, vigorous or feeble, in proportion to the steadiness or fluctuation, adequateness or inadequateness, of the markets on which he must depend for the vent of the surplus which may be produced by his labor; and that such surplus, in the ordinary course of things, will be greater or less in the same proportion....

This idea of an extensive domestic market for the surplus produce of the soil, is of the first consequence. It is, of all things, that which most effectually conduces to a flourishing state of agriculture. If the effect of manufactories should be to detach a portion of the hands which would otherwise be engaged in tillage, it might possibly cause a smaller quantity of lands to be under cultivation; but, by their tendency to procure a more certain demand for the surplus produce of the soil, they would, at the same time, cause the lands which were in cultivation to be better improved and more productive. And while, by their influence, the condition of each individual farmer would be meliorated, the total mass of agricultural production would probably be increased. For this must evidently depend as much upon the degree of improvement, if not more, than upon the number of acres under culture....

The foregoing considerations seem sufficient to establish, as general propositions, that it is the interest of nations to diversify the industrious pursuits of the individuals who compose them; that the establishment of manufactures is calculated not only to increase the general stock of useful and productive labor, but even to improve the state of agriculture in particular,—certainly to advance the interests of those who are engaged in it....

* * * * * *

1. *According to Hamilton, what will be the benefits to the country of an industrial division of labor?*

2. *With industrial development, says Hamilton, "women and children are rendered more useful." Discuss the implications of his point of view.*

12-3 Employers Advertise for Help Wanted in the 1820s

Although most hiring in the early nineteenth century was done by word of mouth, by the 1820s employers in the rapidly expanding industrial economy of New England had begun to advertise in the local papers for skilled and unskilled workers. These notices are taken from the Manufacturers' and Farmers' Journal of Providence, Rhode Island.

SOURCE: Gary Kulik, Roger Parks, and Theodore A. Penn, eds., *The New England Mill Village, 1790–1860* (Cambridge, Mass.: The MIT Press, 1982).

[June 28, 1821]
WANTED,
A mule and Throstle Spinner, and a few Girls from fifteen to twenty years of age, who have been accustomed to tending spinning frames, and can come well recommended....
John C. Dodge, Agent
Tyler Manufacturing Co.,
Attleboro, Massachusetts

[July 2, 1821]
A family who wishes employment in a Cotton Factory, may find suitable encouragement, if they can be recommended to be of good habits, and willing to work, say one reeler, one or two to tend spinning, and one or two to tend drawing and roping....

[November 1, 1821]
The subscriber is in want of a mule Spinner—one who is well versed in the business and can give satisfactory recommendations of his skill and habits, will find liberal encouragement by calling on the subscriber.

Ira P. Evans
N.B. One with family would be preferred.

[April 15, 1822]
The subscribers are in want of eight or ten Girls to weave on Water looms. Those who understand the business may have constant employ, good treatment and liberal wages, by applying to Mr. Kent, at the Hope Factory, Scituate, or to EPHRAIM TALBOT & CO.,
Providence.
N.B. None need apply but those who are willing to work twelve hours a day. One or two good families are also wanted at the above mill....

[April 25, 1822]
Wanted, a family consisting of six or eight persons to work in a Cotton mill, near this town. Two of them must be Spinners; and the remainder work in a Carding Room. None need apply unless well recommended, and are willing to comply to good and necessary regulations; to such a Family liberal wages will be paid, either in cash or otherwise as may be agreed upon....

[April 29, 1822]
Wanted, A man to take charge of a carding room in a cotton factory in Walpole, N.H. One very well acquainted with the business and that could bring good recommendations would meet with good encouragement.
Sampson Drury
Anan Evans

[September 19, 1822]
WANTED—At the Middlesex Factory in Hopkinton [Massachusetts], a man that understands carding, spinning, weaving and repairing a cotton mill. No one need apply without he is master of the business. To such a man good encouragement will be given. Also, a girl that understands taking care of a dresser may meet with good encouragement by applying at the factory in Hopkinton.

[October 24, 1822]
WANTED At the Plainfield Union Factory, in Plainfield [Connecticut], two good machine makers. Inquire of the agent at the Factory, or of David Anthony, agent at Providence.

[December 19, 1822]
WANTED to Hire, a good workman, to repair Cotton Machinery at a Cotton Mill near this town—one with a family to work in a mill, would be preferred.
Philip Allen

[June 28, 1824]
Wanted by the Framingham Manufacturing Company, at Framingham, Mass. 30 miles from Providence, twenty girls, acquainted with spinning and weaving. Also a good Mechanick, acquainted with the operation of machinery....Those answering the above description, will find constant employment and receive good wages, in cash, for their services.

Samuel Murdock, Agent
Framingham

[October 1, 1829]
The subscribers are in want o Twenty-four good [female] Water Loom Weavers, to whom good wages will be given, part cash or all, if particularly required. None need apply unless they are willing to work twelve hours per day, and be subject to good rules and regulations while weaving.
J. Underwood & Co.

* * * * *

1. *Consult a dictionary to be sure you understand all the terms used in these advertisements.*

2. *Using these advertisements as evidence, discuss the qualities and characteristics employers desired in their workers in the 1820s.*

12–4   The Carpenters of Boston Go on Strike in 1825

The first organized strikes of workers in the United States took place immediately after the Revolution, but it was not until the development of industry in the nineteenth century that work stoppages became a common tool of the workers' movement. The following two resolutions—the first issued by the Journeymen Carpenters of Boston, the second by their employers, the Master Carpenters—were published in April, 1825.

SOURCE: John R. Commons, ed., *A Documentary History of American Industrial Society* (Glendale: Arthur H. Clark Company, 1910).

RESOLUTIONS OF JOURNEYMEN CARPENTERS

Notice to house carpenters and housewrights in the country. An advertisement having appeared in the papers of this city, giving information that there is at this time a great demand for workmen in this branch of mechanical business in this city, it is considered a duty to state for the benefit of our brethren of the trade that we are not aware of any considerable demand for labor in this business, as there is, at this time, a very considerable number of journeymen carpenters who are out of employ, and the problable inducement which led to the communication referred to arises from a disposition manifested on the part of the builders in this city to make their own terms as to the price of labor and the number of hours labor which shall hereafter constitute a day's work. It being a well-known fact that the most unreasonable requirements have been hitherto extracted with regard to the terms of labor of journeymen mechanics in this city; and it is further well known that in the cities of New York, Philadelphia, Baltimore, and most of the other cities of much more liberal and equitable course of policy has been adopted by the master-builders, on this subject, giving to their journeymen that fair and liberal support to which they are unquestionably entitled. It is an undoubted fact that, on the present system, it is impossible for a journeyman housewright and house carpenter to maintain a family at the present time with the wages which are now usually given to the journeymen house carpenters in this city.

RESOLUTIONS OF MASTER-CARPENTERS

Resolved, That we learn with surprise and regret that a large number of those who are employed as journeymen in this city have entered into a combination for the purpose of altering the time of commencing and terminating their daily labor from that which has been customary from time immemorial, thereby lessening the amount of labor each day in a very considerable degree.

Resolved, That we consider such a combination as unworthy of that useful and industrious class of the community who are engaged in it; that it is fraught with numerous and pernicious evils, not only as respect their employers but the public at large, and especially themselves; for all journeymen of good character and of skill may expect very soon to become masters and, like us, the employers of others; and by the measure which they are now inclined to adopt they will entail upon themselves the inconvenience to which they seem desirous that we should not be exposed?

Resolved, That we consider the measure proposed, as calculated to exert a very unhappy influence on our apprentices—by seducing them from that course of industry and economy of time to which we are anxious to inure them. That it will expose the journeymen themselves to many temptations and improvident practices from which they are happily secure; while they attend to that wise and salutary maxim of mechanics, "Mind your business." That we consider idleness as the most deadly bane to usefulness and honorable living; and knowing (such is human nature that, where there is no necessity, there is no exertion, we fear and dread the consequences of such a measure upon the morals and well-being of society.)

Resolved, That we cannot believe this project to have originated with many of the faithful and industrious sons of New England but are compelled to consider it an evil of foreign growth, and one which, we hope and trust, will not take root in the favored soil of Massachusetts. And especially that our city, the early rising and industry of whose inhabitants are universally proverbial, may not be infested with the unnatural production.

Resolved, That if such a measure were ever to be proper and necessary, the time has not yet arrived when it is so; if it would ever be just, it cannot be at a time like the present, when builders have generally made their engagements and contracts for the season, having predicated their estimats and prices upon the original state of things in reference to journey men. And we appeal therefore to the good sense, the honesty, and justice of all who are engaged in this combination, and ask them to review their doings, contemplate their consequences, and then act as becomes men of sober sense and of prudence.

Resolved, finally, That we will make no alteration in the manner of employing journeymen as respects the time of commencing and leaving work and that we will employ no man who persists in adhering to the project of which we complain.

* * * * * *

1. *According to the Journeymen Carpenters, what were their employers attempting to accomplish?*

2. *In response to the action of the Journeymen, the Master Carpenters appeal to the ancient system of craft in which "all journeymen of good character and of skill may expect very soon to become masters and, like us, the employers of others." How might the Journeymen have replied?*

12–5 A New England Factory Issues Regulations for Workers in 1825

The Hamilton Manufacturing Company was one of the many textile manufacturers that prospered in the city of Lowell, Massachusetts, in the early nineteenth century. These regulations constituted the contractual conditions under which employees worked for the company. Failure to work according to the rules could result in a worker being blacklisted and prevented from finding further employment in the area.

SOURCE: John R. Commons, ed., *A Documentary History of American Industrial Society* (Glendale: Arthur H. Clark Company, 1910).

Regulations to be observed by all persons employed in the factories of the Hamilton Manufacturing Company. The overseers are to be always in their rooms at the starting of the mill, and not absent unnecessarily during working hours. They are to see that all those employed in their rooms, are in their places in due season, and keep a correct account of their time and work. They may grant leave of absence to those employed under them, when they have spare hands to supply their places, and not otherwise, except in cases of absolute necessity.

All persons in the employ of the Hamilton Manufacturing Company, are to observe the regulations of the room where they are employed. They are not to be absent from their work without the consent of the overseer, except in cases of sickness, and then they are to send him word of the cause of their absence. They are to board in one of the houses of the company and give information at the counting room, where they board, when they begin, or, whenever they change their boarding place; and are to observe the regulations of their boarding-house.

Those intending to leave the employment of the company, are to give at least two weeks' notice thereof to their overseer.

All persons entering into the employment of the company, are considered as engaged for twelve months and those who leave sooner, or do not comply with all these regulations, will not be entitled to a regular discharge.

The company will not employ any one who is habitually absent from public worship on the Sabbath, or known to be guilty of immorality.

A physician will attend once in every month at the

counting-room, to vaccinate all who may need it, free of expense.

Any one who shall take from the mills or the yard, any yarn, cloth or other article belonging to the company, will be considered guilty of stealing and be liable to prosecution.

Payment will be made monthly, including board and wages. The accounts will be made up to the last Saturday but one in every month, and paid in the course of the following week.

These regulations are considered part of the contract, with which all persons entering into the employment of the Hamilton Manufacturing Company, engage to comply.

JOHN AVERY, Agent.

* * * * * *

1. How do these regulations compare with work rules in modern America?

2. A number of the rules involve the moral character of the workers. What gave employers the right to impose these requirements on their employees?

12–6   A Young Woman Writes of the Evils of Factory Life in 1845

The women employed in the textile factories of Lowell, Massachusetts, became nationally famous because of the publication of the Lowell Offering, *a literary magazine sponsored by the manufacturers. The* Offering *painted a rosy picture of life in the mills. But not all the women who worked at Lowell shared these sentiments. The following letter, written by a woman calling herself "Julianna," was rejected by the* Offering *and published in 1845 as a pamphlet entitled* Factory Life As It Is *by the Lowell Female Labor Reform Association, a militant labor organization.*

SOURCE: *Factory Life As It Is, By An Operative* (Lowell, Mass.: Lowell Female Labor Reform Association, 1845).

Among the first which we shall notice, is the tendency it has, at the present time, to destroy all love of order and practice in domestic affairs. It is a common remark, that by the time a young lady has worked in a factory one year, she will lose all relish for the quiet, fireside comforts of life, and the neatness attendant upon order and precision. The truth is, time is wanting, and opportunity, in order to cultivate the mind and form good habits. All is hurry, bustle and confusion in the street, in the mill, and in the overflowing boarding house. If there chance to be an intelligent mind in that crowd which is striving to lay up treasures of knowledge, how unfavorably it is situated! Crowded into a small room, which contains three bed and six females, all possessing the "without end" tongue of woman, what chance is there for *studying?* and much less so for thinking and reflecting?...

Let us look forward into the future, and what does the picture present to our imagination! Methinks I behold the self same females occupying new and responsible stations in society. They are now wives and mothers! But oh! how deficient in everything pertaining to those holy, *sacred* names! Behold what disorder, confusion and disquietude reigns, where quiet, neatness and calm serenity should sanctify and render almost like heaven the home of domestic union and love! Instead of being qualified to rear a family,—to instruct them in the great duties of life—to cultivate and unfold the intellect—to imbue the soul in the true and living principles of right and justice—to teach them the most important of all lessons, the art of being *useful* members in the world, ornaments in society and blessings to all around them,—*they,* themselves, have need to be instructed in the *very first* principles of living well and thinking right. Incarcerated within the walls of a factory, while as yet mere children—drilled there from five till seven o'clock, year after year—thrown into company with all sorts and descriptions of minds, dispositions and intellects, without counsellor or friends to advise—far away from a watchful mother's tender care or father's kind instruction—surrounded on all sides with the vain ostentation of fashion, vanity and light frivolity—beset with temptations without, and the carnal propensities of nature within, what *must,* what *will* be the natural, rational result? What but ignorance, misery, and *premature decay* of both *body* and *intellect?* Our country will be but one great hospital filled with worn out operatives and colored slaves! Those who marry, even, become a curse instead of a help-meet to their husbands, because of having broken the laws of God and their own physical natures, in these modern prisons (alias palaces,) in the gardens of Eden! It has been remarked by some writer that the mother educates the man. Now, if this be a truth, as we believe it is, to a very great extent, what, we would ask, are we to expect, the same system of labor prevailing, will be the mental and intellectual character of the future generations of New England? What but a race weak, sickly, imbecile, both mental and physical? A race fit only for corporation tools and time-serving slaves?

Nobility of America!—producers of all the luxuries and comforts of life! will you not *wake up* on this subject? Will you sit supinely down and let the drones in society fasten the yoke of tyranny, which is already fitted to your necks so cunningly that you do not feel it but slightly,—will you, I say suffer them to rivet that yoke upon you, which has crushed and is crushing its millions in the old world to earth; yea, to starvation and death? Now is the time to answer this all-important question. Shall we not hear the response from every hill and vale, "EQUAL RIGHTS, or death to the corporations"? God grant it, is the fervent prayer of

—JULIANNA

* * * * * *

1. According to "Julianna," what is the worst evil of factory life for women?

2. The writer compares America with "the old world." What is her vision of the economic future of the country?

12-7　A Woman Worker Writes Home to Her Father in 1845

The writings pro and con about the employment of women were often heavy with the language of propaganda. Mary Paul came to Lowell in the mid-1840s from her home in New Hampshire. Her letters home to her father provide a convincing personal view of life in the mills.

SOURCE: Thomas Dublin, ed., *Farm to Factory: Women's Letters, 1870–1860* (New York: Columbia University Press, 1981).

Lowell Dec 21st 1845

Dear Father

I received your letter on Thursday the 14th with much pleasure. I am well which is one comfort. My life and health are spared while others are cut off. Last Thursday one girl fell down and broke her neck which caused instant death. She was coming in or coming out of the mill and slipped down it being very icy. The same day a man was killed by the cars. Another had nearly all of his ribs broken. Another was nearly killed by falling down and having a bale of cotton fall on him. Last Tuesday we were paid. In all I had six dollars and sixty cents paid $4.68 for board. With the rest, I got me a pair of rubbers and a pair of 50 cts shoes. Next payment I am to have a dollar a week beside my board. We have not had much snow the deepest being not more than 4 inches. It has been very warm for winter. Perhaps you would like something about our regulations about going in and coming out of the mill. At 5 o'clock in the morning the bell rings for the folks to get up and get breakfast. At half past six it rings for the girls to get up and at seven they are called into the mill. At half past 12 we have dinner are called back again at one and stay till half past seven. I get along very well with my work. I can doff as fast as any girl in our room. I think I shall have frames before long. The usual time allowed for learning is six months but I think I shall have frames before I have been in three as I get along so fast. I think that the factory is the best place for me and if any girl wants employment I advise them to come to Lowell. Tell Harriet that though she does not hear from me she is not forgotten. I have little time to devote to writing that I cannot write all I want to. There are half a dozen letters which I ought to write to day but I have not time. Tell Harriet I send my love to her and all of the girls. Give my love to Mrs. Clement. Tell Henry this will answer for him and you too for this time.

This from
Mary S. Paul

Lowell Nov 5th 1848

Dear Father

Doubtless you have been looking for a letter from me all the week past. I would have written but wished to find whether I should be able to stand it—to do the work that I am now doing. I was unable to get my old place in the cloth room on the Suffolk or on any other corporation. I next tried the dressrooms on the Lawrence Cor[poration], but did not succe[e]d in getting a place. I almost concluded to give up and go back to Claremont, but thought I would try once more. So I went to my old overseer on the Tremont Cor. I had no idea that he would want one, but he *did*, and I went to work last Tuesday—warping—the same work I used to do.

It is *very* hard indeed and sometimes I think I shall not be able to endure it. I never worked so hard in my life but perhaps I shall get used to it. I shall try hard to do so for there is no other work that I can do unless I spin and that I shall not undertake on any account. I presume you have heard before this that the wages are to be reduced on the 20th of this month. It is *true* and there seems to be a good deal of excitement on the subject but I can not tell what will be the consequence. The companies pretend they are losing immense sums every *day* and therefore they are obliged to lessen the wages, but this seems perfectly absurd to me for they are constantly making *repairs* and it seems to me that this would not be if there were really any danger of their being obliged to *stop* the mills. It is very difficult for any one to get into the mill on any corporation. All seem to be very full of help. I expect to be paid about two dollars a week but it will be dearly earned. I cannot tell how it is but never since I have worked in the mill have I been so very tired as I have for the last week but it may be owing to the long rest I have had for the last six months. I have not told you that I do not board on the Lawrence. The reason of this is because I wish to be nearer the mill and I do no wish to pay the extra $.12-1/2 per week (I should not be obliged to do it if I boarded at 15) and I know that they are not able to give it me. Beside this I am so near I can go and see them as often as I wish. So considering all things I think I have done the best I could....

Give my love to uncle Jerry and aunt Betsey and tell little Lois that "Cousin Carra" thanks her very much

for the *apple* she sent her. Her health is about the same that it was when she was at Claremont. No one has much hope of her ever being any better

Write soon. Yours affectionately

Mary S. Paul

* * * * * *

1. *From Paul's two letters, what are your impressions of life in Lowell for a young woman worker?*

2. *Given the conditions of her work, why do you think Paul writes to her father that "the factory is the best place for me"?*

12–8   A New England Woman Describes the Responsibilities of American Women in 1847

Catherine Beecher was a member of one of the most influential families of nineteenth-century America, including her father the Reverend Lyman Beecher; her brother the Reverend Henry Ward Beecher; and her sister, Harriet Beecher Stowe, author of Uncle Tom's Cabin. In 1847 Catherine wrote an influential book, Treatise on Domestic Economy for Young Ladies at Home and at School, *in which she promoted a domestic ideal for American women, an ideal that has since become known as "the cult of true womanhood." Women's subordination to men, she argued, sheltered them from the harshness of the world of the marketplace and politics and enabled them to work for moral uplift at home.*

SOURCE: Catherine Beecher, *Treatise on Domestic Economy for Young Ladies at Home and at School* (New York: Harper and Brothers, 1847).

...There must be the magistrate and the subject, one of whom is the superior, and the other the inferior. There must be the relations of husband and wife, parent and child, teacher and pupil, employer and employed, each involving the relative duties of subordination. The superior, or, in certain particulars, is to direct, and the inferior is to yield obedience. Society could never go forward, harmoniously, nor could any craft or profession be successfully pursued, unless these superior and subordinate relations be instituted and sustained.

But who shall take the higher, and who the subordinate, stations in social and civil life? This matter, in the case of parents and children, is decided by the Creator. He has given children to the control of parents, as their superiors,

and to them they remain subordinate, to a certain age, or so long as they are members of their household. And parents can delegate such a portion of their authority to teachers and employers, as the interests of their children require.

In most other cases, in a truly democratic state, each individual is allowed to choose for himself, who shall take the position of his superior. No woman is forced to obey any husband but the one she chooses for herself; nor is she obliged to take a husband, if she prefers to remain single. So every domestic, and every artisan or laborer, after passing from parental control, can choose the employer to whom he is to accord obedience, or, if he prefers to relinquish certain advantages, he can remain without taking a subordinate place to any employer.

And the various privileges that wealth secures, are, equally open to all classes. Every man may aim at riches, unimpeded by any law or institution which secures peculiar privileges to a favored class, at the expense of another. Every law, and every institution, is tested by examining whether it secures equal advantages to all; and, if the people become convinced that any regulation sacrifices the good of the majority to the interests of the smaller number, they have power to abolish it....

It appears, then, that it is in America, alone, that women are raised to an equality with the other sex; and that, both in theory and practice, their interests are regarded as of equal value. They are made subordinate in station, only where a regard to their best interests demands it, while, as if in compensation for this, by custom and courtesy, they are always treated as superiors. Universally, in this Country, through every class of society, precedence is given to woman, in all the comforts, conveniences, and courtesies, of life.

In civil and political affairs, American women take no interest or concern, except so far as they sympathize with their family and personal friends; but in all cases, in which they do feel a concern, their opinions and feelings have a consideration, equal, or even superior, to that of the other sex.

In matters pertaining to the education of their children, in the selection and support of a clergyman, in all benevolent enterprises, and in all questions relating to morals or manners, they have a superior influence. In such concerns, it would be impossible to carry a point, contrary to their judgement and feelings; while an enterprise, sustained by them, will seldom fail of success.

If those who are bewailing themselves over the fancied wrongs and injuries of women in this Nation, could only see things as they are, they would know, that, whatever remnants of a barbarous or aristocratic age may remain in our civil institutions, in reference to the interests of women, it is only because they are ignorant of them, or do not use their influence to have them rectified; for it is very certain that there is nothing reasonable, which American women would unite in asking, that would not readily be bestowed....

The success of democratic institutions, as is conceded by all, depends upon the intellectual and moral character of the mass of the people. If they are intelligent and virtuous, democracy is a blessing; but if they are ignorant and wicked, it is only a curse, and as much more dreadful than any other form of civil government, as a thousand tyrants are more to be dreaded than one. It is equally conceded, that the formation of the moral and intellectual character of the young is committed mainly to the female hand. The mother forms the character of the future man; the sister bends the fibres that are hereafter to be the forest tree; the wife sways the heart, whose energies may turn for good or for evil the destinies of a nation. Let the women of a country be made virtuous and intelligent, and the men will certainly be the same. The proper education of a man decides the welfare of an individual; but educate a woman, and the interests or a whole family are secured.

If this be so, as none will deny, then to American women, more than to any others on earth, is committed the exalted privilege of extending over the world those blessed influences, which are to renovate degraded man, and "clothe all climes with beauty."

No American woman, then, has any occasion for feeling that hers is an humble or insignificant lot. The value of what an individual accomplishes, is to be estimated by the importance of the enterprise achieved, and not by the particular position of the laborer. The drops of heaven which freshen the earth, are each of equal value, whether they fall in the lowland meadow, or the princely parterre. The builders of a temple are of equal importance, whether they labor on the foundations, or toil upon the dome....

[The] greater difficulty, peculiar to American women, is, a delicacy of constitution, which renders them early victims to disease and decay.

The fact that the women of this Country are unusually subject to disease, and that their beauty and youthfulness are of shorter continuance than those of the women of other nations, is one which always attracts the attention of foreigners; while medical men and philanthropists are constantly giving fearful monitions as to the extent and alarming increase of this evil. Investigations make it evident, that a large proportion of young ladies, from the wealthier classes, have the incipient stages of curvature of the spine, one of the most sure and fruitful causes of future disease and decay. The writer has heard medical men, who have made extensive inquiries, say, that a very large proportion of the young women at boarding schools, are affected in this way, while many other indications of disease and debility exist, in cases where this particular evil cannot be detected.

In consequence of this enfeebled state of their constitutions, induced by a neglect of their physical education, as soon as they are called to the responsibilities and trials of domestic life, their constitution fails, and their whole existence is rendered a burden. For no woman can enjoy existence, when disease throws a dark cloud over the mind, and incapacitates her for the proper discharge of every duty....

It would seem as if the primeval curse, which has written the doom of pain and sorrow on one period of a young mother's life, in this Country had been extended over all; so that the hour seldom arrives, when "she forgetteth her sorrow for joy that a man is born into the world." Many a mother will testify, with shuddering, that the most exquisite sufferings she ever endured, were not those appointed by Nature, but those, which, for week after week, have worn down health and spirits, when nourishing her child. And medical men teach us, that this, in most cases, results from a debility of constitution, consequent on the mismanagement of early life. And so frequent and so mournful are these, and the other distresses that result from the delicacy of the female constitution, that the writer has repeatedly heard mothers say, that they had wept tears of bitterness over their infant daughters, at the thought of the sufferings which they were destined to undergo; while they cherished the decided wish, that these daughters should never marry.

* * * * *

1. Beecher argued against those "bewailing themselves over the fancied wrongs and injuries of women in this Nation." Who might she have had in mind? How does she answer them?

2. Beecher believed that the greatest problem for American women was their "delicacy of constitution" due to their neglect of "physical education." Is this argument similar to ones you hear today?

Coming to Terms with the New Age, 1820s–1850s

13–1   A Plan to Equalize the Wealth in 1829

Jacksonian Democracy was marked by a concern for the little man and a lessening of federal power. Jackson himself came from rather humble beginnings and this was reflected in his social concerns. This democratization of power was also reflected by the thinkers of Jackson's day and their social policy. One such proponent, Thomas Skidmore, outlines a radical "Plan For Equalizing Property," in his The Rights of Man to Property! *being a Proposition to make it equal among the adults of the present generation: and to provide for its equal transmission…. Skidmore first makes a philosophical argument for his plan, and in the following excerpt, presents a step by step procedure for redistributing wealth.*

SOURCE: Thomas Skidmore, *The Rights of Man to Property!* (New York: A Ming, Jr., 1829).

1. Let a new State Convention be assembled. Let it prepare a new constitution, and let that constitution, after having been adopted by the people, decree an abolition of all debts, both at home and abroad, between citizen and citizen, and between citizen and foreigner. Let it renounce all property belonging to our citizens, without the State. Let it claim all property within the State, both real and personal, of whatever kind it may be, with the exception of that belonging to resident aliens, and with the further exception of so much personal property as may be in the possession of transient owners, not being citizens. Let it order an equal division of all this property among the citizens, of and over the age of maturity, in manner yet to be directed. Let it order all transfers or removals of property, except so much as may belong to transient owners, to cease until the division is accomplished.

2. Let a census be taken of the people, ascertaining and recording in books made for the purpose the name, time when born, as near as may be, and annexing the age, the place of nativity, parentage, sex, color, occupation, domicile or residence, and time of residence since last resident in the State, distinguishing aliens from citizens, and ordering, with the exception of the Agents of Foreign Governments, such as ambassadors, etc., that all such aliens shall be considered as citizens if they have been

resident for the five years next previous to the time when the before mentioned division of property shall have been ordered.

3. Let each citizen, association, corporation, and other persons at the same time when the census is being taken give an inventory of all personal property, of whatever description it may be, and to whomsoever it may belong, in his, her, or their possession. Let also a similar inventory of all real property within the State be taken, whoever may be the owner of it. And from these data let a general inventory be made out of all the real and personal property within the State which does not belong to alien residents or transient owners. To this let there be added all property in the possession of our tribunals of law and equity, and such State property as can be offered up to sale without detriment to the State.

4. Let there be next a dividend made of this amount among all such citizens who shall be of and over the age of eighteen, if this should be fixed as I am inclined to think it should be as the age of maturity; and let such dividend be entered in a book for the purpose to the credit of such persons, male and female.

5. Let public sale be made, as soon after such dividend is made as may be practicable, to the highest bidder of all the real and personal property in the State. Care must be taken that the proper authority be required to divide all divisible property that shall require it into such allotments or parcels as will be likely to cause it to bring the greatest amount at the time of sale.

6. All persons having such credit, on the books before mentioned, are authorized and required to bid for an amount of property falling short not more than ten per cent of the sum placed to their credit and not exceeding it more than ten per cent. Delivery may be made of the whole, if it be real property, and the receiver may stand charged with the overplus. If it be personal property, delivery to be made only to the amount of the dividend unless it be secured.

7. When property, real or personal, is offered for sale which is not in its nature divisible and in its value such as to be of an amount greater than would fall to the lot of any one person, then it shall be proper to receive a joint bid of two or more persons, and these may purchase in conjunction, giving in their names, however, at the time of sale.

8. As it regards personal property which may be secreted or clandestinely put out of the way, order should be given that from the time when any Inventory of any person's property of the kind is made out up to the completion of the General Sale, the owner should be answerable for the forthcoming of so much as may be left in his possession, at the peril of imprisonment for fourteen years, as is now the punishment for the crime of grand larceny, unless good cause were shown to the contrary.

Similar punishment, also, should be visited upon everyone who knowingly gave in a false or defective statement of the property he had in his possession or who, having received his patrimony, goes abroad and receives debts or property which the State has renounced.

9. As the General Sales are closed, their amount should be ascertained, and a new dividend declared. It will then be seen how much this dividend, which may be called a "patrimony," differs from the original dividend. By comparing the amount of each person's purchases with this patrimony, it will be seen whether he is creditor or debtor to the State, and how much, and he will be entitled to receive the same or required to pay it to the State accordingly.

10. There is one exception to the delivering of property to persons who may bid it off. It is to those for whom, from excessive intemperance, insanity, or other incapacitating cause, the law may provide, as it should, proper and suitable trustees or guardians. Under proper regulations, it should be entrusted to *them*.

II. While all this is transacting, persons already arrived at the age of maturity and before they can be put in possession of their own patrimony will die. Of these and others throughout the State, a daily register should be kept from this time forward forever; and so also should be kept another register of the births of those now in minority and of those that shall hereafter be born. The property intended to be given to those who shall thus have received their patrimony in consequence of the General Division and who shall die before the first day of January ensuing the completion of the General Sales shall be divided equally among all those

who shall have arrived at the age of maturity between the time of taking the Census aforesaid and the first day of January just mentioned.

12. An annual dividend forever shall be made of the property left throughout the State by persons dying between the last day of every year and the first day of the next succeeding, among those who throughout the State, male and female, shall have arrived at the age of maturity within such period; and it shall be at their option, after the dividend is made, to receive it in cash or to use the credit of it in the future purchase of other property which the State will have constantly on sale in consequence of the decease of other persons in the ensuing year.

13. Property belonging to persons not citizens, but of transiently resident among us, and dying here, to abide by the laws which govern the state or nation to which such person belonged in the disposal of property in such a situation; provided such state or nation allows the property, or the value thereof, of our citizens dying there and leaving property to be sent home to abide by the operation of our own laws....

* * * * * *

1. Summarize Skidmore's plan. Would this work? Would you be in favor of such a plan?

2. When was Karl Marx's work published relative to Skidmore? What similarities do you see to Marx's plan to redistribute the means of production? What differences?

13–2 *Irish Laborers Get an Endorsement in 1833*

The early 19th century saw a steady influx of immigrants—Italian, Irish, Asian—many of whom were put to the hardest labor in the building of America. There was widespread resentment of the laborers, and numerous articles appeared denouncing them as filthy and lice ridden. But they also had occasional advocates. In the following passage from his Impressions of America *during the years 1833, 1834, and 1835, Tyrone Power describes the working conditions of the Irish laborers toiling on the canal to connect Lake Pontchartrain to New Orleans, and applauds the Irish people.*

SOURCE: Tyrone Power, *Impressions of America* (London: R. Bentley, 1836).

One of the greatest works now in progress here, is the canal planned to connect Lac Pontchartrain with the city [New

Orleans]. In the month of February it was completed to within three miles of the lake; and as it was a pleasant ride to the point where the digging was in progress, I two or three times visited the scene, after its bearings had been explained by the two intelligent persons under whose guidance I first penetrated the swamp.

I only wish that the wise men at home who coolly charge the present condition of Ireland upon the inherent laziness of her population, could be transported to this spot, to look upon the hundreds of fine fellows labouring here beneath a sun that at this winter season was at times insufferably fierce, and amidst a pestilential swamp whose exhalations were foetid to a degree scarcely endurable even for a few moments; wading amongst stumps of trees, mid-deep in black mud, clearing the spaces pumped out by powerful steam-engines; wheeling, digging, hewing, or bearing burdens it made one's shoulders ache to look upon; exposed meantime to every change of temperature, in log-huts, laid down in the very swamp, on a foundation of newly-felled trees, having the water lying stagnant between the floor-logs, whose interstices, together with those of the side-walls, are open, pervious alike to sun or wind, or snow. Here they subsist on the coarsest fare, holding life on a tenure as uncertain as does the leader of a forlorn hope; excluded from all the advantages of civilization; often at the mercy of a hard contractor, who wrings his profits from their blood; and all this for a pittance that merely enables them to exist, with little power to save, or a hope beyond the continuance of the like exertion.

Such are the labourers I have seen here, and have still found them civil and courteous, with a ready greeting for the stranger inquiring into their condition, and a quick jest on their own equipment, which is frequently, it must be admitted, of a whimsical kind.

Here too were many poor women with their husbands; and when I contemplated their wasted forms and haggard sickly looks, together with the close swamp whose stagnant air they were doomed to breathe, whose aspect changeless and deathlike alone met their eyes, and fancied them, in some hour of leisure, calling to memory the green valley and the pure river, or the rocky glen and sparkling brook of their distant home, with all the warmth of colouring the imaginative spirit of the Irish peasant can so well supply, my heart has swelled and my eyes have filled with tears.

I cannot hope to inspire the reader with my feelings upon a mere sketch like this; but if I could set the scene of these poor labourers' exile fairly forth, with all the sad accompaniments detailed; could I show the course of the hardy, healthy pair, just landed, to seek fortune on these long-sighed-for shores, with spirits newly lifted by hope and brighter prospects from the apathy into which compulsory idleness and consequent recklessness had reduced them at home; and then paint the spirit-sinking felt on a first view of the scene of their future labour,—paint the wild revel designed to drown remembrance, and give heart to the newcomers; describe the nature of the toil where exertion is taxed to the uttermost, and the weary frame stimulated by the worst alcohol, supplied by the contractor, at a cheap rate for the purpose of exciting a rivalry of exertion amongst these simple men.

Next comes disease, either a sweeping pestilence that deals, wholesale on its victims, or else a gradual sinking of mind and body; finally, the abode in the hospital, if any comrade is interested enough for the sufferer to bear him to it; else, the solitary log-hut and quicker death. Could these things with their true colours be set forth in detail before the veriest grinder of the poor that ever drove the peasant to curse and quit the soil of his birth, he would cover his eyes from the light of heaven, and feel that he yet possessed a heart and human sympathy.

At such works all over this continent the Irish are the labourers chiefly employed, and the mortality amongst them is enormous,—a mortality I feel certain might be vastly lessened by a little consideration being given to their condition

by those who employ them. At present they are, where I have seen them working here, worse lodged than the cattle of the field; in fact, the only thought bestowed upon them appears to be, by what expedient the greatest quantity of labour may be extracted from them at the cheapest rate to the contractor. I think, however, that a better spirit is in progress amongst the companies requiring this class of labourers; in fact it becomes necessary this should be so, since, prolific as is the country from whence they are drawn, the supply would in a little time cease to keep pace with the demand, and slave labour cannot be substituted to any extent, being much too expensive; a good slave costs at this time two hundred pounds sterling, and to have a thousand such swept off a line of canal in one season, would call for prompt consideration.

Independent of interest, Christian charity and justice should alike suggest that the labourers ought to be provided with decent quarters, that sufficient medical aid should always be at hand, and above all, that the brutalizing, accursed practice of extorting extra labour by the stimulus of corn spirit should be wholly forbidden.

Let it be remembered that, although rude and ignorant, these men are not insensible to good impressions, or incapable of distinguishing between a kindly and paternal care of their well-doing, and the mercenary cold-blooded bargain which exacts the last scruple of flesh it has paid for....

At present the priest is the only stay and comfort of these men; the occasional presence of the minister of God alone reminds them that they are not forgotten of their kind: unfortunate for this interference, they would grow in a short time wholly abandoned and become uncontrollable; unfortunately of these men, who conscientiously fulfill their holy functions, there are but too few,—the climate, and fatigue soon incapacitates all but the very robust. Those who follow the ministry of God in the swamp and in the forest must have cast the pride of flesh indeed out from them, since they brave the martyr's fate without a martyr's triumph....

The gloomy picture of the labourer's condition, which my mention of this canal has drawn from me, may by some be considered overcharged; but I protest I have, on the contrary, withheld details of suffering from heat, and cold, and sickness, which my heart at this moment aches when I recall....

* * * * *

1. *Why would the Irish have come to America to work under such conditions? What was happening in their own country?*

2. *What can you say about the living conditions of the Irish laborers? How did it compare to slave life that you have read about in other accounts?*

13-3 Feminists Hold a Convention, 1848

Elizabeth Cady Stanton was one of the leading feminists of the 19th century. Educated in law, but denied the bar because of her sex, Stanton was active in the abolitionist movement as well as women's issues. It 1848, Stanton organized the Seneca Falls Convention with Lucretia Mott and other feminists at which they drafted their own declaration, which follows, modeled very much on the Declaration of Independence. This declaration is often seen as the formal origin of the women's rights movement.

SOURCE: Elizabeth Cady Stanton, Susan B. Anthony, and Matilda J. Gage, eds., *History of Woman Suffrage* (Rochester, N.Y.: Susan B. Anthony, 1887).

When, in the course of human events, it becomes necessary for one portion of the family of man to assume among the people of the earth a position different from that which they have hitherto occupied, but onto which the laws of nature and of nature's God entitle them, a decent respect to the opinions of mankind requires that they should declare the causes that impel them to such a course.

We hold these truths to be self-evident: that all men and women are created equal; that they are endowed by their Creator with certain inalienable rights; that among these are life, liberty, and the pursuit of happiness; that to secure these rights governments are instituted, deriving their just powers from the consent of the governed. Whenever any form of government becomes destructive of these ends, it is the right of those who suffer from it to refuse allegiance to it and to insist upon the institution of a new government laying its foundation on such principles, and organizing its powers in such form, as to them shall seem most likely to effect their safety and happiness. Prudence, indeed, will dictate that governments long established should not be changed for light and transient causes and accordingly all experience hath shown that mankind are more disposed to suffer, while evils are sufferable, than to right themselves by abolishing the forms to which they were accustomed. But when a long train of abuses and usurpations, pursuing invariably the same object, evinces a design to reduce them under absolute despotism, it is their duty to throw off such government, and to provide new guards for their future security. Such has been the patient sufferance of the women under this government, and such is now the necessity which constrains them to demand the equal station to which they are entitled. The history of mankind is a history of repeated injuries and usurpations on the part of man toward woman, having in direct object the establishment of an absolute tyranny over her. To prove this, let facts be submitted to a candid world.

He has never permitted her to exercise her inalienable right to the elective franchise.

He has compelled her to submit to laws, in the formation of which she had no voice.

He has withheld from her rights which are given to the most ignorant and degraded men—both natives and foreigners.

Having deprived her of this first right of a citizen, the elective franchise, thereby leaving her without representation in the halls of legislation, he has oppressed her on all sides.

He has made her, if married, in the eye of the law, civilly dead.

He has taken from her all right in property, even to the wages she earns.

He has made her, morally, an irresponsible being, as she can commit many crimes with impunity, provided they be done in the presence of her husband.

In the covenant of marriage, she is compelled to promise obedience to her husband, he becoming to all intents and purposes, her master—the law giving him power to deprive her of her liberty, and to administer chastisement.

He has so framed the laws of divorce, as to what shall be the proper causes, and in case of separation, to whom the guardianship of the children shall be given, as to be wholly regardless of the happiness of women—the law, in all cases, going upon a false supposition of the supremacy of man, and giving all power into his hands.

After depriving her of all rights as a married woman, if single, and the owner of property, he has taxed her to support a government which recognizes her only when her property can be made profitable to it.

He has monopolized nearly all the profitable employments, and from those she is permitted to follow, she receives but a scanty remuneration. He closes against her all the avenues to wealth and distinction which he considers most, honorable to himself. As a teacher of theology, medicine, or law, she is not known.

He has denied her the facilities for obtaining a thorough education, all colleges being closed against her.

He allows her in Church, as well as State, but a subordinate position, claiming Apostolic authority for her exclusion from the ministry, and, with some exceptions, from any public participation in the affairs of the Church.

He has created a false public sentiment by giving to the world a different code of morals for men and women, by which moral delinquencies which exclude women from society, are not only tolerated, but deemed of little account in man.

He has usurped the prerogative of Jehovah himself, claiming it as his right to assign for her a sphere of action, when that belongs to her conscience and to her God.

He has endeavored, in every way that he could, to destroy her confidence in her own powers, to lessen her self-respect, and to make her willing to lead a dependent and abject life.

Now, in view of this entire disfranchisement of one-half the people of this country, their social and religious degradation—in view of the unjust laws above mentioned, and because women do feel themselves aggrieved, oppressed, and fraudulently deprived of their most sacred rights, we insist that they have immediate admission to all the rights and privileges which belong to them as citizens of the United States.

In entering upon the great work before us, we anticipate no small amount of misconception, misrepresentation, and ridicule; but we shall use every instrumentality within our power to effect our object. We shall employ agents, circulate tracts, petition the State and National legislatures, and endeavor to enlist the pulpit and the press in our behalf. We hope this Convention will be followed by a series of Conventions embracing every part of the country.

* * * * * *

1. *What were the legal rights of women in 1848? How long was it before women received the right to vote? What do you think the effect of the Seneca Falls Convention Declaration was?*

2. *The abolition of slavery had become a popular issue by the mid-19th century in much of the U.S. Women's issues were still not. Speculate as to why this might have been so.*

13–4   Social Philosopher Advocates Communities, 1840

There were any number of reform movements in the early 19th century from slavery to women's rights, education to the founding of ideal communities, all grappling with the improvement of mankind. One staunch supporter of communal living as a way to improve society was Albert Brisbane. Brisbane studied with Charles Fourier in France, who advocated an elaborate system of phalanxes, or loosely connected ideal communities as the solution to man's ills. In the following essay, Brisbane outlines his plan to set up one of these phalanxes.

For an Association of eighteen hundred to two thousand persons a tract of land three miles square, say in round numbers six thousand acres, will be necessary. A fine stream of water should flow through it. Its surface should be undulating and its soil adapted to a varied cultivation. It should be adjoining a forest, and situated in the vicinity of a large city, which would afford a convenient market for its products.

The first Phalanx being alone and without the aid of neighboring Associations, will have, in consequence of its isolated position, so many voids in attraction, so many passional calms to fear, that it will be necessary to select a fine position adapted to all varieties of cultivation and occupations....

Two thousand persons of different degrees of fortune, of different ages and characters, of varied theoretical and practical knowledge, should be associated. The greatest diversity possible should exist, for the greater the diversity of passions, talents, fortunes, etc., of the members, the easier it will be to harmonize them....

Every possible variety of agricultural pursuits should be carried on in the Association. Three branches of manufactures at least should be organized to afford occupation during rainy days and the winter months; besides various practical branches of the arts and sciences, without including those pursued in the schools.

Seven-eighths of the members should be agriculturalists and manufacturers; the balance capitalists, men of science and artists, who in a small Association of four-hundred persons, would be unnecessary; but we are here describing the largest Association, that of two thousand persons, which should first be understood, as the other is merely a reduction of it.

In laying out the fields and in organizing the workshops of the first Phalanx, it will be necessary to foresee and calculate as far as possible the degree of attraction, which each branch of industry will excite. The plum-tree, for example, is less attractive than the pear-tree; fewer plum pear-trees consequently should be planted. The degree of attraction, which each branch of Industry possesses, will be the only guide to follow in the choice of occupations.

Political-economists would reason differently; they would lay it down as a principle, that those objects should be cultivated, which produced the most. The first Phalanx should avoid this error; it will have to follow a different policy from those which follow it. When Association

SOURCE: Charles Fourier, *Social Science: The Theory of Universal Unity* (New York: American News Co., 1850).

becomes general, it will be necessary to regulate Industry to suit the demands of interest as well as of attraction; but in the first Association a different object is to be attained; the great question is to succeed in inducing eighteen hundred to two thousand persons to work from attraction alone; and should it be found that the cultivation of thistles and briars was more attractive than the cultivation of fruit-trees and flowers, it would be necessary to abandon fruit-trees and flowers for thistles and briars in the first Phalanx. As soon as the two great ends of Association,—*Industrial attraction and Passional equilibrium* are attained, means will be found of extending the sphere of Industry to useful objects, which were neglected in the commencement. *The first and sole aim should be to render Industry Attractive*, without regard to objects cultivated; it should suit its policy to this great end, and solve the problem of *Industrial Attraction* by any and every means within its power.

The internal organization of the Phalanx will, *in the commencement*, be under the direction of a Council, composed of stockholders, distinguished for their wealth or their industrial and scientific acquirements. Women, if there be any capable, will take part with the men; they will in Association be upon a level with them in all business matters, provided they possess the necessary knowledge.

In Association no community of property can exist, nor can any *collective* payments to whole families take place. An account is kept with every member individually, even with children over four and a half years of age; and every person is remunerated according to LABOR, CAPITAL AND SKILL.

Parents, husbands, wives and friends can, as in civilization, put in common, if they wish, what they possess; but the Phalanx in its relations with them, opens on its books an account with each individually, even with the child five years old, the profits of whose industry do not go to the father, but are reserved and constitute, together with legacies, inheritances and interest, a fund, which the Phalanx preserves for him until he is of age.

All lands, machines, furniture, or other objects, brought by members into the Association, are appraised at their cash value, and represented, as well as the monied capital paid in, by transferable shares, which are secured upon the personal and real estate of the Phalanx, that is upon its domain, edifices, flocks, manufactories, etc. The Council transfers to each person the value in shares of the objects, which he has furnished. A person may be a member without being a stockholder, or a stockholder without being a member. In the latter case, he receives no part of the profits, which are awarded to *Labor* and *Skill*.

The annual profits of the Association are, after taking an inventory, divided into three unequal portions, and paid as follows:

Five twelvths *to Labor*:
Four twelvths *to Capital*.
Three twelvths *to Practical and theoretical knowledge*....

Every person may, according to circumstances, receive a part of the three classes of profit, or of any one separately....

The edifice, outhouses and the distribution of the grounds of a Society, whose operations and industry are regulated by Series of groups, must differ prodigiously from the constructions of civilization, from its isolated dwellings and villages, which are adapted to families, between whom very few social relations, and no combination of action, exist. Instead of the confused mass of small houses which compose our towns and villages, and which vie with each other in dirt and ugliness, a Phalanx builds a regular edifice, as far as the land permits. We will add a general description, supposing the location to be a favorable one.

The centre of the Palace should be reserved for quiet occupations; it will contain the dining halls, council rooms, the exchange, library, reading-rooms, etc. In it will also be placed the observatory, the telegraph, the chime of bells and the tower of observation which overlooks the domain, and from which orders can be issued; the range of buildings, which form the centre, will enclose a winter garden and promenade, ornamented with evergreens.

In one of the wings should be located all manufactories and workshops of a noisy nature, like those of carpenters and blacksmiths; in it also should be held assemblages of children engaged in industrial pursuits, who are generally very noisy. Association will avoid by this means a great inconvenience of our cities in almost every street of which some tin or blacksmith, or some learner of the clarinet stuns the ears of fifty families around. In the other wing, the hotel, with apartments and saloons for strangers, should be placed, which would prevent the centre of the Palace from being crowded.

Besides the private rooms and apartments the Palace must contain a great many public halls and saloons for social relations, and for the meetings, occupations and pleasures.... We will take as an example the banquet halls, which will comprise nine saloons of unequal sizes:

1. For persons extremely advanced in age.
2. For children.
3. For the third class of fortune.
2. For the second class of fortune.
1. For the first or richest class.

Adjoining these banquet halls must be small dining rooms for parties or groups, who may wish to eat apart from the large tables. Parties of friends will wish daily to dine by themselves; they can do so in these rooms, where they will be served in the same manner and at the same price as at the large tables....

In Association a man of the most humble fortune will go from his rooms to the public halls and manufactories through galleries, warmed in winter and aired in summer. The inhabitants of the Palace can, in the height of winter, communicate with the workshops, stables, storehouses, bazaars, banquet and ball rooms, public saloons, etc., without knowing whether it rains or blows, whether it is warm or cold....

The Phalanx has no exterior street or uncovered way, exposed to the inclemency of the weather; all quarters of the edifice can be communicated with by means of the large Gallery, which passes along the first story, (that is the story above the basement and the semi-story,) encircling the centre and wings of the entire Palace. At the extremities of this spacious corridor are covered passages, supported by columns, and also underground passages, which form elegant covered ways, leading to every part of the edifice and to the rural buildings....

To pass a winter's day in the Palace of a Phalanx, to visit all parts of it without exposure to the inclemency of the weather, to go to balls or to the opera in light shoes and dress without being incommoded by the cold or having to pass through muddy streets, would be a charm so new that it would alone suffice to render our palaces and cities detestable....

The apartments are rented by the Council to the members....

* * * * *

1.   *Brisbane's community seems enticing. Would you join such a community? Why or why not? What is Brisbane's philosophical basis for this community? Is such a community plausible?*

2.   *The early 19th century was fraught with movements trying to improve the condition of mankind in America. Why do you think such movements were flourishing at this time?*

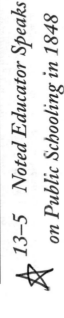

13–5   Noted Educator Speaks on Public Schooling in 1848

Horace Mann has often been called the "father of American public education." Trained as a lawyer, Mann created the Massachusetts Board of Education and then served as its secretary from 1837 to 1848, resigning when he was elected to the United States Congress. Mann was instrumental in establishing teaching as a profession, lengthening school sessions, standardizing textbooks within schools, and seeking public funding for education. Mann's annual reports as state superintendent of schools were filled with observations about education and schooling. The following excerpts touch on just a few of Mann's concerns.

SOURCE: Massachusetts Board of Education, *Annual Reports on Education* (Boston: Horace B. Fuller, 1868).

Without undervaluing any other human agency, it may be safely affirmed that the common school, improved and energized as it can easily be, may become the most effective and benignant of all the forces of civilization. Two reasons sustain this position. In the first place, there is a universality in its operation, which can be affirmed of no other institution whatever. If administered in the spirit of justice and conciliation, all the rising generation may be brought within the circle of its reformatory and elevating influences. And, in the second place, the materials upon which it operates are so pliant and ductile as to be susceptible of assuming a greater variety of forms than any other earthly work of the Creator....

I proceed, then, in endeavoring to show how the true business of the schoolroom connects itself, and becomes identical, with the great interests of society.

The former is the infant, immature state of those interests; the latter their developed, adult state. As "the child is father to the man," so may the training of the schoolroom expand into the institution and fortunes of the State....

According to the European theory, men are divided into classes—some to toil and earn, others to seize and enjoy. According to the Massachusetts theory, all are to have an equal chance for earning, and equal security in the enjoyment of what they earn. The latter tends to equality of condition; the former, to the grossest inequalities. Tried by any Christian standard of morals,...can anyone hesitate, for a moment, in declaring which of the two will produce the greater amount of human welfare?...

Moral education is a primal necessity of social existence. The unrestrained passions of men are not only homicidal, but suicidal; and a community without a conscience would soon extinguish itself....To all doubters, disbelievers, or despairers in human progress, it may still be said, there is one experiment which has never yet been tried....It is expressed in these few and simple words: *"Train up a child in the way he should go; and, when he is old, he will not depart from it."*...But this experiment has never yet been tried. Education has never yet been brought to bear with one-hundredth part of its potential force upon the natures of children, and, through them, upon the character of men and of the race....Here, then, is a new agency, whose powers are but just beginning to be understood, and whose mighty energies hitherto have been but feebly invoked....

But it will be said that this grand result in practical morals is a consummation of blessedness that can never be attained without religion, and that no community will ever be religious without a religious education. Both these propositions I regard as eternal and immutable truths....That our public schools are not theological seminaries, is admitted....They are debarred by law from inculcating the peculiar and distinctive doctrines of any one religious denomination amongst us....But our system earnestly inculcates all Christian morals; it founds its morals on the basis of religion; it welcomes the religion of the Bible....

I hold it...to be one of the excellences, one of the moral beauties, of the Massachusetts system, that there is one place in the land where the children of all the different denominations are brought together for instruction, where the Bible is allowed to speak for itself; one place where the children can kneel at a common altar, and feel that they have a common Father, and where the services of religion tend to create brothers, and not Ishmaelites....

Such, then,...is the Massachusetts system of common schools. Reverently it recognizes and affirms the sovereign rights of the Creator, sedulously and sacredly it guards the religious rights of the creature....In a social and political sense, it is a *free* school-system. It knows no distinction of rich and poor, of bond and free, or between those, who, in the imperfect light of this world, are seeking, through different avenues, to reach the gate of heaven. Without money and without price, it throws open its doors, and spreads the table of its bounty, for all the children of the State. Like the sun, it shines not only upon the good, but upon the evil, that they may become good; and, like the rain, its blessings descend not only upon the just, but upon the unjust, that their injustice may depart from them, and be known no more.

* * * * * *

1. *Mann advocates the public school as the location of moral and Religious education. Do you agree with this philosophy?*

2. *The industrial revolution saw a rapid increase in investment in not only machinery, but in many cases, workers as well, as tasks became more complex. How do you think Mann's ideas fit into this scheme?*

13–6 An African American Advocates Radical Action in 1829

David Walker was a free African American who operated a second-hand clothing shop in Boston and spoke out on abolition. Unlike many abolitionists, Walker advocated violent action, the rebellion of slaves and the killing of masters. The following account, from Walker's pamphlet An Appeal to Blacks.... *illustrates a small rebellion that Walker proposed for the entire South. Fear by slave holders in the South brought the banning of the pamphlet, and even the closing of black churches for fear the slaves would hear Walker's ideas and take them to heart.*

SOURCE: David Walker, *Walker's Appeal, in Four Articles* (Boston: D. Walker, 1830).

To show the force of degraded ignorance and deceit among us, I will give here an extract from a paragraph, which may be found in the Columbian Centinel of this city, for September 9, 1829, on the first part of which, the curious may find an article headed:

"AFRAY AND MURDER"

"PORTSMOUTH, (OHIO) AUG. 22, 1829."

"A most shocking outrage was committed in Kentucky, about eight miles from this place, on 14th inst. A negro driver, by the name of Gordon, who had purchased in Maryland about sixty negroes, was taking them, assisted by an associate named Allen, and the wagoner who conveyed the baggage, to the Mississippi. The men were hand-cuffed and chained together, in the usual manner for driving those poor wretches, while the women and children were suffered to proceed without incumbrance. It appears that, by means of a file the negroes, unobserved, had succeeded in separating the iron which bound their hands, in such a way as to be able to throw them off at any moment. About 8 o'clock in the morning, while proceeding on the state road leading from Greenup to Vanceburg, two of them dropped their shackles and commenced a fight, when the wagoner (Petit) rushed in with his whip to compel them to desist. At this moment, every negro was found to be perfectly at liberty; and one of them seizing a club, gave Petit a violent blow on the head, and laid him dead at his feet; and Allen, who came to his assistance, met a similar fate, from the contents of a pistol fired by another of the gang. Gordon was then attacked, seized and held by one of the negroes, whilst another fired twice at him with a pistol, the ball of which each time grazed his head, but not proving effectual, he was beaten with clubs, and left for dead. They then commenced pillaging the wagon, and with an axe split open the trunk of Gordon, and rifled it of the money, about $2,400. Sixteen of the negroes then took to the woods; Gordon, in the mean time, not being materially injured, was enabled, by the assistance of one of the women, to mount his horse and flee; pursued, however, by one of the gang on another horse, with a drawn pistol; fortunately he escaped with his life barely, arriving at a plantation, as the negro came in sight; who then turned about and retreated."

"The neighbourhood was immediately rallied, and a hot pursuit given—which, we understand, has resulted in the capture of the whole gang and the recovery of the greatest part of the money. Seven of the negro men and one woman, it is said were engaged in the murders, and will be brought to trial at the next court in Greenupsburg."

Here my brethren, I want you to notice particularly in the above article, the *ignorant* and *deceitful actions* of this coloured woman. I beg you to view it candidly, as for ETER-NITY!!!! Here a *notorious wretch*, with two other confederates had SIXTY of them in a gang, driving them like *brutes*—the men all in chains and hand-cuffs, and by the help of God they got their chains and hand-cuffs thrown off, and caught two of the wretches and put them to death, and left him for dead; however, he deceived them, and rising from the ground, this *servile woman* helped him upon his horse, and he made his escape. Brethren, what do you think of this? Was it the natural *fine feelings* of this woman, to save such a wretch alive? I know that the blacks (though they are great cowards) where they have the advantage, or think that there are any prospects of getting it, they murder all before them, in order to subject men to wretchedness and degradation to under them. This is the natural result of pride and avarice. But I declare, the actions of this black woman are really insupportable. For my own part, I cannot think is it was any thing but servile deceit, combined with the most gross ignorance: for we must remember that *humanity, kindness and the fear of the Lord*, does not consist in protecting *devils*. Here is a set of wretches, who had SIXTY of them in a gang, driving them around the country like *brutes*, to dig up gold and silver for them, (which they will get enough of yet). Should the lives of such creatures be spared? Are God and Mammon in league?

What has the Lord to do with a gang of desperate wretches, who go *sneaking about the country like robbers*—light upon his people wherever they can get a chance, binding them with chains and handcuffs, beat and murder them as they would *rattle-snakes*? Are they not the Lord's enemies? Ought they not to be destroyed? Any person who will save such wretch-es from destruction, is fighting against the Lord, and will receive his just recompense. The black men acted like *block-heads*. Why did they not make sure of the wretch? He would have made sure of them, if he could. It is just the way with black men—eight white men can frighten fifty of them; whereas, if you can only get courage into the blacks, I do declare it, that one good black man can put to death six white men; and I give it as a fact, let twelve black men get well armed for battle, and they will kill and put to flight fifty whites. The reason is, the blacks, once you get them started, they glory in death. The whites have had us under them for more than three centuries, murdering, and treating us like brutes; and, as Mr. Jefferson wisely said, they have *never found us out*—they do not know, indeed, that there is an unconquerable disposition in the breasts of the blacks, which, when it is fully awakened and put in motion, will be subdued, only with the destruction of the animal existence. Get the blacks started, and if you do not have a gang of tigers and lions to deal with, I am a deceiver of the blacks and of the whites. How sixty of them could let that wretch escape unkilled, I cannot conceive—they will have to suffer as much for the two whom, they secured, as if they had put one hundred to death; if you commence, make sure work—do not trifle, for they will not trifle with you—they want us for their slaves, and think nothing of murdering us in order to subject us to that wretched condition—therefore, if there is an *attempt* made by us, kill or be killed. Now, I ask you, had you not rather be killed than to be a slave to a tyrant, who takes the life of your mother, wife, and dear little children? Look upon your mother, wife and children, and answer God Almighty; and believe this, that it is no more harm for you to kill a man, who is trying to kill you, than it is for you to take a drink of water when thirsty; in fact, the man who will stand still and let another murder him, is worse than an infidel, and, if he has common sense, ought not to be pitied....

* * * * * *

1. *Many have wondered why more blacks didn't rebel. Walker gives several reasons. What are they? What other reasons might there have been?*

2. *Why were slave owners in the south so afraid of this pamphlet? Why would they have kept slaves from learning to read and write? What are the limitations to a culture that communicates orally, rather than through the written word?*

13–7 Abolitionist Demands Immediate End to Slavery, 1831

William Lloyd Garrison was one of the most prominent leaders of the abolitionist movement. Garrison's journal, the Liberator, was one of the longest lived abolitionist papers, running from 1831 to 1865, with Garrison active in its publication the entire time. The Liberator was feared in the south where its circulation was banned. Garrison took a position of moral abolition, demanding an immediate end to slavery which alienated many of the political abolitionists who sought a slower, more orderly discontinuation. The following is the prospectus which appeared in the first issue of the Liberator.

SOURCE: William Lloyd Garrison, The Words of Garrison (Boston: Houghton, Mifflin, 1905).

…During my recent tour for the purpose of exciting the minds of the people by a series of discourses on the subject of slavery, every place that I visited gave fresh evidence of the fact, that a greater revolution in public sentiment was to be effected in the free states—and particularly in New-England—than at the south. I found contempt more bitter, opposition more active, detraction more relentless, prejudice more stubborn, and apathy more frozen, than among the slave owners themselves. Of course, there were individual exceptions to the contrary. This state of things afflicted, but did not dishearten me. I determined, at every hazard, to lift up the standard of emancipation in the eyes of the nation, within sight of Bunker Hill and in the birth place of liberty. That standard is now unfurled; and long may it float, unhurt by the spoliations of time or the missiles of a desperate foe—yea, till every chain be broken, and every bondman set free! Let southern oppressors tremble—let their secret abettors tremble—let their northern apologists tremble—let all the enemies of the persecuted blacks tremble.

I deem the publication of my original Prospectus unnecessary, as it has obtained a wide circulation. The principles therein inculcated will be steadily pursued in this paper, excepting that I shall not array myself as the political partisan of any man. In defending the great cause of human rights, I wish to derive the assistance of all religions and of all parties.

Assenting to the "self-evident truth" maintained in the American Declaration of Independence, "that all men are created equal and endowed by their Creator with certain

inalienable rights—among which are life, liberty and the pursuit of happiness," I shall strenuously contend for the immediate enfranchisement of our slave population. In Park-street Church, on the Fourth of July, 1829, in an address on slavery, I unreflectingly assented to the popular but pernicious doctrine of gradual abolition. I seize this opportunity to make a full and unequivocal recantation, and thus publicly to ask pardon of my God, of my country, and of my brethren the poor slaves, for having uttered a sentiment so full of timidity, injustice and absurdity. A similar recantation, from my pen, was published in the Genius of Universal Emancipation at Baltimore, in September, 1829. My conscience is now satisfied.

I am aware that many object to the severity of my language; but is there not cause for severity? I will be as harsh as truth, and as uncompromising as justice. On this subject, I do not wish to think, or speak, or write, with moderation. No! no! Tell a man whose house is on fire, to give a moderate alarm; tell him to moderately rescue his wife from the hands of the ravisher; tell the mother to gradually extricate her babe from the fire into which it has fallen;—but urge me not to use moderation in a cause like the present. I am in earnest—I will not equivocate—I will not excuse—I will not retreat a single inch—AND I WILL BE HEARD. The apathy of the people is enough to make every statue leap from its pedestal, and to hasten the resurrection of the dead.

It is pretended, that I am retarding the cause of emancipation, by the coarseness of my invective, and the precipitancy of my measures. The charge is not true. On this question my influence,—humble as it is,—is felt at this moment to a considerable extent, and shall be felt in coming years—not perniciously, but beneficially—not as a curse, but as a blessing; and posterity will bear testimony that I was right. I desire to thank God, that he enables me to disregard "the fear of man which bringeth a snare," and to speak his truth in its simplicity and power….

* * * * *

1. What do you think of Garrison's moral approach to abolition? Does it have a stronger foundation than a political basing of arguments against slavery?

2. Garrison described himself as a radical abolitionist. He advocated absolute immediate reversal of slavery. Do you think this was radical compared to, say, David Walker? Was it more radical than political abolitionists?

13-8   Southern Belle Denounces Slavery, 1838

Angelina Grimke was the daughter of a southern aristocrat and herself a staunch abolitionist. Angelina and her sister, Sarah, moved to Philadelphia, converted to the Quaker religion and became active in the abolition movement. Angelina became dissatisfied with the pacifism of the Quakers and wrote "An Appeal to the Christian Women of the South," which was banned in the South and prompted a call for her arrest in South Carolina. Grimke's position was extremely radical for a southern woman in her day. Grimke's speech, "Bearing Witness Against Slavery," reprinted here, was delivered at the 1838 National Anti-Slavery Convention in Philadelphia. The convention was greeted by an angry mob who waited outside, jeering and throwing rocks for three days, the mob finally storming the building and setting fire to it on the third day.

SOURCE: Carolina Herron, ed., *Selected Works of Angelina Weld Grimke* (New York: Oxford University Press, 1991).

Do you ask, "What has the North to do with slavery?" Hear it, hear it! Those voices without tell us that the spirit of slavery is *here*, and has been roused to wrath by our Conventions; for surely liberty would not foam and tear herself with rage, because her friends are multiplied daily, and meetings are held in quick succession to set forth her virtues and extend her peaceful kingdom. This opposition shows that slavery has done its deadliest work in the hearts of our citizens. Do you ask, then, "What has the North to do?" I answer, cast out first the spirit of slavery from your own hearts, and then lend your aid to convert the South. Each one present has a work to do, be his or her situation what it may, however limited their means or insignificant their supposed influence. The great men of this country will not do this work; the Church will never do it. A desire to please the world, to keep the favor of all parties and of all conditions, makes them dumb on this and every other unpopular subject.

As a Southerner, I feel that it is my duty to stand up here to-night and bear testimony against slavery. I have seen it! I have seen it! I know it has horrors that can never be described. I was brought up under its wing. I witnessed for many years its demoralizing influences and its destructiveness to human happiness. I have never seen a happy slave. I have seen him dance in his chains, it is true, but he was not happy. There is a wide difference between happiness and mirth. Man can not enjoy happiness while his manhood is destroyed. Slaves, however, may be, and

sometimes are mirthful. When hope is extinguished, they say, "Let us eat and drink, for to-morrow we die." [Here stones were thrown at the windows—a great noise without and commotion within.]

What is a mob? What would the breaking of every window be? What would the levelling of this hall be? Any evidence that we are wrong, or that slavery is a good and wholesome institution? What if the mob should now burst in upon us, break up our meeting, and commit violence upon our persons, would that be anything compared with what the slaves endure? No, no; and we do not remember them, "as bound with them," if we shrink in the time of peril, or feel unwilling to sacrifice ourselves, if need be, for their sake. [Great noise.] I thank the Lord that there is yet life enough left to feel the truth, even though it rages at it; that conscience is not so completely seared as to be unmoved by the truth of the living God. [Another outbreak of the mob and confusion in the house.]

How wonderfully constituted is the human mind! How it resists, as long as it can, all efforts to reclaim it from error! I feel that all this disturbance is but an evidence that our efforts are the best that could have been adopted, or else the friends of slavery would not care for what we say and do. The South know what we do. I am thankful that they are reached by our efforts. Many times have I wept in the land of my birth over the system of slavery. I knew of none who sympathized in my feelings; I was unaware that any efforts were made to deliver the oppressed; no voice in the wilderness was heard calling on the people to repent and do works meet for repentance, and my heart sickened within me. Oh, how should I have rejoiced to know that such efforts as these were being made. I only wonder that I had such feelings. But in the midst of temptation I was preserved, and my sympathy grew warmer, and my hatred of slavery more inveterate, until at last I have exiled myself from my native land, because I could no longer endure to hear the wailing of the slave.

I fled to the land of Penn; for here, thought I, sympathy for the slave will surely be found. But I found it not. The people were kind and hospitable, but the slave had no place in their thoughts. I therefore shut up my grief in my own heart. I remembered that I was a Carolinian, from a State which framed this iniquity by law. Every Southern breeze wafted to me the discordant tones of weeping and wailing, shrieks and groans, mingled with prayers and blasphemous curses. My heart sank within me at the abominations in the midst of which I had been born and educated. What will it avail, cried I, in bitterness of spirit, to expose to the gaze of strangers the horrors and pollutions of slavery, when there is no ear to hear nor heart to feel and pray for the slave? But how different do I feel now! Animated with hope, nay, with an assurance of the triumph of liberty and good-will to man, I will lift up my voice like a trumpet, and show this people what they can do to influence the Southern mind and overthrow slavery. [Shouting, and stones against the windows.]

We often hear the question asked, "What shall we do?" Here is an opportunity. Every man and every woman present may do something, by showing that we fear not a mob, and in the midst of revilings and threatenings, pleading the cause of those who are ready to perish. Let me urge every one to buy the books written on this subject; read them, and lend them to your neighbors. Give your money no longer for things which pander to pride and lust, but aid in scattering "the living coals of truth upon the naked heart of the nation"; in circulating appeals to the sympathies of Christians in behalf of the outraged slave.

But it is said by some, our "books and papers do not speak the truth"; why, then, do they not contradict what we say? They can not. Moreover, the South has entreated, nay, commanded us, to be silent; and what greater evidence of the truth of our publications could be desired?

Women of Philadelphia! allow me as a Southern woman, with much attachment to the land of my birth, to entreat you to come up to this work. Especially, let me urge you to petition. Men may settle this and other questions at the ballot-box, but you have no such right. It is only through petitions that you can reach the Legislature. It is, therefore, peculiarly your duty to petition. Do you say, "It does no good!" The South already turns pale at the number sent. They have read the reports of the proceedings of Congress, and there have seen that among other petitions were very many from the women of the North on the subject of slavery. Men who hold the rod over slaves rule in the councils of the nation; and they deny our right to petition and remonstrate against abuses of our sex and our kind. We have these rights, however, from our God. Only let us exercise them, and, though often turned away unanswered, let us remember the influence of importunity upon the unjust judge, and act accordingly. The fact that the South looks jealously upon our measures shows that they are effectual. There is, therefore, no cause for doubting or despair.

It was remarked in England that women did much to abolish slavery in her colonies. Nor are they now idle. Numerous petitions from them have recently been presented to the Queen to abolish the system whose place it supplies. One petition, two miles and a quarter long, has been presented. And do you think these labors will be in vain? Let the history of the past answer. When the women of these States send up to Congress such a petition our legislators will arise, as did those of England, and say: "When all the maids and matrons of the land are knocking at our doors we must legislate." Let the zeal and love, the faith and works of our English sisters quicken ours; that while the slaves continue to suffer, and when they shout for deliverance, we may feel the satisfaction of "having done what we could."

* * * * * *

1. What can you discern about the role of women within the abolitionist movement from Grimke's speech? What specific things are the women doing?

2. What do you think about Grimke's courage? How is it demonstrated within this speech? Why do you think more Southern women did not join her?

SOURCE: Elizabeth Cady Stanton, Susan B. Anthony, and Matilda J. Gage, eds., History of Woman Suffrage (Rochester, NY: Susan B. Anthony, 1887).

13–9 A Black Feminist Speaks Out in 1851

Born into slavery in New York as Isabella, Sojourner Truth was later freed by a subsequent owner and changed her name. In 1843 she started traveling across the country as a missionary. Sojourner later became active in not only the abolitionist movement, but the women's rights movement as well, all of which she worked into her religious message. Having addressed the first National Women's Rights Convention in 1850 at Worcester, Massachusetts, Sojourner was met with hisses by the women at the Ohio Woman's Rights Convention the following year. The women were afraid of getting involved with the abolitionist movement and confusing their own women's issues. However, after Sojourner's speech, which is printed here, she was met with applause and accolades from the audience.

Address to the Ohio Women's Rights Convention

Well, children, where there is so much racket here must be something out of kilter. I think that 'twixt the Negroes of the South and the women at the North, all talking about rights, the white men will be in a fix pretty soon. But what's all this here talking about?

That man over there says that women need to be

helped into carriages, and lifted over ditches, and to have the best place everywhere. Nobody ever helps me into carriages, or over mud-puddles, or gives me any best place! And ain't I a woman? Look at me! Look at my arm. I have ploughed and planted, and gathered into barns, and no man could head me! And ain't I a woman? I could work as much and eat as much as a man—when I could get it—and bear the lash as well! And ain't I a woman? I have borne thirteen children, and seen them most all sold off to slavery, and when I cried out with my mother's grief, none but Jesus heard me! And ain't I a woman?

Then they talk about this thing in the head; what's this they call it? [Intellect, someone whispers.] That's it, honey. What's that got to do with women's rights or Negro's rights? If my cup won't hold but a pint, and yours holds a quart, wouldn't you be mean not to let me have my little half-measure full?

Then that little man in black there, he says women can't have as much rights as men, 'cause Christ wasn't a woman! Where did your Christ come from? Where did your Christ come from? From God and a woman! Man had nothing to do with Him.

If the first woman God ever made was strong enough to turn the world upside down all alone, these women together ought to be able to turn it back, and get it right side up again. And now they is asking to do it, the men better let them.

Obliged to you for hearing me, and now old Sojourner ain't got nothing more to say.

* * * * * *

1.   *Sojourner points out a problem that women of color are still addressing today: what is their role within the feminist movement? Sojourner repeats the same phrase over and over, "And ain't I a woman?" Why was it necessary for her to say this? What was the role of black women in the early women's movements? The abolitionists?*

2.   *Sojourner also illustrates the conflict between rural and urban women within the movement. Why would they be in conflict? What would their different roles have been? What would they still be?*

c h a p t e r   1 4

The Territorial Expansion of the United States, 1830s–1850s

14–1 A Tejano Describes the Beginning of the Texas Revolution in 1835–36

Juan Nepomuceno Seguin (1806–1890) was a member of a prominent Tejano (or native Texan) family of San Antonio. In this memoir, published in 1858, he describes his leadership of the movement for Texan independence and his military service in the rebellion along with the American settlers. Sent from the Alamo with his company to summon reinforcements, he narrowly escaped death at the hands of the Mexican army.

SOURCE: Juan Nepomuceno Seguin, *Personal Memoirs* (1858).

In October 1834, I was Political Chief of the Department of Bejar [in south-central Texas]. Dissatisfied with the reactionary designs of General Santa Anna, who was at that time President of the Republic of Mexico, and endeavored to overthrow the Federal system, I issued a circular, in which I urged every Municipality in Texas to appoint delegates to a convention that was to meet at San Antonio, for the purpose of taking into consideration the impending dangers, and for devising the means to avert them. All the Municipalities appointed their delegates but the convention never met, the General Government having ordered Col. Jose Maria Mendoza to march with his forces from Matamoras to San Antonio, and prevent the meeting of the delegates....

In April 1835, the Governor of Coahuila and Texas [the two Mexican provinces were joined as a single state] called for assistance from the various Departments to resist the aggressions of Santa Anna against that State. I volunteered my services, and received from the political Chief, Don Angel Navarro, the command of a party of National Guards sent from San Antonio to Monclova. In our encounters with the troops of Santa Anna, I was efficiently assisted by Col. B. R. Milam and Maj. John R. Allen. On our withdrawal from Monclova, disgusted with the weakness of the Executive, who had given up the struggle, we pledged ourselves to use all our influence to rouse Texas against the tyrannical government of Santa Anna....

We had agreed that the movement should begin in the center of Texas but not hearing from that quarter, I determined to send an agent to Brazoria [on the Brazos River, where many of the Americans had their settlements], Juan A. Zambrano, with directions to sound the disposition of the people. On the return of the agent, we were apprized that there was a great deal of talk about a revolution, in public meetings, but that the moment for an armed movement was still remote. Our agent was sent to Victoria [in south Texas], and he there called a meeting of the citizens, but the Military Commander of Goliad sent down a detachment of troops to prevent the assembly and arrest the promoters.

We were despairing of a successful issue, when the Military Commander of Texas, informed of the revolutionary feelings which were spreading over the colonies, determined upon removing from the town of Gonzales a piece of artillery, lent to that corporation by the Political Chief Saucedo. This was at the time a delicate undertaking. A lieutenant was detailed to carry it into execution, with orders to use force if necessary. On the same day that the military detachment started for Gonzales, I went to the lower ranchos on the San Antonio River; at Salvador Flores I held a meeting of the neighbors, and induced several to take up arms, well satisfied that the beginning of the revolution was close at hand....

Major Collinsworth, surprising the garrison of Goliad, took possession of that place. So soon as I was informed of that circumstance, I marched with my company to reinforce the Major, but, at the "conquista" crossing on the San Antonio River, I was overtaken by an express from General Stephen F. Austin, who informed me that he was marching on San Antonio, and requested me to join him, in order to attack General Cos. I retraced my steps, after having requested Captain Manuel Flores to go and meet General Austin and inform him of my readiness to comply with his wishes, and that I would take with me all the men I could possibly enlist on my route.

On the 13th of October, I met Austin on the Salado, at the crossing of the Gonzales road, and joined my forces with his small army. Upon this occasion I had the honor to become acquainted with General Sam Houston, who accompanied Austin. On the same day we had a slight encounter with the forces under Cos, who retired into San Antonio. Austin, as Commander-in-Chief of the army, gave me the appointment of Captain....

I was detailed to forage for the army, and was successful in doing so, returning to the camp with a liberal supply of provisions. Our camp was shortly moved to within one mile of the Alamo, whence we proceeded to the "Molino Blanco," and established head-quarters. On the 11th of December we entered the city, and after having taken possession of the houses of the Curate Garza, Vermendi, Flores, and others, we obliged the enemy to capitulate and withdraw towards Laredo.

After the capture of San Antonio, Captain Travis' company and mine were detailed to go in pursuit of the Mexican forces and capture from them a cavallado [a herd of horses] which they had in the Parrita, Laredo road; we succeeded, taking nearly one hundred head of horses, which were sent to San Felipe de Austin, for the benefit of the public service. I was afterwards detailed to the ranchos on the San Antonio river, to see if I could find more horses belonging to the Mexican troops.

On the 2d of January, 1836, I received from the Provisional Government [of Texas] the commission of Captain of Regular Cavalry, with orders to report to Lieutenant-Colonel Travis in San Antonio. On the 22d of February, at 2 o'clock P.M., General Santa Anna took possession of the city, with over 4000 men and in the mean time we fell back on the Alamo.

On the 28th, the enemy commenced the bombardment; meanwhile we met in a Council of War, and taking into consideration our perilous situation, it was resolved by a majority of the council, that I should leave the fort, and proceed with a communication to Colonel Fannin, requesting him to come to our assistance. I left the Alamo on the night of the council....I sent Fannin, by express, the comunication from Travis, informing him at the same time of the critical position of the defenders of the Alamo. Fannin answered me, through Lieutenant Finley, that he had advanced as far as "Rancho Nuevo," but, being informed of the movements of General Urrea, he had countermarched to Goliad, to defend that place; adding, that he could not respond to Travis call, their respective commands being separate, and depending upon General Houston, then at Gonzales, with whom he advised me to communicate. I lost no time in repairing to Gonzales, and reported myself to the General, informing him of the purport of my mission. He commanded me to wait at Gonzales for further orders. General Houston ordered

Captain Salvador Flores with 25 men of my company to the lower ranchos on the San Antonio river, to protect the inhabitants from the depredations of the Indians.

Afterwards, I was ordered to take possession, with the balance of my company, of the "Perra," distant about four miles on the road to San Antonio, with instructions to report every evening at head-quarters. Thus my company was forming the vanguard of the Texan army, on the road to San Antonio. On the 6th of March, I received orders to go to San Antonio with my company and a party of American citizens, carrying, on the horses, provisions for the defenders of the Alamo.

Arrived at the Cibolo, and not hearing the signal gun which was to be discharged every fifteen minutes, as long as the place held out, we retraced out steps to convey to the General-in-Chief the sad tidings. A new party was sent out, which soon came back, having met with Anselmo Verara and Andres Barcena, both soldiers of my company, whom I had left for purposes of observation in the vicinity of San Antonio; they brought the intelligence of the fall of the Alamo. Their report was so circumstantial as to preclude any doubts about that disastrous event.

* * * * *

* * * * * *

1. *Some years after the revolution, Seguin and his family were harassed into leaving Texas for Mexico, and he eventually fought against the Americans during the Mexican War. He wrote this account, addressed "to the American people," to set the record straight and to clear his name. How does Seguin present the origins of the independence movement?*

2. *Seguin mentions both American and Tejano participants in the struggle. What picture of interethnic cooperation emerges from the account?*

14–2 The Texans Declare Their Independence 1836

The Texan independence struggle against the central Mexican state broke out in 1835. As Santa Anna's army of six thousand Mexican soldiers marched on the province, a convention of Americans and Tejanos met to draw up a declaration of independence. This document was printed in both English and Spanish.

SOURCE: Henry Steele Commager, *Documents of American History* (1949); Poore, ed. *Constitutions, Charters, etc.* Part II, pp. 1752–1753.

March 1, 1836

(Poore, ed., *Constitutions, Charters, etc.* Part II, pp. 1752–1753)

WHEREAS, General Antonio Lopez de Santa Anna and other Military Chieftains have, by force of arms, overthrown the Federal Institutions of Mexico, and dissolved the Social Compact which existed between Texas and the other Members of the Mexican Confederacy—Now, the good People of Texas, availing themselves of their natural rights,

SOLEMNLY DECLARE

1st. That they have taken up arms in defence of their Rights and Liberties, which were threatened by the encroachments of military despots, and in defence of the Republican Principles of the Federal Constitution of Mexico of eighteen hundred and twenty-four.

2d. That Texas is no longer, morally or civilly, bound by the compact of Union; yet, stimulated by the generosity and sympathy common to a free people they offer their support and assistance to such of the Mexican Confederacy as will take up arms against their military despotism.

3d. That they do not acknowledge, that the present authorities of the nominal Mexican Republic have the right to govern within the limits of Texas.

4th. That they will not cease to carry on war against the said authorities, whilst their troops are within the limits of Texas.

5th. That they hold it to be their right, during the disorganization of the Federal System and the reign of despotism, to withdraw from the Union, to establish an independent Government, or to adopt such measures as they may deem best calculated to protect their rights and liberties; but that they will continue faithful to the Mexican Government so long as that nation is governed by the Constitution and Laws that were formed for the government of the Political Association.

6th. That Texas is responsible for the expenses of their Armies now in the field.

7th. That the public faith of Texas is pledged for the payment of any debts contracted by her Agents.

8th. That she will reward by donations in Land, all who volunteer their services in her present struggle, and receive them as Citizens.

These DECLARATIONS we solemnly avow to the world, and call GOD to witness their truth and sincerity; and invoke defeat and disgrace upon our heads should we prove guilty of duplicity.

RICHARD ELLIS, *President.*

* * * * * *

1. *Why, according to this declaration, did the Texans declare independence?*

2. *Many suspect that the independence movement was inspired by the goal of joining Texas to the United States. Can this idea be supported by this declaration? How do you assess the declaration of the intention to "continue faithful to the Mexican Government"?*

14–3 A Newspaper Man Declares the "Manifest Destiny" of the United States in 1845

The journalist John L. O'Sullivan (1813–1895), an enthusiastic Jacksonian Democrat, first coined the phrase "manifest destiny" in this article supporting the Annexation of Texas, printed in the Democratic Review for July 1845. O'Sullivan was later involved in other movements to annex additional territories, such as the Spanish colony of Cuba in the Caribbean.

SOURCE: *Democratic Review* (1845).

It is time for opposition to the Annexation of Texas to cease.…It is time for the common duty of Patriotism to the Country to succeed:—or if this claim will not be recognized, it is at least time for common sense to acquiesce with decent grace in the inevitable and the irrevocable.…Why, were other reasoning wanting, in favor of now elevating this question of the reception of Texas into the Union, out of the lower region of our past party dissentions, up to its proper level of a high and broad nationality, it surely is to be found, found abundantly, in the manner in which other nations have undertaken to intrude themselves into it, between us and the proper parties to the case, in a spirit of hostile interference against us, for the avowed object of thwarting our policy and hampering our power, limiting our greatness and checking the fulfilment of our manifest destiny to overspread the continent allotted by Providence for the free development of our yearly multiplying millions. This we have seen done by England, our old rival and enemy; and by France, strangely coupled with her against us, under the influence of the Anglicism strongly tinging the policy of her present prime minister, Guizot.…

It is wholly untrue, and unjust to ourselves, the pretence that the Annexation has been a measure of spoliation, unrightful and unrighteous—of military conquest under forms of peace and law—of territorial aggrandizement at the expense of justice, and justice due by a double sanctity to the weak. This view of the question is wholly unfounded, and has been before so amply refuted in these pages, as well as in a thousand other modes, that we shall not again dwell upon it. The independence of Texas was complete and absolute. It was an independence, not only in fact but of right. No obligation of duty towards Mexico tended in the least degree to restrain our right to effect the desired recovery of the fair province once our own—whatever motives of policy might have prompted a more deferential consideration of her feelings and her pride, as involved in the question. If Texas became peopled with an American population, it was by no contrivance of our government, but on the express invitation of that of Mexico herself; accompanied with such guaranties of State independence, and the maintenance of a federal system analogous to our own, as constituted a compact fully justifying the strongest measures of redress on the part of those afterwards deceived in this guaranty, and sought to be enslaved under the yoke imposed by its violation. She was released, rightfully and absolutely released, from all Mexican allegiance, or duty of cohesion to the Mexican political body, by the acts and fault of Mexico herself, and Mexico alone. There never was a clearer case. It was not revolution; it was resistance to revolution; and resistance under such circumstances as left independence the necessary resulting state, caused by the abandonment of those with whom her former federal association had existed. What then can be more preposterous than all the clamor by Mexico and the Mexican interest, against Annexation, as a violation of any rights of hers, any duties of ours?...

Nor is there any just foundation for the charge that Annexation is a great pro-slavery measure—calculated to increase and perpetuate that institution. Slavery had nothing to do with it. Opinions were and are greatly divided, both at the North and South, as to the influence to he exerted by it on Slavery and the Slave States. That it will tend to facilitate and hasten the disappearance of Slavery from all the northern tier of the present Slave States, cannot surely admit of serious question. The greater value in Texas of the slave labor now employed in those States, must soon produce the effect of draining off that labor southwardly, by the same unvarying law that bids water descend the slope that invites it. Every new Slave State in Texas will make at least one Free State from among those in which that institution now exists—to say nothing of those portions of Texas on which slavery cannot spring and grow—to say nothing of the far more rapid growth of new States in the free West and Northwest, as these fine regions are overspread by the emigration fast flowing over them from Europe, as well as from the Northern and Eastern States of the Union as it exists. On the other hand, it is undeniably much gained for the cause of the eventual voluntary abolition of slavery, that it should have been thus drained off towards the only outlet which appeared to furnish much probability of the ultimate disappearance of the negro race from our borders. The Spanish-Indian-American populations of Mexico, Central America and South America, afford the only receptacle capable of absorbing that race whenever we shall be prepared to slough it off—to emancipate it from slavery, and (simultaneously necessary) to remove it from the midst of our own. Themselves already of mixed and confused blood, and free from the "prejudices" which among us so insuperably forbid the social amalgamation which can alone elevate the Negro race out of a virtually servile degrada-

tion even though legally free, the regions occupied by those populations must strongly attract the black race in that direction; and as soon as the destined hour of emancipation shall arrive, will relieve the question of one of its worst difficulties, if not absolutely the greatest.

No—Mr. Clay was right when he declared that Annexation was a question with which slavery had nothing to do. The country which was the subject of Annexation in this case, from its geographical position and relations, happens to be—or rather the portion of it now actually settled, happens to be—a slave country. But a similar process might have taken place in proximity to a different section of our Union; and indeed there is a great deal of Annexation yet to take place, within the life of the present generation, along the whole line of our northern border. Texas has been absorbed into the Union in the inevitable fulfilment of the general law which is rolling our population westward; the connexion of which with that ratio of growth in population which is destined within a hundred years to swell our numbers to the enormous population of *two hundred and fifty millions* (if not more), is too evident to leave us in doubt of the manifest design of Providence in regard to the occupation of this continent. It was disintegrated from Mexico in the natural course of events, by a process perfectly legitimate on its own part, blameless on ours; and in which all the censures due to wrong, perfidy and folly, rest on Mexico alone. And possessed as it was by a population which was in truth but a colonial detachment from our own, and which was still bound by myriad ties of the very heartstrings to its old relations, domestic and political, their incorporation into the Union was not only inevitable, but the most natural, right and proper thing in the world—and it is only astonishing that there should be any among ourselves to say it nay.

California will, probably, next fall away from the loose adhesion which, in such a country as Mexico, holds a remote province in a slight equivocal kind of dependence on the metropolis. Imbecile and distracted, Mexico never can exert any real governmental authority over such a country. The impotence of the one and the distance of the other, must make the relation one of virtual independence; unless, by stunting the province of all natural growth, and forbidding that immigration which can alone develope its capabilities and fulfil the purposes of its creation, tyranny may retain a military dominion which is no government in the legitimate sense of the term. In the case of California this is now impossible. The Anglo-Saxon foot is already on its borders. Already the advance guard of the irresistible army of Anglo-Saxon emigration has begun to pour down upon it, armed with the plough and the rifle, and marking its trail with schools and colleges, courts and representative halls, mills and meeting-houses. A population will soon be in actual occupation of California, over which it will be idle for Mexico to dream of dominion. They will necessarily become independent. All this without agency of our government, without responsibility of our people—in the natural flow of events, the spontaneous working of principles, and the adaptation of the tendencies and wants of the human race to the elemental circumstances in the midst of which they find themselves placed. And they will have a right to independence—to self-government—to the possession of the homes conquered from the wilderness by their own labors and dangers, sufferings and sacrifices—a better and a truer right than the artificial title of sovereignty in Mexico a thousand miles distant, inheriting from Spain a title good only against those who have none better. Their right to independence will be the natural right of self-government belonging to any community strong enough to maintain it—distinct in position, origin and character, and free from any mutual obligations of membership of a common political body, binding it to others by the duty of loyalty and compact of public faith. This will be their title to independence; and by this title, there can be no doubt that the population now fast streaming down upon California will both assert and maintain that independence.

Away, then, with all idle French talk of *balances of power* on the American Continent. There is no growth in Spanish America! Whatever progress of population there may be in the British Canadas, is only for their own early severance of their present colonial relation to the little

island three thousand miles across the Atlantic; soon to be followed by Annexation, and destined to swell the still accumulating momentum of our progress. And whatsoever may hold the balance, though they should east into the opposite scale all the bayonets and cannon, not only of France and England, but of Europe entire, how would it kick the beam against the simple solid weight of the two hundred and fifty or three hundred millions—and American millions—destined to gather beneath the flutter of the stripes and stars, in the fast hastening year of the Lord 1945?

* * * * * *

1. What role does the growth of population play in O'Sullivan's ideas about "manifest destiny?" How does he explain Texas's break from Mexico? Why does he predict the eventual separation of California?

2. O'Sullivan attempts to show that the annexation of Texas has nothing to do with slavery. Why?

3. How would you describe O'Sullivan's views of race? In what ways is "manifest destiny" for him tied up with his belief in the superiority of "Anglo-Saxon" peoples?

14–4   A Young Pioneer Writes of Her Journey to California in 1846 with the Donner Party

Virginia Reed (1833–1921) was thirteen years old at the time of her overland journey with the ill-fated Donner Party. This letter, which she wrote home to her cousin after reaching California, appears here with her own spelling preserved but with some punctuation added for clarity. Virginia provided a remarkable account of the hardships of the journey using the ordinary speech and syntax of western Americans of the mid-nineteenth century.

SOURCE: Kenneth L. Holmes, ed., Covered Wagon Women (1983).

Napa Vallie, California
May 16th 1847

My Dear Cousan,

I take this oppertunity to write to you to let you now that we are all Well at presant and hope this letter may find you all well to. My dear Cousan I am a going to Write to you about our trubels geting to California. We had good luck til we come to big Sangy there we lost our best yoak of oxons. We come to Brigers Fort & we lost another ox. We sold some of our provisions & baut a yoak of Cows & oxen & they pursuaded us to take Hastings cut of over the salt plain. They said it saved 3 Hondred miles, we went that road & we had to go through a long drive of 40 miles With out water or grass. Hastings said it was 40 but i think it was 80 miles. We traveld a day and night & a nother day and at noon pa went on to see if he coud find Water, he had not bin gone long till some of the oxen give out and we had to leve the Wagons and take the oxen on to water. One of the men staid with us and others went on with the cattel to water. Pa was a coming back to us with Water and met the men & thay was about 10 miles from water. Pa said they get to water that night, and the next day to bring the cattel back for the wagons and bring some Water. Pa got to us about noon. The man that was with us took the horse and went on to water. We wated thare. Thought they would com. We thought we start and walk to Mr doners wagons that night. We took what little water we had and some bread and started. Pa caried Thomos and all the rest of us walk.

We got to Donner and thay were all a sleep so we laid down on the ground. We spred one shawl down we laid doun on it a spred another over us and then put the dogs on top. It was the coldes night you most ever saw. The wind blew and if it haden bin for the dogs we would have Frosen....

[Virginia's father was forced to hurry ahead in order to get provisions in California.] We had to Walk all the time we was a traviling up the Truckee river. We met 2 Indians that we had sent out for propessions to Suter Fort. Thay had met pa, not fur from Suters Fort. He looked very bad. He had not ate but 3 times in 7 days and thes days with out any thing. His horse was not abel to carrie him. Thay give him a horse and he went on. So we cashed some more of our things all but what we could pack on one mule and we started. Martha and James rode behind the two Indians. It was a raing then in the Vallies and snowing on the mountains so we went on that way 3 or 4 days tell we come to the big mountain or the Callifornia Mountain. The snow then was about 8 feet deep. Thare was some wagons thare. Thay said thay had attempted to cross and could not, well we thought we would try it so we started and thay started again with thare wagons. The snow was then way to the muels side. The farther we went up the deeper the snow got so the wagons could not go. So thay packed thare oxons and started with us carring a child a piece and driving the oxons in snow up to thare wast. The mule Martha and the Indian was on was the best one so thay went and broak the road and that Indian was the Pilot. So we went on that way 2 miles and the mules kept faling down in the snow head formost and the Indian said he could not find the road. We stoped and let the Indian and man go on to hunt the road. Thay went on and found the road to the top of the mountain and come back and said they thought we could git over if it did not snow any more. Well the Woman were all so tirder caring there Children that thay could not go over that night. So we made a fire and got something to eat & ma spred down a bufalorobe & we all laid down on it & spred something over us & ma sit up by the fire & it snowed one foot on top of the bed so we got up in the morning & the snow was so deep we could not go over & we had to go back to the cabin & build more cabins & stay thare all Winter without Pa.

We had not the first thing to eat. Ma maid arrangements for some cattel giving 2 for 1 in Callifonia. We seldom thot of bread for we had not had any since [words unreadable] & the cattel was so poor thay could note hadley git up when thay laid down. We stoped thare the 4th of November & staid till March and what we had to eat i cant hardely tell you & we had that man & Indians to fee. Well thay started over a foot and had to come back so thay made snow shoes and started again & it come on a storme & thay had to come back. It would snow 10 days

before it would stop. Thay wated tell it stoped & started again. I was a goeing with them & I took sick & could not go—thare was 15 started & thare was 7 got throw. 5 Weman & 2 men. It come a storme and thay lost the road & got out of provisions & the ones that got throwe had to eat them that Died.

Not long after thay started we got out of provisions & had to put Martha at one cabin, James at another, Thomas at another, & Ma & Elizea & Milt Eliot & I dried up what littel meat we had and started to see if we could get across & had to leve the childrin. O Mary you may think that hard to leve theme with strangers & did not now wether we would see them again or not. We could hardle get a way from them but we told theme we would bring them Bread & then thay was willing to stay. We went & was out 5 days in the mountains. Elie giv out & had to go back. We went on a day longer. We had to lay by a day & make snow shows & we went on a while and coud not find the road & we had to turn back. I could go on very well while i thougt we were giting along but as soone as we had to turn back i coud hadley git along but we got to the cabins that night. I froze one of my feet verry bad & that same night thare was the worst storme we had that winter & if we had not come back that night we would never got back. We had nothing to eat but ox hides. O Mary I would cry and wish I had what you all wasted. Eliza had to go to Mr Graves cabin & we staid at Mr Breen. Thay had meat all the time & we had to kill littel cash the dog & cat him. We ate his head and feet & hide & evry thing about him. O my Dear Cousin you dont now what trubel is. Yet a many a time we had on the last thing a cooking and did not now whet the next would come from but there was awl wais some way provided.

There was 15 in the cabon we was in and half of us had to lay a bed all the time. Thare was 10 starved to death. There we was hadley abel to walk. We lived on a little cash a week and after Mr Breen would cook his meat we would take the bones and boil them 3 or 4 days at a time. Ma went down to the other caben and got half a hide carried it in snow up to her wast.

It snowed and would cover the cabin all over so we could not git out for 2 or 3 days. We would have to cut pieces of the loges in sied to make a fire with. I coud hardly eat the hides and had not eat anything 3 days. Pa stated out to us with provisions and then came a storme and he could not go. He cash his provision and went back on the other side of the bay to get compana of men and the San Wakien [San Juaquin] got so hye he could not crose. Well thay Made up a Compana at Suters Fort and sent out. We had not ate any thing for 3 days & we had onely a half a hide and we was out on top of the cabin and we seen them a coming.

O my Dear Cousin you dont now how glad i was. We run and met them. One of them we knew. We had traveled with them on the road. They staid thare 3 days to recruet a little so we could go. Thare was 20 started. All of us started and went a piece and Martha and Thomas giv out & so the men had to take them back. Ma and Eliza, James and I come on. And o Mary that was the hades thing yet to come on and liev them thar. Did not now but what thay would starve to Death. Martha said, well ma if you never see me again do the best you can. The men said thay could hadly stand it. It maid them all cry but they said it was better for all of us to go on for if we was to go back we would eat that much more from them. Thay give them a littel meat and flore and took them back and we come on. We went over great hye mountain as strait as stair steps in snow up to our knees. Little James walk the hole way over all the mountain in snow up to his waist. He said every step he took he was a gitting higher Pa and something to eat. The Bears took the provision the men had washed and we had but very little to eat.

When we had traveld 5 days travel we met Pa with 13 men going to the cabins. O Mary, you do not now how glad we was to see him: We had not seen him for months. We thought we woul never see him again. He heard we was coming and he made some seet cakes to give us. He said he would see Martha and Thomas the next day. He went to tow days what took us 5 days. Some of the compana was eating from them that Died but Thomas &

Martha had not ate any, Pa and the men started with 12 people....

O Mary I have not wrote you half of the truble we have had but I have Wrote you anuf to let you now that you dont now what truble is. But thank the Good god we have all got throw and the onely family that did not eat human flesh. We have left every thing but i dont cair for that. We have got through but Dont let this letter dishaten anybody and never tak no cutofs and hury along as fast as you can.

* * * * * *

1. *Using evidence drawn from this letter, discuss the organization of the overland journey; the importance of the family unit to the enterprise, and the cooperation of traveling companies.*

2. *Judging from her letter, what did Virginia Reed consider the worst horror of this disasterous episode?*

3. *"Don't let this letter dishaten anybody," Virginia concludes. How do you explain her continuing optimism at the end of such a harrowing journey?*

14–5   The President Asks Congress to Declare War on Mexico in 1846

President James Polk delivered this war message on May 11, 1846, and Congress declared war two days later. The most controversial aspect of the message was Polk's assertion that "Mexico has passed the boundary of the United States, has invaded our territory and shed American blood upon the American soil." When Texas was a province of Mexico, its southern boundary had been the Nueces River. After the revolution, the Texas nation claimed all the territory between the Nueces and the Rio Grande, but Mexico had consistently disputed this claim.

To the Senate and House of Representatives:

The existing state of the relations between the United States and Mexico renders it proper that I should bring the subject to the consideration of Congress....

In my message at the commencement of the present session I informed you that upon the earnest appeal both

SOURCE: William Macdonald, ed., Select Documents Illustrative of the History of the United States, 1776–1861 (1905), pp. 310–311.

of the Congress and convention of Texas I had ordered an efficient military force to take a position "between the Nueces and the Del Norte." This had become necessary to meet a threatened invasion of Texas by the Mexican forces, for which extensive military preparations had been made. The invasion was threatened solely because Texas had determined, in accordance with a solemn resolution of the Congress of the United States, to annex herself to our Union, and under these circumstances it was plainly our duty to extend our protection over her citizens and soil.

This force was concentrated at Corpus Christi, and remained there until after I had received such information from Mexico as rendered it probable, if not certain, that the Mexican Government would refuse to receive our envoy.

Meantime Texas, by the final action of our Congress, had become an integral part of our Union. The Congress of Texas, by its act of December 19, 1836, had declared the Rio del Norte to be the boundary of that Republic. Its jurisdiction had been extended and exercised beyond the Nueces. The country between that river and the Del Norte had been represented in the Congress and in the convention of Texas, had thus taken part in the act of annexation itself, and is now included within one of our Congressional districts. Our own Congress had, moreover, with great unanimity, by the act approved December 31, 1845, recognized the country beyond the Nueces as a part of our territory by including within our own revenue system, and a revenue officer to reside within that district has been appointed by and with the advice and consent of the Senate. It became, therefore, of urgent necessity to provide for the defense of that portion of our country. Accordingly, on the 13th of January last instructions were issued to the general in command of these troops to occupy the left bank of the Del Norte. This river, which is the southwestern boundary of the State of Texas, is an exposed frontier.

The movement of the troops to the Del Norte was made by the commanding general under positive instructions to abstain from all aggressive acts toward Mexico or Mexican citizens and to regard the relations between that Republic and the United States as peaceful unless she should declare war or commit acts of hostility indicative of a state of war....

The Mexican forces at Matamoras assumed a belligerent attitude, and on the 12th of April General Ampudia, then in command, notified General Taylor to break up his camp within twenty-four hours and to retire beyond the Nueces River, and in the event of his failure to comply with these demands announced that arms, and arms alone, must decide the question. But no open act of hostility was committed until the 24th of April. On that day General Arista, who had succeeded to the command of the Mexican forces, communicated to General Taylor that "he considered hostilities commenced and should prosecute them." A party of dragoons of 63 men and officers were on the same day dispatched from the American camp up the Rio del Norte, on its left bank, to ascertain whether the Mexican troops had crossed or were preparing to cross the river, "became engaged with a large body of these troops, and after a short affair, in which some 16 were killed and wounded, appear to have been surrounded and compelled to surrender."...

The cup of forbearance had been exhausted even before the recent information from the frontier of the Del Norte. But now, after reiterated menaces, Mexico has passed the boundary of the United States, has invaded our territory and shed American blood upon the American soil. She has proclaimed that hostilities have commenced, and that the two nations are now at war.

As war exists, and, notwithstanding all our efforts to avoid it, exists by the act of Mexico herself, we are called upon by every consideration of duty and patriotism to vindicate with decision the honor, the rights, and the interests of our country....

In further vindication of our rights and defense of our territory. I invoke the prompt action of Congress to recognize the existence of the war, and to place at the disposition of the Executive the means of prosecuting the war with vigor, and thus hastening the restoration of peace....

* * * * * *

1.   How does Polk support the claim that the land beyond the Nueces River is American soil?

2.   Can you reconstruct the Mexican view of the war's origins from Polk's message?

14–6 An Illinois Representative Attacks President Polk's View of the War in 1848

Abraham Lincoln of Illinois, elected to the House of Representatives in 1846, was one of the northern Whigs who opposed the Mexican War. In December of 1847, in a series of questions or "interrogatories," Lincoln publicly challenged President Polk to show the spot where the Mexicans shed "American blood on the American soil." Unimpressed with the President's response, Lincoln gave this sharply critical speech in his congressional district, where he was ridiculed as "spotty Lincoln."

SOURCE: Congressional Globe (1848).

The President, in his first war message of May, 1846, declares that the soil was ours on which hostilities were commenced by Mexico, and he repeats that declaration almost in the same language in each successive annual message, thus showing that he deems that point a highly essential one. In the importance of that point I entirely agree with the President. To my judgment it is the very point upon which he should be justified, or condemned. In his message of December, 1846, it seems to have occurred to him, as is certainly true, that title—ownership—to soil or anything else is not a simple fact, but is a conclusion following on one or more simple facts; and that it was incumbent upon him to present the facts from which he concluded the soil was ours on which the first blood of the war was shed....

Now, I propose to try to show that the whole of this—issue and evidence—is from beginning to end the sheerest deception. The issue, as he presents it, is in these words: "But there are those who, conceding all this to be true, assume the ground that the true western boundary of Texas is the Nueces, instead of the Rio Grande; and that, therefore, in marching our army to the east bank of the latter river, we passed the Texas line and invaded the territory of Mexico." Now this issue is made up of two affirmatives and no negative. The main deception of it is that it assumes as true that one river or the other is necessarily the boundary; and cheats the superficial thinker entirely out of the idea that possibly the boundary is somewhere between the two, and not actually at either. A further deception is that it will let in evidence which a true issue would exclude. A true issue made by the President would be about as follows: "I say the soil was ours, on which the first blood was shed; there are those who say it was not."

I now proceed to examine the President's evidence as applicable to such an issue.... His first item is that the Rio Grande was the western boundary of Louisiana, as we purchased it of France in 1803; and seeming to expect this to be disputed, he argues over the amount of nearly a page to prove it true; at the end of which he lets us know that by the treaty of 1819 we sold to Spain the whole country from the Rio Grande eastward to the Sabine. Now, admitting for the present that the Rio Grande was the boundary of Louisiana, what, under heaven, had that to do with the present boundary between us and Mexico? How, Mr. Chairman, the line that once divided your land from mine can still be the boundary between us after I have sold my land to you is to me beyond all comprehension. And how any man, with an honest purpose only by proving the truth, could ever have thought of introducing such a fact to prove such an issue is equally incomprehensible. His next piece of evidence is that "the Republic of Texas always claimed this river (Rio Grande) as her western boundary." That is not true, in fact. Texas has claimed it, but she has not always claimed it. There is at least one distinguished exception. Her State constitution—the republic's most solemn and well-considered act; that which may, without impropriety, be called her last will and testament, revoking all others—makes no such claim. But suppose she had always claimed it. Has not Mexico always claimed the contrary? So that there is but claim against claim, leaving nothing proved until we get back to the claims and find which has the better foundation....

I next consider the President's statement that Santa Anna in his treaty with Texas recognized the Rio Grande as the western boundary of Texas. Besides the position so often taken, that Santa Anna while a prisoner of war, a captive, could not bind Mexico by a treaty, which I deem conclusive—besides this, I wish to say something in relation to this treaty, so called by the President, with Santa Anna....I believe I should not err if I were to declare that during the first ten years of the existence of that document it was never by anybody called a treaty—that it was never so called till the President, in his extremity, attempted by so calling it to wring something from it in justification of himself in connection with the Mexican war. It has none of the distinguishing features of a treaty. It does not call itself a treaty....It is stipulated therein that the Mexican forces should evacuate the territory of Texas, passing to the other side of the Rio Grande; and in another article it is stipulated that, to prevent collisions between the armies, the Texas army should not approach nearer than within five leagues—of what is not said, but clearly, from the object stated, it is of the Rio Grande. Now, if this is a treaty recognizing the Rio Grande as the boundary of Texas, it contains the singular features of stipulating that Texas shall not go within five leagues of her own boundary.

Next comes the evidence of Texas before annexation, and the United States afterward, exercising jurisdiction beyond the Nueces and between the two rivers. This actual exercise of jurisdiction is the very class or quality of evidence we want. It is excellent so far as it goes; but does it go far enough? He tells us it went beyond the Nueces, but he does not tell us it went to the Rio Grande. He tells us jurisdiction was exercised between the two rivers, but he does not tell us it was exercised over all the territory between them. Some simple-minded people think it is possible to cross one river and go beyond it without going all the way to the next, that jurisdiction may be exercised between two rivers without covering all the country between them. I know a man, not very unlike myself, who exercises jurisdiction over a piece of land between the Wabash and the Mississippi; and yet so far is this from being all there is between those rivers that it is just one hundred and fifty-two feet long by fifty feet wide, and not part of it much within a hundred miles of either. He has a neighbor between him and the Mississippi—that is, just across the street, in that direction—whom I am sure he could neither persuade nor force to give up his habitation; but which nevertheless he could certainly annex, if it were to be done by merely standing on his own side of the street and claiming it, or even sitting down and writing a deed for it....

I am now through the whole of the President's evidence; and it is a singular fact that if any one should declare the President sent the army into the midst of a settlement of Mexican people who had never submitted, by consent or by force, to the authority of Texas or of the United States, and that there and thereby the first blood of the war was shed, there is not one word in all the President has said which would either admit or deny the declaration. This strange omission it does seem to me could not have occurred but by design. My way of living leads me to be about the courts of justice; and there I have sometimes seen a good lawyer, struggling for his client's neck in a desperate case, employing every artifice to work round, befog, and cover up with many words some point arising in the case which he dared not admit and yet could not deny. Party bias may help to make it appear so, but with all the allowance I can make for such bias, it still does appear to me that just such, and from just such necessity, is the President's struggle in this case.

...Now, sir, for the purpose of obtaining the very best evidence as to whether Texas had actually carried her revolution to the place where the hostilities of the present war commenced, let the President answer the interrogatories I proposed, as before mentioned, or some other similar ones. Let him answer fully, fairly, and candidly. Let him answer with facts and not with arguments. Let him remember he sits where Washington sat, and so remembering, let him answer as Washington would answer. As a nation should not, and the Almighty will not, be evaded, so let him attempt no evasion—no equivocation. And, if, so answering, he can show that the soil was ours where the first blood of the war was shed,—that it was not within an inhabited country, or, if within such, that the inhabitants had submitted themselves to the civil authority of Texas or of the United States, and that the same is true of the site of Fort Brown,—then I am with him for his justification. In that case I shall be most happy to reverse the vote I gave the other day. I have a selfish motive for desiring that the President may do this—I expect to gain some votes, in connection with the war, which, without his so doing, will be of doubtful propriety in my own judgment, but which will be free from the doubt if he does so. But if he can not or will not do this,—if on any pretense or no pretense he shall refuse or omit it—then I shall be fully convinced of what I more than suspect already—that he is deeply conscious of being in the wrong; that he feels the blood of this war, like the blood of Abel, is crying to Heaven against him; that originally having some strong motive—what, I will not stop now to give my opinion concerning—to involve the two countries in a war, and trusting to escape scrutiny by fixing the public gaze upon the exceeding brightness of military glory—that attractive rainbow that rises in showers of blood—that serpent's eye that charms to destroy,—he plunged into it, and has swept on and on till, disappointed in his calculation of the ease with which Mexico might be subdued, he now finds himself he knows not where. How like the half-insane mumbling of a fever dream is the whole war part of his late message!...

* * * * * *

1. *What is Lincoln's argument in this speech? What is his primary objective in attacking Polk's rationale for the war?*

2. *Lincoln was renowned for his storytelling. Examine the ways in which he attempts to appeal to his constituents in this speech.*

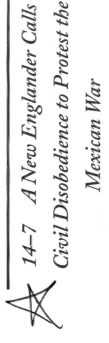

14–7   A New Englander Calls Civil Disobedience to Protest the Mexican War

The essayist and naturalist Henry David Thoreau (1817–1862) objected to slavery and the Mexican War. When he refused to pay his poll tax, declaring that he could not condone a government that supported such things, the constable of his town of Concord, Massachusetts, locked him in jail until one of his relatives paid the tax for him. In the famous essay of 1849, "Civil Disobedience," from which the following document is drawn, Thoreau defended his actions.
SOURCE: Elizabeth P. Peabody, ed. *Aesthetic Papers* (1849).

I heartily accept the motto—"That government is best which governs least;" and I should like to see it acted up to more rapidly and systematically. Carried out, it finally amounts to this, which also I believe—"That government is best which governs not at all;" and when men are prepared for it, that will be the kind of government which they will have. Government is at best but an expedient; but most governments are usually, and all governments are sometimes, inexpedient. The objections which have been brought against a standing army, and they are many and weighty, and deserve to prevail, may also at last be brought against a standing government. The standing army is only an arm of the standing government. The government itself, which is only the mode which the people have chosen to execute their will, is equally liable to be abused and perverted before the people can act through it. Witness the present Mexican war, the work of comparatively a few individuals using the standing government as their tool; for, in the outset, the people would not have consented to this measure.

How does it become a man to behave toward this American government to-day? I answer that he cannot without disgrace be associated with it. I cannot for an instant recognize that political organization as *my* government which is the *slave's* government also.

All men recognize the right of revolution; that is, the right to refuse allegiance to and to resist the government, when its tyranny or its inefficiency are great and unendurable. But almost all say that such is not the case now. But such was the case, they think, in the Revolution of '75. If one were to tell me that this was a bad govern-ment because it taxed certain foreign commodities brought to its ports, it is most probable that I should not make an ado about it, for I can do without them; all machines have their friction; and possibly this does enough good to counterbalance the evil. At any rate, it is a great evil to make a stir about it. But when the friction comes to have its machine, and oppression and robbery are organized, I say, let us not have such a machine any longer. In other words, when a sixth of the population of a nation which has undertaken to be the refuge of liberty are slaves, and a whole country is unjustly overrun and conquered by a foreign army, and subject to military law, I think that it is not too soon for honest men to rebel and revolutionize. What makes this duty the more urgent is the fact, that the country so overrun is not our own, but ours is the invading army....

Practically speaking, the opponents to a reform in Massachusetts are not a hundred thousand politicians at the South, but a hundred thousand merchants and farm-ers here, who are more interested in commerce and agri-culture than they are in humanity, and are not prepared to do justice to the slave and to Mexico, *cost what it may.* I quarrel not with far-off foes, but with those who, near at home, co-operate with, and do the bidding of those far away, and without whom the latter would be harmless. We are accustomed to say, that the mass of men are unprepared; but improvement is slow, because the few are not materially wiser or better than the many. It is not so important that many should be as good as you, as that there be some absolute goodness somewhere; for that will leaven the whole lump. There are thousands who are *in opinion* opposed to slavery and to the war, who yet in effect do nothing to put an end to them; who, esteeming themselves children of Washington and Franklin, sit down with their hands in their pockets, and say that they know not what to do, and do nothing; who even postpone the question of freedom to the question of free-trade, and quietly read the prices-current along with the latest advices from Mexico, after dinner, and, it may be, fall asleep over them both....obey them, or shall we endeav-or to amend them, and obey them until we have succeed-ed, or shall we transgress them at once? Men generally, under such a government as this, think that they ought to wait until they have persuaded the majority to alter them. They think that, if they should resist, the remedy would be worse than the evil. But it is the fault of the govern-ment itself that the remedy *is* worse than the evil. *It* makes it worse. Why is it not more apt to anticipate and provide for reform? Why does it not cherish its wise minority? Why does it cry and resist before it is hurt? Why does it not encourage its citizens to be on the alert to point out its faults, and *do* better than it would have them? Why does it always crucify Christ, and excommu-nicate Copernicus and Luther, and pronounce Washington and Franklin rebels?...

If the injustice is part of the necessary friction of the machine of government, let it go, let it go; perchance it will wear smooth,—certainly the machine will wear out. If the injustice has a spring, or a pulley, or a rope, or a crank, exclusively for itself, then perhaps you may con-sider whether the remedy will not be worse than the evil; but if it is of such a nature that it requires you to be the agent of injustice to another, then, I say, break the law. Let your life be a counter friction to stop the machine. What I have to do is to see, at any rate, that I do not lend myself to the wrong which I condemn.

As for adopting the ways which the State has pro-vided for remedying the evil, I know not of such ways. They take too much time, and a man's life will be gone. I have other affairs to attend to. I came into this world, not chiefly to make this a good place to live in, but to live in it, be it good or bad. A man has not everything to do, but something; and because he cannot do *every thing,* it is not necessary that he should do *something* wrong. It is not my business to be petitioning the governor or the leg-islature any more than it is theirs to petition me; and if they should not hear my petition, what should I do then? But in this case the State has provided no way: its very Constitution is the evil. This may seem to be harsh and stubborn and unconciliatory; but it is to treat with the utmost kindness and consideration the only spirit that can appreciate or deserves it. So is all change for the better, like birth and death which convulse the body.

Under a government which imprisons any unjustly, the true place for a just man is also in prison. The proper place to-day, the only place which Massachusetts has provided for her freer and less desponding spirits, is in her prisons, to be put out and locked out of the State by her own act, as they have already put themselves out by their principles. It is there that the fugitive slave, and the Mexican prisoner on parole, and the Indian come to plead the wrongs of his race, should find them; on that separate, but more free and honorable ground, where the State places those who are not *with* her, but *against* her,—the only house in a slave-state in which a free man can abide with honor. If any think that their influence would be lost there, and their voices no longer affict the ear of the State, that they would not be as an enemy with-in its walls, they do not know by how much truth is stronger than error, nor how much more eloquently and effectively he can combat injustice who has experienced a little in his own person. Cast your whole vote, not a strip of paper merely, but your whole influence. A minor-ity is powerless while it conforms to the majority; it is not even a minority then; but it is irresistible when it clogs by its whole weight. If the alternative is to keep all just men in prison, or give up war and slavery, the State will not hesitate which to choose. If a thousand men were not to pay their tax-bills this year, that would not be a violent and bloody measure, as it would be to pay them, and enable the State to commit violence and shed innocent blood. This is, in fact, the definition of a peaceable revolution, if any such is possible. If the tax-gatherer, or any other public officer, asks me, as one has done, "But what shall I do?" my answer is, "If you really wish to do anything, resign our office." When the subject has resigned his allegiance, and the officer has resigned his office, then the revolution is accomplished. But even suppose blood should flow. Is there not a sort of blood shed when the conscience is wounded? Through this wound a man's real manhood and immortality flow out, and he bleeds to an everlasting death. I see this blood flowing now....

* * * * * *

1. *What is Thoreau's assessment of the Mexican War? How does his account compare with those given by James Polk and Abraham Lincoln?*

2. *Thoreau declares about laws: "If it is of such a nature that it requires you to be the agent of injustice to another; then, I say, break the law." Do you agree or disagree with his views?*

3. *Compare Thoreau's vision of American government with that of John L. O'Sullivan. How do they differ on the issues of slavery and expansion? What, if any, political values do they share?*

14–8 An Indian Chief Discusses the Difference Between His People and the Americans in 1854

Chief Seattle (1786–1866) was leader of the Suquamish and Duwamish tribes of the Puget Sound when the United States acquired the Pacific Northwest. A smallpox epidemic that decimated his people led him to the conclusion that American rule over the Indians was inevitable, and he ceded the land on which the city of Seattle, named for him, now stands. In this speech, Seattle focused on the occasion of that cession, Seattle focused critically on the differences between Indians and Americans. Renowned as a great orator; he delivered this speech in his native language, but it was translated and transcribed by an American who was present.

SOURCE: W. C. Vanderwerth, *Indian Oratory* (1971), pp. 1770–1772.

Yonder sky that has wept tears of compassion upon my people for centuries untold, and which to us appears changeless and eternal, may change. Today is fair. Tomorrow it may be overcast with clouds. My words are like the stars that never change. Whatever Seattle says the great chief at Washington can rely upon with as much certainty as he can upon the return of the sun or the seasons. The White Chief says that Big Chief at Washington sends us greetings of friendship and goodwill. This is kind of him for we know he has little need of our friendship in return. His people are many. They are like the grass that covers vast prairies. My people are few. They resemble the scattering trees of a storm-swept plain. The great—and I presume—good White Chief sends us word that he wishes to buy our lands but is willing to allow us enough to live comfortably. This indeed appears just, even generous, for the Red Man no longer has rights that he need respect, and the offer may be wise also, as we are no longer in need of an extensive country.

There was a time when our people covered the land as the waves of a wind-ruffled sea cover its shell paved floor, but that time long since passed away with the greatness of tribes that are now but a mournful memory. I will not dwell on, nor mourn over, our untimely decay, nor reproach my paleface brothers with hastening it as we too may have been somewhat to blame.

Youth is impulsive. When our young men grow angry at some real or imaginary wrong, and disfigure their faces with black paint, it denotes that their hearts are black, and that they are often cruel and relentless, and our old men and old women are unable to restrain them. Thus it has ever been. Thus it was when the white man first began to push our forefathers westward. But let us hope that the hostilities between us may never return. We would have everything to lose and nothing to gain. Revenge by young men is considered gain, even at the cost of their own lives, but old men who stay at home in times of war, and mothers who have sons to lose, know better.

Our good father at Washington—for I presume he is now our father as well as yours, since King George has moved his boundaries further north—our great and good father, I say, sends us word that if we do as he desires he will protect us. His brave warriors will be to us a bristling wall of strength, and his wonderful ships of war will fill our harbors so that our ancient enemies far to the northward—the Hydas and Tsimpsians—will cease to frighten our women, children, and old men. Then in reality will he be our father and we his children. But can that ever be? Your God is not our God! Your God loves your people and hates mine. He folds his strong protecting arms lovingly about the pale face and leads him by the hand as a father leads his infant son—but

He has forsaken His red children—if they really are His. Our God, the Great Spirit, seems also to have forsaken us. Your God makes your people wax strong every day. Soon they will fill all the land. Our people are ebbing away like a rapidly receding tide that will never return. The white man's God cannot love our people or He would protect them. They seem to be orphans who can look nowhere for help. How then can we be brothers? How can your God become our God and renew our prosperity and awaken in us dreams of returning greatness? If we have a common heavenly father He must be partial—for He came to His paleface children. We never saw Him. He gave you laws but had no word for his red children whose teeming multitudes once filled this vast continent as stars fill the firmament. No; we are two distinct races with separate origins and separate destinies. There is little in common between us.

To us the ashes of our ancestors are sacred and their resting place is hallowed ground. You wander far from the graves of your ancestors and seemingly without regret. Your religion was written upon tables of stone by the iron finger of your God so that you could not forget. The Red Man could never comprehend nor remember it. Our religion is the traditions of our ancestors—the dreams of our old men, given them in the solemn hours of night by the Great Spirit; and the visions of our sachems, and is written in the hearts of our people.

Your dead cease to love you and the land of their nativity as soon as they pass the portals of the tomb and wander way beyond the stars. They are soon forgotten and never return. Our dead never forget the beautiful world that gave them being. They still love its verdant valleys, its murmuring rivers, its magnificent mountains, sequestered vales and verdant lined lakes and bays, and ever yearn in tender, fond affection over the lonely hearted living, and often return from the Happy Hunting Ground to visit, guide, console and comfort others.

Day and night cannot dwell together. The Red Man has ever fled the approach of the White Man, as the morning mist flees before the morning sun.

However, your proposition seems fair and I think that my people will accept it and will retire to the reservation you offer them. Then we will dwell in peace, for the words of the Great White Chief seem to be the words of nature speaking to my people out of dense darkness.

It matters little where we pass the remnant of our days. They will not be many. The Indians' night promises to be dark. Not a single star of hope hovers above his horizon. Sad-voiced winds moan in the distance. Grim fate seems to be on the Red Man's trail, and wherever he goes he will hear the approaching footsteps of his destroyer and prepare stoically to meet his doom, as does the wounded doe that hears the approaching footsteps of the hunter.

A few more moons. A few more winters—and not one of the descendants of the mighty hosts that once moved over his broad land or lived in happy homes, protected by the Great Spirit, will remain to mourn over the graves of a people—once more powerful and hopeful than yours. But why should I mourn at the untimely fate of my people? Tribe follows tribe, and nation follows nation, like the waves of the sea. It is the order of nature, and regret is useless. Your time of decay may be distant, but it will surely come, for even the White Man whose God walked and talked with him as friend with friend, cannot be exempt from the common destiny. We may be brothers after all. We will see.

We will ponder your proposition and when we decide will let you know. But should we accept it, I here and now make this condition that we will not be denied the privilege without molestation of visiting at any time the tombs of our ancestors, friends and children. Every part of this soil is sacred in the estimation of my people. Every hillside, every valley, every plain and grove, has been hallowed by some sad or happy event in days long vanished. Even the rocks, which seem to be dumb and dead as they swelter in the sun along the silent shore, thrill with memories of stirring events connected with the lives of my people, and the very dust upon which you now stand responds more lovingly to their footsteps than to yours, because it is rich with the blood of our ancestors and our bare feet are conscious of the sympathetic touch. Our departed braves, fond mothers, glad, happy-hearted maidens, and even our little children who lived here and rejoiced here for a brief season, will love these somber solitudes and at eventide they greet shadowy returning spirits. And when the last Red Man shall have perished, and the memory of my tribe shall have become a myth among the White Men, these shores will swarm with the invisible dead of my tribe, and when your children's children think themselves alone in the field, the store, the shop, upon the highway, or in the silence of the pathless woods, they will not be alone. In all the earth there is no place dedicated to solitude. At night when the streets of your cities and villages are silent and you think them deserted, they will throng with the returning hosts that once filled them and still love this beautiful land. The White Man will never be alone.

Let him be just and deal kindly with my people, for the dead are not powerless. Dead, did I say? There is no death, only a change of worlds.

* * * * * *

1. According to Seattle, what are the most important differences between the Indian people and white Americans?

2. Seattle had converted to Catholicism in the 1830s, but by the time he delivered this address he seems to have returned to his native religious beliefs. What is his view of the white man's religion in 1854?

14–9 A Californio Describes the "Bear Flag" Insurrection in California

Mariano Guadalupe Vallejo (1808–1890) was a Mexican soldier who before the American acquisition of California accumulated a fortune in California land and cattle. He was one of the Californios, the wealthy land barons who controlled the Mexican province before American acquisition. By the time he related the story of this life in the 1870s, his estate had been reduced to a few acres surrounding his home in Sonoma, in the northern part of the state. In this passage, he gave his views of the American-led insurrection of 1846.

SOURCE: Paul Lauter et al., eds., *The Heath Anthology of American Literature* (1990), pp. 1957–1959.

On the fourth day that Mr. Ide was in command at the Sonoma *plaza* and when he saw that a great number of Americans and foreigners had hurried in to place themselves under his protection, being fearful lest the Californians would attack them on their *ranchos* should they continue to live scattered over the country, he issued a document in which he set forth the reasons that had impelled him to refuse to recognize the authority of the Mexican government. The original proclamation, which was very brief, merely stated that, since the lives of foreigners were in imminent danger, he had felt it his duty to declare Alta California independent and that, counting as he did upon the definite support and cooperation of the "fighting men" who had rallied around him, he aimed to do all he could to prevent the Californians or the Mexicans from recovering the military post and arms which the valor of his men had seized from them. This is approximately what "Captain" Ide read aloud before the original proclamation was destroyed and that a few weeks later another was drawn up which, it was said, contained a list of the wrongs which the Mexican authorities had perpetrated against United States citizens.

After the reading of the Commander-in-chief's proclamation, they proceeded with great ceremony to hoist the flag by virtue of which those who had assaulted my home and who had by that time appropriated to themselves two hundred fifty muskets and nine cannon proposed to carry on their campaign.

This flag was nothing more nor less than a strip of white cotton stuff with a red edge and upon the white part, almost in the center, were written the words "California

Republic." Also on the white part, almost in the center, there was painted a bear with lowered head. The bear was so badly painted, however, that it looked more like a pig than a bear. The material for the flag was furnished, according to some, by Mrs. Elliot; according to others by Mrs. Sears. I also heard it said that Mrs. Grigsby furnished it.

Those who helped to prepare, sew and paint the flag were the following young men: Alexander Todd, Thomas Cowie and Benjamin Duell. The latter was the one who suggested that a star be painted near the mouth of the bear. Of course, both the bear and the star were very badly drawn, but that should not be wondered at, if one takes into consideration the fact that they lacked brushes and suitable colors.

The running up of this queer flag caused much fear to the families of the Californians established in the neighborhood of Sonoma, Petaluma and San Rafael, for they realized that the instigators of the uprising that had disturbed the tranquility of the frontier had made up their minds to rule, come what might, and, as the rumor had been spread far and wide that Ide and his associates had raised the bear flag in order to enjoy complete liberty and not be obliged to render any account of their activities to any civilized governments, the ranchers, who would have remained unperturbed should the American flag have been run up in Sonoma and who would have considered it as the harbinger of a period of progress and enlightenment, seized their *machetes* and guns and fled to the woods, determined to await a propitious moment for getting rid of the disturbers of the peace. Strange to relate, the first victim that the ranchers sacrificed was the painter of the "Bear Flag," young Thomas Cowie, who, along with P. Fowler, was on his way to Fitch's ranch to get one-eyed Moses Carson (brother of the famous explorer Colonel Kit Carson), who was employed as an overseer by Captain Henry Fitch, to give them a half barrel of powder he had locked up in one of the storage closets of his farmhouse. Fowler and Cowie were taken by surprise at the Yulupa Rancho by the party operating under the command of Captains Padilla and Ramón Carrillo, who at the request of the people had assumed direction of the hostilities it had been decided to undertake against "the Bears." Neither of the two extemporaneous commanders thought it right to take the lives of their young captives, upon whom there had been found letters that proved beyond any doubt that Moses Carson and certain others of the Americans employed at the Fitch Ranch were in accord with Ide, Merritt and others of those who had made up their minds to put an end to Mexican domination in California; so they decided to tie them up to a couple of trees while they deliberated as to what should be done with the captives, whose fate was to be decided at the meeting that night to which had been summoned all the ranchers who by their votes had shared in entrusting command of the Californian forces to those wealthy citizens, Padilla and Carrillo. I am of the opinion that the lives of Cowie and Fowler would have been spared, had it not been that a certain Bernardo García, better known under the name of "Three-fingered Jack," taken advantage of the darkness of the night, approached the trees to which the captives were tied and put an end to their existence with his well-sharpened dagger.

After committing the two murders I have just told about, Bernardo García entered the lonely hut in which Padilla, Carrillo and others had met and were discussing as to what disposition should be made of the prisoners. Without waiting for them to ask him any questions, he said to his compatriots, "I thought you here were going to decide to free the prisoners and, as that is not for the good of my country, I got ahead of you and took the lives of the Americans who were tied to the trees."

Those few words, spoken with the greatest of sangfroid by the wickedest man that California had produced up to that time, caused all who heard him to shudder. No one dared to object to what had been done, however, for they knew that such a step would have exposed them to falling under the knife of the dreaded Bernardo García, who for years past had been the terror of the Sonoma frontier.

Equally with the relatives of the unfortunate youths, Cowie and Fowler, I regretted their premature death, for, in spite of the fact that they belonged to a group of audacious men who had torn me from the bosom of my family and done as they pleased with my horses, saddles and arms, I did not consider that the simple fact that they were the bearers of a few letters made them deserving of the supreme penalty. Until that fatal June 21st, neither they nor their companions had shed any Mexican blood and it was not right for the Mexicans to begin a war *à outrance*, that could not help but bring very grievous consequences upon them and their families....

Some years ago (in 1868) when I was in Monterey, my friend, David Spence, showed me a book entitled "History of California," written by an author of recognized merit by the name of Franklin Tuthill, and called my attention to that part of the gentleman's narrative where he expresses the assurance that the guerrilla men whom Captain Fremont sent in pursuit of the Californian, Joaquín de la Torre, took nine field pieces from the latter. I could not help but be surprised when I read such a story, for I know for a fact that Captain de la Torre had only thirty cavalrymen under his command who as their only weapons carried a lance, carbine, saber and pistol. I think that Mr. Tuthill would have done better if, instead of inventing the capture of nine cannon, he had devoted a few lines to describing the vandal-like manner in which the "Bear" soldiers sacked the Olom-palí Rancho and maltreated the eighty year old Dámaso Rodríguez, Alférez retired, whom they beat so badly as to cause his death in the presence of his daughters and granddaughters. Filled with dismay, they gathered into their arms the body of the venerable old man who had fallen as a victim of the thirst for blood that was the prime mover of the guerrilla men headed by Mr. Ford.

I should indeed like to draw a veil over such a black deed, but the inexorable impartiality that is the guiding light of the historian prevents me from passing over a fact that so helps to reveal the true character of the men who on June 14, 1846, assaulted the *plaza* at Sonoma at a time when its garrison was in the central part of the *Departamento* busy curbing raids by the barbarous heathen. Let my readers not think that it is my desire to open up wounds that have healed over by now. I am very far from harboring any such thought, for ever since Alta California became a part of the great federation of the United States of North [America], I have spared no effort to establish upon a solid and enduring basis those sentiments of union and concord which are so indispensable for the progress and advancement of all those who dwell in my native land, and, so long as I live, I propose to use all the means at my command to see to it that both races cast a stigma upon the disagreeable events that took place on the Sonoma frontier in 1846. If before I pass on to render an account of my acts to the Supreme Creator, I succeed in being a witness to a reconciliation between victor and vanquished, conquerors and conquered, I shall die with the conviction of not having striven in vain.

In bringing this chapter to a close, I will remark that, if the men who hoisted the "Bear Flag" had raised the flag that Washington sanctified by his abnegation and patriotism, there would have been no war on the Sonoma frontier, for all our minds were prepared to give a brotherly embrace to the sons of the Great Republic, whose enterprising spirit had filled us with admiration. Ill-advisedly, however, as some say, or dominated by a desire to rule without let or hindrance, as others say, they placed themselves under the shelter of a flag that pictured a bear, an animal that we took as the emblem of rapine and force.

* * * * *

1. *Vallejo continually refers to the responsibilities of the historian. What does he think a historian should do? Does he live up to his own standards?*

2. *What is the significance of the Bear Flag as a symbol of the war in Sonoma? Who resisted the Bear Flag revolt? Why?*

3. *What similarities and/or differences does this event have in common with the war of independence in Texas?*

14–10   An American Army Officer Describes the Beginning of the California Gold Rush in 1848

Colonel R. B. Mason was commander of the First Dragoons of the U.S. Army in California when he wrote this letter to the Adjutant General in Washington, D.C., on August 17, 1848. His account was one of the first descriptions of Gold Rush California to appear in the East.

SOURCE: Joseph Warren Revere, *A Tour of Duty in California* (1849).

HEADQUARTERS 10TH MILITARY DEPOT
MONTEREY, CALIFORNIA SIR:
AUG. 17, 1848

SIR:

I have the honor to inform you that, accompanied by Lieutenant W.T. Sherman, I started on the twelfth of June last, to make a tour through the northern part of California. My principal purpose, however, was to visit the newly-discovered gold 'placer' in the Valley of the Sacramento. We reached San Francisco on the twentieth, and found that all, or nearly all its male inhabitants had gone to the mines. The town, which a few months before was so busy and thriving, was then almost deserted.

On the evening of the twenty-fifth, the horses of the escort were crossed to Sousolito in a launch, and on the following day we resumed the journey to Sutter's Fort, where we arrived on the morning of the second of July. Along the whole route, mills were lying idle, fields of wheat were open to cattle and horses, houses vacant, and farms going to waste. At Sutter's there was more life and business. Launches were discharging their cargoes at the river, and carts were hauling goods to the fort, where already were established several stores, a hotel, &c., (a Captain Sutter had only two mechanics in his employ, (a wagon-maker and blacksmith), to whom he was then paying ten dollars a day. Merchants pay him a monthly rent of one hundred dollars per room; and while I was there, a two-story house in the fort was rented as a hotel for five hundred dollars a month.

At the urgent solicitation of many gentlemen, I delayed there to participate in the first public celebration of our national anniversary at that fort, but on the fifth resumed the journey and proceeded twenty-five miles up the American fork, to a point on it known as the Lower Mines, or Mormon Diggings. The hill-sides were thickly strewn with canvass tents and bush arbors; a store was

erected, and several boarding shanties in operation. The day was intensely hot, yet about two hundred men were at work in the full glare of the sun, washing for gold—some with tin pans, some with close-woven Indian baskets, but the greater part had a rude machine, known as the cradle. This is on rockers, six or eight feet long, open at the foot, and at its head has a coarse grate, or sieve; the bottom is rounded, with small cleets nailed across. Four men are required to work this machine: one digs the ground in the bank close by the stream; another carries it to the cradle and empties it on the grate; a third gives a violent rocking motion to the machine; while a fourth dashes on water from the stream itself.

The sieve keeps the coarse stones from entering the cradle, the current of water washes off the earthy matter, and the gravel is gradually carried out at the foot of the machine, leaving the gold mixed with a heavy fine black sand above the first cleets. The sand and gold mixed together are then drawn off through auger holes into the pan below, are dried in the sun, and afterwards separated by blowing off the sand. A party of four men thus employed at the lower mines averaged one hundred dollars a day. The Indians and those who have nothing but pans or willow baskets, gradually wash out the earth, and separate the gravel by hand, leaving nothing but the gold mixed with sand, which is separated in the manner before described. The gold in the lower mines is in fine bright scales, of which I send several specimens....

The most moderate estimate I could obtain from men acquainted with the subject, was, that upwards of four thousand men were working in the gold district, of whom more than one-half were Indians; and that from thirty to fifty thousand dollars' worth of gold, if not more, was daily obtained. The entire gold district, with very few exceptions of grants made some years ago by the Mexican authorities, is on land belonging to the United States. It was a matter of serious reflection to me, how I could secure to the government certain rents or fees for the privilege of procuring this gold; but upon considering the large extent of country, the character of people engaged, and the small scattered force at my command, I resolved not to interfere, but to permit all to work freely, unless broils and crimes should call for interference. I was surprised to learn that crime of any kind was very infrequent, and that no thefts or robberies had been committed in the gold district.

All live in tents, in bush arbors, or in the open air; and men have frequently about their persons thousands of dollars worth of this gold, and it was to me a matter of surprise that so peaceful and quiet state of things should continue to exist. Conflicting claims to particular spots of ground may cause collisions, but they will be rare, as the extent of country is so great, and the gold so abundant, that for the present there is room enough for all. Still the government is entitled to rents for this land, and immediate steps should be devised to collect them, for the longer it is delayed the more difficult it will become.

The discovery of these vast deposits of gold has entirely changed the character of Upper California. Its people, before engaged in cultivating their small patches of ground, and guarding their herds of cattle and horses, have all gone to the mines, or are on their way thither. Laborers of every trade have left their work-benches, and tradesmen their shops. Sailors desert their ships as fast as they arrive on the coast, and several vessels have gone to sea with hardly enough hands to spread a sail. Two or three are now at anchor in San Francisco with no crew on board. Many desertions, too, have taken place from the garrisons within the influence of these mines; twenty-six soldiers have deserted from the post of Sonoma, twenty-four from that of San Francisco, and twenty-four from Monterey. For a few days the evil appeared so threatening, that grave danger existed that the garrisons would leave in a body. I shall spare no exertions to apprehend and punish deserters, but I believe no time in the history of our country has presented such temptations to desert as now exist in California.

The danger of apprehension is small, and the prospect of high wages certain; pay and bounties are trifles, as laboring men at the mines can now earn in *one day* more than double a soldier's pay and allowances for a month, and even the pay of a lieutenant or captain cannot hire a servant. A carpenter or mechanic would not listen to an offer of less than fifteen or twenty dollars a day. Could any combination of affairs try a man's fidelity more than this? I really think some extraordinary mark of favor should be given to those soldiers who remain faithful to their flag throughout this tempting crisis. No officer can now live in California on his pay, money has so little value; the prices of necessary articles of clothing and subsistence are so exorbitant, and labor so high, that to hire a cook or servant has become an impossibility, save to those who are earning from thirty to fifty dollars a day. This state of things cannot last forever. Yet from the geographical position of California, and the new character it has assumed as a mining country, prices of labor will always be high, and will hold out temptations to desert. If the government wish to prevent desertions here on the part of men, and to secure zeal on the part of officers, their pay must be increased very materially.

Many private letters have gone to the United States giving accounts of the vast quantity of gold recently discovered, and I have no hesitation now in saying that there is more gold in the country drained by the Sacramento and San Joaquin rivers, than will pay the cost of the present war with Mexico a hundred times over. No capital is required to obtain this gold, as the laboring man wants nothing but his pick and shovel and tin pan, with which to dig and wash the gravel; and many frequently pick gold out of the crevices of the rocks with their butcher-knives, in pieces from one to six ounces.

Mr. Dye, a gentleman residing in Monterey, and worthy of every credit, has just returned from Feather River. He tells me that the company to which he belonged worked seven weeks and two days, with an average of fifty Indians, (washers?), and that their gross product was two hundred and seventy-three pounds of gold. His share, (one seventh), after paying all expenses, is about thirty-seven pounds, which he brought with him and exhibited in Monterey. I see no laboring man from the mines who does not show his two, three, or four pounds of gold. A soldier of the artillery company returned here a few days ago from the mines, having been absent on furlough twenty days. He made by trading and working during that time one thousand five hundred dollars. During these twenty days he was travelling ten or eleven days, leaving but a week, in which he made a sum of money greater than he receives in pay, clothes, and rations during a whole enlistment of five years. These statements appear incredible, but they are true.

The 'placer' gold is now substituted as the currency in this country; in trade it passes freely at sixteen dollars per ounce; as an article of commerce its value is not yet fixed. The only purchase I made was at twelve dollars the ounce. That is about the present cash value in the country, although it has been sold for less. The great demand for goods and provisions made by the sudden development in wealth, has increased the amount of commerce at San Francisco very much, and it will continue to increase.

I have the honor to be, your most ob't, serv't,

R.B. MASON
Colonel First Dragoons, Commanding

* * * * * *

1. How did the discovery of gold affect the economy of northern California?

2. What role did Indians play in the recovery of gold from the rivers? How were their lives changed by the Gold Rush?

3. In what ways did the Gold Rush, as described in this account, exemplify the frontier mythology of America?

chapter 15

The Coming Crisis, 1848–1861

15-1 The Lincoln-Douglas Debates, 1858

The fourth joint debate between Abraham Lincoln and Stephen Douglas took place in Charleston, Illinois on September 18, 1858. The Charleston debate was, in many ways, a homecoming for Lincoln since he had lived for many years in a neighboring town. He was the crowd favorite. Douglas did his best to tarnish the local hero, however, by accusing Lincoln of favoring black citizenship and equal rights for free slaves. Such a position would have been extremely unpopular at this time in antebellum Illinois.

SOURCE: Robert W. Johannsen, *The Lincoln-Douglas Debates of 1858* (New York: Oxford University Press, 1965), 195–200.

Mr. Lincoln said in his first remarks that he was not in favor of the social and political equality of the negro with the white man. Every where up north he has declared that he was not in favor of the social and political equality of the negro, but he would not say whether or not he was opposed to negroes voting and negro citizenship. I want to know whether he is for or against negro citizenship? He declared his utter opposition to the Dred Scott decision, and advanced as a reason that the court had decided that it was not possible for a negro to be a citizen under the Constitution of the United States. If he is opposed to the Dred Scott decision for that reason, he must be in favor of conferring the right and privilege of citizenship upon the negro! I have been trying to get an answer from him on that point, but have never yet obtained one, and I will show you why. In every speech made in the north he quoted the Declaration of Independence to prove that all men were created equal, and insisted that the phrase "all men," included the negro as well as the white man, and that the equality rested upon Divine law. Here is what he said on that point:

"I should like to know if, taking this old Declaration of Independence, which declares that all men are equal upon principle, and making exceptions to it, where will it stop? If one man says it does not mean a negro, why may not another say it does not mean some other man? If that declaration is not the truth, let us get the statute book in which we find it and bear it out."

Lincoln maintains there that the Declaration of Independence asserts that the negro is equal to the white man, and that under Divine law, and if he believes so it was rational for him to advocate negro citizenship, which, when allowed, puts the negro on an equality under the law. I say to you in all frankness, gentlemen, that in my opinion a negro is not a citizen, cannot be, and ought not to be, under the Constitution of the United States. I will not even qualify my opinion to meet the declaration of one of the Judges of the Supreme Court in the Dred Scott case, "that a negro descended from African parents, Who was imported into this country as a slave is not a citizen, and cannot be." I say that this Government was established on the white basis. It was made by white men, for the benefit of white men and their posterity forever, and never should be administered by any except white men. I declare that a negro ought not to be a citizen, whether his parents were imported into this country as slaves or not, or whether or not he was born here. It does not depend upon the place a negro's parents were born, or whether they were slaves or not, but upon the fact that he is a negro, belonging to a race incapable of self-government, and for that reason ought not to be on an equality with white men....

...In conclusion, let me ask you why should this Government be divided by a geographical line—arraying all men North in one great hostile party against all men South? Mr. Lincoln tells you, in his speech at Springfield, "that a house divided against itself cannot stand; that this Government, divided into free and slave States, cannot endure permanently; that they must either be all free or all slave; all one thing or all the other." Why cannot this Government endure divided into free and slave States, as our fathers made it? When this Government was established by Washington, Jefferson, Madison, Jay, Hamilton, Franklin, and the other sages and patriots of that day, it was composed of free States and slave States, bound together by one common Constitution. We have existed and prospered from that day to this thus divided, and have increased with a rapidity never before equaled in wealth, the extension of territory, and all the elements of power and greatness, until we have become the first nation of the face of the globe. Why can we not thus continue to prosper? We can if we will live up to and execute the Government upon those principles upon which our fathers established it. During the whole period of our existence Divine Providence has smiled upon us, and showered upon our nation richer and more abundant blessings than have ever been conferred upon any other.

Mr. Lincoln's Rejoinder

FELLOW CITIZENS:...Judge Douglas has said to you that he has not been able to get from me an answer to the question whether I am in favor of negro citizenship. So far as I know, the Judge never asked me the question before. He shall have no occasion to ever ask it again, for I tell him very frankly that I am not in favor of negro citizenship....Now my opinion is that the different States have the power to make a negro a citizen under the Constitution of the United States if they choose. The Dred Scott decision decides that they have not that power. If the State of Illinois had that power I should be opposed to the exercise of it. This is all I have to say about it.

Judge Douglas has told me that he heard my speeches north and my speeches south—that he had heard me at Ottawa and at Freeport in the north, and recently at Jonesboro in the south, and there was a very different cast of sentiment in the speeches made at the different points. I will not charge upon Judge Douglas that he willfully misrepresents me, but I call upon every fair-minded man to take these speeches and read them, *and I dare him to point out any difference between my speeches north and south.* While I am here perhaps I ought to say a word, if I have the time, in regard to the latter portion of the Judge's speech, which was a sort of declamation in reference to my having said I entertained the belief that this Government would not endure, half slave and half free. I have said so, and I did not say it without what seemed to me to be good reasons. It perhaps would require more time than I have now to set forth these reasons in detail; but let me ask you a few questions. Have we ever had any peace on this slavery question? When are we to have peace upon it if it is kept in the position it now occupies? How are we ever to have peace upon it? That is an important question. To be sure, if we will all stop and allow Judge Douglas and his friends to march on in their present career until they plant the institution all over the nation, here and wherever else our flag waves, and we acquiesce in it, there will be peace. But let me ask Judge Douglas how he is going to get the people to do that? They have been wrangling over this question for at least forty years. This was the cause of the agitation resulting in the Missouri Compromise—this produced the troubles at the annexation of Texas, in the acquisition of the territory acquired in the Mexican war. Again, this was the trouble which was quieted by the Compromise of 1850, when it was settled, *"forever,"* as both the great political parties declared in their National Conventions. That "forever" turned out to be just four years, *when Judge Douglas himself reopened it.* When is it likely to come to an end? He introduced the Nebraska bill in 1854 to put *another end* to the slavery agitation. He

promised that it would finish it all up immediately....Now he tells us again that it is all over, and the people of Kansas have voted down the Lecompton Constitution....Now, at this day in the history of the world we can no more foretell where the end of this slavery agitation will be than we can see the end of the world itself. The Nebraska-Kansas bill was introduced four years and a half ago, and if the agitation is ever to come to an end, we may say we are four years and a half nearer the end. So, too, we can say we are four years and a half nearer the end of the world; and we can just as clearly see the end of the world as we can see the end of this agitation. The Kansas settlement did not conclude it. If Kansas should sink to-day, and leave a great vacant space in the earth's surface, this vexed question would still be among us. I say, then, there is no way of putting an end to the slavery agitation amongst us but to put it back upon the basis where our fathers placed it, no way but to keep it out of our new Territories—to restrict it forever to the old States where it now exists. Then the public mind *will* rest in the belief that it is in the course of ultimate extinction. That is one way of putting an end to the slavery agitation.

The other way is for us to surrender and let Judge Douglas and his friends have their way and plant slavery over all the States—cease speaking of it as in any way a wrong—regard slavery as one of the common matters of property, and speak of negroes as we do of our horses and cattle. But while it drives on in its state of progress as it is now driving, and as it has driven for the last five years, I have ventured the opinion, and I say to-day, that we will have no end to the slavery agitation until it takes one turn or the other. I do not mean that when it takes a turn toward ultimate extinction it will be in a day, nor in a year, nor in two years. I do not suppose that in the most peaceful way ultimate extinction would occur in less than a hundred years at least; but that it will occur in the best way for both races, in God's own good time, I have no doubt. But, my friends, I have used up more of my time than I intended on this point.

* * * * *

1. *Lincoln answers Douglas's accusation of favoring black citizenship by making very clear that he is against it. What, instead, does Lincoln favor? How does he propose to achieve his goal?*

2. *For Lincoln and Douglas, the most important issue facing the future of the Union is the extension of slavery. Why does Douglas believe that the Union can afford to have both slave and free states? Why does Lincoln disagree with him?*

15-2   Northern State Defies Fugitive Slave Act, 1855

Prior to the Fugitive Slave Act of 1850, many northern states had used personal liberty laws to delay the return of runaway slaves. The laws had not been passed for slaves, but rather to protect individual citizens and provide them with due process of law. The Fugitive Slave Act of 1850, however, angered many northern states who did indeed pass new personal liberty laws in defiance of the act. The Massachusetts Personal Liberty Act of 1855 was just one of these acts. The following sections from the act provide the penalties for those helping to return slaves, as well as outlining the rights of captured slaves.

SOURCE: Massachusetts, *Acts and Resolves* (Boston: Little, Brown, 1855).

Sec. 2. The meaning of the one hundred and eleventh chapter of the Revised Statutes is hereby declared to be, that every person imprisoned or restrained of his liberty is entitled, as of right and of course, to the writ of *habeas corpus*, except in the cases mentioned in the second section of that chapter.

Sec. 3. The writ of *habeas corpus* may be issued by the supreme judicial court, the court of common pleas, by any justice's court or police court of any town or city, by any court of record, or by any justice of either of said courts, or by any judge of probate; and it may be issued by any justice of the peace, if no magistrate above named is known to said justice of the peace to be within five miles of the place where the party is imprisoned or restrained, and it shall be returnable before the supreme judicial court, or any one of the justices thereof, whether the court may be in session or not, and in term time or vacation....

Sec. 6. If any claimant shall appear to demand the custody or possession of the person for whose benefit such writ is sued out, such claimant shall state in writing the facts on which he relies, with precision and certainty; and neither the claimant of the alleged fugitive, nor any person interested in his alleged obligation to service or labor, shall be permitted to testify at the trial of the issue; and no confessions, admissions or declarations of the alleged fugitive against himself shall be given in evidence. Upon every question of fact involved in the issue, the burden of proof shall be on the claimant, and the facts alleged and necessary to be established, must be proved by the testimony of at least two credible witnesses, or other legal evidence equivalent thereto, and by the rules of evidence known and secured by the common law; and no *ex parte* deposition or affidavit shall be received in

proof in behalf of the claimant, and no presumption shall arise in favor of the claimant from any proof that the alleged fugitive or any of his ancestors had actually been held as a slave, without proof that such holding was legal.

Sec. 7. If any person shall remove from the limits of this Commonwealth, or shall assist in removing therefrom, or shall come into the Commonwealth with the intention of removing or of assisting in the removing therefrom, or shall procure or assist in procuring to be so removed, any person being in the peace thereof who is not "held to service or labor" by the "party" making "claim," or who has not "escaped" from the "party" making "claim," within the meaning of those words in the constitution of the United States, on the pretence that such person is so held or has so escaped, or that his "service or labor" is so "due," or with the intent to subject him to such "service or labor," he shall be punished by a fine of not less than one thousand, nor more than five thousand dollars, and by imprisonment in the State Prison not less than one, nor more than five years....

Sec. 9. No person, while holding any office of honor, trust, or emolument, under the laws of this Commonwealth, shall, in any capacity, issue any warrant or other process, or grant any certificate, under or by virtue of an act of congress...or shall in any capacity, serve any such warrant or other process.

Sec. 10. Any person who shall grant any certificate under or by virtue of the acts of congress, mentioned in the preceding section, shall be deemed to have resigned any commission from the Commonwealth which he may possess, his office shall be deemed vacant, and he shall be forever thereafter ineligible to any office of trust, honor or emolument under the laws of this Commonwealth.

Sec. 11. Any person who shall act as counsel or attorney for any claimant of any alleged fugitive from service or labor, under or by virtue of the acts of congress mentioned in the ninth section of this act, shall be deemed to have resigned any commission from the Commonwealth that he may possess, and he shall be thereafter incapacitated from appearing as counsel or attorney in the courts of this Commonwealth....

Sec. 14. Any person holding any judicial office under the constitution or laws of this Commonwealth, who shall continue, for ten days after the passage of this act, to hold the office of United States commissioner, or any office...which qualifies him to issue any warrant or other process...under the [Fugitive Slave Acts] shall be deemed to have violated good behavior, to have given sufficient reason for the loss of public confidence, and furnished sufficient ground either for impeachment or for removal by address.

Sec. 15. Any sheriff, deputy sheriff, jailer, coroner, constable, or other officer of this Commonwealth, or the police of any city or town, or any district, county, city or town officer, or any officer or other member of the vol-unteer militia of this Commonwealth, who shall hereafter arrest...any person for the reason that he is claimed or adjudged to be a fugitive from service or labor, shall be punished by fine...and by imprisonment....

Sec. 16. The volunteer militia of the Commonwealth shall not act in any manner in the seizure...of any person for the reason that he is claimed or adjudged to be a fugitive from service or labor....

Sec. 19. No jail, prison, or other place of confine-ment belonging to, or used by, either the Commonwealth of Massachusetts or any county therein, shall be used for the detention or imprisonment of any person accused or convicted of any offence created by [the Federal Fugitive Slave Acts]...or accused or convicted of obstructing or resisting any process, warrant, or order issued under either of said acts, or of rescuing, or attempting to rescue, any person arrested or detained under any of the provi-sions of either of the said acts.

* * * * * *

1. *How does this act defy the Fugitive Slave Act of 1850? What are some of the specific points that would be in conflict?*

2. *Where was the abolitionist movement centered? What cities? What relationship do you think that has to this act?*

15-3 A New England Writer Portrays Slavery in 1852

Although she authored several books on New England, Harriet Beecher Stowe was best known for her portrayal of slavery in Uncle Tom's Cabin. The daughter of the most important Puritan preacher of her day, Stowe had a long concern with humanitarian causes. The death of one of Stowe's children prompted her to become involved with the abolitionist movement. Uncle Tom's Cabin outraged the south and solidified the anti-slavery movement in the north. Some even feel the book was one of the factors that brought on the Civil War. The following section finds Uncle Tom, recently purchased by the cruel Simon Legree, on his way to Legree's plantation.

SOURCE: Harriet Beecher Stowe, *Uncle Tom's Cabin; or, Life among the Lowly* (Boston: J.P. Jewett, 1851).

Trailing wearily behind a rude wagon, and over a ruder road, Tom and his associates faced onward.

In the wagon was seated Simon Legree; and the two women, still fettered together, were stowed away with some baggage in the back part of it, and the whole com-pany were seeking Legree's plantation, which lay a good distance off.

It was a wild, forsaken road, now winding through dreary pine barrens, where the wind whispered mournfully, and now over log causeways, through long cypress swamps, the doleful trees rising out of the slimy, spongy ground, hung with long wreaths of funereal black moss, while ever and anon the loathsome form of the moccasin snake might be seen sliding among broken stumps and shattered branch-es that lay here and there, rotting in the water.

It is disconsolate enough, this riding, to the stranger, who, with well-filled pocket and well-appointed horse, threads the lonely way on some errand of business; but wilder, drearier, to the man enthralled, whom every weary step bears further from all that man loves and prays for.

So one should have thought, that witnessed the sunken and dejected expression on those dark faces; the wistful, patient weariness with which those sad eyes rested on object after object that passed them in their sad journey.

Simon rode on, however, apparently well pleased, occasionally pulling away at a flask of spirit, which he kept in his pocket.

"I say, *you*" he said, as he turned back and caught a glance at the dispirited faces behind him! "Strike up a song, boys,—come!"

The men looked at each other, and the *"come"* was repeated, with a smart crack of the whip which the driver carried in his hands. Tom began a Methodist hymn.

"Jerusalem, my happy home,
Name ever dear to me!
When shall my sorrow have an end,
Thy joys when shall—"

"Shut up, you black cuss!" roared Legree; "did ye think I wanted any o' yer infernal old Methodism? I say, tune up, now, something real rowdy,—quick!"

One of the other men struck up one of those unmean-ing songs, common among the slaves.

"Mas'r see'd me cotch a coon,
High boys, high!
He laughed to split,—d'ye see the moon,
Ho! ho! ho! boys, ho!
Ho! yo! hi—e! oh!"

The singer appeared to make up the song to his own

pleasure, generally hitting on rhyme, without much attempt at reason; and all the party took up the chorus, at intervals,

"Ho! ho! ho! boys, ho!
High—e—oh! high—e—oh!"

It was sung very boisterously, and with a forced attempt at merriment; but no wail of despair, no words of impassioned prayer, could have had such a depth of woe in them as the wild notes of the chorus. As if the poor, dumb heart, threatened,—prisoned,—took refuge in that inarticulate sanctuary of music, and found there a language in which to breathe its prayer to God! There was a prayer in it, which Simon could not hear. He only heard the boys singing noisily, and was well pleased; he was making them "keep up their spirits."

"Well, my little dear," said he, turning, to Emmeline, and laying his hand on her shoulder, "we're almost home!"

When Legree scolded and stormed, Emmeline was terrified; but when he laid his hand on her, and spoke as he now did, she felt as if she had rather he would strike her. The expression of his eyes made her soul sick, and her flesh creep. Involuntarily she clung closer to the mulatto woman by her side, as if she were her mother.

"You didn't ever wear ear-rings," he said, taking hold of her small ear with his coarse fingers.

"No, Mas'r!" said Emmeline, trembling and looking down.

"Well, I'll give you a pair, when we get home, if you're a good girl. You needn't be so frightened; I don't mean to make you work very hard. You'll have fine times with me, and live like a lady,—only be a good girl."

Legree had been drinking to that degree that he was inclining to be very gracious; and it was about this time that the enclosures of the plantation rose to view. The estate had formerly belonged to a gentleman of opulence and taste, who had bestowed some considerable attention to the adornment of his grounds. Having died insolvent, it had been purchased, at a bargain, by Legree, who used it, as he did everything else, merely as an implement for money-making. The place had the ragged, forlorn appearance, which is always produced by the evidence that the care of the former owner has been left to go to utter decay.

What was once a smooth-shaven lawn before the house, dotted here and there with ornamental shrubs, was now covered with frowsy tangled grass, with horse-posts set up, here and there, in it, where the turf was stamped away, and the ground littered with broken pails, cobs of corn, and other slovenly remains. Here and there, a mildewed jessamine or honeysuckle hung raggedly from some ornamental support, which had been pushed to one side by being used as a horse-post. What once was a large

garden was now all grown over with weeds, through which, here and there, some solitary exotic reared its forsaken head. What had been a conservatory had now no window-sashes, and on the mouldering shelves stood some dry, forsaken flower-pots, with sticks in them, whose dried leaves showed they had once been plants.

The wagon rolled up a weedy gravel walk, under a noble avenue of China trees, whose graceful forms and ever-springing foliage seemed to be the only things there that neglect could not daunt or alter,—like noble spirits, so deeply rooted in goodness, as to flourish and grow stronger amid discouragement and decay.

The house had been large and handsome. It was built in a manner common at the South; a wide verandah of two stories running round every part of the house, into which every outer door opened, the lower tier being supported by brick pillars.

But the place looked desolate and uncomfortable; some windows stopped up with boards, some with shattered panes, and shutters hanging by a single hinge,—all telling of coarse neglect and discomfort.

Bits, of board, straw, old decayed barrels and boxes, garnished the ground in all directions; and three or four ferocious-looking dogs, roused by the sound of the wagon-wheels, came tearing out, and were with difficulty restrained from laying hold of Tom and his companions, by the effort of the ragged servants who came after them.

"Ye see what ye'd get!" said Legree, caressing the dogs with grim satisfaction, and turning to Tom and his companions. "Ye see what ye'd get, if ye try to run off. These yer dogs has been raised to track niggers; and they'd jest as soon chaw one on ye up as eat their supper. So, mind yerself! How now, Sambo!" he said, to a ragged fellow, without any brim to his hat, who was officious in his attentions. "How have things been going?"

"Fust rate, Mas'r."

"Quimbo," said Legree to another, who was making demonstrations to attract his attention, "ye minded what I telled ye?"

"Guess I did, didn't I?"

These two colored men were the two principal hands on the plantation. Legree had trained them in savageness and brutality as systematically as he had his bull-dogs; and, by long practice in hardness and cruelty, brought their whole nature to about the same range of capacities. It is a common remark, and one that is thought to militate strongly against the character of the race, that the Negro overseer is always more tyrannical and cruel than the white one. This is simply saying that the Negro mind has been more crushed and debased than the white. It is no more true of this race than of every oppressed race, the world over. The slave is always a tyrant, if he can get a chance to be one.

Legree, like some potentates we read of in history, governed his plantation by a sort of resolution of forces. Sambo and Quimbo cordially hated each other; the plantation hands, one and all, cordially hated them; and, by playing off one against another, he was pretty sure, through one or the other of the three parties, to get informed of whatever was on foot in the place.

Nobody can live entirely without social intercourse; and Legree encouraged his two black satellites to a kind of coarse familiarity with him,—a familiarity, however, at any moment liable to get one or the other of them into trouble; for, on the slightest provocation, one of them always stood ready, at a nod, to be a minister of his vengeance on the other.

As they stood there now by Legree, they seemed an apt illustration of the fact that brutal men are lower even than animals. Their coarse, dark, heavy features; their great eyes, rolling enviously on each other; their barbarous, guttural, half-brute intonation; their dilapidated garments fluttering in the wind,—were all in admirable keeping with the vile and unwholesome character of everything about the place.

"Here, you Sambo," said Legree, "take these yer boys down to the quarters; and here's a gal I've got for you," said he, as he separated the mulatto woman from Emmeline, and pushed her towards him;—"I promised to bring you one, you know."

The woman gave a sudden start, and, drawing back, said, suddenly,

"O, Mas'r! I left my old man in New Orleans."

"What of that, you—;won't you want one here? None o' your words,—go long!" said Legree, raising his whip.

"Come, mistress," he said to Emmeline, "you go in here with me."

A dark, wild face was seen, for a moment, to glance at the window of the house; and, as Legree opened the door, a female voice said something, in a quick, imperative tone. Tom, who was looking, with anxious interest, after Emmeline, as she went in, noticed this, and heard Legree answer angrily, "You may hold your tongue! I'll do as I please, for all you!"

Tom heard no more; for he was soon following Sambo to the quarters. The quarters was a little sort of street of rude shanties, in a row, in a part of the plantation, far off from the house. They had a forlorn, brutal, forsaken air. Tom's heart sank when he saw them. He had been comforting himself with the thought of a cottage, rude, indeed, but one which he might make neat and quiet, and where he might have a shelf for his Bible, and a place to be alone out of his laboring hours. He looked into several; they were mere rude shells, destitute of any species of furniture, except a heap of straw, foul with dirt, spread confusedly over the floor, which was merely the bare ground, trodden hard by the tramping of innumerable feet.

"Which of these will be mine?" said he, to Sambo, submissively.

"Dunno; ken turn in here, I spose," said Sambo; "spects thar's room for another thar; thar's a pretty smart heap o' niggers to each on 'em, now; sure, I dunno what I's to do with more."

* * * * * *

1. If Uncle Tom's Cabin was indeed one of the factors in starting the Civil War, what does this say about the role of fiction in history? Is it worthy of consideration by historians? Why would this book have inflamed the south? Why would it have been so widely read in the north?

2. How does Stowe's portrayal of slave life compare with actual accounts you have read elsewhere?

15–4 An African American Decries the Fourth of July in 1852

Frederick Douglass escaped from slavery in 1838 and made his way to New England. By 1841, Douglass was relating his experiences at abolitionist meetings throughout the eastern states. Douglass's book, the Narrative of the Life of Frederick Douglass (1845), forced him to flee to England as he had revealed his place of escape. However, liberal friends purchased Douglass's freedom and he was able to return to Rochester and start his abolitionist newspaper, the North Star. Active in the freedom railroad, Douglass continued to lecture and write on slavery. The following section is taken from a speech in Rochester, N.Y. on July 5, 1852 in which Douglass asks, "What to a Slave is the Fourth of July?"

SOURCE: Frederick Douglass, What to a Slave is the Fourth of July? (Rochester, NY: The author, 1852).

...Fellow-citizens, pardon me, allow me to ask, why am I called upon to speak here to-day? What have I, or those I represent, to do with your national independence? Are the great principles of political freedom and of natural justice, embodied in that Declaration of Independence, extended to us? and am I, therefore, called upon to bring our humble offering to the national altar, and to confess the benefits and express devout gratitude for the blessings resulting from your independence to us?

Would to God, both for your sakes and ours, that an affirmative answer could be truthfully returned to these questions! Then would my task be light, and my burden easy and delightful. For *who* is there so cold, that a nation's sympathy could not warm him? Who so obdurate and dead to the claims of gratitude, that would not thankfully acknowledge such priceless benefits? Who so stolid and selfish, that would not give his voice to swell the hallelujahs of a nation's jubilee, when the chains of servitude had been torn from his limbs? I am not that man. In a case like that, the dumb might eloquently speak, and the "lame man leap as an hart."

But, such is not the state of the case. I say it with a sad sense of the disparity between us. I am not included within the pale of this glorious anniversary! Your high independence only reveals the immeasurable distance between us. The blessings in which you, this day, rejoice, are not enjoyed in common. The rich inheritance of justice, liberty, prosperity and independence, bequeathed by your fathers, is shared by you, not by me. The sunlight that brought life and healing to you, has brought stripes and death to me. This Fourth [of] July is *yours*, not *mine. You* may rejoice, *I* must mourn. To drag a man in fetters into the grand illuminated temple of liberty, and call upon him to join you in joyous anthems, were inhuman mockery and sacrilegious irony. Do you mean, citizens, to mock me, by asking me to speak today? If so, there is a parallel to your conduct. And let me warn you that it is dangerous to copy the example of a nation whose crimes, towering up to heaven, were thrown down by the breath of the Almighty, burying that nation in irrecoverable ruin! I can to-day take up the plaintive lament of a peeled and woe-smitten people!

"By the rivers of Babylon, there we sat down. Yea! we wept when we remembered Zion. We hanged our harps upon the willows in the midst thereof. For there, they that carried us away captive, required of us a song; and they who wasted us required of us mirth, saying, Sing us one of the songs of Zion. How can we sing the Lord's song in a strange land? If I forget thee, O Jerusalem, let my right hand forget her cunning. If I do not remember thee, let my tongue cleave to the roof of my mouth."

Fellow-citizens; above your national, tumultuous joy, I hear the mournful wail of millions! whose chains, heavy and grievous yesterday, are, to-day, rendered more intolerable by the jubilee shouts that reach them. If I do forget, if I do not faithfully remember those bleeding children of sorrow this day, "may my right hand forget her cunning, and may my tongue cleave to the roof of my mouth!" To forget them, to pass lightly over their wrongs, and to chime in with the popular theme, would be treason most scandalous and shocking, and would make me a reproach before God and the world. My subject, then, fel-

low-citizens, is AMERICAN SLAVERY. I shall see, this day, and its popular characteristics, from the slave's point of view. Standing, there, identified with the American bond-man, making his wrongs mine, I do not hesitate to declare, with all my soul, that the character and conduct of this nation never looked blacker to me than on this 4th of July! Whether we turn to the declarations of the past, or to the professions of the present, the conduct of the nation seems equally hideous and revolting. America is false to the past, false to the present, and solemnly binds herself to be false to the future. Standing with God and the crushed and bleeding slave on this occasion, I will, in the name of humanity which is outraged, in the name of liberty which is fettered, in the name of the constitution and the Bible, which are disregarded and trampled upon, dare to call in question and to denounce, with all the emphasis I can command, everything that serves to per-petuate slavery—the great sin and shame of America! "I will not equivocate; I will not excuse"; I will use the severest language I can command; and yet not one word shall escape me that any man, whose judgement is not blinded by prejudice, or who is not at heart a slaveholder, shall not confess to be right and just.

But I fancy I hear some one of my audience say, it is just in this circumstance that you and your brother abolitionists fail to make a favorable impression on the public mind. Would you argue more, and denounce less, would you persuade more, and rebuke less, your cause would be much more likely to succeed. But, I submit, where all is plain there is nothing to be argued. What point in the anti-slavery creed would you have me argue? On what branch of the subject do the people of this country need light? Must I undertake to prove that the slave is a man? That point is conceded already. Nobody doubts it. The slaveholders themselves acknowledge it in the enact-ment of law, for their government. They acknowledge it when they punish disobedience on the part of the slave. There are seventy-two crimes in the State of Virginia, which, if committed by a black man, (no matter how ignorant he be), subject him to the punishment of death; while only two of the same crimes will subject a white man to the like punishment. What is this but the acknowl-edgement that the slave is a moral, intellectual and responsible being? The manhood of the slave is conced-ed. It is admitted in the fact that Southern statute books are covered with enactments forbidding, under severe fines and penalties, the teaching of the slave to read or to write. When you can point to any such laws, in reference to the beasts of the field, then I may consent to argue the manhood of the slave. When the dogs in your streets, when the fowls of the air, when the cattle on your hills, when the fish of the sea, and the reptiles that crawl, shall be unable to distinguish the slave from a brute, *then* will I argue with you that the slave is a man!...

* * * * * *

1. What is Douglass's central argument? Do you agree?

2. Douglass's tone is almost insulting. What effect do you think this might have had on his audience? Why would he have consciously adopted it?

15–5 A Slave Sues for Freedom in 1857

Although several slaves had previously sued for freedom, Dred Scott v. Sandford, or the Dred Scott decision, is by far the most famous case. The crux of the case was that Scott, a slave, had been taken to a slave-free territory by his master; and thus, being technically free, was always free. Scott later sued for his freedom on this basis. However, the case became a legal nightmare. All nine justices of the Supreme Court wrote opinions, and it is still not entirely clear what was decided. The court ruled that Scott was not a citizen, and thus had no right to sue. But at the behest of President Buchanan, the court tried to decide the political issue of slavery in court. The basic finding was that slaves were property and could never be citizens, and hence never sue in court. Also, as property, slaves and slavery could not be prohibited in free states or territories because it would deprive an owner of his property. The case only further fueled the growing slavery/anti-slavery factionalism in Congress, and was another step on the road to the civil war. The following excerpt from Chief Justice Taney's opinion describes the slave as property.

SOURCE: Cases Argued and Adjudged in the Supreme Court (1857).

Chief Justice Taney delivered the opinion of the Court.

The question is simply this: Can a negro, whose ancestors were imported into this country, and sold as slaves, become a member of the political community formed and brought into existence by the constitution of the United States, and as such become entitled to all the rights, and privileges, and immunities, guaranteed by that instrument to the citizen? One of which rights is the privilege of suing in a court of the United States in the cases specified in the constitution....

...These powers, and others, in relation to rights of person, which it is not necessary here to enumerate, are, in express and positive terms, denied to the general government; and the rights of private property have been guarded with equal care. Thus the rights of property are united with the rights of person and placed on the same ground by the Fifth Amendment to the Constitution, which provides that no person shall be deprived of life, liberty, and property without due process of law. And an act of Congress which deprives a citizen of the United States of his liberty or property, without due process of law, merely because he came himself or brought his property into a particular territory of the United States, and who had committed no offense against the laws, could hardly be dignified with the name of due process of law....

It seems, however, to be supposed that there is a difference between property in a slave and other property, and that different rules may be applied to it in expounding the Constitution of the United States. And the laws and usages of nations, and the writings of eminent jurists upon the relation of master and slave and their mutual rights and duties, and the powers which governments may exercise over it, have been dwelt upon in the argument.

But, in considering the question before us, it must be borne in mind that there is no law of nations standing between the people of the United States and their government and interfering with their relation to each other. The powers of the government and the rights of the citizen under it are positive and practical regulations plainly written down. The people of the United States have delegated to it certain enumerated powers and forbidden it to exercise others. It has no power over the person or property of a citizen but what the citizens of the United States have granted. And no laws or usages of other nations, or reasoning of statesmen or jurists upon the relations of master and slave, can enlarge the powers of the government or take from the citizens the rights they have reserved. And if the Constitution recognizes the right of property of the master in a slave, and makes no distinction between that description of property and other property owned by a citizen, no tribunal, acting under the authority of the United States, whether it be legislative, executive, or judicial, has a right to draw such a distinction or deny to it the benefit of the provisions and guaranties which have been provided for the protection of private property against the encroachments of the government.

Now, as we have already said in an earlier part of this opinion, upon a different point, the right of property in a slave is distinctly and expressly affirmed in the Constitution. The right to traffic in it, like an ordinary article of merchandise and property, was guaranteed to the citizens of the United States, in every state that might desire it, for twenty years. And the government in express terms is pledged to protect it in all future time if the slave escapes from his owner. That is done in plain words—too plain to be misunderstood. And no word can be found in the Constitution which gives Congress a greater power over slave property or which entitles property of that kind to less protection than property of any other description. The only power conferred is the power coupled with the duty of guarding and protecting the owner in his rights.

Upon these considerations it is the opinion of the Court that the act of Congress which prohibited a citizen from holding and owning property of this kind in the territory of the United States north of the line therein mentioned is not warranted by the Constitution and is therefore void; and that neither Dred Scott himself, nor any of his family, were made free by being carried into this territory; even if they had been carried there by the owner with the intention of becoming a permanent resident.

* * * * *

1. *What is the status of slaves as declared in this decision? What are the legal justifications?*

2. *Why would the Supreme Court have become involved in what was essentially a political, rather than legal, issue?*

3. *Why would the South have been happy with this decision and the North enraged? Why would this case have fueled the fires of war?*

15-6   A Senatorial Candidate Addresses the Question of Slavery in 1858

The quintessential American politician, Abraham Lincoln was a self-made man, self-educated, and had risen to power based on his wit and honesty. Having studied the law on his own, Lincoln had become one of the most successful lawyers in Illinois, and in 1858 was running against Stephan A. Douglas for the United States Senate. In his famous "The House Divided Speech," part of which appears here, Lincoln argues that the United States cannot be half slave and half free. In the following section, Lincoln discusses the Kansas-Nebraska Bill which allowed new territories to decide slavery for themselves, nullifying the earlier Missouri Compromise.

SOURCE: Philip Van Doren Stern, ed., *The Life and Writings of Abraham Lincoln* (New York: The Modern Library, 1940).

If we could first know where we are, and whither we are tending, we could better judge what to do, and how to do it. We are now far into the fifth year since a policy was initiated with the avowed object and confident promise of putting an end to slavery agitation. Under the operation of that policy that agitation has not only not ceased, but has constantly augmented. In my opinion, it will not cease until a crisis shall have been reached and passed. "A house divided against itself can not stand." I believe this Government can not endure permanently half slave and half free. I do not expect the Union to be dissolved—I do not expect the house to fall—but I do expect it will cease to be divided. It will become all one thing, or all the other. Either the opponents of slavery will arrest the further spread of it, and place it where the public mind shall rest in the belief that it is in course of ultimate extinction; or its advocates will push it forward till it shall become alike lawful in all the States, old as well as new, North as well as South.

Have we no tendency to the latter condition? Let any one who doubts carefully contemplate that now almost complete legal combination—piece of machinery, so to speak—compounded of the Nebraska doctrine and the Dred Scott decision. Let him consider not only what work the machinery is adapted to do, and how well adapted; but also let him study the history of its construction, and trace, if he can, or rather fail, if he can, to trace the evidences of design and concert of action among its chief master-workers from the beginning.

The new year of 1854 found slavery excluded from more than half the States by State Constitutions, and from most of the national territory by Congressional prohibition. Four days later commenced the struggle which ended in repealing that Congressional prohibition. This opened all the national territory to slavery, and was the first point gained.

But, so far, Congress only had acted; and an indorsement by the people, real or apparent, was indispensable to save the point already gained and give chance for more. This necessity had not been overlooked, but had been provided for, as well as might be, in the notable argument of "squatter sovereignty," otherwise called "sacred right of self-government," which latter phrase, though expressive of the only rightful basis of any government, was so perverted in this attempted use of it as to amount to just this: that if any one man choose to enslave another, no third man shall be allowed to object. That argument was incorporated into the Nebraska Bill itself, in the language which follows: "It being the true intent and meaning of this act not to legislate slavery into any Territory or State, nor to exclude it therefrom; but to leave the people thereof perfectly free to form and regulate their domestic institutions in their own way, subject only to the Constitution of the United States."

Then opened the roar of loose declamation in favor of "squatter sovereignty" and "sacred right of self-government."

"But," said opposition members; "let us amend the bill so as to expressly declare that the people of the territory may exclude slavery." "Not we," said the friends of the measure; and down they voted the amendment.

While the Nebraska Bill was passing through Congress, a law case involving the question of a Negro's freedom, by reason of his owner having voluntarily taken him first into a free State and then a territory covered by the Congressional prohibition, and held him as a slave for a long time in each, was passing through the U.S. Circuit Court for the District of Missouri and both the Nebraska Bill and law suit were brought to a decision in the same month of May, 1854. The Negro's name was "Dred Scott," which name now designates the decision finally made in the case.

Before the then next Presidential election, the law case came to and was argued in the Supreme Court of the United States; but the decision of it was deferred until after the election. Still, before the election, Senator Trumbull, on the floor of the Senate, requested the leading advocate of the Nebraska Bill to state his opinion whether the people of a territory can constitutionally exclude slavery from their limits; and the latter answered, "That is a question for the Supreme Court."

The election came. Mr. Buchanan was elected, and the indorsement, such as it was, secured. That was the second point gained. The indorsement, however, fell short of a clear popular majority by nearly four hundred thousand votes, and so, perhaps, was not overwhelmingly reliable and satisfactory. The outgoing President, in his last annual message, as impressively as possible echoed back upon the people the weight and authority of the indorsement.

The Supreme Court met again; did not announce their decision, but ordered a re-argument. The Presidential inauguration came, and still no decision of the court; but the incoming President, in his Inaugural Address, fervently exhorted the people to abide by the forthcoming decision, whatever it might be. Then, in a few days came the decision.

This was the third point gained.

The reputed author of the Nebraska Bill finds an early occasion to make a speech at this capitol indorsing the Dred Scott decision, and vehemently denouncing all opposition to it. The new President, too, seizes an early occasion to indorse and strongly construe that decision, and to express his astonishment that any different view had ever been entertained!

At length a squabble springs up between the President and the author of the Nebraska Bill, on the mere question of fact, whether the Lecompton Constitution was or was not, in any just sense, made by the people of Kansas; and in that quarrel the latter declares that all he wants is a fair vote for the people, and that he cares not whether slavery be voted down or voted up. I do not understand his declaration that he cares not whether slavery be voted down or voted up to be intended by him other than as an apt definition of the policy he would impress upon the public mind—the principle for which he declares he has suffered much, and is ready to suffer to the end....

* * * * * *

1. What are the central points of the Kansas-Nebraska Act [Nebraska Bill] as outlined in Lincoln's speech? Where does it leave the issue of slavery?

2. Judging from Lincoln's speech, what is his personal position on slavery?

15–7   An Abolitionist Is Given the Death Sentence in 1859

John Brown was one of the most radical abolitionists in the movement. Actively advocating armed violence in the name of anti-slavery, Brown made several raids in the name of freeing of slaves. Brown and his followers attacked several pro-slavery settlers in Lawrence, Kansas and hacked them to death. Brown also killed a slaveowner and freed several slaves in Missouri. In October of 1859, Brown attacked and seized the U.S. Arsenal at Harpers Ferry, Virginia in his hopes to arm the slaves for rebellion. Brown was captured after a deadly battle with federal and state troops and charged with murder, treason, and insurrection. He was hanged on December 2, 1859. Brown lost the battle, but he won the war against slavery, having increased the pressure to end slavery nationwide. His speech after his conviction was printed in several newspapers, and is reproduced here.

SOURCE: John Brown, *Address of John Brown to the Virginia Court at Charles Town* (NP: n.p., 1859)

I have, may it please the Court, a few words to say.

In the first place, I deny everything but what I have all along admitted; of a design on my part to free slaves.

I intended certainly to have made a clean thing of that matter, as I did last winter, when I went into Missouri and there took slaves without the snapping of a gun on either side, moving them through the country, and finally leaving them in Canada. I designed to have done the same thing again on a larger scale. That was all I intended. I never did intend murder, or treason, or the destruction of property, or to exercise or incite slaves to rebellion, or to make insurrection.

I have another objection, and that is that it is unjust that I should suffer such a penalty. Had I interfered in the manner which I admit, and which I admit has been fairly proved—for I admire the truthfulness and candor of the greater portion of the witnesses who have testified in this case—Had I so interfered in behalf of the rich, the powerful, the intelligent, the so-called great, or in behalf of any of their friends, either father, mother, brother, sister, wife or children, or any of that class, and suffered and sacrificed what I have in this interference, it would have been all right. Every man in this Court would have deemed it an act worthy of reward rather than punishment.

This Court acknowledges, too, as I suppose, the validity of the law of God. I see a book kissed, which I suppose to be the Bible, or at least the New Testament, which teaches me that all things whatsoever I would that men should do to me, I should do even so to them. It teaches me, further, to remember them that are in bonds as bound with them. I endeavored to act up to that instruction. I say I am yet too young to understand that a God is any respecter of persons. I believe that to have interfered as I have done, as I have always freely admitted I have done, in behalf of His despised poor, I did no wrong, but right. Now, if it is deemed necessary that I should forfeit my life for the furtherance of the ends of justice, and mingle my blood further with the blood of my children and

with the blood of millions in this slave country whose rights are disregarded by wicked, cruel, and unjust enactments, I say, let it be done.

Let me say one word further. I feel entirely satisfied with the treatment I have received on my trial. Considering all the circumstances, it has been more generous than I expected. But I feel no consciousness of guilt. I have stated from the first what was my intention, and what was not. I never had any design against the liberty of any person, nor any disposition to commit treason or incite slaves to rebel or make any general insurrection. I never encouraged any man to do so, but always discouraged any idea of that kind.

Let me say, also, in regard to the statements made by some of those who were connected with me, I hear it has been stated by some of them that I have induced them to join me. But the contrary is true. I do not say this to injure them, but as regretting their weakness. Not one but joined me of his own accord, and the greater part at their own expense. A number of them I never saw, and never had a word of conversation with, till the day they came to me, and that was for the purpose I have stated.

Now, I have done.

* * * * *

1. *Thoreau advocated civil disobedience. And the revolutionary fathers certainly took the law into their own hands and engaged in violence in protest of Britain. Why are John Brown's acts against slavery seen in a different light? What is the status of slaves at this time?*

2. *What do you think of Brown's actions? Was he right to take them?*

SOURCE: Henry Steele Commager, *Documents of American History* (N.Y.: Appleton-Century-Crofts, 1948).

15–8 Lincoln Is Elected and Southern Secession Begins in 1860

As Lincoln was elected president, South Carolina seceded from the union and advocated that the other slave-holding states do likewise. The state of South Carolina issued two papers, An Address to the People of the Slaveholding States, *and the* Declaration of the Causes of Secession. *The* Declaration *of December 24, 1860, is printed here after the actual* Ordinance of Secession, *passed four days before. The secession was the culmination of a long smoldering fight over the rights of states to govern themselves, which had centered around the issue of slavery.*

An Ordinance to Dissolve the Union between the State of South Carolina and other States united with her under the compact entitled the Constitution of the United States of America:

We, the people of the State of South Carolina, in Convention assembled, do declare and ordain, and it is hereby declared and ordained, that the ordinance adopted by us in Convention, on the 23d day of May, in the year of our Lord 1788, whereby the Constitution of the United States of America was ratified, and also all Acts and parts of Acts of the General Assembly of this State ratifying the amendments of the said Constitution, are hereby repealed, and that the union now subsisting between South Carolina and other States under the name of the United States of America is hereby dissolved.

The people of the State of South Carolina in Convention assembled, on the 2d day of April, A.D. 1852, declared that the frequent violations of the Constitution of the United States by the Federal Government, and its encroachments upon the reserved rights of the States, fully justified this State in their withdrawal from the Federal Union; but in deference to the opinions and wishes of the other Slaveholding States, she forbore at that time to exercise this right. Since that time these encroachments have continued to increase, and further forbearance ceases to be a virtue.

And now the State of South Carolina having resumed her separate and equal place among nations, deems it due to herself, to the remaining United States of America, and to the nations of the world, that she should declare the immediate causes which have led to this act.

In 1787, Deputies were appointed by the States to revise the articles of Confederation; and on 17th September, 1787, these Deputies recommended, for the adoption of the States, the Articles of Union, known as the Constitution of the United States.

...Thus was established by compact between the States, a Government with defined objects and powers, limited to the express words of the grant.... We hold that the Government thus established is subject to the two great principles asserted in the Declaration of Independence; and we hold further, that the mode of its formation subjects it to a third fundamental principle, namely, the law of compact. We maintain that in every compact between two or more parties, the obligation is mutual; that the failure of one of the contracting parties to perform a material part of the agreement, entirely releases the obligation of the other; and that, where no arbiter is provided, each party is remitted to his own judgment to determine the fact of failure, with all its consequences.

In the present case, that fact is established with certainty. We assert that fourteen of the States have deliberately refused for years past to fulfil their constitutional obligations, and we refer to their own statutes for the proof.

The Constitution of the United States, in its fourth Article, provides as follows:

"No person held to service or labor in one State is under the laws thereof, escaping into another, shall, in consequence of any law or regulation therein, be discharged from such service or labor, but shall be delivered up, on claim of the party to whom such service or labor may be due."

This stipulation was so material to the compact that without it that compact would not have been made. The greater number of the contracting parties held slaves, and they had previously evinced their estimate of the value of such a stipulation by making it a condition in the Ordinance for the government of the territory ceded by Virginia, which obligations, and the laws of the General government, have ceased to effect the objects of the Constitution. The States of Maine, New Hampshire, Vermont, Massachusetts, Connecticut, Rhode Island, New York, Pennsylvania, Illinois, Indiana, Michigan, Wisconsin and Iowa, have enacted laws at which either nullify the acts of Congress, or render useless any attempt to execute them. In many of these States the fugitive is discharged from the service of labor claimed, and in none of them has the State Government complied with the stipulation made in the Constitution. The State of New Jersey, at an early day, passed a law in conformity with her constitutional obligation; but the current of Anti-Slavery feeling has led her more recently to enact laws which render inoperative the remedies provided by her own laws and by the laws of Congress. In the State of New York even the right of transit for a slave has been denied by her tribunals; and the States of Ohio and Iowa have refused to surrender to justice fugitives charged with murder, and with inciting servile insurrection in the State of Virginia. Thus the constitutional compact has been deliberately broken and disregarded by the non-slaveholding States; and the consequence follows, that South Carolina is released from her obligation....

We affirm that these ends for which this Government was instituted have been defeated, and the Government itself has been destructive of them by the action of the non-slaveholding States. Those States have assumed the right of deciding upon the propriety of our domestic institutions; and have denied the rights of property established in fifteen of the States and recognized by the Constitution; they have denounced as sinful the institution of Slavery; they have permitted the open establishment among them of societies, whose avowed object is to disturb the peace of and eloin the property of the citizens of other States. They have encouraged and assisted thousands of our slaves to leave their homes; and those who remain, have been incited by emissaries, books, and pictures, to servile insurrection.

For twenty-five years this agitation has been steadily increasing, until it has now secured to its aid the power of the common Government. Observing the *forms* of the Constitution, a sectional party has found within that article establishing the Executive Department, the means of subverting the Constitution itself. A geographical line has been drawn across the Union, and all the States north of that line have united in the election of a man to the high office of President of the United States whose opinions and purposes are hostile to Slavery. He is to be intrusted with the administration of the common Government, because he has declared that "Government cannot endure permanently half slave, half free," and that the public mind must rest in the belief that Slavery is in the course of ultimate extinction.

This sectional combination for the subversion of the Constitution has been aided, in some of the States, by elevating to citizenship persons who, by the supreme law of the land, are incapable of becoming citizens; and their votes have been used to inaugurate a new policy, hostile to the South, and destructive of its peace and safety.

On the 4th of March next this party will take possession of the Government. It has announced that the South shall be excluded from the common territory, that the Judicial tribunal shall be made sectional, and that a war must be waged against Slavery until it shall cease throughout the United States.

The guarantees of the Constitution will then no longer exist; the equal rights of the States will be lost. The Slaveholding States will no longer have the power of self-government, or self-protection, and the Federal Government will have become their enemy.

Sectional interest and animosity will deepen the irritation; and all hope of remedy is rendered vain, by the fact that the public opinion at the North has invested a great political error with the sanctions of a more erroneous religious belief.

We, therefore, the people of South Carolina, by our delegates in Convention assembled, appealing to the Supreme Judge of the world for the rectitude of our intentions, have solemnly declared that the Union heretofore existing between this State and the other States of North America is dissolved, and that the State of South Carolina has resumed her position among the nations of the world, as a separate and independent state, with full power to levy war, conclude peace, contract alliances, establish commerce, and to do all other acts and things which independent States may of right do.

* * * * *

1. *Did the Constitution give states the right to secede? Review the statute.*

2. *What was at stake in South Carolina's decision to leave the union? What economic factors were involved? What northern business interests would be affected by southern secession? Where were goods manufactured? Where were raw materials obtained?*

15–9   *A New President Is Sworn In, in 1861*

Lincoln took his presidential oath on the Capitol steps March 4, 1861. A month before, seven states had seceded from the union. A month later, the first shots of the Civil War were fired at Fort Sumpter, and four more states seceded. Lincoln became president of a nation at the brink of civil war, on the edge of self-destruction. In his inaugural address, Lincoln made a last ditch effort to reconcile the differences between the states. Lincoln appealed to the southern states to rejoin the union, but he also made it clear that secession was illegal and that he would take whatever steps were necessary to maintain the integrity of the union. Part of Lincoln's speech is printed here.

SOURCE: James D. Richardson, ed., *A Compilation of the Messages and Papers of the President, 1789–1897* (Washington, D.C.: Government Printing Office, 1896-99).

most ample evidence to the contrary has all the while existed and been open to their inspection. It is found in nearly all the published speeches of him who now addresses you. I do but quote from one of those speeches when I declare that—I have no purpose, directly or indirectly, to interfere with the institution of slavery in the States where it exists. I believe I have no lawful right to do so, and I have no inclination to do so....

...Before entering upon so grave a matter as the destruction of our national fabric, with all its benefits, its memories, and its hopes, would it not be wise to ascertain precisely why we do it? Will you hazard so desperate a step while there is any possibility that any portion of the ills you fly from have no real existence? Will you, while the certain ills you fly to are greater than all the real ones you fly from, will you risk the commission of so fearful a mistake?

All profess to be content in the Union if all constitutional rights can be maintained. Is it true, then, that any right plainly written in the Constitution has been denied? I think not....

No organic law can ever be framed with a provision specifically applicable to every question which may occur in practical administration. No foresight can anticipate nor any document of reasonable length contain express provisions for all possible questions. Shall fugitives from labor be surrendered by national or by State authority? The Constitution does not expressly say. *May Congress*

...Apprehension seems to exist among the people of the Southern States that by the accession of a Republican Administration their property and their peace and personal security are to be endangered. There has never been any reasonable cause for such apprehension. Indeed, the

prohibit slavery in the Territories? The Constitution does not expressly say. *Must* Congress protect slavery in the Territories? The Constitution does not express-ly say.

From questions of this class spring all our con-stitutional controversies, and we divide upon them into majorities and minorities. If the minority will not acquiesce, the majority must, or the Government must cease. There is no other alternative, for continuing the Government is acquiescence on one side or the other. If a minority in such case will secede rather than acquiesce, they make a precedent which in turn will divide and ruin them, for a minority of their own will secede from them whenever a majority refuses to be controlled by such minority. For instance, why may not any portion of a new confederacy a year or two hence arbitrarily secede again, precisely as portions of the present Union now claim to secede from it? All who cherish disunion sentiments are now being edu-cated to the exact temper of doing this.

Is there such perfect identity of interests among the States to compose a new union as to produce har-mony only and prevent renewed secession?

Plainly the central idea of secession is the essence of anarchy. A majority held in restraint by constitutional checks and limitations, and always changing easily with deliberate changes of popular opinions and sentiments, is the only true sovereign of a free people. Whoever rejects it does of necessity fly to anarchy or to despotism. Unanimity is impossible. The rule of a minority, as a permanent arrangement, is wholly inadmissible; so that, rejecting the majority principle, anarchy or despotism in some form is all that is left.

One section of our country believes slavery is *right* and ought to be extended, while the other believes it is *wrong* and ought not to be extended. This is the only sub-stantial dispute....

Physically speaking, we can not separate. We can not remove our respective sections from each other nor build an impassable wall between them. A husband and wife may be divorced and go out of the presence and beyond the reach of each other, but the different parts of our country can not do this. They can not but remain face to face, and intercourse, either amicable or hostile, must continue between them. Is it possible, then, to make that intercourse more advantageous or more satisfactory *after* separa-tion than *before*? Can aliens make treaties easier than friends can make laws? Can treaties be more faithful-ly enforced between aliens than laws can among friends? Suppose you go to war, you can not fight always; and when, after much loss on both sides and no gain on either, you cease fighting, the identical old questions, as to terms of intercourse, are again upon you....

Why should there not be a patient confidence in the ultimate justice of the people? In our present differences, is either party without faith of being in the right? If the Almighty Ruler of Nations, with His eternal truth and justice, be on your side of the North, or on yours of the South, that truth and that justice will surely prevail by the judgment of this great tribunal of the American people.

By the frame of the Government under which we live this same people have wisely given their pub-lic servants but little power for mischief, and have with equal wisdom provided for the return of that lit-tle to their own hands at very short intervals. While the people retain their virtue and vigilance no Administration by any extreme of wickedness or folly can very seriously injure the Government in the short space of four years.

My countrymen, one and all, think calmly and *well* upon this whole subject. Nothing valuable can be lost by taking time. If there be an object to *hurry* any of you in hot haste to a step which you would never take *deliberately*, that object will be frustrated by tak-ing time; but no good object can be frustrated by it. Such of you as are now dissatisfied still have the old Constitution unimpaired, and, on the sensitive point, the laws of your own framing under it; while the new Administration will have no immediate power, if it would, to change either. If it were admitted that you who are dissatisfied hold the right side in the dispute, there still is no single good reason for precipitate action. Intelligence, patriotism, Christianity, and a firm reliance on Him who has never yet forsaken this favored and are still competent to adjust in the best way all our present difficulty.

In *your* hands, my dissatisfied fellow-country-men, and not in *mine*, is the momentous issue of civil war. The Government will not assail *you*. You can have no conflict without being yourselves the aggres-sors. *You* have no oath registered in heaven to destroy the Government, while I shall have the most solemn one to "preserve, protect, and defend it."

I am loath to close. We are not enemies, but friends. We must not be enemies. Though passion may have strained it must not break our bonds of affection. The mystic chords of memory, stretching from every battlefield and patriot grave to every liv-ing heart and hearthstone all over this broad land, will yet swell the chorus of the Union, when again touched, as surely they will be, by the better angels of our nature.

* * * * * *

1. Lincoln reveals a firm grasp of constitutional law in his inaugural address. What are Lincoln's legal reasons for declaring the Confederate States of America illegal?

2. What are the legal decisions affecting slavery at this time? What is the legal status of slavery? What is the status of slaves?

3. Arrange for yourself the sequence of major national events at this time. When do the southern states secede? When is the confederacy formed? When does the Civil War start? When is slavery declared illegal? When does the war end?

c h a p t e r   1 6

The Civil War, 1861–1865

16–1 A Civil War Nurse Writes of Conditions of Freed Slaves, 1864

Cornelia Hancock, like Mary Ann Bickerdyke and many other women, volunteered as a nurse during the Civil War. She tended the wounded during various battles and served in the Second Corps Hospital for nearly two years from 1863 through the end of the war. After her service at the Battle of Gettysburg, Hancock worked in the Contraband Hospital near Washington D.C. treating the recently freed slaves. There she encountered the divergence between abolitionist rhetoric and the realities facing free blacks. She served the Contraband Hospital for four months before rejoining the troops at the front.

SOURCE: Henrietta Stratton Jaquette, ed., *South After Gettysburg: Letters of Cornelia Hancock from the Army of the Potomac* (Philadelphia: University of Pennsylvania Press, 1937), 40–43.

Dear William[1]

Where are the people who have been professing such strong abolition proclivity for the last thirty years?—certainly not in Washington laboring with these people whom they have been clamoring to have freed. They are freed now or at least many of them, and herded together in filthy huts, half clothed. And, what is worse than all, guarded over by persons who have not a proper sympathy for them.

I have been in the Washington Contraband Hospital for the past two months—it is in close proximity to the Camp of Reception—and I have had ample opportunity to see these people, the persons in charge of them, and the whole mode of proceeding with them. Their wants are great and appeal in every way for aid from the North. Their idea of freedom is exemption from labor. And those who are industrious and do labor we find much neglected on the part of employers in paying. Consequently there is much less inducement for them to labor than there otherwise would be. To get them to labor is the earnest desire of everyone working for the interest of these people—for they *must* be self-supporting—they should not remain paupers upon the government as they now are.

[1] Her brother.

They are totally ignorant of the mere rudiments of learning, not one in one hundred can read so as to be understood. The laws were very stringent in the slave states on that subject....

The situation of the Camp is revolting to a degree, 12 or 14 persons occupy a room not 15 ft. square, do all their cooking, eating, etc. therein. The Camp has but one well of water and that out of order most of the time. All the water used by nearly 1,000 persons is carted from Washington so one can judge of the cleanliness of the Camp.

In "the hall," consisting of nothing conducive to comfort, neither light nor beds, probably some fifty sleep and the consequence is in a few days several of these people are seized with some aggravated disease and have to be carried to the hospital on stretchers and lay there to be supported by this same government that the authorities here say refuses to give them better accommodations when they first arrive. Now, I maintain an ounce of preventative would be worth a pound of cure, if the object is to save the government expense.

...The order now is to remove all contrabands south of the Potomac. It may be better there than here, but we remain under the same authority and let me state emphatically that nothing for the permanent advancement of these people can be effected until the whole matter is removed from the military authority and vested in a separate bureau whose *sole object* is that protection and elevation of these people.

...And the only way to ever get justice done to these people is to separate the whole matter from the military authority, make a separate bureau, have men at the head of this bureau with living souls in them large enough to realize that a contraband is a breathing *human being* capable of being *developed*, if not so now. Let them have the power to appoint officers to have charge of these camps, good energetic, anti-slavery persons who will take an interest in the improvement of those under their charge. I feel this to be the duty of every individual to urge upon every senator and congressman that this step be taken, but meanwhile as we stand at our present, our needs are very pressing and any contributions of any kind of clothing, old or new, shoes and stockings especially, both men's and women's, will prevent much immediate suffering. There is much charity being extended to our poor soldiers and I would not that any one should withhold one mite from them, but I maintain that persons living in their comfortable homes in the North should give liberally to those so sadly situated as these forlorn contrabands, as well as to the soldiers. A national Sanitary Commission for the Relief of Colored Persons of this class would save lives and a great deal of suffering. The slaves generally get free when our army advances; they come into our lines several hundred at a time, follow the

Cornelia Hancock
Jan. 1864

army for a while, then come into Washington, some probably having walked 50 miles. One woman carried one child in her arms and dragged two by her side. Judge of the condition of that woman when she arrives. Should not some comfortable quarters await her weary body?

Thy sister,
Cornelia H.

* * * * * *

1.   From Cornelia Hancock's letter to her brother, what do we know about the manner in which former slaves were treated? How does she think that these problems should be fixed?

2.   What problems did former slaves face once they were freed? How were they able to overcome these obstacles? What kind of a reception did they receive in the North?

3.   Why do you think that Hancock looks to the government to provide shelter and protection for black people? Why do you think she proposes a separate government bureau for assistance to the freed slaves?

16–2   President Abraham Lincoln Issues the Emancipation Proclamation on January 1, 1863

The "contraband" proclamation of General Butler was followed by the antislavery actions of other generals in the field, but hoping to maintain the support of the border states, Lincoln overruled these orders. By mid-1862, however, both Congressional and public opinion were moving toward a more radical position, and in July the President read his Cabinet a preliminary draft of a general Emancipation Proclamation. It was issued as a preliminary proclamation on September 22, and made formal and definitive on January 1, 1863.

SOURCE: *United States Statutes at Large* 12: 1268—69.

By the President of the United States of America: A Proclamation.

Whereas on the 22d day of September, A.D. 1862, a proclamation was issued by the President of the United States, containing, among other things, the following, to wit:

"That on the 1st day of January, A.D. 1863, all persons held as slaves within any State or designated part of a State the people whereof shall then be in rebellion against the United States shall be then, thenceforward, and forever free; and the executive government of the United States, including the military and naval authority thereof, will recognize and maintain the freedom of such persons and will do no act or acts to repress such persons, or any of them, in any efforts they may make for their actual freedom.

"That the executive will on the 1st day of January aforesaid, by proclamation, designate the States and parts of States, if any, in which the people thereof, respectively, shall then be in rebellion against the United States; and the fact that any State or the people thereof shall on that day be in good faith represented in the Congress of the United States by members chosen thereto at elections wherein a majority of the qualified voters of such States shall have participated shall, in the absence of strong countervailing testimony, be deemed conclusive evidence that such State and the people thereof are not then in rebellion against the United States."

Now, therefore, I, Abraham Lincoln, President of the United States, by virtue of the power in me vested as Commander-in-Chief of the Army and Navy of the United States in time of actual armed rebellion against the authority and government of the United States, and as a fit and necessary war measure for suppressing said rebellion, do, on this 1st day of January, A.D. 1863, and in accordance with my purpose so to do, publicly proclaimed for the full period of one hundred days from the first day above mentioned, order and designate as the States and parts of States wherein the people thereof, respectively, are this day in rebellion against the United States the following, to wit:

Arkansas, Texas, Louisiana (except the parishes of St. Bernard, Plaquemines, Jefferson, St. John, St. Charles, St. James, Ascension, Assumption, Terrebonne, Lafourche, St. Mary, St. Martin, and Orleans, including the city of New Orleans), Mississippi, Alabama, Florida, Georgia, South Carolina, North Carolina, and Virginia (except the forty-eight counties designated as West Virginia, and also the counties of Berkeley, Accomac, Northhampton, Elizabeth City, York, Princess Anne, and Norfolk, including the cities of Norfolk and Portsmouth), and which excepted parts are for the present left precisely as if this proclamation were not issued.

And by virtue of the power and for the purpose aforesaid, I do order and declare that all persons held as slaves within said designated States and parts of States are, and henceforward shall be, free; and that the Executive Government of the United States, including the military and naval authorities thereof, will recognize and maintain the freedom of said persons.

And I hereby enjoin upon the people so declared to be free to abstain from all violence, unless in necessary self-defense; and I recommend to them that, in all cases when allowed, they labor faithfully for reasonable wages.

And I further declare and make known that such persons of suitable condition will be received into the armed service of the United States to garrison forts, positions, stations, and other places, and to man vessels of all sorts in said service.

And upon this act, sincerely believed to be an act of justice, warranted by the Constitution upon military necessity, I invoke the considerate judgment of mankind and the gracious favor of Almighty God.

* * * * * *

1. *To what areas did the Emancipation Proclamation apply? Why were the slave states of Missouri, Kentucky, and Tennessee, for example, not included? Why were certain parishes and counties in Louisiana and Virginia excepted?*

2. *President Lincoln assumed the authority to abolish slavery in the Confederate states "as a necessary war measure." Explain his logic.*

16-3   The Working-Men of Manchester, England, Write to President Lincoln on the Question of Slavery in 1862

While the government of Great Britain was sympathetic to the South, most working people in England favored the Union because of their opposition to slavery. On December 31, 1862, an assembly of factory workers in Manchester urged President Lincoln to go the full distance and make emancipation the law of the entire land.
SOURCE: Frank Moore, *The Rebellion Record: A Diary of American Events*, 11 volumes (New York: G. P. Putnam and D. Van Nostrand, 1861–68), 7-344.

To Abraham Lincoln, President of the United States:

As citizens of Manchester, assembled at the Free-Trade Hall, we beg to express our fraternal sentiments toward you and your country. We rejoice in your greatness as an outgrowth of England, whose blood and language you share, whose orderly and legal freedom you have applied to new circumstances, over a region immeasurably greater than our own. We honor your Free States, as a singularly happy abode for the working millions where industry is honored. One thing alone has, in the past, lessened our sympathy with your country and our confidence in it—we mean the ascendency of politicians who not merely maintained negro slavery, but desired to extend and root it more firmly. Since we have discerned, however, that the victory of the free North, in the war which has so sorely distressed us as well as afflicted you, will strike off the fetters of the slave, you have attracted our warm and earnest sympathy. We joyfully honor you,

as the President, and the Congress with you, for many decisive steps toward practically exemplifying your belief in the words of your great founders: "All men are created free and equal." You have procured the liberation of the slaves in the district around Washington, and thereby made the centre of your Federation visibly free. You have enforced the laws against the slave-trade, and kept up your fleet against it, even while every ship was wanted for service in your terrible war. You have nobly decided to receive ambassadors from the negro republics of Hayti and Liberia, thus forever renouncing that unworthy prejudice which refuses the rights of humanity to men and women on account of their color. In order more effectually to stop the slave-trade, you have made with our Queen a treaty, which your Senate has ratified, for the right of mutual search. Your Congress has decreed freedom as the law forever in the vast unoccupied or half unsettled Territories which are directly subject to its legislative power. It has offered pecuniary aid to all States which will enact emancipation locally, and has forbidden your Generals to restore fugitive slaves who seek their protection. You have entreated the slave-masters to accept these moderate offers; and after long and patient waiting, you, as Commander-in-Chief of the Army, have appointed to-morrow, the first of January, 1863, as the day of unconditional freedom for the slaves of the rebel States. Heartily do we congratulate you and your country on this humane and righteous course. We assume that you cannot now stop short of a complete uprooting of slavery. It would not become us to dictate any details, but there are broad principles of humanity which must guide you. If complete emancipation in some States be deferred, though only to a predetermined day, still in the interval, human beings should not be counted chattels. Women must have the rights of chastity and maternity, men the rights of husbands, masters the liberty of manumission. Justice demands for the black, no less than for the white, the protection of law—that his voice be heard in your courts. Nor must any such abomination be tolerated as slave-breeding States, and a slave market—if you are to earn the high reward of all your sacrifices, in the approval of the universal brotherhood and of the Divine Father. It is for your free country to decide whether any thing but immediate and total emancipation can secure the most indispensable rights of humanity against the inveterate wickedness of local laws and local executives. We implore you, for your own honor and welfare, not to faint in your providential mission. While your enthusiasm is aflame, and the tide of events runs high, let the work be finished effectually. Leave no root of bitterness to spring up and work fresh misery to your children. It is a mighty task, indeed, to reorganize the industry not only of four millions of the colored race, but of five millions of whites. Nevertheless, the vast progress you have made in the short space of twenty months fills us with hope that every stain on your freedom will shortly be removed, and that the erasure of that foul blot upon civilization and Christianity—chattel slavery—during your Presidency will cause the name of Abraham Lincoln to be honored and revered by posterity. We are certain that such a glori-ous consummation will cement Great Britain to the United States in close and enduring regards. Our interests, moreover, are identified with yours. We are truly one people, though locally separate. And if you have any ill-wishers here, be assured they are chiefly those who oppose liberty at home, and that they will be powerless to stir up quarrels between us, from the very day in which your country becomes, undeniably and without exception, the home of the free. Accept our high admiration of your firmness in upholding the proclamation of freedom.

* * * * *

1. The Civil War and the blockade of the South created a cotton famine in England and closed many of the textile mills. Why, then, did these workers identify with the Union cause?

2. While "the tide of events runs high," wrote the Manchester workers, "let the work be finished effectually." What did they mean by this?

16-4   President Lincoln Responds to the Working-Men of Manchester on the Subject of Slavery in 1863

On January 19, 1863, two weeks after the Emancipation Proclamation had taken effect, Lincoln replied to the Manchester workers. His letter is an effective summary statement of his position on the prosecution of the war.
SOURCE: Philip Van Doren Stern, ed., *The Life and Writings of Abraham Lincoln* (New York: The Modern Library, 1940):718—49.

To the Working-Men of Manchester:

I have the honor to acknowledge the receipt of the address and resolutions which you sent me on the eve of the new year. When I came, on the 4th of March, 1861, through a free and constitutional election to preside in the Government of the United States, the country was found at the verge of civil war. Whatever might have been the cause, or whosoever the fault, one duty, paramount to all others, was before me, namely, to maintain and preserve at once the Constitution and the integrity of the Federal Republic. A conscientious purpose to perform this duty is the key to all the measures of administration which have been and to all which will hereafter be pursued. Under our frame of government and my official oath, I could not depart from this purpose if I would: It is not always in the power of governments to enlarge or restrict the scope of moral results which follow the policies that they may deem it necessary for the public safety from time to time to adopt.

I have understood well that the duty of self-preservation rests solely with the American people; but I have at the same time been aware that favor or disfavor of foreign nations might have a material influence in enlarging or prolonging the struggle with disloyal men in which the country is engaged. A fair examination of history has served to authorize a belief that the past actions and influences of the United States were generally regarded as having been beneficial toward mankind. I have, therefore, reckoned upon the forbearance of nations. Circumstances—to some of which you kindly allude—induce me especially to expect that if justice and good faith should be practised by the United States, they would encounter no hostile influence on the part of Great Britain. It is now a pleasant duty to acknowledge the demonstration you have given of your desire that a spirit of amity and peace toward this country may prevail in the councils of your Queen, who is respected and esteemed in your own country only more than she is by the kindred nation which has its home on this side of the Atlantic.

I know and deeply deplore the sufferings which the working-men at Manchester, and in all Europe, are called to endure in this crisis. It has been often and studiously represented that the attempt to overthrow this government, which was built upon the foundation of human rights, and to substitute for it one which should rest exclusively on the basis of human slavery, was likely to obtain the favor of Europe. Through the action of our disloyal citizens, the working-men of Europe have been subjected to severe trials, for the purpose of forcing their sanction to that attempt. Under the circumstances, I cannot but regard your decisive utterances upon the question as an instance of sublime Christian heroism which has not been surpassed in any age or in any country. It is indeed an energetic and reinspiring assurance of the inherent power of truth and of the ultimate and universal triumph of justice, humanity, and freedom. I do not doubt that the sentiments you have expressed will be sustained by your great nation; and, on the other hand, I have no hesitation in assuring you that they will excite admiration, esteem, and the most reciprocal feelings of friendship among the American people. I hail this interchange of sentiment, therefore, as an augury that whatever else may happen, whatever misfortune may befall your country or my own, the peace and friendship which now exist between the two nations will be, as it shall be my desire to make them, perpetual.

ABRAHAM LINCOLN.

* * * * *

1. Despite the fact that the Emancipation Proclamation was then in effect, Lincoln avoids a discussion of slavery. Why?

2. According to Lincoln, the duty of the President is "to maintain and preserve at once the Constitution and the integrity of the Federal Republic." In what way is this the key to understanding Lincoln's position?

16-5   The New York Times Prints Opinion on the New York City Draft Riots in 1863

The Conscription Act of 1863 made all men aged 20–45 liable to military service. Men could avoid the draft, however, by paying $300 or finding a substitute, a provision that led directly to riots in several cities. But none equalled the fighting in the streets of the working-class districts of New York City from July 13–16. There were over $1.5 million in property losses and hundreds of casualties—including scores of African Americans lynched from street lamps. Union forces fresh from the Battle of Gettysburg were required to restore order. In the midst of the disorder, The New York Times printed the following letter from one of the rioters and its own editorial opinion on July 15, 1863.

SOURCE: The New York Times, July 15, 1863.

MONDAY NIGHT—UP TOWN.

To the Editor of the New-York Times:

You will, no doubt, be hard on us rioters tomorrow morning, but that 300-dollar law has made us nobodies, vagabonds and cast-outs of society, for whom nobody cares when we must go to war and be shot down. We are the poor rabble, and the rich rabble is our enemy by this law. Therefore we will give our enemy battle right here, and ask no quarter. Although we got hard fists, and are dirty without, we have soft hearts, and have clean consciences within, and that's the reason we love our wives and children more than the rich, because we got not much besides them; and we will not go and leave them at home for to starve.... Why don't they let the nigger kill the slave-driving race and take possession of the South, as it belongs to them.

A POOR MAN, BUT A MAN FOR ALL THAT.

The mob in our City is still rampant. Though the increasing display of armed force has done something to check its more flagrant outrages, it is yet wild with fury, and panting for fresh havoc. The very fact of its being withstood seems only to give it, for the time, new malignity; just as the wild beast never heaves with darker rage than when he begins to see that his way is barred. The monster grows more dangerous as he grows desperate....

It is too true that there are public journals who try to dignify this mob by some respectable appellation. The Herald characterizes it as the people, and the World as the laboring men of the City. These are libels that ought to have paralyzed the fingers that penned them. It is ineffably infamous to attribute to the people, or to the laboring men of this metropolis, such hideous barbarism as this horde has been displaying. The people of New-York and the laboring men of New-York are not incendiaries, nor robbers, nor assassins. They do not hunt down men whose only offence is the color God gave them; they do not chase, and insult, and beat women; they do not pillage an asylum for orphan children, and burn the very roof over those orphans' heads. They are civilized beings, valuing law and respecting decency; and they regard with unqualified abhorrence the doings of the tribe of savages that have sought to bear rule in their midst.

This mob is not the people, nor does it belong to the people. It is for the most part made up of the very vilest people.

elements of the City. It has not even the poor merit of being what mobs usually are—the product of mere ignorance and passion. They talk, or rather did talk at first, of the oppressiveness of the Conscription law; but three-fourths of those who have been actively engaged in violence have been boys and young men under twenty years of age, and not at all subject to the Conscription. Were the Conscription law to be abrogated to-morrow, the controlling inspiration of the mob would remain all the same. It comes from sources quite independent of that law, or any other—from malignant hate toward those in better circumstances, from a craving for plunder, from a love of commotion, from a barbarous spite against a different race, from a disposition to bolster up the failing fortunes of the Southern rebels. All of these influences operate in greater or less measure upon any person engaged in this general defiance of law; and all concerned have generated a composite monster more hellish than the triple-headed Cerberus....

You may as well reason with the wolves of the forest as with these men in their present mood. It is quixotic and suicidal to attempt it. The duties of the executive officers of this State and City are not to debate, or negotiate, or supplicate, but to *execute the laws.* To execute means to enforce *by authority.* This is their *only* official business. Let it be promptly and sternly entered upon with all the means now available, and it cannot fail of being carried through to an overwhelming triumph of public order. It may cost blood—much of it perhaps; but it will be a lesson to the public enemies, whom we always have, and must have in our midst, that will last for a generation. Justice and mercy, this time, unite in the same behest— *Give them grape, and a plenty of it....*

OBJECT OF THE MOB. If this mob was originated in a passionate spirit of resistance to the Conscription law, it very soon changed its purpose, and assumed the character merely of a mob for robbery, plunder and arson. This is shown in the rifling of houses, hotels and stores, and the assaults and felonies upon the persons of unoffending citizens. Some of the ringleaders are noted thieves, who have served out several terms in Sing Sing and other penitentiaries and prisons. Hundreds of the workmen who joined with the crowd on Monday were, of course, as honest as the average of us, but they were at once joined by all the knaves of the City, who saw in the occasion an opportunity for plunder such as had never before presented itself. They made good use of their opportunity, as hundreds of unfortunate citizens can testify. The whole thing, if it continues, bids fair to become a gigantic mob of plunderers, with no more reference to the Conscription than to the Koran. It is remarkable, and almost incredible, how infectious this spirit becomes. A man who joins in such a mob as this may never have stolen a pin's worth in his life before, but when a jewelry store like that up town, or a mansion like those in Fifth-avenue, is broken into, the temptation is almost irresistible to rush in, and obtain a share of things. If this affair is allowed to go on, if it be not promptly put down, it will quickly result in a state of things such as was never before known in a civilized city. It is now a question of the protection of firesides, property and persons against general plunder. It has nothing to do with the conscription.

LAW AND LIBERTY.—It has heretofore been the boast of this country that liberty regulated by law was the principle which governed its citizens. The most perfect freedom to every man in every relation of life—freedom of person, of speech and in the pursuit of happiness, has been our glory, while the universally upheld governance of law has been the safety both of ourselves and of our liberty. The dominance of the mob strikes at the root of this great and special American principle. It reverts us back to semi-barbarism, and throws us forward into despotism. A mob is un-American, anti-American. Every grievance can here be remedied, every wrong can here be righted by *law,* which has its power in the will of the people and "its fountain in the bosom of God." It will be a dark day for the liberties of America, for its honor, its greatness, its power, its glory, when this excrescence of European despotism fastens itself upon our free institutions and society. Every man who prides himself in the name of American must use his determined efforts to drive back this black and deadly tide of human depravity.

* * * * *

1. *According to the letter, the rioters were responding to the injustice of the Conscription Act, something disputed by the editorial. Consider the language of class in these documents.*

2. *Discuss the following statement: "Let the nigger kill the slave-driving race and take possession of the South, as it belongs to them."*

16—6 An African American Soldier Writes to the President Appealing for Equality in 1863

James Henry Gooding was a 26-year-old corporal in the 54th Massachusetts Infantry Regiment (Volunteers) when he wrote to President Lincoln on September 28, 1863, complaining that African American soldiers were paid three dollars a month less than their white counterparts. Only two months before, hundreds of the men of the 54th Massachusetts had lost their lives in the heroic storming of Fort Wagner in South Carolina. At war's end, Congress finally equalized the pay of black and white soldiers, but by that time Gooding had died a prisoner of war at the notorious Andersonville prison camp in Georgia.

SOURCE: Herbert Aptheker, A Documentary History of the Negro People in the United States (New York: Citadel Press, 1990): 482–84.

Your Excellency, Abraham Lincoln:

Your Excellency will pardon the presumption of an humble individual like myself, in addressing you, but the earnest solicitation of my comrades in arms besides the genuine interest felt by myself in the matter is my excuse, for placing before the Executive head of the Nation our Common Grievance.

On the 6th of the last Month, the Paymaster of the Department informed us, that if we would decide to receive the sum of $10 (ten dollars) per month, he would come and pay us that sum, but that, on the sitting of Congress, the Regt. would, in his opinion, be allowed the other 3 dollars. He did not give us any guarantee that this would be, as he hoped; certainly he had no authority for making any such guarantee, and we cannot suppose him acting in any way interested.

Now the main question is, are we Soldiers, or are we Laborers? We are fully armed, and equipped, have done all the various duties pertaining to a Soldier's life, have conducted ourselves to the complete satisfaction of General Officers, who were, if anything, prejudiced against us, but who now accord us all the encouragement and honors due us; have shared the perils and labor of reducing the first strong-hold that flaunted a Traitor Flag; and more, Mr. President, to-day the Anglo-Saxon Mother, Wife, or Sister are not alone in tears for departed Sons, Husbands and Brothers. The patient, trusting descendant of Afric's Clime have dyed the ground with blood, in defence of the Union, and in measure the cruelties of the iron heel of oppression,

which in years gone by, the very power their blood is now being spilled to maintain, ever ground them in the dust.

But when the war trumpet sounded o'er the land, when men knew not the Friend from the Traitor, the Black man laid his life at the altar of the Nation,—and he was refused. When the arms of the Union were beaten, in the first year of the war, and the Executive called for more food for its ravenous maw, again the black man begged the privilege of aiding his country in her need, to be again refused.

And now he is in the War, and how has he conducted himself? Let their dusky forms rise up, out of the mires of James Island, and give the answer. Let the rich mould around Wagner's parapets be upturned, and there will be found an eloquent answer. Obedient and patient and solid as a wall are they. All we lack is a paler hue and a better acquaintance with the alphabet.

Now your Excellency, we have done a Soldier's duty. Why can't we have a Soldier's pay? You caution the Rebel chieftain, that the United States knows no distinction in her soldiers. She insists on having all her soldiers of whatever creed or color, to be treated according to the usages of War. Now if the United States exacts uniformity of treatment of her soldiers from the insurgents, would it not be well and consistent to set the example herself by paying all her soldiers alike?

We of this Regt. were not enlisted under any "contraband" act. But we do not wish to be understood as rating our service of more value to the Government than the service of the ex-slave. Their service is undoubtedly worth much to the Nation, but Congress made express provision touching their case, as slaves freed by military necessity, and assuming the Government to be their temporary Guardian. Not so with us. Freemen by birth and consequently having the advantage of thinking and acting for ourselves so far as the Laws would allow us, we do not consider ourselves fit subjects for the Contraband act.

We appeal to you, Sir, as the Executive of the Nation, to have us justly dealt with. The Regt. do pray that they be assured their service will be fairly appreciated by paying them as American Soldiers, not as menial hirelings. Black men, you may well know, are poor; three dollars per month, for a year, will supply their needy wives and little ones with fuel. If you, as Chief Magistrate of the Nation, will assure us of our whole pay, we are content. Our Patriotism, our enthusiasm will have a new impetus, to exert our energy more and more to aid our Country. Not that our hearts ever flagged in devotion, spite the evident apathy displayed in our behalf, but we feel as though our Country spurned us, now we are sworn to serve her. Please give this a moment's attention.

ready to fight. How do you evaluate this claim?

1. *Gooding argued that when others rebelled or refused to serve, African American men were*

* * * * *

2. *What was the justification for paying African American soldiers less?*

16-7   A Nurse Writes of the Destruction on the Battlefields of Virginia in 1863

Clara Barton was a schoolteacher when the war began, but she responded to the emergency by becoming a battlefield nurse. In her writings she focused on her personal ministry to the wounded, but in fact her greatest accomplishment was as a leader and organizer. She was instrumental in rationalizing the delivery of medical supplies to the front lines, and later became the principal founder of the American Red Cross.

SOURCE: Perry H. Epler, *Life of Clara Barton* (New York: Macmillan, 1915).

At 10 o'clock Sunday (August 31) our train drew up at Fairfax Station. The ground, for acres, was a thinly wooded slope—and among the trees on the leaves and grass, were laid the wounded who were pouring in by scores of wagon loads, as picked up on the field under the flag of truce. All day they came and the whole hillside was covered. Bales of hay were broken open and scattered over the ground like littering for cattle, and the sore, famishing men were laid upon it.

And when the night shut in, in the mist and darkness about us, we knew that standing apart from the world of anxious hearts, throbbing over the whole country, we were a little band of almost empty handed workers literally by ourselves in the wild woods of Virginia, with 3000 suffering men crowded upon the few acres within our reach.

After gathering up every available implement or convenience for our work, our domestic inventory stood 2 water buckets, 5 tin cups, 1 camp kettle, 1 stewpan, 2 lanterns, 4 bread knives, 3 plates, and a 2-quart tin dish, and 3000 guests to serve....

You generous thoughtful mothers and wives have not forgotten the tons of preserves and fruits with which you filled our hands. Huge boxes of these stood beside that railway track. Every can, jar, bucket, bowl, cup or tumbler, when emptied, that instant became a vehicle of mercy to convey some preparation of mingled bread and wine or soup or coffee to some helpless famishing sufferer who partook of it with the tears rolling down his bronzed cheeks and divided his blessings between the

hands that fed him and his God. I never realized until that day how little a human being could be grateful for and that day's experience also taught me the utter worthlessness of that which could not be made to contribute directly to our necessities. The bit of bread which would rest on the surface of a gold eagle was worth more than the coin itself.

But the most fearful scene was reserved for the night. I have said that the ground was littered with dry hay and that we had only two lanterns, but there were plenty of candles. The wounded were laid so close that it was impossible to move about in the dark. The slightest misstep brought a torrent of groans from some poor mangled fellow in your path.

Consequently here were seen persons of all grades from the careful man of God who walked with a prayer upon his lips to the careless driver hunting for his lost whip,—each wandering about among this hay with an open flaming candle in his hands.

The slightest accident, the mere dropping of a light could have enveloped in flames this whole mass of helpless men.

How we watched and pleaded and cautioned as we worked and wept that night! How we put socks and slippers upon their cold, damp feet, wrapped your blankets and quilts about them, and when we had no longer these to give, how we covered them in the hay and left them to their rest!...

The slight, naked chest of a fair-haired lad caught my eye, and dropping down beside him, I bent low to draw the remnant of his torn blouse about him, when with a quick cry he threw his left arm across my neck and, burying his face in the folds of my dress, wept like a child at his mother's knee. I took his head in my hands and held it until his great burst of grief passed away.

"And do you know me?" he asked at length, "I am Charley Hamilton, who used to carry your satchel home from school!" My faithful pupil, poor Charley. That mangled right arm would never carry a satchel again.

About three o'clock in the morning I observed a surgeon with his little flickering candle in hand approaching me with cautious step far up in the wood. "Lady," he said as he drew near, "will you go with me? Out on the hills is a poor distressed lad, mortally wounded and dying. His piteous cries for his sister have touched all our hearts and none of us can relieve him but rather seem to distress him by our presence."

By this time I was following him back over the

bloody track, with great beseeching eyes of anguish on every side looking up into our faces, saying so plainly, "Don't step on us."

"He can't last half an hour longer," said the surgeon as we toiled on. "He is already quite cold, shot through the abdomen, a terrible wound." By this time the cries became plainly audible to me.

"Mary, Mary, sister, Mary, come,—O come, I am wounded, Mary! I am shot. I am dying—Oh come to me—I have called you so long and my strength is almost gone—Don't let me die here alone. O Mary, Mary, come!"

Of all the tones of entreaty to which I have listened, and certainly I have had some experience of sorrow, I think these sounding through that dismal night, the most heart-rending. As we drew near some twenty persons attracted by his cries had gathered around and stood with moistened eyes and helpless hands waiting the change which would relieve them all. And in the midst, stretched upon the ground, lay, scarcely full grown, a young man with a graceful head of hair, tangled and matted, thrown back from a forehead and a face of livid whiteness. His throat was bare. His hands, bloody, clasped his breast, his large, bewildered eyes turning anxiously in every direction. And ever from between his ashen lips pealed that piteous cry of "Mary! Mary! Come."

I approached him unobserved, and motioning the lights away, I knelt by him alone in the darkness. Shall I confess that I intended if possible to cheat him out of his terrible death agony? But my lips were truer than my heart, and would not speak the word "Brother," I had willed them to do. So I placed my hands upon his neck, kissed his cold

forehead and laid my cheek against his.

The illusion was complete; the act had done the false-hood my lips refused to speak. I can never forget that cry of joy. "Oh Mary! Mary! You have come? I knew you would come if I called you and I have called you so long. I could not die without you, Mary. Don't cry, darling, I am not afraid to die now that you have come to me. Oh, bless you. Bless you, Mary." And he ran his cold, blood-wet hands about my neck, passed them over my face, and twined them in my hair, which by this time had freed itself from fasten-ings and was hanging damp and heavy upon my shoulders. He gathered the loose locks in his stiffened fingers and holding them to his lips continued to whisper through them "Bless you, bless you, Mary!" And I felt the hot tears of joy trickling from the eyes I had thought stony in death. This encouraged me, and wrapping his feet closely in blankets and giving him such stimulants as he could take I seated myself on the ground and lifted him on my lap, and draw-ing the shawl on my own shoulders also about his I bade him rest....

* * * * * *

1. Some historians have suggested that through her writing Barton carefully created the image of "the angel of the battlefield." Can you find evidence for such an interpretation?

2. How do Barton's descriptions compare with the Civil War photographs of the aftermath of battle?

16–8 President Abraham Lincoln Delivers the Gettysburg Address in 1863

The Battle of Gettysburg, July 1–3, 1863, was the most destructive and decisive combat of the Civil War turning back the Southern invasion of Pennsylvania. In combination with the defeat of the South at the Battle of Vicksburg on the Mississippi (July 4), the Confederacy was doomed. On November 19, 1963 President Lincoln read the following short address to a crowd assembled to mark the dedication of a national cemetery on the site of the Gettysburg battlefield. Contrary to popular belief the speech was immediately hailed as the most eloquent statement of the North's war aims.

SOURCE: Philip Van Doren Stern, The Life and Writings of Abraham Lincoln (New York: Modern Library, 1940).

Four score and seven years ago our fathers brought forth on this continent, a new nation, conceived in Liberty, and ded-icated to the proposition that all men are created equal.

Now we are engaged in a great civil war, testing whether that nation, or any nation so conceived and so dedicated, can long endure. We are met on a great battle-field of that war. We have come here to dedicate a portion of that field, as a final resting place for those who here gave their lives that that nation might live. It is altogether fitting and proper that we should do this.

But, in a larger sense, we can not dedicate—we can not consecrate—we can not hallow—this ground. The brave men, living and dead, who struggled here, have consecrated it, far above our poor power to add or detract. The world will little note, nor long remember what we say here, but it can never forget what they did here. It is for us the living, rather, to be dedicated here to the unfinished work which they who fought here have thus far so nobly advanced. It is rather for us to be here dedicated to the great task remaining before us—that from these honored dead we take increased devotion to that cause for which they gave the last full measure of devotion—that we here highly resolve that these dead shall not have died in vain—that this nation, under God, shall have a new birth of freedom—and that government of the people, by the people, for the people, shall not perish from the earth.

* * * * *

1.   Compare the sentiments Lincoln expressed here with his letter to the Manchester workers. Discuss the similarities and differences.

2.   President Lincoln was unwilling to make the abolition of slavery a principal policy of his administration, but here he dedicates the nation to "a new birth of freedom." Did the Gettysburg Address amount to a restatement of the goals of the war?

16–9   A Union Captain Describes Sherman's March to the Sea in 1864

David P. Conyngham was not only an officer in General William T. Sherman's Army of the Republic, but a newspaper correspondent for the New York Herald. His account of the Southern campaign included many convincing anecdotes of ordinary life during war:

SOURCE: David P. Conyngham, *Sherman's March Through the South* (New York: Sheldon & Co., 1865).

It was no unusual thing to see our pickets and skirmishers enjoying themselves very comfortably with the rebels, drinking bad whiskey, smoking and chewing worse tobacco, and trading coffee and other little articles. The rebels had no coffee, and our men plenty, while the rebels had plenty of whiskey; so they very soon came to an understanding. It was strange to see men, who had been just pitted in deadly conflict, trading, and bantering, and chatting, as if they were the best friends in the world. They discussed a battle with the same gusto they would a cock-fight, or horse-race, and made inquiries about their friends, as to who was killed, and who not, in the respective armies. Friends that have been separated for years have met in this way. Brothers who parted to try their fortune have often met on the picket line, or on the battle-field. I once met a German soldier with the head of a dying rebel on his lap. The stern veteran was weeping, whilst the boy on his knee looked pityingly into his face. They were speaking in German, and from my poor knowledge of the language, all I could make out was, that they were brothers; that the elder had come out here several years before; the younger followed him, and being informed that he was in Macon, he went in search of him, and got conscripted; while the elder brother, who was in the north all the time, joined our army. The young boy was scarcely twenty, with light hair, and a soft, fair complexion. The pallor of death was on his brow, and the blood was flowing from his breast, and gurgled in his throat and mouth, which the other wiped away with his handkerchief. When he could speak, the dying youth's conversation was of the old home in Germany, of his brothers and sisters, and dear father and mother, who were never to see him again.

In those improvised truces, the best possible faith was observed by the men. These truces were brought about chiefly in the following manner. A rebel, who was heartily tired of his crippled position in his pit, would call out, "I say, Yank!"

"Well, Johnny Reb," would echo from another hole or tree.

"I'm going to put out my head; don't shoot."

"Well, I won't."

The reb would pop up his head; the Yank would do the same.

"Hain't you got any coffee, Johnny?"

"Na'r a bit, but plenty of rot-gut."

"All right; we'll have a trade."

They would meet, while several others would follow the example, until there would be a regular bartering mart established. In some cases the men would come to know each other so well, that they would often call out,—"Look out, reb; we're going to shoot," or "Look out, Yank, we're going to shoot," as the case may be.

On one occasion the men were holding a friendly *reunion* of this sort, when a rebel major came down in a great fury, and ordered the men back. As they were going back, he ordered them to fire on the Federals. They refused, as they had made a truce. The major swore and stormed, and in his rage he snatched the gun from one of the men, and fired at a Federal soldier, wounding him. A cry of execration at such a breach of faith rose from all the men, and they called out, "Yanks, we couldn't help it." At night these men deserted into our lines, assigning as a reason, that they could not with honor serve any longer in an army that thus violated private truces....

Our campaign all through Central Georgia was one delightful picnic. We had little or no fighting, and good living. The farm-yards, cellars, and cribs of the planters kept ourselves and animals well stored with provisions and forage, besides an occasional stiff horn of something strong and good, which, according to the injunctions of holy writ, we took "for our stomachs' sake."

Indeed, the men were becoming epicures. In passing through the camp one night, I saw a lot of jolly soldiers squatted outside the huts in true gypsy style, and between them a table richly stocked with meats and fowls of different kinds, flanked by several bottles of brandy.

They were a jolly set of scamps—talked, laughed, jested, and cracked jokes and bottles in smashing style.

Chase's financial speculations were nothing to theirs; and as for their war schemes, Stanton's and Halleck's were thrown in the shade by them. On the subject of eating they were truly eloquent, and discussed the good things before them with the gusto of a Beau Brummel.

They thought campaigning in Georgia about the pleasantest sort of life out, and they wondered what would become of the poor dog-gone folks they had left with their fingers in their mouths, and little else to put in them.

Many of our foragers, scouts, and hangers-on of all classes, thought, like Cromwell, that they were doing the work of the Lord, in wantonly destroying as much property as possible. Though this was done extensively in Georgia, it was only in South Carolina that it was brought to perfection.

When we reached Milledgeville, we had about thirty days' extra marching rations.

It is impossible to enter into the details of the many ways an army can live on the country. Besides the regular detailed forage parties, there are the officers' servants and cooks, black and white, all wanting something nice for massa general or the captain's mess. Some of these black and white rascals draw largely on the mess fund, with the honest intention of paying for what they get, but somehow forget doing so....

War is very pleasant when attended by little fighting, and good living at the expense of the enemy.

To draw a line between stealing and taking or appropriating everything for the subsistence of an army would puzzle the nicest casuist. Such little freaks as taking the last chicken, the last pound of meal, the last bit of bacon, and the only remaining scraggy cow, from a poor woman and her flock of children, black or white not considered, came under the order of legitimate business. Even crockery; bed-covering, or cloths, were fair spoils. As for plate, or jewelry, or watches, these were things rebels had no use for. They might possibly convert them into gold, and thus enrich the Confederate treasury.

Men with pockets plethoric with silver and gold coin; soldiers sinking under the weight of plate and free bedding materials; lean mules and horses, with the richest trappings of Brussels carpets, and hangings of fine chenille; negro wenches, particularly good-looking ones, decked in satin and silks, and sporting diamond ornaments; officers with sparkling rings, that would set Tiffany in raptures,—gave color to the stories of hanging up or fleshing an "old cuss," to make him shell out.

A planter's house was overrun in a jiffy; boxes, drawers, and escritoirs were ransacked with a laudable zeal, and emptied of their contents. If the spoils were ample, the depredators were satisfied, and went off in peace; if not, everything was torn and destroyed, and most likely the owner was tickled with sharp bayonets into a confession where he had his treasures hid. If he escaped, and was hiding in a thicket, this was *prima facie* evidence that he was a skulking rebel; and most likely some ruffian, in his zeal to get rid of such vipers, gave him a dose of lead, which cured him of his Secesh tendencies. Sorghum barrels were knocked open, beehives rifled, while their angry swarms rushed frantically about. Indeed, I have seen a soldier knock a planter down because a bee stung him. Hogs are bayonetted, and then hung in quarters on the bayonets to bleed; chickens, geese, and turkeys are knocked over and hung in garlands from the saddles and around the necks of swarthy negroes; mules and horses are fished out of the swamps; cows and calves, so wretchedly thin that they drop down and perish on the first day's march, are driven along, or, if too weak to travel, are shot, lest they should give aid to the enemy.

Should the house be deserted, the furniture is smashed in pieces, music is pounded out of four hundred dollar pianos with the ends of muskets. Mirrors were wonderfully multiplied, and rich cushions and carpets carried off to adorn teams and war-steeds. After all was cleared out, most likely some set of stragglers wanted to enjoy a good fire, and set the house, debris of furniture, and all the surroundings, in a blaze. This is the way Sherman's army lived on the country. They were not ordered to do so, but I am afraid they were not brought to task for it much either.

* * * * * *

1. *There is an appealing quality to Conyngham's account of the common humanity of the soldiers from both sides. Could such a description have been written during the war?*

2. *Conyngham was a supporter of the Union. Do you think his political sympathies affected his description of "living off the country?"*

16–10   A Southern Lady Recounts the Fall of Richmond in 1865

Constance Cary Harrison wrote the following letter to her mother and brother from Richmond, Virginia, as the city fell to Union forces on April 4, 1865. The writer was a member of the plantation aristocracy.

SOURCE: Mrs. Burton Harrison, *Recollection, Grave and Gay* (New York: Charles Scribner's Sons, 1911), pp. 210–215.

Grace Street, Richmond, April 4, 1865.

MY PRECIOUS MOTHER AND BROTHER:

I write you this jointly, because I can have no idea where Clarence is. Can't you imagine with what a heavy heart I begin it—? The last two days have added long years to my life. I have cried until no more tears will come, and my heart throbs to bursting night and day. When I bade you good-bye, dear, and walked home alone, I could not trust myself to give another look after you. All that evening the air was full of farewells as if to the dead. Hardly anybody went to bed. We walked through the streets like lost spirits till nearly daybreak. My dearest mother, it is a special Providence that has spared you this! Your going to nurse poor Bert at this crisis has saved you a shock I never can forget. With the din of the enemy's wagon trains, bands, trampling horses, fifes, hurrahs and cannon ever in my ears, I can hardly write coherently. As you desired, in case of trouble, I left our quarters and came over here to be under my uncle's wing. In Aunt M.'s serious illness the house is overflowing; there was not a room or a bed to give me, but that made no difference, they insisted on my staying all the same. Up under the roof there was a lumber-room with two windows and I paid an old darkey with some wrecks of food left from our housekeeping, to clear it out, and scrub floor and walls and windows, till all was absolutely clean. A cot was found and some old chairs and tables—our own bed linen was brought over, and here I write in comparative comfort, so don't bother about me!

Hardly had I seemed to have dropped upon my bed that dreadful Sunday night—or morning rather—when I was wakened suddenly by four terrific explosions, one after the other, making the windows of my garret shake. It was the blowing up, by order of the Secretary of the Navy, of our gunboats on the James, the signal for an all-day carnival of thundering noise and flames. Soon the fire spread, shells in the burning aresenals began to explode, and a smoke arose that shrouded the whole town, shutting out every vestige of blue sky and April sunshine. Flakes of fire fell around us, glass was shattered, and chimneys fell, even

so far as Grace Street from the scene.

By the middle of the day poor Aunt M.'s condition became so much worse in consequence of the excitement, the doctor said she positively could not stand any further sudden alarm. His one comfort is that you, his dear sister, are taking care of his wounded boy of whom his wife has been told nothing. It was suggested that some of us should go to head-quarters and ask, as our neighbors were doing, for a guard for the house where an invalid lay so critically ill. Edith and I were the volunteers for service, and set out for the Capitol Square, taking our courage in both hands. Looking down from the upper end of the square, we saw a huge wall of fire blocking out the horizon. In a few hours no trace was left of Main, Cary, and Canal Streets, from 8th to 18th Streets, except tottering walls and smouldering ruins. The War Department was sending up jets of flame. Along the middle of the streets smouldered a long pile, like street-sweepings, of papers torn from the different departments' archives of our beloved Government, from which soldiers in blue were picking out letters and documents that caught their fancy. The Custom House was the sole building that defied the fire amongst those environing the Square. The marble Statesman on the Monument looked upon queer doings that day, inside the enclosure from which all green was soon scorched out, or trampled down by the hoofs of cavalry horses picketted at intervals about it. Mr. Reed's Church, Mrs. Stanard's house, the Prestons' house, are all burned; luckily the Lee house and that side of Franklin stand uninjured. General Lee's house has a guard camped in the front yard.

We went on to the head-quarters of the Yankee General in charge of Richmond, that day of doom, and I must say we were treated with perfect courtesy and consideration. We saw many people we knew on the same errand as ourselves. We heard stately Mrs.—and the—'s were there to ask for food, as their families were starving. Thank God, we have not fallen to that! Certainly, her face looked like a tragic mask carved out of stone.

A courteous young lieutenant was sent to pilot us out of the confusion, and identify the house, over which a guard was immediately placed. Already the town wore the aspect of one in the Middle Ages smitten by pestilence. The streets filled with smoke and flying fire were empty of the respectable class of inhabitants, the doors and shutters of every house tight closed.…

The ending of the first day of occupation was truly horrible. Some negroes of the lowest grade, their heads turned by the prospect of wealth and equality, together with a mob of miserable poor whites, drank themselves mad with liquor scooped from the gutters. Reinforced, it was said, by convicts escaped from the penitentiary, they tore through the streets, carrying loot from the burnt district.

(For days after, even the kitchens and cabins of the better class of darkies displayed handsome oil paintings and mirrors, rolls of stuff, rare books, and barrels of sugar and whiskey.) One gang of drunken rioters dragged coffins sacked from undertakers, filled with spoils from the speculators' shops, howling so madly one expected to hear them break into the Carmagnole. Thanks to our trim Yankee guard in the basement, we felt safe enough, but the experience was not pleasant.

Through all this strain of anguish ran like a gleam of gold the mad vain hope that Lee would yet make a stand somewhere—that Lee's dear soldiers would give us back our liberty.

Dr. Minnegerode has been allowed to continue his daily services and I never knew anything more painful and touching than that of this morning when the Litany was *sobbed out* by the whole congregation.

A service we went to the same evening at the old Monumental I never shall forget. When the rector prayed for, 'the sick and wounded soldiers and all in distress of mind or body,' there was a brief pause, filled with a sound of weeping all over the church. He then gave out the hymn: 'When gathering clouds around I view.' There was no organ and a voice that started the hymn broke down in tears. Another took it up, and failed likewise. I, then, with a tremendous struggle for self-control, stood up in the corner of the pew and sang alone. At the words, 'Thou Savior see'st the tears I shed,' there was again a great burst of crying and sobbing all over the church. I Wanted to break down dreadfully, but I held on and carried the hymn to the end. As we left the church, many people came up and squeezed my hand and tried to speak, but could not. Just then a splendid military band was passing, the like of which we had not heard in years. The great swell of its triumphant music seemed to mock the shabby broken-spirited congregation defiling out of the gray old church buried in shadows, where in early Richmond days a theatre with many well-known citizens was burned! That was one of the tremendous moments of feeling I experienced that week....

* * * * * *

1. *In the late nineteenth century Southerners came to refer to the Civil War as the "lost cause." Is any of that attitude displayed in this letter?*

2. *Harrison implies that even "the better class of darkies" participated in looting the city. What are the limitations of her perspective on these events?*

chapter 17

Reconstruction, 1863–1877

17–1 Charlotte Forten,
Life on the Sea Islands, 1864

In 1862, after Union troops captured Port Royal off the coast of South Carolina, the surrounding Sea Islands became the site of the first major attempts to aid freed people. Charlotte Forten was part of a wealthy free black family in Philadelphia. She was one of many northern teachers who volunteered to help educate ex-slaves and demonstrate that African Americans were capable of self-improvement. The following selection, published in 1864, was compiled from letters she wrote to her friend, the poet John Greenleaf Whittier.

SOURCE: Atlantic Monthly (1864).

The Sunday after our arrival we attended service at the Baptist Church. The people came in slowly; for they have no way of knowing the hour, except by the sun. By eleven they had all assembled, and the church was well filled. They were neatly dressed in their Sunday attire, the women mostly wearing clean, dark frocks, with white aprons and bright-colored head-hand-kerchiefs. Some had attained to the dignity of straw hats with gay feathers, but these were not nearly as becoming nor as picturesque as the handkerchiefs. The day was warm, and the windows were thrown open as if it were summer, although it was the second day of November. It was very pleasant to listen to the beautiful hymns, and look from the crowd of dark, earnest faces within, upon the grove of noble oaks without. The people sang, "Roll, Jordan, roll," the grandest of all their hymns. There is a great, rolling wave of sound through it all….

Harry, the foreman on the plantation, a man of a good deal of natural intelligence, was most desirous of learning to read. He came in at night to be taught, and learned very rapidly. I never saw any one more determined to learn. We enjoyed hearing him talk about the "gun-shoot,"—so the people call the capture of Bay Point and Hilton Head. They never weary of telling you "how Massa run when he hear de fust gun."

"Why didn't you go with him, Harry?" I asked.

"Oh, Miss, 't was n't 'cause Massa did n't try to 'suade me. He tell we dat de Yankees would shoot we, or would sell we to Cuba, an' do all de wust tings to we, when dey come, 'Berry well, Sar,' says I. 'If I go wid you, I be good

as dead. If I stay here, I can't be no wust; so if I got to dead, I might's well dead here as anywhere. So I'll stay here an' wait for de "dam Yankees." 'Lor', Miss, I knowed he was n't tellin' de truth all de time."

"But why didn't you believe him, Harry?"

"Dunno, Miss; somehow we hear de Yankees was our friends, an' dat we'd be free when dey come, an' 'pears like we believe dat."

I found this to be true of nearly all the people I talked with, and thought it strange they should have had so much faith in the Northerners. Truly, for years past, they had but little cause to think them very friendly. Cupid told us that his master was so daring as to come back, after he had fled from the island, at the risk of being taken prisoner by our soldiers; and that he ordered the people to get all the furniture together and take it to a plantation on the opposite side of the creek, and to stay on that side themselves. "So," said Cupid, "dey could jus' sweep us all up in a heap, an' put us in de boat. An' he telled me to take Patience—dat's my wife—an' de chil'en down to a certain pint, an' den I could come back, if I choose. Jus' as if I was gwine to be sich a goat!" added he, with a look and gesture of ineffable contempt. He and the rest of the people, instead of obeying their master, left the place and hid themselves in the woods; and when he came to look for them, not one of all his "faithful servants" was to be found. A few, principally house-servants, had previously been carried away.

In the evenings, the children frequently came in to sing and shout for us. These "shouts" are very strange,—in truth, almost indescribable. It is necessary to hear and see in order to leave any clear idea of them. The children form a ring, and move around in a kind of shuffling dance, singing all the time. Four or five stand apart, and sing very energetically clapping their hands, stamping their feet, and rocking their bodies to and fro. These are the musicians, to whose performance the shouters keep perfect time. The grown people on this plantation did not shout, but they do on some of the other plantations. It is very comical to see little children, not more than three or four years old, entering into the performance with all their might. But the shouting of the grown people is rather solemn and impressive otherwise. We cannot determine whether it has a religious character or not. Some of the people tell us that it has, others that it has not. But as the shouts of the grown people are always in connection with their religious meetings, it is probable that they are the barbarous expression of religion, handed down to them from their African ancestors, and destined to pass away under the influence of Christian teachings. The people on this island have no songs. They sing only hymns, and most of these are sad. Prince, a large black boy from a neighboring plantation, was the principal shouter among the children. It seemed impossible for him to keep still for a moment. His performances were most amusing speci-mens of Ethiopian gymnastics. Amaretta the younger, a cunning, kittenish little creature of only six years old, had a remarkably sweet voice. Her favorite hymn, which we used to hear her singing to herself as she walked through the yard, is one of the oddest we have heard:—

"What makes ole Satan follow me so?
Satan got nuttin' 't all fur to do wid me.
CHORUS
"Tiddy Rosa, hold your light!
Bradder Tony, hold your light!
All de member, hold bright light
On Canaan's shore!"

This is one of the most spirited shouting-tunes. "Tiddy" is their word for sister.

A very queer-looking old man came into the store one day. He was dressed in a complete suit of brilliant Brussels carpeting. Probably it had been taken from his master's house after the "gun-shoot"; but he looked so very dignified that we did not like to question him about it. The people called him Doctor Crofts,—which was, I believe, his master's name, his own being Scipio. He was very jubilant over the new state of things, and said to Mr. H.,—"Don't hab me feelins hurt now. Used to hab me feel-ins hurt all de time. But don't hab 'em hurt now no more." Poor old soul! We rejoiced with him that he and his brethren no longer have their "feelins" hurt, as in the old time.

* * * * * *

1. How would you describe Forten's attitudes toward the freed people of the Sea Islands? What differences seem apparent between their world and the one she comes from?

2. How does Forten compare the Sea Island religious practices to those that she is used to? Why were they so different?

3. What feelings do the Sea Islanders express toward education and freedom?

17-2 Lincoln's Second Inaugural Address, 1865

In the summer of 1864 Abraham Lincoln's reelection chances looked bleak. Public opinion on the war and emancipation remained deeply divided, and many Radical Republicans lacked confidence in the President. But General Sherman's capture of Atlanta in September lifted northern morale and contributed to Lincoln's victory over Democratic candidate General George B. McClellan. Lincoln's Second Inaugural was one of the briefest yet most memorable ever delivered.
SOURCE: *Richardson, ed., Messages and Papers, Vol. VI, p. 276 ff.*

Lincoln's Second Inaugural Address

FELLOW-COUNTRYMEN:—At this second appearing to take the oath of the presidential office there is less occa-sion for an extended address than there was at the first. Then a statement somewhat in detail of a course to be pur-sued seemed fitting and proper. Now, at the expiration of four years, during which public declarations have been constantly called forth on every point and phase of the great contest which still absorbs the attention and engrosses the energies of the nation, little that is new could be presented. The progress of our arms, upon which all else chiefly depends, is as well known to the public as to myself, and it is, I trust, reasonably satisfactory and encouraging to all. With high hope for the future, no pre-diction in regard to it is ventured.

On the occasion corresponding to this four years ago all thoughts were anxiously directed to an impending civil war. All dreaded it, all sought to avert it. While the inaugural address was being delivered from this place, devoted altogether to *saving* the Union without war, insurgent agents were in the city seeking to *destroy* it without war—seeking to dissolve the Union and divide effects by negotiation. Both parties deprecated war, but one of them would *make* war rather than let the nation survive, and the other would *accept* war rather than let it perish, and the war came.

One eighth of the whole population was colored slaves, not distributed generally over the Union, but local-ized in the southern part of it. These slaves constituted a peculiar and powerful interest. All knew that this interest was somehow the cause of the war. To strengthen, perpet-uate, and extend this interest was the object for which the insurgents would rend the Union even by war, while the Government claimed no right to do more than to restrict the territorial enlargement of it. Neither party expected for the war the magnitude or the duration which it has already attained. Neither anticipated that the *cause* of the conflict might cease with or even before the conflict itself should cease. Each looked for an easier triumph, and a result less fundamental and astounding. Both read the same Bible and pray to the same God, and each invokes His aid against the other. It may seem strange that any men should dare to ask a just God's assistance in wring-ing their bread from the sweat of other men's faces, but let us judge not, that we be not judged. The prayers of both could not be answered fully. The Almighty has His own purposes. "Woe unto the world because of offenses; for it must needs be that offenses come, but woe to that man by whom the offense cometh." If we shall suppose that American slavery is one of those offenses which, in the providence of God, must needs come, but which, having continued through His appointed time, He now wills to remove, and that He gives to both North and South this terrible war as the woe due to those by whom the offense came, shall we discern therein any departure from those divine attributes which the believers in a living God always ascribe to Him? Fondly do we hope, fervently do we pray, that this mighty scourge of war may speedily pass away. Yet, if God wills that it continue until all the wealth piled by the bonds-man's two hundred and fifty years of unrequited toil shall be sunk, and until every drop of blood drawn with the lash shall be paid by another drawn with the sword, as was said three thousand years ago, so still it must be said, "The judgments of the Lord are true and righteous alto-gether."

With malice toward none, with charity for all, with firmness in the right as God gives us to see the right, let us strive on to finish the work we are in, to bind up the nation's wounds, to care for him who shall have borne the battle and for his widow and his orphan, to do all which may achieve and cherish a just and lasting peace among ourselves and with all nations.

* * * * *

1. *To what extent does the address outline Lincoln's plan for Reconstruction?*

2. *How would you compare the Second Inaugural to the First Inaugural in tone and style? How do both treat the issue of slavery?*

17–3   The Freedmen's Bureau Bill, 1865

Congress established the Bureau of Refugees, Freedmen, and Abandoned Lands to provide aid for freed people and to oversee free labor arrangements in the South. President Andrew Johnson's policy of liberally pardoning ex-confederates and returning their land frustrated Bureau commissioner General O. O. Howard's efforts to resettle freed people on confiscated lands. Congress extended the life of the Bureau in 1866 over Johnson's veto. Always underfunded, the Bureau nonetheless succeeded in helping establish schools, overseeing free labor contracts, and providing legal support for freed people.

SOURCE: Henry Steele Commager, *Documents of American History* (1973); U.S. *Statutes at Large*, Vol. XIII, p. 507ff.

AN ACT TO ESTABLISH A BUREAU FOR THE RELIEF OF FREEDMEN AND REFUGEES

Be it enacted, That there is hereby established in the War Department, to continue during the present war of rebel-lion, and for one year thereafter, a bureau of refugees, freedmen, and abandoned lands, to which shall be com-mitted, as hereinafter provided, the supervision and man-agement of all abandoned lands, and the control of all subjects relating to refugees and freedmen from rebel states, or from any district of country within the territory embraced in the operations of the army, under such rules and regulations as may be prescribed by the head of the bureau and approved by the President. The said bureau shall be under the management and control of a commis-sioner to be appointed by the President, by and with the advice and consent of the Senate....

SEC. 2. That the Secretary of War may direct such issues of provisions, clothing, and fuel, as he may deem needful for the immediate and temporary shelter and sup-ply of destitute and suffering refugees and freedmen and their wives and children, under such rules and regulations as he may direct.

SEC. 3. That the President may, by and with the advice and consent of the Senate, appoint an assistant commissioner for each of the states declared to be in insurrection, not exceeding ten in number, who shall, under the direction of the commissioner, aid in the execu-tion of the provisions of this act;...And any military offi-cer may be detailed and assigned to duty under this act without increase of pay or allowances....

SEC. 4. That the commissioner, under the direction of the President, shall have authority to set apart, for the use of loyal refugees and freedmen, such tracts of land within the insurrectionary states as shall have been aban-doned, or to which the United States shall have acquired title by confiscation or sale, or otherwise, and to every male citizen, whether refugee or freedman, as aforesaid, there shall be assigned not more than forty acres of such land, and the person to whom it was so assigned shall be protected in the use and enjoyment of the land for the term of three years at an annual rent not exceeding six per centum upon the value of such land, as it was appraised by the state authorities in the year eighteen hundred and sixty, for the purpose of taxation, and in case no such appraisal can be found, then the rental shall be based upon the estimated value of the land in said year, to be ascertained in such manner as the commissioner may by regulation prescribe. At the end of said term, or at any time during said term, the occupants of any parcels so assigned may purchase the land and receive such title thereto as the United States can convey, upon paying therefor the value of the land, as ascertained and fixed for the purpose of determining the annual rent aforesaid....

1. *How does the Bill treat the issue of abandoned lands in the South? What hope did it offer freed people?*

* * * * *

17–4 Black Code of Mississippi, 1865

In the aftermath of Emancipation, southern states passed a variety of laws known as "Black Codes." Although these codes varied from state to state, they were all aimed at tightly controlling the lives and labor of newly freed people. The codes angered Congress and the northern public, who viewed them as southern attempts to roll back Emancipation and subvert Reconstruction. The Civil Rights Act of 1866, the Fourteenth Amendment, and the Military Reconstruction Act of 1867 were all designed in part to counter the Black Codes.

SOURCE: Henry Steele Commager, *Documents in American History* (1973):
Laws of Mississippi, 1865, p. 82ff.

BLACK CODE OF MISSISSIPPI, 1865

1. CIVIL RIGHTS OF FREEDMEN IN MISSISSIPPI

Sec. 1. *Be it enacted....* That all freedmen, free negroes, and mulattoes may sue and be sued, implead and be impleaded, in all the courts of law and equity of this State, and may acquire personal property, and choses in action, by descent or purchase, and may dispose of the same in the same manner and to the same extent that white persons may: *Provided,* That the provisions of this section shall not be so construed as to allow any freedman, free negro, or mulatto to rent or lease any lands or tenements except in incorporated cities or towns, in which places the corporate authorities shall control the same....

Sec. 3....All freedmen, free negroes, or mulattoes who do now and have heretofore lived and cohabited together as husband and wife shall be taken and held in law as legally married, and the issue shall be taken and held as legitimate for all purposes; that it shall not be lawful for any freedman, free negro, or mulatto to intermarry with any white person; nor for any white person to intermarry with any freedman, free negro, or mulatto; and any person who shall so intermarry, shall be deemed guilty of felony, and on conviction thereof shall be confined in the State penitentiary for life; and those shall be deemed freedmen, free negroes, and mulattoes who are of pure negro blood, and those descended from a negro to the third generation, inclusive, though one ancestor in each generation may have been a white person....

Sec. 6....All contracts for labor made with freedmen, free negroes, and mulattoes for a longer period than one month shall be in writing, and in duplicate, attested and read to said freedman, free negro, or mulatto by a beat, city or county officer, or two disinterested white persons of the county in which the labor is to be performed, of which each party shall have one; and said contracts shall be taken and held as entire contracts, and if the laborer shall quit the service of the employer before the expiration of his term of service, without good cause, he shall forfeit his wages for that year up to the time of quitting.

Sec. 7....Every civil officer shall, and every person may, arrest and carry back to his or her legal employer any freedman, free negro, or mulatto who shall have quit the service of his or her employer before the expiration of his or her term of service without good cause; and said officer and person shall be entitled to receive for arresting and carrying back every deserting employe aforesaid the sum of five dollars, and ten cents per mile from the place of arrest to the place of delivery; and the same shall be paid by the employer, and held as a set-off for so much against the wages of said deserting employe: *Provided,* that said arrested party, after being so returned, may appeal to the justice of the peace or member of the board of police of the county, who, on notice to the alleged employer, shall try summarily whether said appellant is legally employed by the alleged employer, and has good cause to quit said employer; either party shall have the right to appeal to the county court, pending which the alleged deserter shall be remanded to the alleged employer or otherwise disposed of, as shall be right and just; and the decision of the county court shall be final....

Sec. 9....If any person shall persuade or attempt to persuade, entice, or cause any freedman, free negro, or mulatto to desert from the legal employment of any person before the expiration of his or her term of service, or shall knowingly employ any such deserting freedman, free negro, or mulatto, or shall knowingly give or sell to any such deserting freedman, free negro, or mulatto, any food, raiment, or other thing, he or she shall be guilty of a misdemeanor, and, upon conviction, shall be fined not less than twenty-five dollars and not more than two hundred dollars and the costs; and if said fine and costs shall not be immediately paid, the court shall sentence said convict to not exceeding two months' imprisonment in the county jail and he or she shall moreover be liable to the party injured in damages: *Provided*, if any person shall, or shall attempt to, persuade, entice, or cause any freedman, free negro, or mulatto to desert from any legal employment of any person, with the view to employ said freedman, free negro, or mulatto without the limits of this State, such person, on conviction, shall be fined not less than fifty dollars, and not more than five hundred dollars and costs; and if said fine and costs shall not be immediately paid, the court shall sentence said convict to not exceeding six months imprisonment in the county jail....

2. MISSISSIPPI APPRENTICE LAW

(LAWS OF MISSISSIPPI, 1865, p. 86.)

Sec. 1....It shall be the duty of all sheriffs, justices of the peace, and other civil officers of the several counties in this State, to report to the probate courts of their respective counties semi-annually, at the January and July terms of said courts, all freedmen, free negroes, and mulattoes, under the age of eighteen, in their respective counties, who are orphans, or whose parent or parents have not the means or who refuse to provide for and support said minors; and thereupon it shall be the duty of said probate court to order the clerk of said court to apprentice said minors to some competent and suitable person, on such terms as the court may direct, having a particular care to the interest of said minor: *Provided*, that the former owner of said minors shall have the preference when, in the opinion of the court, he or she shall be a suitable person for that purpose....

Sec. 3....In the management and control of said apprentice, said master or mistress shall have the power to inflict such moderate corporal chastisement as a father or guardian is allowed to inflict on his or her child or ward at common law. *Provided*, that in no case shall cruel or inhuman punishment inflicted.

Sec. 4....If any apprentice shall leave the employment of his or her master or mistress, without his or her consent, said master or mistress may pursue and recapture said apprentice, and bring him or her before any justice of the peace of the county, whose duty it shall be to remand said apprentice to the service of his or her master or mistress; and in the event of a refusal on the part of said apprentice so to return, then said justice shall commit said apprentice to the jail of said county, on failure to give bond, to the next term of the county court; and it shall be the duty of said court at the first term thereafter to investigate said case, and if the court shall be of opinion that said apprentice left the employment of his or her master or mistress without good cause, to order him or her to be punished, as provided for the punishment of hired freedmen, as may be from time to time provided for by law for desertion, until he or she shall agree return to the service of his or her master or mistress...if the court shall believe that said apprentice had good cause to quit his said master or mistress, the court shall discharge said apprentice from said indenture, and also enter a judgment against the master or mistress for not more than one hundred dollars, for the use and benefit of said apprentice....

3. MISSISSIPPI VAGRANT LAW

(LAWS OF MISSISSIPPI, 1865, p. 90)

Sec. 1. *Be it enacted*, etc.... That all rogues and vagabonds, idle and dissipated persons, beggars, jugglers, or persons practicing unlawful games or plays, runaways, common drunkards, common night-walkers, pilferers, lewd, wanton, or lascivious persons, in speech or behavior, common railers and brawlers, persons who neglect their calling or employment, misspend what they earn, or do not provide for the support of themselves or their families, or dependents, and all other idle and disorderly persons, including all who neglect all lawful business, habitually misspend their time by frequenting houses of ill-fame, gaming-houses, or tippling shops, shall be deemed and considered vagrants, under the provisions of this act, and upon conviction thereof shall be fined not exceeding one hundred dollars, with all accruing costs, and be imprisoned at the discretion of the court, not exceeding ten days.

Sec. 2....All freedmen, free negroes and mulattoes in this State, over the age of eighteen years, found on the second Monday in January, 1866, or thereafter, with no lawful employment or business, or found unlawfully assembling themselves together, either in the day or night time, and all white persons so assembling themselves with freedmen, free negroes or mulattoes, or usually associating with freedmen, free negroes or mulattoes, on terms of equality, or living in adultery or fornication with a freed woman, free negro or mulatto, shall be deemed vagrants, and on conviction thereof shall be fined in a sum not exceeding, in the case of a freedman, free negro or mulatto, fifty dollars, and a white man two hundred dollars, and imprisoned at the discretion of the court, the free negro not exceeding ten days, and the white man not exceeding six months....

4. PENAL LAWS OF MISSISSIPPI

(LAWS OF MISSISSIPPI, 1865, p. 165.)

Sec. 1. *Be it enacted*,...That no freedman, free negro, or

mulatto, not in the military service of the United States government, and not licensed so to do by the board of police of his or her county, shall keep or carry fire-arms of any kind, or any ammunition, dirk or bowie knife, and on conviction thereof in the county court shall be punished by fine, not exceeding ten dollars, and pay the costs of such proceedings, and all such arms or ammunition shall be forfeited to the informer; and it shall be the duty of every civil and military officer to arrest any freedman, free negro, or mulatto found with any such arms or ammunition, and cause him or her to be committed to trial in default of bail.

2....Any freedman, free negro, or mulatto committing riots, routs, affrays, trespasses, malicious mischief, cruel treatment to animals, seditious speeches, insulting gestures, language, or acts, or assaults on any person, disturbance of the peace, exercising the function of a minister of the Gospel without a license from some regularly organized church, vending spirituous or intoxicating liquors, or committing any other misdemeanor, the punishment of which is not specifically provided for by law, shall, upon conviction thereof in the county court, be fined not less than ten dollars, and not more than one hundred dollars, and may be imprisoned at the discretion of the court, not exceeding thirty days.

Sec. 3....If any white person shall sell, lend, or give to any freedman, free negro, or mulatto any firearms, dirk or bowie knife, or ammunition, or any spirituous or intoxicating liquors, such person or persons so offending, upon conviction thereof in the county court of his or her county, shall be fined not exceeding fifty dollars, and may be imprisoned, at the discretion of the court, not exceeding thirty days....

Sec. 5....If any freedman, free negro, or mulatto, convicted of any of the misdemeanors provided against in this act, shall fail or refuse for the space of five days, after conviction, to pay the fine and costs imposed, such person shall be hired out by the sheriff or other officer, at public outcry, to any white person who will pay said fine and all costs, and take said convict for the shortest time.

* * * * * *

1. How did these laws limit the freedom of movement of ex-slaves? Why was this so important to the Mississippi legislature?

2. Apprenticeship laws provoked especially bitter complaints from African Americans. How would you explain this?

3. Why did the Black Codes pay so much attention to limiting the social lives of freed people, for example, sexuality, drinking, recreation?

17–5 Frederick Douglass, Speech to the American Anti-Slavery Society, 1865

Congress approved the Thirteenth Amendment abolishing slavery in February, 1865, and the Union's final military victory over the Confederacy that spring assured the destruction of the slave system. The American Anti-Slavery Society, long in the forefront of the abolitionist movement, met in May, 1865, to discuss its future. Black leader Frederick Douglass addressed the Society, urging it not to disband but to continue the fight against racial discrimination.

SOURCE: Philip S. Foner, ed., The Life and Writings of Frederick Douglass, Vol. IV (1955).

...I do not wish to appear here in any fault-finding spirit, or as an impugner of the motives of those who believe that the time has come for this Society to disband. I am conscious of no suspicion of the purity and excellence of the motives that animate the President of this Society [William Lloyd Garrison], and other gentlemen who are in favor of its disbandment. I take this ground; whether this Constitutional Amendment [the thirteenth] is law or not, whether it has been ratified by a sufficient number of States to make it law or not, I hold that the work of Abolitionists is not done. Even if every State in the Union had ratified that Amendment, while the black man is confronted in the legislation of the South by the word "white," our work as Abolitionists, as I conceive it, is not done. I took the ground, last night, that the South, by unfriendly legislation, could make our liberty, under that provision, a delusion, a mockery, and a snare, and I hold that ground now. What advantage is a provision like this Amendment to the black man, if the Legislature of any State can to-morrow declare that no black man's testimony shall be received in a court of law? Where are we then? Any wretch may enter the house of a black man, and commit any violence he pleases; if he happens to do it only in the presence of black persons, he goes unwhipt of justice. ['Hear, hear.'] And don't tell me that those people down there have become so just and honest all at once that they will not pass laws denying to black men the right to testify against white men in the courts of law. Why, our Northern States have done it. Illinois, Indiana and Ohio have done it. Here, in the midst of institutions that have gone forth from old Plymouth Rock, the black man has been excluded from testifying in the courts of law; and if the Legislature of every Southern State to-morrow pass a law, declaring that no Negro shall testify in any courts of law, they will not violate that provision of the Constitution. Such laws exist now at the South, and they might exist under this provision of the Constitution, that there shall be neither slavery not involuntary servitude in any State of the Union....

Slavery is not abolished until the black man has the ballot. While the Legislatures of the South retain the right to pass laws making any discrimination between black and white, slavery still lives there. [Applause.] As Edmund Quincy once said, "While the word 'white' is on the statute-book of Massachusetts, Massachusetts is a slave State. While a black man can be turned out of a car in Massachusetts, Massachusetts is a slave State. While a slave can be taken from old Massachusetts, Massachusetts is a slave State." That is what I heard Edmund Quincy say twenty-three or twenty-four years ago. I never forget such a thing. Now, while the black man can be denied a vote, while the Legislatures of the South can take from him the right to keep and bear arms, as they can—would not allow a Negro to walk with a cane where I came from, they would not allow five of them to assemble together—the work of the Abolitionists is not finished. Notwithstanding the provision in the Constitution of the United States, that the right to keep and bear arms shall not be abridged, the black man has never had the right either to keep or bear arms; and the Legislatures of the States will still have the power to forbid it, under this Amendment. They can carry on a system of unfriendly legislation, and will they not do it? Have they not got prejudice there to do it with? Think you, that because they are for the moment in the talons and beak of our glorious eagle, instead of the slave being there, as formerly, that they are converted? I hear of the loyalty at Wilmington, the loyalty at South Carolina—what is it worth?

["Not a straw."]

Not a straw. I thank my friend for admitting it. They are loyal while they see 200,000 sable soldiers, with glistening bayonets, walking in their midst. [Applause.] But let the civil power of the South be restored, and the old prejudices and hostility to the Negro will revive. Aye, the very fact that the Negro has been used to defeat this rebellion and strike down the standards of the Confederacy will be a stimulus to all their hatred, to all their malice, and lead them to legislate with greater stringency towards

this class than ever before. [Applause.] The American people are bound—bound by their sense of honor (I hope by their sense of honor, at least, by a just sense of honor), to extend the franchise to the Negro; and I was going to say, that the Abolitionists of the American Anti-Slavery Society were bound to "stand still, and see the salvation of God," until that work is done. [Applause.] Where shall the black man look for support, my friends, if the American Anti-Slavery Society fails him? ["Hear, hear."] From whence shall we expect a certain sound from the trumpet of freedom, when the old pioneer, when this Society that has survived mobs, and martyrdom, and the combined efforts of priest-craft and state-craft to suppress it, shall all at once subside, on the mere intimation that the Constitution has been amended, so that neither slavery not involuntary servitude shall hereafter be allowed in this land? What did the slaveholders of Richmond say to those who objected to arming the Negro, on the ground that it would make him a freeman? Why, they said, "The argument is absurd. We may make these Negroes fight for us; but while we retain the political power of the South, we can keep them in their subordinate positions." That was the argument; and they were right. They might have employed the Negro to fight for them, and while they retained in their hands power to exclude him from political rights, they could have reduced him to a condition similar to slavery. They would not call it slavery, but some other name. Slavery has been fruitful in giving itself names. It has been called "the peculiar institution," "the social system," and the "impediment," as it was called by the General conference of the Methodist Episcopal Church. It has been called by a great many names, and it will call itself by yet another name; and you and I and all of us had better wait and see what new form this old monster will assume, in what new skin this old snake will come forth. [Loud applause.]

* * * * * *

1. *What rights does Douglass see as crucial to establishing full citizenship for African Americans?*

2. *How does Douglass compare black civil rights in the northern and southern states?*

3. *What course does Douglass advise for dealing with the defeated Confederacy?*

17–6 The Civil Rights Act of 1866

Passed over President Johnson's veto in April 1866, the Civil Rights Act provided the first statutory definition of American citizenship. By conferring citizenship rights upon freed people, it negated the Supreme Court's Dred Scott decision of 1857, which had held that a black person could not be a citizen of the United States. The Civil Rights Act proposed that the federal government guarantee the principle of equality before the law, regardless of race.

SOURCE: Henry Steele Commager, *Documents of American History* (1973), pp. 14–15: *U.S. Statues at Large,* Vol. XIV, p. 27ff.

An Act to protect all Persons in the United States in their Civil Rights, and furnish the Means of their Vindication.

Be it enacted, That all persons born in the United States and not subject to any foreign power, excluding Indians not taxed, are hereby declared to be citizens of the United States; and such citizens, of every race and color, without regard to any previous condition of slavery or involuntary servitude, except as a punishment for crime whereof the party shall have been duly convicted, shall have the same right, in every State and Territory in the United States, to make and enforce contracts, to sue, be parties, and give evidence, to inherit, purchase, lease, sell, hold, and convey real and personal property, and to full and equal benefit of all laws and proceedings for the security of person and property, as is enjoyed by white citizens, and shall be subject to like punishment, pains, and penalties, and to none other, any law, statute, ordinance, regulation, or custom, to the contrary notwithstanding.

SEC. 2. *And be it further enacted,* That any person who, under color of any law, statute, ordinance, regulation, or custom, shall subject, or cause to be subjected, any inhabitant of any State or Territory to the deprivation of any right secured or protected by this act, or to different punishment, pains or penalties on account of such person having at any time been held in a condition of slavery or involuntary servitude, except as a punishment for crime whereof the party shall have been duly convicted, or by reason of his color or race, than is prescribed for the punishment of white persons, shall be deemed guilty of a misdemeanor, and, on conviction, shall be punished by fine not exceeding one thousand dollars, or imprisonment not exceeding one year, or both, in the discretion of the court.

SEC. 3. *And be it further enacted,* That the district courts the United States,…shall have, exclusively of the courts of the several States, cognizance of all crimes and

offences committed against the provisions of this act, and also, concurrently with the circuit courts of the United States, of all causes, civil and criminal, affecting persons who are denied or cannot enforce in the *courts* or judicial tribunals of the State or locality where they may be any of the rights secured to them by the first section of this act.…

SEC. 4. *And be it further enacted,* That the district attorneys, marshals, and deputy marshals of the United States, the commissioners appointed by the circuit and territorial courts of the United States, with powers of arresting, imprisoning, or bailing offenders against the laws of the United States, the officers and agents of the Freedmen's Bureau, and every other officer who may be specially empowered by the President of the United States, shall be, and they are hereby, specially authorized and required, at the expense of the United States, to institute proceedings against all and every person who shall violate the provisions of this act, and cause him or them to be arrested and imprisoned, or bailed, as the case may be, for trial before such court of the United States or territorial court as by this act has cognizance of the offence.…

SEC. 8. *And be it further enacted,* That whenever the President of the United States shall have reason to believe that offences have been or are likely to be committed against the provisions of this act within any judicial district, it shall be lawful for him, in his discretion, to direct the judge, marshal, and district attorney of such district to attend at such place within the district, and for such time as he may designate, for the purpose of the more speedy arrest and trial of persons charged with a violation of this act; and it shall be the duty of every judge or other officer, when any such requisition shall be received by him, to attend at the place and for the time therein designated.

SEC. 9. *And be it further enacted,* That it shall be lawful for the President of the United States, or such person as he may empower for that purpose, to employ such part of the land or naval forces of the United States, or of the militia, as shall be necessary to prevent the violation and enforce the due execution of this act.

SEC. 10. *And be it further enacted,* That upon all questions of law arising in any cause under the provisions of this act a final appeal may be taken to the Supreme Court of the United States.

* * * * *

1.   How does the act specifically define civil rights and those who may enjoy them?

2.   What provisions does the act make for enforcement of these rights?

17–7 President Johnson's Veto of the Civil Rights Act, 1866

The Civil Rights Act was the first major piece of legislation to become law over a president's veto. Johnson's veto message helped make the estrangement between Congress and the President irreparable. Johnson's constitutional arguments induced Congress to enact the Fourteenth Amendment, which forbade individual states to deprive citizens of the "equal protection of the laws."

SOURCE: Richardson, ed., *Messages and Papers*, Vol. VI, p. 405ff.

WASHINGTON, D.C., *March 27, 1866. To the Senate of the United States:*

I regret that the bill, which has passed both Houses of Congress, entitled "An act to protect all persons in the United States in their civil rights and furnish the means of their vindication," contains provisions which I can not approve consistently with my sense of duty to the whole people and my obligations to the Constitution of the United States. I am therefore constrained to return it to the Senate, the House in which it originated, with my objections to its becoming a law.

By the first section of the bill all persons born in the United States and not subject to any foreign power, excluding Indians not taxed, are declared to be citizens of the United States.... It does not purport to give these classes of persons any status as citizens of States, except that which may result from their status as citizens of the United States. The power to confer the right of State citizenship is just as exclusively with the several States as the power to confer the right of Federal citizenship is with Congress.

The right of Federal citizenship thus to be conferred on the several excepted races before mentioned is now for the first time proposed to be given by law. If, as is claimed by many, all persons who are native born already are, by virtue of the Constitution, citizens of the United States, the passage of the pending bill can not be necessary to make them such. If, on the other hand, such persons are not citizens, as may be assumed from the proposed legislation to make them such, the grave question presents itself whether, when eleven of the thirty-six States are unrepresented in Congress at the present time, it is sound policy to make our entire colored population and all other excepted classes citizens of the United States. Four millions of them have just emerged from slavery into freedom.…It may also be asked whether it is necessary that they should be declared citizens in order that they may be

secured in the enjoyment of the civil rights proposed to be conferred by the bill. Those rights are, by Federal as well as State laws, secured to all domiciled aliens and foreigners, even before the completion of the process of naturalization; and it may safely be assumed that the same enactments are sufficient to give like protection and benefits to those for whom this bill provides special legislation. Besides, the policy of the Government from its origin to the present time seems to have been that persons who are strangers to and unfamiliar with our institutions and our laws should pass through a certain probation, at the end of which, before attaining the coveted prize, they must give evidence of their fitness to receive and to exercise the rights of citizens as contemplated by the Constitution of the United States. The bill in effect proposes a discrimination against large numbers of intelligent, worthy, and patriotic foreigners, and in favor of the negro, to whom, after long years of bondage, the avenues to freedom and intelligence have just now been suddenly opened.…

The first section of the bill also contains an enumeration of the rights to be enjoyed by these classes so made citizens "in every State and Territory in the United States." These rights are "to make and enforce contracts; to sue, be parties, and give evidence; to inherit, purchase, lease, sell, hold, and convey real and personal property," and to have "full and equal benefit of all laws and proceedings for the security of person and property as is enjoyed by white citizens." So, too, they are made subject to the same punishment, pains, and penalties in common with white citizens, and to none other. Thus a perfect equality of the white and colored races is attempted to be fixed by Federal law in every State of the Union over the vast field of State jurisdiction covered by these enumerated rights. In no one of these can any State ever exercise any power of discrimination between the different races.…

Hitherto every subject embraced in the enumeration of rights contained in this bill has been considered as exclusively belonging to the States. They all relate to the internal police and economy of the respective States. They are matters which in each State concern the domestic condition of its people, varying in each according to its own peculiar circumstances and the safety and well-being of its own citizens. I do not mean to say that upon all these subjects there are not Federal restraints—as, for instance, in the State power of legislation over contracts there is a Federal limitation that no State shall pass a law impairing the obligations of contracts; and, as to crimes, that no State shall pass an *ex post facto* law; and, as to money, that no State shall make anything but gold and silver a legal tender; but where can we find a Federal prohibition against the power of any State to discriminate, as do most of them, between aliens and citizens, between artificial persons, called corporations, and natural persons, in the right to hold real estate? If it be granted that Congress can repeal all State laws discriminating between whites and blacks in the subjects covered by this bill, why, it may be asked, may not Congress repeal in the same way all State laws discriminating between the two races on the subjects of suffrage and office? If Congress can declare by law who shall hold lands, who shall testify, who shall have capacity to make a contract in a State, then Congress can by law also declare who, without regard to color or race, shall have the right to sit as a juror or as a judge, to hold any office, and, finally, to vote "in every State and Territory of the United States." As respects the Territories, they come within the power of Congress, for as to them the lawmaking power is the Federal power; but as to the States no similar provision exists vesting in Congress the power "to make rules and regulations" for them.

The object of the second section of the bill is to afford discriminating protection to colored persons in the full enjoyment of all the rights secured to them by the preceding section....

This provision of the bill seems to be unnecessary, as adequate judicial remedies could be adopted to secure the desired end without invading the immunities of legislators, always important to be preserved in the interest of public liberty; without assailing the independence of the judiciary, always essential to the preservation of individual rights; and without impairing the efficiency of ministerial officers, always necessary for the maintenance of public peace and order. The remedy proposed by this section seems to be in this respect not only anomalous, but unconstitutional; for the Constitution guarantees nothing with certainty if it does not insure to the several States the right of making and executing laws in regard to all matters arising within their jurisdiction, subject only to the restriction that in cases of conflict with the Constitution and constitutional laws of the United States the latter should be held to be the supreme law of the land....

The fourth section of the bill provides that officers and agents of the Freedmen's Bureau shall be empowered to make arrests, and also that other officers may be specially commissioned for that purpose by the President of the United States. It also authorizes circuit courts of the United States and the superior courts of the Territories to appoint, without limitation, commissioners, who are to be charged with the performance of *quasi* judicial duties. The fifth section empowers the commissioners so to be selected by the courts to appoint in writing, under their hands, one or more suitable persons from time to time to execute warrants and other processes described by the bill. These numerous official agents re made to constitute a sort of police, in addition to the military, and are authorized to summon a *posse comitatus*, and even to call to their aid such portion of the land and naval forces of the United States, or of the militia, "as may be necessary to the performance of the duty with which they are charged." This extraordinary power is to be conferred upon agents irresponsible to the Government and to the people, to whose number and the discretion of the commissioners is the only limit, and in whose hands such authority might be made a terrible engine of wrong, oppression, and fraud....

The ninth section authorizes the President, or such person as he may empower for that purpose, "to employ such part of the land or naval forces of the United States, or of the militia, as shall be necessary to prevent the violation and enforce the due execution of this act." This language seems to imply a permanent military force, that to be always at hand, and whose only business is to be the enforcement of this measure over the vast region on where it is intended to operate....

In all our history, in all our experience as people living under Federal and State law, no such system as that contemplated by the details of this bill has ever before been proposed or adopted. They establish for the security of the colored race safeguards which go infinitely beyond any that the General Government has ever provided for the white race. In fact, the distinction of race and color is by the bill made to operate in favor of the colored and against the white race. They interfere with the municipal legislation of the States, with the relations existing exclusively between a State and its citizens, or between inhabitants of the same State—an absorption and assumption of power by the General Government which, if acquiesced in, must sap and destroy our federative system of limited powers and break down the barriers which preserve the rights of the States. It is another step, or rather stride, toward centralization and the concentration of all legislative powers in the National Government. The tendency of the bill must be to resuscitate the spirit of rebellion and to arrest the progress of those influences which are more closely drawing around the States the bonds of union and peace....

ANDREW JOHNSON.

* * * * *

1. *What is Johnson's "states rights" argument against the notion of federal citizenship?*

2. *How do Johnson's racial views mesh with his constitutional interpretation?*

3. *How and why does Johnson extend his argument to a critique of the Freedmen's Bureau?*

17–8   The First Reconstruction Act, 1867

Radical Republicans made President Johnson's intransigence the central issue in the election campaign of 1866. Northern voters overwhelmingly rejected Johnson's policies and strengthened the Radicals' control of Congress. At the same time, all the southern states (except Tennessee) rejected the Fourteenth Amendment. In response, Congress passed the following act in March, 1867, outlining the main principles of Congressional Reconstruction.

SOURCE: Henry Steele Commager, *Documents in American History* (1973): *U.S. Statutes at Large*, Vol. XIV, p. 428ff.

An Act to provide for the more efficient Government of the Rebel States

WHEREAS no legal State governments or adequate protection for life or property now exists in the rebel States of Virginia, North Carolina, South Carolina, Georgia, Mississippi, Alabama, Louisiana, Florida, Texas, and Arkansas; and whereas it is necessary that peace and good order should be enforced in said States until loyal and republican State governments can be legally established: Therefore,

Be it enacted, That said rebel States shall be divided into military districts and made subject to the military authority of the United States as hereinafter prescribed, and for that purpose Virginia shall constitute the first district; North Carolina and South Carolina the second district; Georgia, Alabama, and Florida the third district; Mississippi and Arkansas the fourth district; and Louisiana and Texas the fifth district.

SEC. 2. That it shall be the duty of the President to assign to the command of each of said districts an officer of the army, not below the rank of brigadier-general, and to detail a sufficient military force to enable such officer to perform his duties and enforce his authority within the district to which he is assigned.

SEC. 3. That it shall be the duty of each officer assigned as aforesaid, to protect all persons in their rights of persons and property, to suppress insurrection, disorder, and violence, and to punish, or cause to be punished, all disturbers of the public peace and criminals; and to this end he may allow local civil tribunals to take jurisdiction of and to try offenders, or, when in his judgment it may be necessary for the trial of offenders, he shall have power to organize military commissions or tribunals for that purpose, and all interference under color of State authority with the exercise of military authority, under

this act, shall be null and void.

SEC. 4. That all persons put under military arrest by virtue of this act shall be tried without unnecessary delay, and no cruel or unusual punishment shall be inflicted, and no sentence of any military commission or tribunal hereby authorized, affecting the life or liberty of any person, shall be executed until it is approved by the officer in command of the district, and the laws and regulations for the government of the army shall not be affected by this act, except in so far as they conflict with its provisions: *Provided,* That no sentence of death under the provisions of this act shall be carried into effect without the approval of the President.

SEC. 5. That when the people of any one of said rebel States shall have formed a constitution of government in conformity with the Constitution of the United States in all respects, framed by a convention of delegates elected by the malc citizens of said State twenty-one years old and upward, of whatever race, color, or previous condition, who have been resident in said State for one year previous to the day of such election, except such as may be disfranchised for participation in the rebellion or for felony at common law, and when such constitution shall provide that the elective franchise shall be enjoyed by all such persons as have the qualifications herein stated for electors of delegates, and when such constitution shall be ratified by a majority of the persons voting on the question of ratification who are qualified as electors for delegates, and when such constitution shall have been submitted to Congress for examination and approval, and Congress shall have approved the same, and when said State, by a vote of its legislature elected under said constitution, shall have adopted the amendment to the Constitution of the United States, proposed by the Thirty-ninth Congress, and known as article fourteen, and when said article shall havc become a part of the Constitution of the United States said State shall be declared entitled to representation in Congress, and senators and representatives shall be admitted therefrom on their taking the oath prescribed by law, and then and thereafter the preceding sections of this act shall be inoperative in said State: *Provided,* That no person excluded from the privilege of holding office by said proposed amendment to the Constitution of the United States, shall be eligible to election as a member of the convention to frame a constitution for any of said rebel States, nor shall any such person vote for members of such convention.

SEC. 6. That, until the people of said rebel States shall be by law admitted to representation in the Congress of the United States, any civil governments which may exist therein shall be deemed provisional only, and in all respects subject to the paramount authority of the United States at any time to abolish, modify, control, or supersede the same; and in all elections to any office under such provisional governments all persons shall be entitled to vote, and none others, who are entitled to vote, under the provisions of the fifth section of this act; and no persons shall be eligible to any office under any such provisional governments who would be disqualified from holding office under the provisions of the third article of said constitutional amendment.

* * * * * *

1. *Why did Congress define its Reconstruction policy in military terms?*

2. *What provisions did it make for the readmission of southern states to the Union? How did these differ from the policy followed by President Johnson?*

17–9 *Organization and Principles of the Ku Klux Klan, 1868*

Founded in Pulaski, Tennessee, in 1866, the Ku Klux Klan spread quickly throughout the South under the leadership of former Confederate General Nathan Bedford Forrest, its first Grand Wizard. The Klan became a potent instrument of terror against freed people, their white allies, and Republican state governments. The Klan was strongest in rural areas and operated locally, with little central control. Most Klan leaders came from local landholding and professional elites.

SOURCE: Walter L. Fleming, ed., *The Ku Klux Klan* (1905), p. 154ff.

This Organization shall be styled and denominated, the Order of the * * *

APPELLATION

ORGANIZATION AND PRINCIPLES OF THE KLU KLUX KLAN

CREED

We, the Order of the * * *, reverentially acknowledge the majesty and supremacy of the Divine Being, and recognize the goodness and providence of the same. And we recognize our relation to the United States Government, the supremacy of the Constitution, the Constitutional Laws thereof, and the Union of States thereunder.

CHARACTER AND OBJECTS OF THE ORDER

This is an institution of Chivalry, Humanity, Mercy, and Patriotism; embodying in its genius and its principles all that is chivalric in conduct, noble in sentiment, generous in manhood, and patriotic in purpose; its peculiar objects being

First: To protect the weak, the innocent, and the defenseless, from the indignities, wrongs, and outrages of the lawless, the violent, and the brutal; to relieve the injured and oppressed; to succor the suffering and unfortunate, and especially the widows and orphans of Confederate soldiers.

Second: To protect and defend the Constitution of the United States, and all laws passed in conformity thereto, and to protect the States and the people thereof from all invasion from any source whatever.

Third: To aid and assist in the execution of all constitutional laws, and to protect the people from unlawful seizure, and from trial except by their peers in conformity to the laws of the land.

TITLES

Sec. I. The officers of this Order shall consist of a Grand Wizard of the Empire, and his ten Genii; a Grand Dragon of the Realm, and his eight Hydras; a Grand Titan of the Dominion, and his six Furies; a Grand Giant of the Province, and his four Goblins; a Grand Cyclops of the Den, and his two Night Hawks; a Grand Magi, a Grand Monk, a Grand Scribe, a Grand Exchequer, a Grand Turk, and a Grand Sentinel.

Sec. 2. The body politic of this Order shall be known and designated as "Ghouls."

TERRITORY AND ITS DIVISIONS

Sec. 1. The territory embraced within the jurisdiction of this Order shall be coterminous with the States of Maryland, Virginia, North Carolina, South Carolina, Georgia, Florida, Alabama, Mississippi, Louisiana, Texas, Arkansas, Missouri, Kentucky, and Tennessee; all combined constituting the Empire.

Sec. 2. The Empire shall be divided into four departments, the first to be styled the Realm, and coterminous with the boundaries the several States; the second to be styled the Dominion and to be coterminous with such counties as the Grand Dragons of the several Realms may assign to the charge of the Grand Titan. The third to be styled the Province, and to be coterminous with the several counties; *provided* the Grand Titan may, when he deems it necessary, assign two Grand Giants to one Province, prescribing at the same time, the jurisdiction of each. The fourth department to be styled the Den, and shall embrace such part of a Province as the Grand Giant shall assign to the charge of a Grand Cyclops....

INTERROGATIONS TO BE ASKED

1st. Have you ever been rejected, upon application for membership in the * *, or have you ever been expelled from the same?

2d. Are you now, or have you ever been, a member of the Radical Republican party, or either of the organizations known as the "Loyal League" and the "Grand Army of the Republic?"

3d. Are you opposed to the principles and policy of the Radical party, and to the Loyal League, and the Grand Army of the Republic, so far as you are informed of the character and purposes of those organizations?

4th. Did you belong to the Federal army during the late war, and fight against the South during the existence of the same?

5th. Are you opposed to negro equality, both social and political?

6th. Are you in favor of a white man's government in this country?

7th. Are you in favor of Constitutional liberty, and a Government of equitable laws instead of a Government of violence and oppression?

8th. Are you in favor of maintaining the Constitutional rights of the South?

9th. Are you in favor of the reenfranchisement and emancipation of the white men of the South, and the restitution of the Southern people to all their rights, alike proprietary, civil, and political?

10th. Do you believe in the inalienable right of self-preservation of the people against the exercise of arbitrary and unlicensed power?....

...9. The most profound and rigid secrecy concerning any and everything that relates to the Order, shall at all times be maintained.

10. Any member who shall reveal or betray the secrets of this Order, shall suffer the extreme penalty of the law.

* * * * * *

1. *How do the Klan "Interrogations" for prospective members reflect the lingering ideals of the Confederacy?*

2. *Why did the Klan place so much emphasis upon ritual secrecy and grand titles?*

17–10 *Blanche K. Bruce, Speech in the Senate, 1876*

Born a slave in Virginia, Blanche K. Bruce grew up in Missouri, where he established the state's first school for African Americans during the Civil War. After the war he moved to Mississippi, where he became a Republican political organizer and a large landowner in the Delta region. Bruce won election to the U.S. Senate in 1874, where he was the first African American to serve a full term. Bruce here protests violent election frauds in his home state.

SOURCE: *Congressional Record, 44th Congress, 1st Session* (1876).

The conduct of the late election in Mississippi affected not merely the fortunes of partisans—as the same were necessarily involved in the defeat or success of the respective parties to the contest—but put in question and jeopardy the sacred rights of the citizen; and the investigation contemplated in the pending resolution has for its object not the determination of the question whether the offices shall be held and the public affairs of that State be administered by democrats or republicans, but the higher and more important end, the protection in all their purity and significance of the political rights of the people and the free institutions of the country....

The evidence in hand and accessible will show beyond peradventure that in many parts of the State corrupt and violent influences were brought to bear upon the registrars of voters, thus materially affecting the character of the voting or poll lists; upon the inspectors of election, prejudicially and unfairly thereby changing the number of votes cast; and, finally, threats and violence were practiced directly upon the masses of voters in such measures and strength as to produce grave apprehensions for their personal safety and as to deter them from the exercise of their political franchises....

It will not accord with the laws of nature or history to brand colored people a race of cowards. On more than one historic field, beginning in 1776 and coming down to this centennial year of the Republic, they have attested in blood their courage as well as a love of liberty. I ask Senators to believe that no consideration of fear or personal danger has kept us quiet and forbearing under the provocations and wrongs that have so sorely tried our souls. But feeling kindly toward our white fellow-citizens, appreciating the good purposes and offices of the better classes, and, above all, abhoring a war of races, we determined to wait until such time as an appeal to the good sense and justice of the American people could be made....

The sober American judgment must obtain in the South as elsewhere in the Republic, that the only distinctions upon which parties can be safely organized and in harmony with our institutions are differences of opinion relative to principles and policy of government, and that differences of religion, nationality, or race can neither with safety nor propriety be permitted for a moment to enter into the party contests of the day. The unanimity with which the colored voters act with a party is not referable to any race prejudice on their pan. On the contrary, they invite the political co-operation of their white brethren, and vote as a unit because proscribed as such. They deprecate the establishment of the color line by the opposition, not only because the act is unwise and wrong in principle, but because it isolates them from the white men of the South, and forces them, in sheer self-protection and against their inclination, to act seemingly upon the basis of a race prejudice that they neither respect nor entertain. As a class they are free from prejudices, and have no uncharitable suspicions against their white fellow-citizens, whether native born or settlers from the Northern States. They not only recognize the equality of citizenship and the right of every man to hold, without proscription any position of honor and trust to which the confidence of the people may elevate him; but owing nothing to race, birth, or surroundings, they, above all other classes in the community, are interested to see prejudices drop out of both politics and the business of the country, and success in life proceed only upon the integrity and merit of the man who seeks it.... But withal, as they progress in intelligence and appreciation of the dignity of their prerogatives as citizens, they, as an evidence of growth begin to realize the significance of the proverb,

"When thou doest well for thyself, men shall praise thee;" and are disposed to exact the same protection and concession of rights that are conferred upon other citizens by the Constitution, and that, too, without the humiliation involved in the enforced abandonment of their political convictions....

I have confidence, not only in my country and her institutions, but in the endurance, capacity, and destiny of my people. We will, as opportunity offers and ability serves, seek our places, sometimes in the field of letters, arts, sciences, and the professions. More frequently mechanical pursuits will attract and elicit our efforts; more still of my people will find employment and livelihood as the cultivators of the soil. The bulk of this people—by surroundings, habits, adaptation, and choice—will continue to find their homes in the South, and constitute the masses of its yeomanry. We will there probably, of our own volition and more abundantly than in the past, produce the great staples that will contribute to the basis of foreign exchange, aid in giving the nation a balance of trade, and minister to the wants and comfort and build up the prosperity of the whole land. Whatever our ultimate position in the composite civilization of the Republic and whatever varying fortunes attend our career, we will not forget our instincts for freedom nor our love of country,

* * * * * *

1. Bruce cultivated a reputation as a racial moderate in Reconstruction politics. How does his speech reflect this?

2. What political and economic strategies does he recommend for freed people?

17—11 A Sharecrop Contract, 1882

During the Reconstruction era, sharecropping emerged as the most common method of organizing and financing southern agriculture. Large plantations, no longer worked by gangs of slaves, were broken up into small plots worked by individual families. The following contract typifies the sort of formal arrangements that many thousands of poor black and white farmers made with local landowners.

SOURCE: Grimes Family Papers, Southern Historical Collection, University of North Carolina, Chapel Hill, in Robert D. Marcus and David Burner, eds., *America Firsthand* (1992), pp. 306—308.

To every one applying to rent land upon shares, the following conditions must be read, and *agreed to.*

To every 30 or 35 acres, I agree to furnish the team, plow, and farming implements, except cotton planters, and I *do not* agree to furnish a cart to every cropper. The croppers are to have half of the cotton, corn and fodder (and peas and pumpkins and potatoes if any are planted) if the following conditions are compiled with, but—if not—they are to have only two fifths (2/5). Croppers are to have no part or interest in the cotton seed raised from the crop planted and worked by them. No vine crops of any description, that is, no watermelons, muskmelons,...squashes or anything of that kind, except peas and pumpkins, and potatoes, are to be planted in the cotton or corn. All must work under my direction. All plantation work to be done by the croppers. My part of the crop to be *housed* by them, and the fodder and oats to be hauled about and put in the house. All the cotton must be topped about

1st August. If any cropper fails from any cause to save all the fodder from his crop, I am to have enough fodder to make it equal to one half of the whole if the whole amount of fodder had been saved.

For every mule or horse furnished by me there must be 1000 good sized rails...hauled, and the fence repaired as far as they will go, the fence to be torn down and put up from the bottom if I so direct. All croppers to haul rails and work on fence whenever I may order. Rails to be split when I may say. Each cropper to clean out every ditch in his crop, and where a ditch runs between two croppers, the cleaning out of that ditch is to be divided equally between them. Every ditch bank in the crop must be shrubbed down and cleaned off before the crop is planted and must be cut down every time the land is worked with his hoe and when the crop is "laid by," the ditch banks must be left clean of bushes, weeds, and seeds. The cleaning out of all ditches must be done by the first of October. The rails must be split and the fence repaired before corn is planted.

Each cropper must keep in good repair all bridges in his crop or over ditches that he has to clean out and when a bridge needs repairing that is outside of all their crops, then any one that I call on must repair it.

Fence jams to be done as ditch banks. If any cotton is planted on the land outside of the plantation fence, I am to have *three fourths* of all the cotton made in those patches, that is to say, no cotton must be planted by croppers in their home patches.

All croppers must clean out stables and fill them with straw, and haul straw in front of stables whenever I direct. All the cotton must be manured, and enough fertilizer must be brought to manure each crop highly, the croppers to pay for one half of all manure bought, the quantity to be purchased for each crop must be left to me.

No cropper to work off the plantation when there is any work to be done on the land he has rented, or when his work is needed by me or other croppers. Trees to be cut down on Orchard, House field & Evanson fences, leaving such as I may designate.

Road field to be planted from the *very edge of the ditch to the fence*, and all the land to be planted close up to the ditches and fences. *No stock of any kind* belonging to croppers to run in the plantation after crops are gathered.

If the fence should be blown down, or if trees should fall on the fence outside of the land planted by any of the croppers, any one or all that I may call upon must put it up and repair it. Every cropper must feed, or have fed, the team he works, Saturday nights, Sundays, and every morning before going to work, beginning to feed his team (morning, noon, and night *every day in the*

week) on the day he rents and feeding it to and including the 31st day of December. If any cropper shall from any cause fail to repair his fence as far as 1000 rails will go, or shall fail to clean out any part of his ditches, or shall fail to leave his ditch banks, any part of them, well shrubbed and clean when his crop is laid by, or shall fail to clean out stables, fill them up and haul straw in front of them whenever he is told, he shall have only two-fifths (2/5) of the cotton, corn, fodder, peas and pumpkins made on the land he cultivates.

If any cropper shall fail to feed his team Saturday nights, all day Sunday and all the rest of the week, morning/noon, and night, for every time he so fails he must pay me five cents.

No corn nor cotton stalks must be burned, but must be cut down, cut up and plowed in. Nothing must be burned off the land except when it is *impossible to plow it in.*

Every cropper must be responsible for all gear and farming implements placed in his hands, and if not returned must be paid for unless it is worn out by use.

Croppers must sow & plow in oats and haul them to the crib, but *must have no part of them.* Nothing to be sold from their crops, nor fodder nor corn to be carried out of the fields until my rent is all paid, and all amounts they owe me and for which I am responsible are paid in full.

I am to gin & pack all the cotton and charge every cropper an eighteenth of his part, the cropper to furnish his part of the bagging, ties, & twine.

The sale of every cropper's part of the cotton to be made by me when and where I choose to sell, and after deducting all they owe me and all sums that I may be responsible for on their accounts, to pay them their half of the net proceeds. Work of every description, particularly the work on fences and ditches, to be done to my satisfaction, and must be done over until I am satisfied that it is done as it should be.

No wood to burn, nor light wood, nor poles, nor timber for boards, nor wood for any purpose whatever must be gotten above the house occupied by Henry Beasley—nor must any trees be cut down nor any wood used for any purpose, except for firewood, without my permission.

* * * * * *

1. *What responsibilities does the landowner agree to take on in the contract? How do these differ from the cropper?*

2. *What distinctions are made between the growing and selling of cotton and other crops?*